GARDENS IN EDWARDIAN ENGLAND

a facsimile reprint of the classic work

Gardens Old and New
The Country House & its
Garden Environment

THE ENTRANCE GATE CLEEVE PRIOR ﻌﻌﻌﻌ

GARDENS IN EDWARDIAN ENGLAND

ANTIQUE COLLECTORS' CLUB

© Country Life
an imprint of Newnes Books
a division of Hamlyn Publishing Group Ltd.

World copyright reserved
ISBN 0 907462 84 7

First published by Country Life Ltd.
as ''Country Gardens Old and New''
This reprint published in 1985 for the Antique Collectors' Club
by the Antique Collectors' Club Ltd.

**Printed in England by the Antique Collectors' Club Ltd.
Woodbridge, Suffolk, England**

Publisher's note

When this book was originally published it was entitled "Gardens Old and New". It was felt that to publish an edition in 1985 under the same title could be misleading and it might be assumed that the book would include gardens up to the present day.

The book includes essays on the famous gardens of the Edwardian era which are discussed in the light of the then up-to-date thinking on garden design. As such it is an important record of gardening history.

This is a facsimile reprint apart from the title and the slightly reduced size overall. The delightful cartouched running headings, which include the original title on occasion, have been left untouched.

IN TIME OF WAR.

FROM THE PAINTING BY G. D. LESLIE, R.A.

INTRODVCTION

Horas non numero nisi serenas

EDMVND·J·SVLLIVAN·

MID the many controversies which have arisen in regard to the character of gardens, no one has ever been found to doubt that they should possess a definite relation to the houses they adorn. There have been different views as to what that relation should be. Some have demanded harmony, others contrast. There are those who look upon gardening as merely a form of architecture, maintaining that a garden is really the extension of the house into its surroundings, and we may say that they enter the pleasaunce of their choice from within outwards. Another school of gardeners, on the other hand, has considered gardening as the approach of wild Nature, subjected and glorified, to the dwelling-place, and these enter their pleasure ground, as it were, from without inwards. There have been exaggerations on both sides. The architect has sometimes tended to a too severe formality ; the landscape gardener has often broken down the barriers of the quaint and homelike, the stately and the dignified, to make way for some tame substitute, or some extravagant futility. A quaint idea, expressed by old Sir Uvedale Price, which had something of reason in it, was that there should be a progressive breaking of style—formality near the house, landscape character beyond, and the native wild outside.

But amid the war of conflicting schools, the broad fact remains that the house and the garden are one. It was not until the friends of Mr. Justice Shallow had entered his Gloucestershire garden and orchard, there, in an arbour, to partake of a last year's pippin of his own "graffing," with a dish of carraways, that Falstaff could declare the cavaliero-justice and coram to possess "a goodly dwelling, and a rich." Here, manifestly, Shakespeare recognised the right relation between the house and its garden, and, indeed, though one should be fair as Camelot and the other gay as Armida's, each would be a marred creation without the other.

THE SUMMER-HOUSE IN THE QUAD GARDEN, KELLY HOUSE, TAVISTOCK.

Such a close relation almost inevitably brings some degree of formality into a garden, as may be seen in examples of every period, except of one comparatively recent. This is a broad truth, notwithstanding certain famous poetical descriptions dating from old times, which seem to tend to the contrary, and may, indeed, have foreshadowed a breaking away from the older style, such, for example, as Milton's account of the Garden of Eden, and that which Tasso has given of Armida's enchanted pleasaunce, where in the scented ways no trace remained of the gardener's hand, for " nowhere appeared the art which all this had wrought."

A BORDER AT PENSHURST.

"So with the rude the polished mingled was,
    That natural seemèd all and every part;
    Nature would Craft in counterfeiting pass,
    And imitate her imitator Art."

Notwithstanding such poetical descriptions of gardens of landscape or woodland character, it would be no difficult matter to show that formality has almost universally prevailed in some degree—if only in the shape of a well-kept hedge or a sequestered alley —as will, indeed, be revealed in the plates which accompany the accounts of English gardens in this book. It is, moreover, curious to observe how, amid change, a certain constancy has existed in gardening methods, revealing the essential basis of the art, which gives us the gardener as the creator of an appendage to the house.

It has been observed that Sir Walter Scott impressed a certain wide-reading public with a love for the fresh beauties of wild Nature, and helped to inspire a taste which, under the influence of other writers also of the romantic school, acquired force among us, and

was not without its influence upon the gardening art. And, yet, let us with Scott and Waverley lift the latch of the wicket door that reveals the old garden at Tully Veolan, where the hero is welcomed by Rose Bradwardine and her hospitable sire. It is a perfect picture of an old garden. Here is Alexander Saunderson, half butler, half gardener, working at Miss Rose's garden in the parterre, sheltered from the blasts by a close yew hedge, while the venerable house looks over it, clothed with fruit trees and evergreens ; over the terrace also, with its grotesque animals and huge sundials, and below it over a garden " kept with great accuracy," exhibiting a profusion of flowers and " evergreens cut into grotesque forms," whence we descend level by level to the octangular garden-house overlooking the stream, there surprised by the dam into temporary tranquillity.

Let us then go back to the Tuscan gardens of Pliny the Younger nearly 1,800 years before. " In the front of the portico is a sort of terrace, consisting of several members, embellished with various figures and bounded with a box hedge, from whence you descend by an easy slope, adorned with the representation of divers animals in box, answering alternately to each other, into a lawn overspread with the soft — I had almost said the liquid—acanthus ; this is surrounded by a walk enclosed with tonsile evergreens, shaped into a variety of forms. Beyond it is the Gestatio, laid out in the form of a circus, ornamented in the middle with box cut in numberless different figures, together with a plantation of shrubs, prevented by the shears from shooting up too high ; the whole is fenced in by a wall

THE HEDGE OF YEW, BOX, AND HOLLY AT HALL BARN.

covered by box, rising by different ranges to the top. On the outside of the wall lies a meadow that owes as many beauties to Nature as all I have been describing within does to Art; at the end of which are several other meadows and fields interspersed with thickets." Here surely is a remarkable illustration of the historical continuity which has existed in the methods of garden design, and which is not without suggestion to the modern gardener.

This partial constancy of character found existing in garden-making from ancient times to the present—and the instances might have been many times multiplied—leads us to enquire what are the features and characteristics which have been found in well-designed gardens? One notable point to be observed is that the garden must not only be appropriate to the house, but to the situation in which it lies. What is suitable to the steep hillside will not befit the plain; what is right in the vicinity of a classic mansion would be out of place near one built in a more picturesque style. Few minds, again, can be contented with pleasure grounds which are

to garden design, or to conclude that because one character is present another is necessarily excluded. The world of gardening is wide enough, and has room and verge enough, for all—alike for those who love the mossy terrace shadowed by beech or lime, the fantastic yew cut by the topiary hand, or the still canal, where the birds "float double, swan and shadow"; or, again, for those who delight in gentle meads, undulating slopes, and waters winding by the wood. All these may find their pleasure in a well-designed garden, if the garden be but appropriate to the house and the situation, and there be a reasonable predominance of the architectural character in those parts of it which neighbour the structure. There may well be terraces, one or many, as at ancient Haddon and at Clevedon Court, with garden-houses perhaps at the angles of a pleasant enclosure, and a wealth of fragrant flowers, greeting the spring, rich in the summer days, and bright still when autumn has blown, to delight the sense with the glories of the garden world. There will certainly always be lawns to give their unfailing green, and perhaps grass walks through

THE TERRACE STAIRWAY AT ALTON TOWERS.   "*Country Life.*"

devoid of marked features, and even the landscape gardener has recognised this fact by erecting curious ruins, hermits' retreats, temples of classic deities, and other like buildings, which, though they must be condemned as mostly futile, are yet a plain indication of what has been suggested. The desire for some marked character in gardens was no doubt largely responsible for that subdivision which is commonly found in them. It accounts, also, for the many attempts which have been made to give variety of level. It may be said, indeed, that the chief distinction of gardens is subdivision and difference of level, with the terraced formation that results from the latter. The enclosures and the various levels have been marked by masonry or by hedges, but some kind of marking or distinction there has usually been. Features are requisite to accentuate the design, and there is no good garden in which character is not enforced. It was the craving for accentuating features that led to all the extravagance of the old tree-cutter and pleacher.

It would be, of course, a mistake to be dogmatic in regard

woods, or bowling greens for the pleasure of many. In short, we may see that no rigid lines need be drawn, and that good sense will always create or maintain a garden of character appropriate. We may discover, too, amid the warring words of the advocates of one style of gardening or another, that it is, after all, no worse to trim a tree than a lawn—that the difference is in degree not in kind, that all gardening is in a measure formal, and that it was only the extravagance of the old topiary gardeners that brought them into contempt and ridicule. Bacon did not like "images cut out of juniper or other garden stuff." " They are for children," he said; but he liked well low hedges with some "pretty pyramids," and even "fair columns upon frames of carpenter's work." The mount in the midst, which had been a feature of mediæval gardens, was also to his taste, and he would have placed " a fine banqueting house upon the top." His stately hedge enclosed the garden, and his alleys marked the formality of it.

The old Englishman dearly loved an enclosed garden, bounded by tall hedges of beech or yew, well cut and trimmed

HEVER CASTLE AND THE LILY-DECKED MOAT.

by such methods as Evelyn himself describes. There were leafy bowers and long alleys, with pyramid yews, perhaps, in his pleasaunce, and a rich orchard beyond. It was a place like Leonato's garden, where Hero and Ursula walked beneath the apple trees, while Beatrice stole

> " Into the pleached bower,
> Where honeysuckles ripened by the sun,
> Forbid the sun to enter ; like favourites,
> Made proud by princes, that advance their pride
> Against that power that bred it."

Fine terraces of excellent masonry, with ascents, perhaps, of many steps, adorned with quaint statuary—good garden architecture, in a word —combined with quaint " clipped greens," were in this pleasaunce. There was little exaggeration in such a garden, and it was not until later that Pope could laugh at the fantastic things that awoke his ridicule. He knew an eminent cook who had beautified his country seat with a coronation dinner in greens, where the champion on horseback was flourishing at one end of the table, and the queen at the other. Sarcasm kills much, and though we may laugh with Pope, it is to be feared that his satire was not without an ill effect. " Adam and Eve in yew ; Adam a little shattered by the fall of the tree of knowledge in the great storm ; Eve and the serpent very flourishing. Noah's Ark in holly, the ribs a little damaged for the want of water. The Tower of Babel not yet finished. St. George, in box ; his arm scarce long enough, but will be in a condition to stick the dragon by next April. An old maid-of-honour, in wormwood." Excellent fooling, indeed !

But, at the same time, let us remember that formal quaintness, sometimes tending to exaggeration, was the delight of our more cultured ancestors, and of the famous men of England and the Continent. It was found at Penshurst and Moor Park, at Hampton Court and Levens, just as at Versailles and St. Cloud, and at the Ludovisi, Medici, Doria Pamphili, and other

THE MOON AND CRESCENT LAKES AT STUDLEY ROYAL.

THE OLD BOWLING GREEN AT SUTTON PLACE, GUILDFORD.

stately gardens of Rome. Thus does Taine speak of the characters embodied at the Villa Albani : "No liberty is left to Nature ; all is artificial. The lawns are hemmed in by enormous hedges taller than a man, thick as walls, and forming geometrical angles, of which the apices all point to one centre. The flower-beds are enclosed by small box frames ; they comprise designs, and resemble well-bordered carpets in a regular medley of graduated colours." And in this way did Rousseau sneer at the fashioner of verdant conceits : "With what disdain would he enter this simple and modest place, with what contempt have all these weeds uprooted! What fine avenues he would open out, what beautiful alleys he would pierce, what fine goose-feet and what fine trees like parasols and fans ! What finely-fretted trellises, what beautifully drawn yew hedges, finely squared and rounded! What fine

Moor Park in Hertfordshire lay upon the side of a hill, which naturally led to a terraced formation, and the great parlour opened upon the terrace fronting the house, which was about 300 paces long, and broad in proportion, the border being set with standard laurels at intervals. From this walk were three flights of steps, disposed at the middle and the ends, by which a descent was made into a very large parterre. Gravel walks crossed this space, dividing it into quarters, and it was adorned with fountains and statues. Above, and at each end of the terrace, were summer-houses, and along the sides of the parterre were covered ways or cloisters open to the garden, and ending with two other summer-houses. Over these two cloisters two terraces extended from the main terrace, with balustrades, and were entered through the summer-houses first described. Here was an enclosure, such as may still be found, though

THE TERRACES, TISSINGTON HALL, DERBYSHIRE.

bowling greens of fine English turf—rounded, squared, sloped, ovaled ! What fine yews carved into dragons, pagodas, marmosets—every kind of monster ! " Indeed, in the descriptions both of those who loved the old gardening and those who extolled the charms of the rival school, we find ample evidence of the permanence—we may even say the essential permanence—of something of formality in gardening style.

A type of the seventeenth century garden, devoid of such exaggerations as Pope derided, was that at Moor Park in Hertfordshire, made famous by the description of Sir William Temple, and formal in character like the famous garden of his own Moor Park near Farnham. There were many great gardens of the class in that century, as at Theobalds, the place of the Lord Treasurer Burleigh, and at Wilton and Penshurst.

with infinite variation, at Montacute, Blickling, Hatfield, Ham House, and many other great places in the land. From the middle of the parterre at Moor Park was a descent by many steps, in two flights on either side of a grotto, into the lower garden, where was an orchard, and here the walks were all green, as well as a grotto (prototype of many) embellished with shells, rockwork, and fountains. Thus we see, as has been suggested, how the seventeenth century Englishman carried his house, as it were, into his garden, and loved the shadowed alley in the hot summer days, the delectable coolness of the evening air on his terrace, and the green lawns where he sped his well-turned bowls.

There were other features of these old gardens which are not found alluded to in Sir William Temple's description of Moor Park, though some of them remain to this day from the

A GARDEN IN SEVILLE—THE CASA DE PILATOS.

GARDEN ARCHITECTURE AT CLIFTON HALL, NOTTINGHAM.

investing it with something more of the work of creative fancy. They are own brothers to the dial, to the trellised pergola, where we seek the summer shade, and the balustrade, where the roses cluster, and fling out their fragrance in the sun. Many people will exclaim with Charles Lamb, when they encounter some garden monitor of the fleeting hours, " What a dull thing is a clock, with its ponderous embowelments of lead or brass, its pert or solemn dulness of communication, compared with the simple altar-like structure and silent heart-language of the old dial ! " Such things as the gate and the dial belonged to the sweet sequestered and enclosed gardens of our seventeenth-century sires, and they have a right place also in our own.

But the enclosed garden did not give complete content. Something more was needed than stately seclusion to an age that had learned to look much abroad upon a newly opening world, and garden design, under the influence of Italy and France, soon began to admit an outlook through some beautiful clairvoyée, or along the twilight vista of an elm or beechen avenue, to what lay beyond. The great exemplar of garden work in the new manner was the famous Frenchman, André le Nôtre, the creator of the celebrated gardens at Versailles, Chantilly, St. Cloud, and Meudon, and of the terrace at Fontainebleau. Planting began now, as an extension of the garden, to form a scheme of which the house was generally the focus, though sometimes a column or a temple became the centre of the arrangement. Great avenues stretched through the park into the neighbouring woods, while in the lower grounds there were formal waters, circular basins, or long, still canals, sheltered on every side, and reflecting mighty elms and beeches, which spread their leafy canopies

gardens of that time. Those noble iron gates fashioned under the hammer of that man of fame, the smith, were

overhead, and often a classic temple or leaden deities or heroes stood at the margin. Hampton Court is, of course,

hanging between lofty piers, with balls or sculptured animals on the top. They are found still in the gardens of Italy, France, and Spain, and are numerous yet in some of the gardens of England. The smith, like the builder, has been a powerful auxiliary of the gardener. Force and character are added by the work they have done together. The labour of the Continent was at our service, and the native worker found ample scope for his skill. Look at that glorious Spanish gate, at the gates of Ragley, Compton Beauchamp, Tissington, Norton Conyers, and many other houses of olden times, and you will see what the united skill of the worker in iron and stone or brick can do to add to the beauty and interest of our gardens. Such gates as these are fitting entrances to the realm of beauty within. They mark its enclosure as a beautiful garden nobly guarded,

THE GARDEN STEPS AT CHARLTON HOUSE.

A SUNDIAL AT HENBURY, GLOUCESTERSHIRE.

and Wise, his gardeners, arranged the terraces and planted the lime avenues, but the splendid yews and laurels belong to the time of Charles II., and were placed there by his gardener, Rose. Along the river-side were rich grilles of magnificent ironwork, of which some are now in South Kensington. Other gardens were there also, including the Pond Garden of an earlier date, belonging to the palace of the Tudors, and on the other side stretched out the park of Bushey, with the long avenue—horse-chestnut and lime—and the great Diana fountain.

But a recoil from the grandiose manner of Le Nôtre and his school soon found expression. Huet, the famous Bishop of Soissons and Avranches, very shortly after Le Nôtre's time, spoke sarcastically of his water-effects, and of the taste of the century which nothing pleased unless it were costly. In our own country, Pope, some of whose satires have been alluded to, exclaimed that the grand style of gardening was contrary to the simplicity of Homer, and proceeded to lay out

the great illustration of the grand manner in England, but it exists also at Castle Howard, Melbourne, and many other places. It was a style that belonged to palaces and to great houses, and that lent itself in no degree to the needs of the smaller gardens of the land. It cannot be adopted, except upon a large scale, without failure, and some of the minor features by which it was accompanied do not commend themselves to modern taste.

The classic pleasaunce had come originally from Italy, and the famous Ludovisi Gardens, which have been often described, were a fine type of stately gardening at its best. There were numerous alleys in them, orange groves, and cypress copses, fountains, statues, and vases. A French writer of the beginning of the eighteenth century, Charles de Brosses, the translator of Sallust, who contrasted these gardens with those of the Tuileries, regarded them with particular pleasure, because they had been Sallust's gardens in ancient times. He remarked that the Italians followed their own tastes, and adapted their gardens to their climate. They wished to have green trees all the year round, grass in their walks instead of gravel, long and palisaded ways, giving shelter in the noonday heat, and many fountains, statues, and architectural accessories for their satisfaction. This, indeed, was the great age of garden architecture, and, still, what can be more delightful than to tread some mossy stairway, shadowed by an ancient lime or a hollow walnut tree, with the sculptured vase or the twisted urn at its sides, which our garden-loving ancestors trod of yore?

It was William III. who chiefly popularised in England the grandiose style of the Continent. and Hampton Court is our most splendid example of the school of Le Nôtre. The greatest effort of William was in the fine semi-circular gardens, with the three radiating avenues, and the long water, in the Home Park beyond. This great canal was formed under the King's personal direction, and London

A FINE GARDEN COMPOSITION AT PENSHURST.

a fanciful garden of his own, with the famous grotto under the Teddington Road.

Perhaps the best feature that remains to these days of such old gardens is the yew hedge, that dominant mark of many English pleasaunces, which gives them a particular distinction, and favours that character of enclosure which has been alluded to as almost essential in good garden design. Evelyn claimed the credit of bringing the yew into fashion, " as well for a defence as for a succedaneum to cypress, whether in hedges or pyramids, conic spires, bowls, and what other shapes. I do again name the yew for hedges as preferable for beauty and a stiff defence to any plant I have seen." There is still at Albury a hedge 10ft. high and a quarter of a mile long, said to have been designed by Evelyn for the Earl of Arundel, and there are yew hedges at Bishopsbourne, near Canterbury, believed to have been planted by Richard Hooker in 1595, and now about 14ft. high

Here was a change of view that was quite fundamental. With a sunk fence instead of a hedge, and wild nature taken into the gardening plan, the sequestered pleasure ground that had delighted the old Englishman was swept away. There had been foreshadowing of the change that was to come, not only in the pages of Milton and Tasso, but in the writings of many observers. Sir Henry Wotton had remarked " a certain contrariety between building and gardening, for as fabrics should be regular, so gardens should be irregular, or at least be cast into a very wild regularity." Sidney, too, brings the hero of " Arcadia " into a place that was " neither field, garden, nor orchard ; or, rather, it was both field, garden, and orchard." The new landscape style had soon a great vogue in England. Kent was the designer who chiefly worked the change, followed by Brown and many more. Walpole ascribed to Kent genius in striking out the " great system from the twilight of imperfect

CRAFTSMAN'S WORK AT COMPTON BEAUCHAMP, BERKSHIRE.

and 10ft. thick. This book illustrates many notable yew and other hedges which derive their character from those times.

Walpole was as firm as Pope in his opposition to the formal style, and, in writing on " Modern Gardening," he makes a remark which is extremely important for an understanding of the change then beginning. Hitherto enclosure by hedges, terraces, or balustrades had been considered essential, but Walpole thought it a " capital stroke " that walls for boundaries began to be destroyed, and that, instead of a hedge, a sunk fence, the ha-ha, was invented. " No sooner was this simple enchantment made than levelling, mowing, and rolling followed. The contiguous ground of the park without the sunk fence was to be harmonised with the lawn within, and the garden in its turn was to be set free from its prim regularity, that it might assort with the wilder country without."

essays." " He leaped the fence, and saw that all Nature was a garden." Landscape, which had hitherto been without, was now to be brought within. " The great principles on which he worked were perspective, and light and shade. Groups of trees broke too uniform or too extensive a lawn ; evergreens and woods were opposed to the glare of the champain, and where the view was less fortunate, or so much exposed as to be beheld at once, he blotted out some parts by thick shades, to divide it into variety, or to make the richest scene more enchanting by reserving it to a farther advance of the spectator's step. Thus, selecting favourite objects, and veiling deformities by screens of plantation, sometimes allowing the rudest waste to add its foil to the richest theatre, he realised the compositions of the greatest masters in painting. Where objects were wanting to animate his horizon, his taste as an architect could bestow immediate termination. His buildings, his seats, his temples, were more the works of his pencil than of his compasses. We owe the restoration of Greece and the diffusion of architecture to his skill in landscape.''

It cannot be said that posterity has altogether sanctioned the exalted view which Horace Walpole expressed of the achievements of Kent. In striving to do away with the old formality, the landscape gardener had introduced a formality of his own, chiefly discernible in the curious embellishments which he found it necessary to add in order to give features to replace those he had sometimes wantonly destroyed. Kent's greatest works were at Esher and Claremont, at Rousham in Oxfordshire, at Lord Burlington's villa at Chiswick, and in the additions which he made to the plans of Bridgman and Vanbrugh at Lord Cobham's place at Stowe The gardens at Stowe, famous at the time, awoke the enthusiasm of many. Thus did Dr. Cotton poetise :

Copyright. *"Country Life."*
THE OLD GATEWAY AT FRANKS.

" It puzzles much the sages' brains
Where Eden stood of yore ;
Some place it in Arabia's plains,
Some say it is no more.

" But Cobham can these tales confute,
As all the curious know ;
For he has prov'd beyond dispute
That Paradise is Stowe."

Kent's popularity brought him many followers and imitators. Mr. Philip Southcote, at Woburn Farm in Surrey, had an embellished place at the time, in which the farm itself was part of his garden conception. Shenstone was a great exponent of the landscape manner, and had a notable example of it at his place at the Leasowes, and the Hon. Charles Hamilton, destroying nothing, like some landscape gardeners, created Pains Hill in Surrey. As George Mason said, who wrote in 1768, Pains Hill has the mark of creative genius, and it is one of the most remarkable examples of the landscape style. But the greatest of all the followers of Kent was Lancelot Brown. Unlike others of his school, Brown did not attempt to form his style upon the works of Claude or Poussin, but went direct to Nature herself, and there would have been little cause to find fault with what he did, if, in doing it, he had not swept away so many characteristic features of the gardens of former times. Lord Cobham, in whose kitchen garden he had worked, recommended him to the Duke of Grafton at Wakefield Lodge, in Northamptonshire, where he directed the formation of a large lake. Blenheim was his favourite triumph, and in speaking of the water-effect there, he exultingly exclaimed

Copyright. *' Country Life."*
THE TERRACE WALK AT LOSELEY PARK, SURREY.

THE GREAT GATES AT RAGLEY HALL, WARWICKSHIRE.

that the Thames would never forgive him. Lord Cobham himself, in his elegy upon Blenheim, written at Oxford in 1727, thus speaks of the famous park and lake :

> "Not the vale
> Of Tempe, fam'd in song, nor Ida's grove
> Such beauty boasts. Amid the mazy gloom
> Of this romantic wilderness once stood
> The bow'r of Rosamonda, hapless fair.
> . . . .
> But see where, flowing with a nobler stream,
> A limpid lake of purest water rolls
> Beneath the wide-stretch'd arch, stupendous work
> Through which the Danube might collected pour
> His spacious urn ! Silent awhile and smooth
> The current glides, till, with an headlong force
> Broke and disorder'd, down the steep it falls
> In loud cascades ; the silver sparkling foam
> Glitters relucent in the dancing ray."

But the landscape gardeners, as has been remarked, soon found that their efforts did not meet with universal approbation. Repton, who swept away the terraces at Burley-on-the-Hill, and was a great exponent of the new methods,

AN ENTRANCE TO TISSINGTON.

explained that his idea was always to display natural beauties and to conceal defects, to convey the impression of size and to remove visible boundaries, and, in short, to give to his garden the freedom of Nature, refusing to have in it objects of mere convenience or comfort if they were incapable of being embodied in such a design. The argument is, perhaps, its own confutation. Those who were seeking a garden could not discover one in such a creation as Repton proposed, and a school arose which either urged a middle course or a return to the older style. Sir Uvedale Price, whose opinion has been cited, was one of the former ; Payne Knight, who wrote " The Landscape," apparently of the latter. He craved for the moss-grown terrace and the ancient avenue, seeking for some object to mark " the flat insipid plain." He had no satisfaction in seeing a house

> "'Midst shaven lawns that far around it creep,
>   In one eternal undulating sweep,
>   And scatter'd clumps that nod at one another,
>   Each stiffly waving to its formal brother."

The pure landscape can, in fact, have no dominating place in the garden. Its gentle sweep and fertile aspect form a pleasant outlook when the garden itself has been explored.

It will not be overlooked, indeed—and the point is of importance—that gardens such as these have no direct or necessary relation to the house. They might well be public gardens, and quite apart from any dwelling whatever. They embody an attempt to adapt Nature according to the conception of the picturesque school, and have nothing in common with the pleached alleys and sequestered bowers of Elizabethan and Stuart gardens. The romantic taste had come as a recoil from the great formality which had crept over garden design, and the idea of sequestered calm had mostly vanished from such places. They were pastoral landscapes or woodland scenes, beautiful in their kind, green and fruitful wildernesses, such as Boccaccio might have loved or Poussin painted, and their walks were so artfully planned that they seemed interminable. As Disraeli says of Armine Place, in " Henrietta Temple," there is no point in an ideal landscape garden where the

AN OLD GATE AND SUNDIAL, NORTON CONYERS, YORKSHIRE.

keenest eye can detect a limit. " Sometimes you wandered
in those arched and winding walks dear to pensive spirits.
Sometimes you emerged on a plot of turf blazing in the
sunshine, a small and bright savannah, and gazed with
wonder on the group of black and mighty cedars that rose
from its centre, with their sharp and spreading foliage.
The beautiful and vast blended together ; and the moment
after you had beheld with delight a bed of geraniums or
of myrtles, you found yourself in an amphitheatre of Italian
pines." In all this there is much that is attractive, and much
that is satisfying to the sense, but the domestic character is
not there. The link that binds the house to the garden is
wanting, and, in attempting to imitate the wilfulness or the
wildness of Nature, the designer has, indeed, made a garden,
but not one that forms, as the domestic garden should, a part
of the house to which it belongs.

We must look, indeed, for something more than the sloping

style of the later Renaissance. In those southern gardens
where noble stairs led up through terraced steeps, amid ilex
and lemon, and where the air was heavy with the fragrance of
the orange trees, marble deities looked out over the spires of
the cypresses, or stood reflected below in the silent pool. In
Le Nôtre's Théâtre d'Eau at Versailles, with its curtain and
wings, Jupiter on an Eagle, and Mars and Pluto were at the
ends of the formal alleys. Cupids of bronze held vases in the
Allée d'Eau from which water fell into marble basins, and for
the Bassin de Neptune, Bouchardon, Lemoigne, and Adam
sculptured the sea god, with trident, and Tritons and children.
English gardens had like adornments, and

"The Herald Mercury
New-lighted on a heaven-kissing hill,"

the Kneeling Slave, and the richly wrought vase, were
frequently produced in lead. Terminal figures stood in
rows or semi-circles against hedges of yew, and the sages

THE TERRACE AT RISLEY.   "Country Life."

mead, the woodland park, and the winding lake ; we must
hope to find something in the way of enclosure, something
of good architecture, something, perhaps, of good garden
sculpture. The terrace that borders the house will lend itself
to the gardener's hand. It may be shadowed by noble trees,
it may be bordered by the greenest turf, and be festooned with
a host of climbers, but it will be an architectural feature, and
our first step from the house to the garden. Good garden
architecture is indeed a necessity in any garden of character.
If there be sculpture, it must be of the best, and not always
will the gleaming marble appear so suitable against some dark
bank of trees as the more subtle tones that gather upon the
ancient figure of lead.

In the work of the sculptor we have, indeed, an aid to
garden effect that no school of gardening has ever despised.
It appeared least, perhaps, in the earlier gardens of England,
but its use was common in Italy and France in the stately

of Greece and Rome looked out over the gardens of
Englishmen.

But sculpture is as much in place in the landscape as in
the formal garden, and is even more necessary in order to
replace the features of a more strongly marked style,
as the creators of such gardens quickly recognised. Yet
there is, perhaps, no more difficult thing than to use
garden sculpture well. It should occupy the right place,
or none at all, and only the judicious eye can direct the
choice. This is especially true of the human figure, for the
urn and vase are sometimes almost necessary upon the terrace
or by the garden stair. A peculiarly happy effect, full of
suggestion in its character, is that of the ascent to the upper
lawn at Clifton, which we illustrate here.

But in truth the garden world is inexhaustible in character
and variety, as this book will show. Here the florist and
the architect have had their common ground, and here the

THE ROSE WALK AT HECKFIELD PLACE, HAMPSHIRE.

craftsman in metal has found high opportunities of displaying his skill. But, whatever be its individual character, the garden of our choice, as William Morris said, should look both orderly and rich, and it should be well fenced from the outside world. It should "look like a thing never to be seen except near a house, and should, in fact, look like a part of the house."

This is no meaningless saying, because it is in the garden governed by the house, its time-consecrated architecture, its immovable boundaries, the old oak and the ineradicable old timber within sight, and thus by the general fitness of things. "I am quite of opinion that a garden should look as though it belonged to the house, and the house as though it were conscious of and approved the garden. In passing from one to the other, one should experience no sense of discord, but the sensations produced by the one should be continued, with a delicate difference, by the other."

There is thus abundant room for individuality in garden work. The house is no dumb thing to the labourer in this field. It suggests to him a character and inspires him with the ideas of design. From its features he learns how to call the craftsman in stone or metal to his aid. If his be an old garden, where the ancient worker has completed an appropriate conception already, there is still room, in the embodiment of the new triumphs of the florist, or in varying the inner disposition of the pleasaunce, for manifold successes. But the true lover of the garden will make a way for himself. He will reject nothing of floral beauty, which is after all the chiefest of the gardener's means, and there will be no time of the year in which his garden is devoid of radiance. His garden is a romantic realm of never-failing charm, even though small it be. Fortunate is he who looks out from his terrace with its mossy parapet, where the peacock, perchance, shakes out its purple glories, to such a world of his own. Roses are clustering on the wall, or flinging out their fragrance below in the sun, mingled with the rare perfume of the aromatic azalea. Along the edge of the lawn his flower-border is glorious with the queenly lily, the dark blue monk's-hood, the tall hollyhock, the spiked veronica, the red lychnis, radiant phloxes, proud pæonies, the tall spires of foxgloves and larkspurs, and a multitude of fair denizens of the parterre. Richness characterises the whole, and the sentinel yews, the hedges, and box edgings, are there to give order and distinction, with the right degree of formality that belongs to the structure that

THE KNEELING SLAVE IN LEAD AT MELBOURNE.

that the house-dweller wins Nature to himself. In "The Garden that I Love" Mr. Alfred Austin has expressed some truths felicitously. "A garden that one makes oneself becomes associated with one's personal history and that of one's friends, interwoven with one's tastes, preferences, and character, and constitutes a sort of unwritten but withal manifest autobiography." And yet it is even better when we can read in it also the history of men who have gone before, and when, as the same writer says, the garden character is

is adorned. The moral sundial, the splashing fountain, the sheltered arbour, and the fragrant pergola, all have their places in such a garden. Nor need the landscape, and the woodland with the lake, be contemned. These lie outside the enclosed gardens, and all are beautiful and entrancing in their degree and place. The final fact is simple after all, and the garden designer must make it his own. It is that the house and the garden are the two parts of a single whole, and happy is he who can best interpret their sweet relationship.

THE GARDEN GATE AT RISLEY.

"*Country Life.*"

SUMMER-HOUSE TERRACE AT CLEVEDON COURT.

GARDENS OLD·&·NEW

CLEVEDON COURT, SOMERSET, . .
THE SEAT OF . . .
SIR EDMUND H. ELTON, Bart.

THIS volume could open with no better illustration of English gardening than is found at Clevedon Court. It is one of those places where the advocates of rival schools may meet upon common ground. The terraced character of the garden springs naturally, as it were, from the soil; not as in Dutch gardens, in which, on the level land, terraces were raised artificially; for we find here a pleasaunce whose terraces are the natural outcome of the gardener's art on the steep slope of the hill. The formality is

Copyright.

"Country Life."

THE ASCENT TO THE TERRACES.

such as appeals to every eye. It does not disdain the help of the florist nor of the collector of fine specimen trees. On the contrary, it claims all that the world of cultivated Nature can appropriately bestow. The background of foliage is superb, the various levels are charming, their bouquets of flowers are fair and fragrant, and below stretch the lawns, with their trim flower-beds breaking into the landscape features beyond. The garden, by the nature of the case, is architectural, as all old gardens were, and it has features that arrest the eye and arouse the imagination. Here is a place that has received broad and effective treatment; radiant colour, applied with bold character and yet with a palette not too garish, finds its counterpoise in the magnificent hill of foliage, and befits the mellow stonework and admirable forms of that typical English abode.

The design at Clevedon embodies at least two of the main distinctions of old gardens. The place has subdivision and change of level; there are walls and hedges, umbrageous masses and fine individual trees, and the appropriateness of the conception to the house and the site will impress every beholder, and gives to the gardens a character of great and welcome repose, and the design is frank and altogether charming. The subtle beauty of the place consists largely in the purely domestic nature of the garden. Its successive terraces belong, as we may say, to cultured leisure, and afford scope to all that fancy may suggest in the distribution of flower-beds or the character of borders. The old Englishman dearly loved such places. He would, perhaps, have added the character of inclosure, which is not noticeable at Clevedon Court except as imparted by the terracing, but his mind was attuned to the sequestered charm of a verdant terrace, like velvet to the tread, with a festooned walk on one side and a wall rising to the trees overhanging, and a well-cut hedge on the other, beyond which was the outlook over the pleasaunce of his pride. All may sound very formal to unimaginative ears; but Clevedon Court is a standing and visible proof of the merit of an old garden not closed to the nurseryman, nor unreceptive of modern ideas, but based in principle upon the garden character of an earlier time. Happy indeed is he who has such a sunny hillside upon which to work out his garden fancies as we find at this sweet Somersetshire home, with its rare surroundings, and the perfectly beautiful mansion as a centre-piece, though no place can lie outside the domain of the gardener's skill.

This beautiful land of Somerset, by the "Severn Sea," has many a noble home and radiant garden within its spacious bounds.

THE FORMAL GARDENS ON THE NORTH FRONT.

Hill and hollow, wood and meadow, the tangled brake and the heathery moor, the orchard richly fruited and the green corn yellowing for the sickle all the summer long, villages nestling in the hollows with thatched roofs, gay in the estival days, warm within when the winter winds blow, the lanes where the roses hang overhead from the hedges, the tall elms and beeches full in their leafage, or bare but beautiful when October has blown—this is the Somersetshire land. And that part of the county which is near the Severn has charms quite its own, as you may see from the pictures of Clevedon Court. Lying along the great estuary, Somersetshire looks—sometimes indeed from sandy flats but far more often from swelling hills—across to distant Wales ; and there is much of hill at Clevedon Court, which has developed the garden, shaped as we see.

The house is a wonderful architectural pile in this green and glorious setting. Here are parts of a mansion that stood in Edwardian days, when the warder kept watch at the heavily buttressed and portcullised door, and, grafted upon them, the most beautiful features of Tudor and Jacobean times. There exist still the winding stairways by which the watchman ascended to the outlook towers, the chapel in which olden worshippers knelt, the rooms where gentlemen in doublet and hose and ladies in ruff and farthingale dwelt. A place about which romance seems to linger and that fancy may people with many fair imaginings. Clevedon Court is a notable house even in a county that contains such splendid and interesting places as Montacute, Dunster, Brympton, and Venn House, to name no more of the many mansions of Somerset. Fire dealt unkindly with the west front in 1882, when the Elizabethan library, with its fireplace carved with the arms and badges of the Wakes, was burned ; but tasteful hands have made all good again, and Nature has lent her aid, so that now the fine old place is vested with luxuriant creepers, myrtles climbing almost to the gables, and thickly blossoming magnolias and fragrant roses adorning the walls. It is garlanded, indeed, just as such places should be—beautified, but not concealed.

The Wakes, who were the ancient possessors of Clevedon, parted with it to the Digbys, Earls of Bristol, who again sold it to the family of the present possessor in 1709. Sir Charles Elton, the sixth Baronet, so well described the place in his poem, entitled "The Two Brothers," published in 1830, that some

THE SOUTH TERRACE.

A NOBLE HILLSIDE GARDEN—THE BOWLING GREEN.

part of it may appropriately be quoted:

"I stood upon a lawn whose greensward spread
Smooth-levelled by the scythe; two mulberry trees
Beyond it stretched their old and foliaged arms;
Th' acacia quiver'd in the wind; the thick
And deep-leaved laurel darken'd the recess
Of massive buttresses; the mansion's walls,
Grey in antiquity, were tapestried o'er
With the fig's downy leaves, and roses climb'd
Clustering around the casement's gothic panes.
With terraces and verdant slopes, where pines
Arch'd their plumed boughs, and fruits espalier-trained
Were mix'd with myrtles and with arbute-trees,
The scene behind look'd sylvan; higher rose
The bounding hill, whose turfy paths were track'd
Up the bare herbage, gnarled with scatter'd crags
And topt with straggling fir, or chestnut broad;
A sweet, yet solemn landscape, for it spoke
Of sacred home."

Copyright. "Country Life."

THE WEST FRONT.

It was the poet's successor, Sir Arthur Hallam Elton, who did much to make the place more beautiful by judiciously laying out the grounds and planting trees on the hills. In his time Tennyson, Hallam, and Thackeray were frequent visitors to Clevedon Court. Old friendship existed between the Eltons and the Hallams, and Henry Hallam, the historian, had married Sir Charles Elton's sister. It will be remembered how Tennyson refers to the Hallams' burial-place in the churchyard at Clevedon:

"The Danube to the Severn gave
The darken'd heart that beat no more;
They laid him by the pleasant shore,
And in the hearing of the wave."

The hand of taste, inspired by the love of the beautiful,

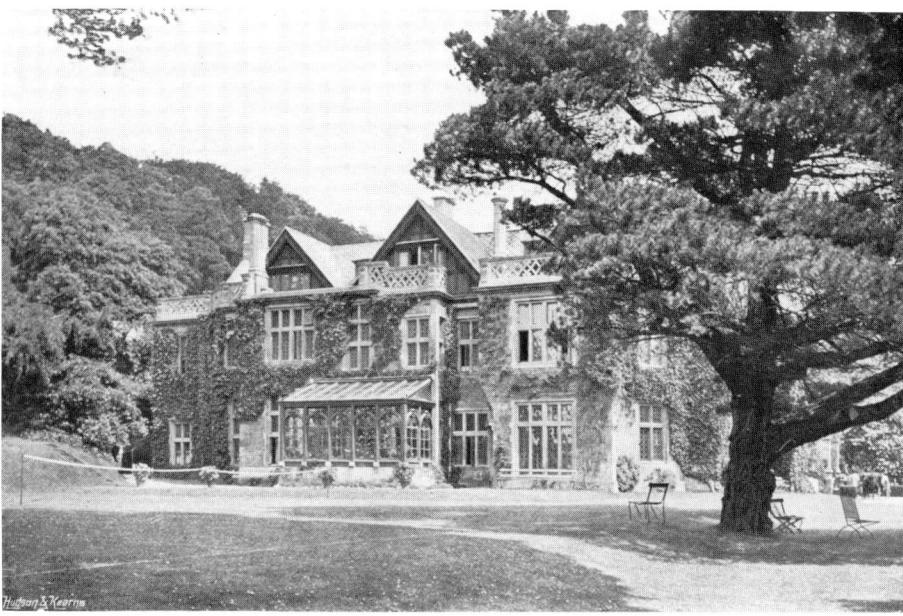

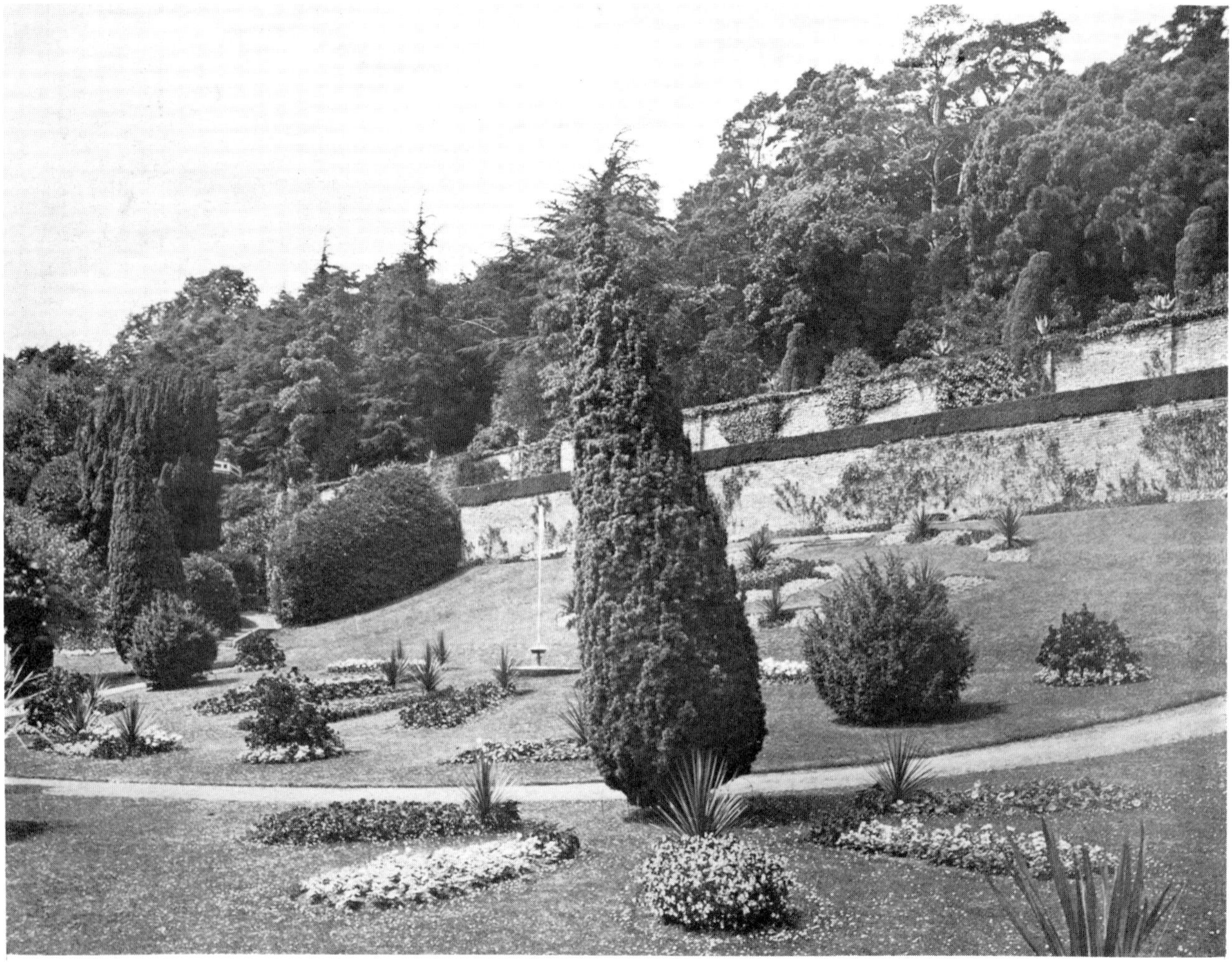

Copyright. Country Life.'

"THE PRETTY GARDEN."

A FINE COMPOSITION OF FOLIAGE. WALL, GRASS, TERRACE, AND HEDGE.

has ruled the adornment and maintenance of Clevedon Court. Its chief charm is in that terraced character of its garden, to which allusion has been made. The configuration of the land dictated the special form, and we may go far indeed before we find terraces so beautiful as these. There are terraces both above and below, for the house stands in the midst of the steep slope, and the effect is doubly charming. The artistic merits of a terrace have been disputed by some gardeners, but they cannot be gainsaid when they are displayed in such a situation and manner as we discover here. It will not be inappropriate to quote what Mr. Blomfield and Mr. Thomas say in defence of terraces in their volume, "The Formal Garden in England": "The terrace is admitted, even by the landscapist, to be desirable near the house. In the first place it presents to the eye a solid foundation for the house to start from, and gives the house itself greater importance by raising it above the level of the adjacent grounds, and again it is healthier. There is something uncomfortable in the idea of a house placed flat on the ground or down in a hole. It need not be necessarily damp, but one always imagines that it will, and that the timber will decay and the plaster moulder, and rats run over the floor; but when the house starts from a terrace it at least looks dry and the house enables you to see the garden."

But Clevedon Court is neither flat on the ground nor down in a hole, and an excellent idea of the garden beauty can be gathered from the accompanying illustrations. The appropriate terraces which have grown out of this condition are distinguished by the special character and are the glory of the place. Mossy and picturesque walls support these fine terraces. They combine luxuriant richness in plant and flower life, adorning the grass

"*Country Life.*"
FROM TERRACE TO TERRACE.

"*Country Life.*"
A FLOWER BORDER.

and garlanding the walls, with hedges and the trimness of well-clipped, smooth-shaven lawns. It cannot be forgotten that a garden must be appropriate, not only to the house, but to the situation. What is suitable on the crest or the slope of a hill might be altogether out of place on a flat, though even in such conditions it would be easy to point out low terraces that are a success. Generally speaking, however, it is true to say that a terrace cannot be a triumph unless there be the initial advantage of a slope. But the character of terraces also varies very much. These at Clevedon have little in common with the romantic terrace at Haddon, but are just as beautiful. Where we cannot go wrong is in adorning our terraces with green turf, a multitude of flowers, and sometimes with the shadowing of trees, with walls never bare, and parapets and balustrades touched with the greens of mosses. To linger on these terraces, looking out over the landscape, is a true delight, and no place could be more attractive for a quiet game of bowls. When a pastime such as this famous diversion of old times can be enshrined in such scenes as these we cannot wonder at its new popularity.

As our pictures reveal, Clevedon Court is a leafy place with masses of foliage garlanding everything with richness, but flowers are also abundant, and contrast their splendour with the dark hues of conifers and evergreens. Arches of roses perfume the air as we walk along, vases of fragrant flowers flank the pathway, and tall yews cast their shadows over the greenest of turf. Light and shadow are here singularly effective in their charm of variety. But to describe further what is so well depicted is unnecessary here. Clevedon Court, in the general character of its gardens, is scarcely excelled in England, and few places are more beautiful than this delightful Somersetshire home.

GARDENS OLD·&·NEW

LEVENS HALL, WESTMORELAND,
THE SEAT OF · · ·
MR. J. F. BAGOT.

APPROPRIATELY does this volume contain an account of the glorious garden depicted, because, among all the famous gardens of England there is none to compare in its kind with Levens. Here, in a glorious part of Westmoreland, stepping into the seat of ancient gentility, did Colonel James Graham, Grahme, or Graeme, younger brother of Sir Richard Graham of Netherby, and an astute courtier of Charles II. and James II., create, with the help of Beaumont, the disciple of Le Nôtre, and the French gardener whom James had employed at Hampton Court, a pleasaunce of the date and to his mind, which remains, well tended and maintained, just as it was formed about 200 years ago. Nowhere can we find anything so interesting or quaint to tell of the outdoor taste of the time. Lord Stanhope, in his "History of England," where he writes of the change of character in the gardens of the days of George III., speaks thus of the steadfast character of Levens: "So complete has the change proved that at present, throughout the whole of England, there remains, perhaps, scarcely more than one private garden presenting in all its parts an entire and true sample of the old designs; this is at the fine old seat of Levens, near Kendal. There, along a wide extent of terraced walks and walls, eagles of holly and peacocks of yew still find each returning summer their wings clipped and their talons pared. There, a stately monument of the old promenoirs—such as the Frenchmen taught our fathers, rather, I should say, to build than plant —along which, in days of old, stalked the gentlemen with periwigs and swords, the ladies in hoops and furbelows, may still be seen to this day." It was, perhaps, scarcely correct to say that the Frenchmen taught us all this. For did not the spirit come equally from Holland, to be grafted upon a similar character already existing in the gardening fashions here at home?

But before we describe the garden it will be well to say a little about Levens and its old possessors, for the principle we wish to enforce is that house and garden are, or should be, intimately associated, and that the character of one corresponds with the other. In the case of Levens a good deal may properly be attributed to the house and its successive owners.

The country surrounding the mansion is very fine in its character, richly varied and broken, with green meadows and the prospect of lofty fells; and the river Kent flows down, with a picturesque fall above the park—Levens Force—and many

Copyright.   "Country Life."

AN EARLY MORNING PICTURE.

BEECH ARCHES IN THE FRUIT GARDEN.

AN ARCH OF MOUNTAIN ASH AND CLEMATIS.

a turbulent race through the rocks, with foam and angry roar, to silent shallows shadowed by overhanging trees. Ancient oaks and mighty beeches seem to carry us back to a distant day, and the picturesque " peel " tower, about which the house has grown, reminds us of turbulent times, when the Scots were wont to sweep down and carry off flocks and herds — times marked, within many a mile of the border country, by these grey old peels, standing generally solitary, or converted to the humble uses of the farm. The garden at Levens, therefore, finds its contrast and background in a singularly picturesque and romantic region. Each is the foil to the other. The garden gains by its relationship with the varied scenery of its surroundings, and these offer greater enjoyment when we pass out to them from amid the well-shorn hedges and quaint garden features of the ancient pleasaunce of the Grahams.

Levens came by purchase, in the reign of Henry II., to the hands of Henry de Redman, or Redmayne, and during the ownership of the place by his family the original rugged tower of Levens was built, and it is probable that Alan de Bellingham, of Burnside and Hilsington, Treasurer of Berwick and Deputy-Warden of the Marches, who bought the estate from the Redmans in 1487, remodelled the place. The Bellinghams held Levens about 200 years. Their memories linger about it, and there still remain their badges of the bugle and the deer, while in a window of the inner drawing-room, painted round a shield of arms, is the dog Latin inscription :

" Amicus Amico Alanus,
    Belliger, Belligero Bellinghamus."

James Bellingham, Alan's great-grandson, afterwards knighted by James I., practically invested Levens with its present character, and he doubtless had a quaint formal garden, with trim walks and hedges, if without the wealth of topiary work which it has to-day, for his pleasure. We know that he had a bowling-green, for the very bowls with his crest remain. Before his time the great hall of the house stretched, with an open roof, westward from the tower, but he remodelled it entirely, and to him is due much of the lavish and beautiful adornment of the structure, with its rich panelling, rare and elaborate mantels, armorial glass, badges of the Tudors and of his own house, the mullioned

THE TOPIARY GARDEN—LOOKING TOWARDS THE STABLES.

QUAINT CREATIONS IN YEW.

BRIGHT FLOWERS IN HAPPY CONTRAST.

THE HOUSE FROM THE GARDEN.

windows and latticed panes of the time, wainscot of oak, and beautiful plaster work, lovely Spanish embossed leather, and much else that is beautiful of the Stewart age.

Such was the house which came to Sir James Graham, the creator of its gardens, in 1690. He bought it, or won it at the gaming table, from Alan Bellingham, the last of his race, "an ingenious but unhappy young man, who consumed a vast estate."

This Graham of "the Netherby clan" was, as befitted his name, a cavalier, who had spent a turbulent youth in the French Army, and was concerned much in the Jacobite risings. He stood high in the Royal favour, and was Master of the Buck-hounds and Lieutenant of Windsor Forest, and he accompanied James in his flight to Rochester; but he managed to escape some of the pains and penalties that were imposed on men less adroit, and, when the new settlement was effected, he lived much at Levens, working at the gardens he loved, except that his Parliamentary duties—for he was member for Westmoreland until 1722 — took him in the session to London. There is reason to know that Graham kept up his correspon-dence with his old associates, and Mrs. Bagot of Levens, in a charming sketch of her home, says: "If stones could speak, what secrets these walls might disclose, what plots of portentous importance they might reveal, could we but hear the talk of Grahme and his guests in the Gilded Parlour, as the wine flowed and the toast was received ' To the King over the Water ' !"

By the marriage of the Jacobite colonel's only daughter,

A NOTABLE GARDEN STUDY OF CHARMING EFFECT.

the house passed to Henry Bowes Howard, Earl of Berkshire, and descended through female heirs to successive owners. It appears to have been well cared for throughout its history, but never more so than now, when it possesses the old-world quaintness that conjures up before us the very spirit of the older time. Before we pass out into the garden, we may, in fancy, be privileged to drink the ancient toast from a goblet called a " constable," filled with " a unique and bitter compound of the genus of ale," while, as custom dictates, we stand on one leg—" Luck to Levens while the Kent flows ! "

There is a portrait at Levens of M. Beaumont, " professor of the topiary art " to James II., who created the gardens under the direction of Colonel Graham. They seem to have been begun about the year 1701, and have the quaintest charm, in their trim and grotesque character, that can be imagined. There are old-world formal gardens in many places still ; Scotland has yet some dear old pleasaunces, like

yew, and bushes cut into globes and cones, or even into judges' wigs and grotesque birds, shall we have no glow of floral beauty ? Levens is a standing demonstration to the contrary, for its ancient topiary work is associated with flowers in great and varied profusion, which are enhanced in effect by the dark greens of the trees and bushes. Evidently the law maxim, " Inclusio unius est exclusio alterius," has no force in the verdant and floral courts of the gardening world, and, then, so enthusiastic a lover of the " natural " style of gardening as Batty Langley, who was a boy when Levens was designed, included cones of evergreens among the adornments of his " beautiful rural garden."

The terrace in front of the house commands a fine view of the noble country in which Levens lies. From the eastern end of the terrace extends the formal garden. There Nature and Art have certainly worked hand in hand, and the abundant fecundity of one has been matched by the patient labour and

FROM   THE   SOUTH.

that sweet region at Tully Veolan, where Rose Bradwardine walked with Waverley. There are recent gardens of the old character, too. But, go where we will, we shall find nothing in its kind to rival ancient Levens. No other place in England possesses so much old and curious topiary work. In the introduction to this volume something of the history of topiary gardening in England is told. From mere quaintness grew its extravagance, it became fashionable in extreme developments, and the bitter satire of Pope and others killed it entirely. But the *topiarius* is an ancient functionary in the garden, who was known even to Pliny, and throughout his history he has certainly invested his verdant realm with a great deal of curious charm. Levens is the happiest example of his skill that England possesses, and is happily illustrative of a point that must be insisted upon—that the adoption of one masterful feature of gardening does not involve the banishment of the charms of others. Because we have trim borders of box or

extraordinary skill of the other. Colour and the quaintness of peculiar beauty crowns the conjoint work. It is an ideal and grotesque world we enter when we tread the pleasure-place of Colonel Graham and of M. Beaumont, the gardener who came from France. Fantastic forms rise in yew, strange and remarkable, as far as the eye can reach—a peacock here, a huge umbrella-like construction there, an archway, a lion and a crown, a helmet bigger than any man could wear, and a host of other such creations, all shaped out of the " ductile yew," except that some of the smaller adornments are in box. A bewildering world of gardening, some may say ! We rest in a green arbour, shaped after the fashion of a judge's wig, to wonder what some strange animal or figure can be. " At last," says Mrs. Bagot, in an account she has written of this marvellous pleasaunce, " I see you pause in bewilderment over some weird contorted figures of box, which form a complete circle round a small rose garden. Are they

A PEEP OF THE HOUSE.

fish, flesh, or fowl ?   Neither.   It is Queen Elizabeth and her
maids of honour these quaint little bushes are striving to
imitate ; this one, see, has a ruff and a crown.   Uncover and
bend to the Virgin Queen ! ''   We are more prepared, perhaps,
to salute the memory of the dead gardeners who created such
a world of wonder, as well as the taste of those at the present
day who know so well how such a place should be maintained.
The mention of the rose garden suggests the other picture to
which we have alluded.   For a multitude of glorious flowers
stand with radiant faces upturned in these formal beds, or
droop their fragrant blossoms in clusters towards the ground.
Trailing branches of roses extend between the formidable
topiary monsters.   What a carpet it is we tread on !   Gorgeous
are the things that now attract us—stately lilies, tall lupines,
blushing pæonies, the fuchsia, pansy, salvia, bergamot, and
pink.   These are here, with a crowd of other garden glories ;

rise hollyhocks, dahlias, and sunflowers, while below there
is a wealth of gay blossoms in every season of the year.
Masses of beautiful climbers clothe the grey old stone.
Indeed, wherever we go at Levens we are greeted by flowers
in profusion, which, as we say again, is proof that formal
character is no bar to the gayer delights of the garden.
Levens has also a beautiful park, very rich in all the charm
that arises from the varied configuration and abundant
foliage that are everywhere characteristic of Westmoreland.
    There is an old sundial also to delay us — that
charming feature of the English garden.   It stood, says
Charles Lamb, as '' the garden god of Christian gardens.''
If its business use may be superseded by more elaborate
inventions, its moral uses, its beauty, might have pleaded
for its continuance.   It spoke of moderate labours, of pleasures
not protracted after sunset, of temperance, and good hours.

A GARDEN PICTURE FROM A WINDOW.   "Country Life."

and to walk by high beech, yew, or holly hedges with such
neighbours is simply delightful.
    We pass in and out among the charms of the garden,
noticing pots and tubs of rare flowers, which add points of
beauty in many places, and ever glad to turn to the quaint old
house, vested with jasmine, purple clematis, and brilliant
nasturtium.   Or we may set out from our arbour of green,
where a curious old portrait of Colonel Graham hangs in the
branches of a tree, may pass along the beautiful turf walks,
so pleasant to walk on, with avenues of old apple trees, and
York and Lancaster roses blossoming freely below, to the large
square bowling green, a scene of singular attraction, where the
old game is played once more.   Now we think of gentlemen
with wigs and clouded canes exhibiting, with biassed bowls,
their calculated skill ; of the rippling laughter of ladies in
silks and satins, with paint and patches, too, greeting with
Schadenfreude those who lamentably fail.   Or, again, we
pace the terrace with the well-managed border, from which

It was the primitive clock, the horologe of the first world.
Adam could scarce have missed it in Paradise.   It was the
measure appropriate for sweet plants and flowers to spring
by, for the birds to apportion their silver warblings by,
for flocks to pasture and be led to fold by.   The '' shepherd
carved it out quaintly in the sun ; and, turning philosopher
by the very occupation, provided it with mottoes more
touching than tombstones.''
    Here, then, at this quaint and interesting Northern
seat are grass walks, beautiful flowery borders, an ancient
bowling green, a charming park with a fine avenue of oaks
a mile in length, and noble individual trees of oak, sycamore,
beech, chestnut, and elm.   In truth, Levens Hall is unique
and offers many distinct characters.   It has the advantages
that belong to a glorious country, which add so much to the
beauty of its park, and it has a garden gay with flowers
throughout the year, yet more famous still for the historic
trees clipped by the topiary hand.

GARDENS OLD·&·NEW

BULWICK HALL, NORTHAMPTON, THE SEAT OF . . MRS. TRYON.

SWEET and beautiful Bulwick has a garden suggestive to many. Here is no grand style, no lordly avenue, no imposing terrace; only the dear charm of the old domestic garden, the beauty and fragrance of the individual flower and the broad colour masses, of the verdant lawn and the grass walk, of the long border and the thickly-trellised and clustered wall, of the quaint pillar, and the gate fashioned by the hammer of the old craftsman. Nothing here is beyond the compass of many. It is such a garden as the loving hand may flush with a greater charm. We may fancy that here the flowers must love to grow, responding to the love that is bestowed upon them. " The Larkspur listens —I hear, I hear ! And the Lily whispers—I wait." It is a garden both orderly and rich, neither copying the wilful wildness of Nature, nor donning the formal bonds of a more grandiose style, fenced in from the outer world and belonging truly to the house it adorns. Simplicity rules its character,

from the broad flagged way that leads in from the arched entrance to the sequestered paths where the lily and larkspur and splendid hollyhock neighbour the queenly rose in the companionage of many a fair and fragrant friend.

Bulwick Hall itself is a building of plain and substantial character, older than some of its features would suggest, for it was built in the seventeenth century, and is entered by a remarkable and unusual classic colonnade bearing the date 1672. There are the picturesque features of moss-grown gate-posts, those curious segmental steps below the house, and gates and rails of hammered iron belonging to that time, and other interesting evidences of old habitation.

But nothing is so attractive at Bulwick Hall as the park and gardens. Of the former, it is enough to say that it is large, and that it pleasantly clothes with its woodland beauties hills of attractive contour and character. Many fine trees are here, well grown and rich in leafage, disposed in groups

THE LONG GARDEN.

and belts, and making a lovely sylvan landscape, for the house stands upon the southern slope of the hills that separate the county of Northampton from the Welland.

At one time the place was occupied by Lord and Lady Henry Grosvenor, and it presented in their time, as it does in the hands of Mrs. Tryon now, a notable example of artistic garden arrangement. The entrance by the colonnade and the delightful vista through the long garden, which is disclosed at the gateway, are characteristic, and tufts of African lilies (Agapanthus umbellatus) are in the path of greyish flagstone, and the vases are filled with summer flowers.

Look where we may the arrangement is simple and pleasing. There is no attempt at the elaborate, imposing, or ornate. A wealth of flowers boldly grouped, filling the fragrant borders, fine shrubberies, and well-disposed ornamental trees, are the materials which produce the delightful effect.

It is pleasant to descend from the higher terrace by the

garden, and another traverses it from east to west. At the end of the long walk referred to are the splendid iron gates leading into the park, which it is said a local crafts-man made. However that may be, they are an exceedingly fine piece of work, and, with the lofty pillars between which they hang, make a very charming picture indeed, and one quite characteristic of the old English garden.

We may turn to the left at the gate of the long garden to reach the rose garden, first passing a fine old evergreen oak, upon which time has left its mark, for chains and props now support its boughs. The rose garden is beautiful, as such gardens should be, and is protected from the north and east winds by walls, while a yew hedge is on the other hand, through an opening in which we enter the lower garden, devoted to vegetables and kitchen produce, and having a walk through the centre. Here, again, there are flowers, the place thus forming a flower reserve, in which the gay

THE IRON GATES LEADING TO THE PARK.

mans on to the level sward of the bowling green by the steps with iron railings of Dutch craftsmanship, caressed by ivy, ampelopsis, and climbing roses. At the foot a long border of mixed irises and another border filled with herbaceous plants add a great charm to the secluded green. Then we may retrace our steps to the mansion, and pass between the lofty ball-capped pillars, with their wide open gates clustered with roses and other climbers, to survey the fragrant beauties of the long garden, the extent of which is about 150yds. Here the cool grassy walk is flanked by glowing borders, which are backed by tall holly hedges, generally well clipped at the top, and with standards rising boldly at intervals. The shiny leaves of the dense hollies throw the flower borders into relief with fine effect. The grass walks at Bulwick are one of its features—there is little or no gravel in the neighbourhood—and are particularly pleasant to tread. In addition to the walk in the long garden, a grassy way runs round the whole

border is happily associated with the large leaves, herbs, and fruit trees of the kitchen garden. The chief merit of the gardens at Bulwick is that flowers are every-where. The borders of hardy plants are simply glorious in their wealth of harmonious colour from early spring to late autumn, and the irises flanking the creeper-covered walls are delightful. Exotic plants, also, if we may so call them—geraniums and so forth—are not wanting. In Lord Henry Grosvenor's time at Bulwick the carnations were mag-nificent. One bed of the Ketton Rose variety was 25yds. long and 6ft. wide, and 15,000 flowers of good form were open at the same time. A host of lovely climbers add a great charm to this beautiful garden. Roses, honeysuckle, sweet peas, and everlasting peas, with many other beautiful clinging plants, are there. Everything is leafy, green, and full of colour.

As Mr. Robinson remarks in his "English Flower Garden," the pleasure grounds at Bulwick do not astonish by showy

THE OLD GARDEN.

THE BOWLING GREEN.

display. They are rather modest as regards flower-gardening in immediate relation to the house, but are charming in their little side gardens and long and pretty borders and vistas, and their delightful grass walks. The character, as we have said, is quite distinct from the usual effect in formal and elaborate gardens, and is very fresh and attractive. But much of

the beauty of the place arises also from the abundance of fine trees and shrubs, and the remarkable leafiness of the surroundings. The colour effects in the autumn are superb, and at a time when many gardens have lost their summer charm that at Bulwick is still beautiful, owing to the well-chosen variety of flowering plants that fill its beds and borders.

CURIOUS SEGMENTAL STEPS.

A GARDEN WALK.

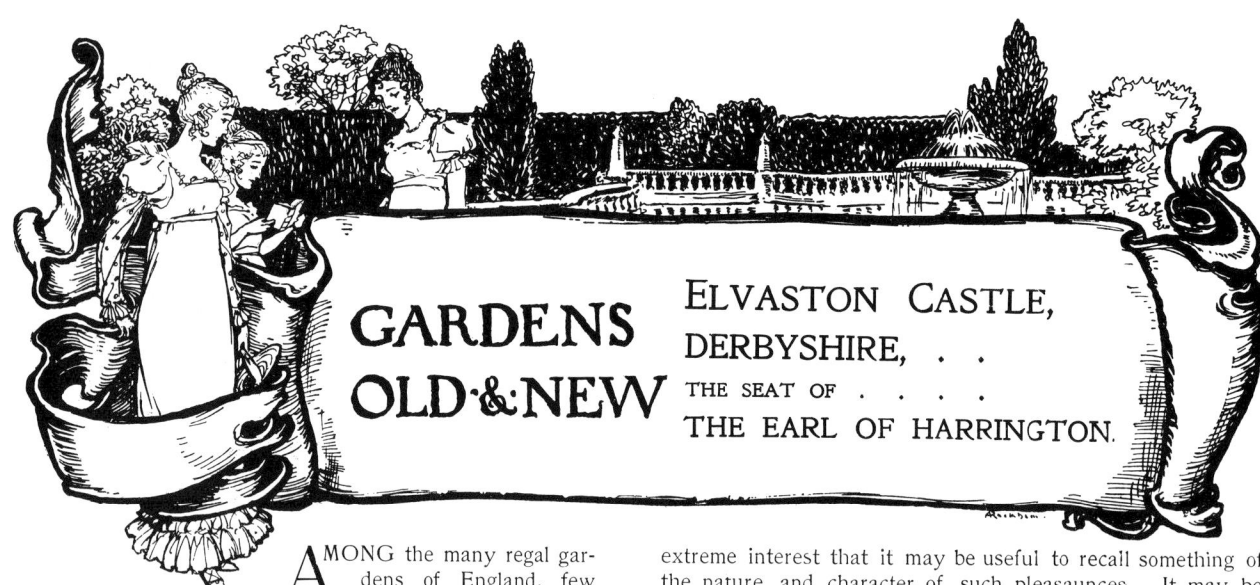

GARDENS OLD & NEW

ELVASTON CASTLE, DERBYSHIRE, . .

THE SEAT OF . . . . THE EARL OF HARRINGTON.

AMONG the many regal gardens of England, few are more remarkable than those of the Earl of Harrington at Elvaston, in Derbyshire. There are many fine gardens in which topiary features exist—pyramids, columns, and globes of yew, with glorious hedges trimmed and cut to the evenness of a wall, but not even at Levens is there anything so characteristic as the quaint and curious creations of Elvaston. The history of the gardens has something of an element of enchantment about it, and we may well wonder to witness the formation of such gardens in modern days. We have already said something about topiary gardens, but the subject is of such extreme interest that it may be useful to recall something of the nature and character of such pleasaunces. It may be conceded freely that verdant sculpture may be carried too far. It is apt to be dissociated, though there is no valid reason why it should be, from the sweeter charms that we look for in gardens. Yet the cutting of trees has always exercised a fascination over gardeners. Rightly used, they have regarded it as investing gardens with attractive quaintness, and yet with sequestered calm. Delightful truly it is to cross a green court enclosed with fine yew hedges, to pass between lofty, pillared urns filled with flowers, through gates, perhaps, of beaten iron, and then to enter a curious world which the cunning hand of the *topiarius* is tending, where we find

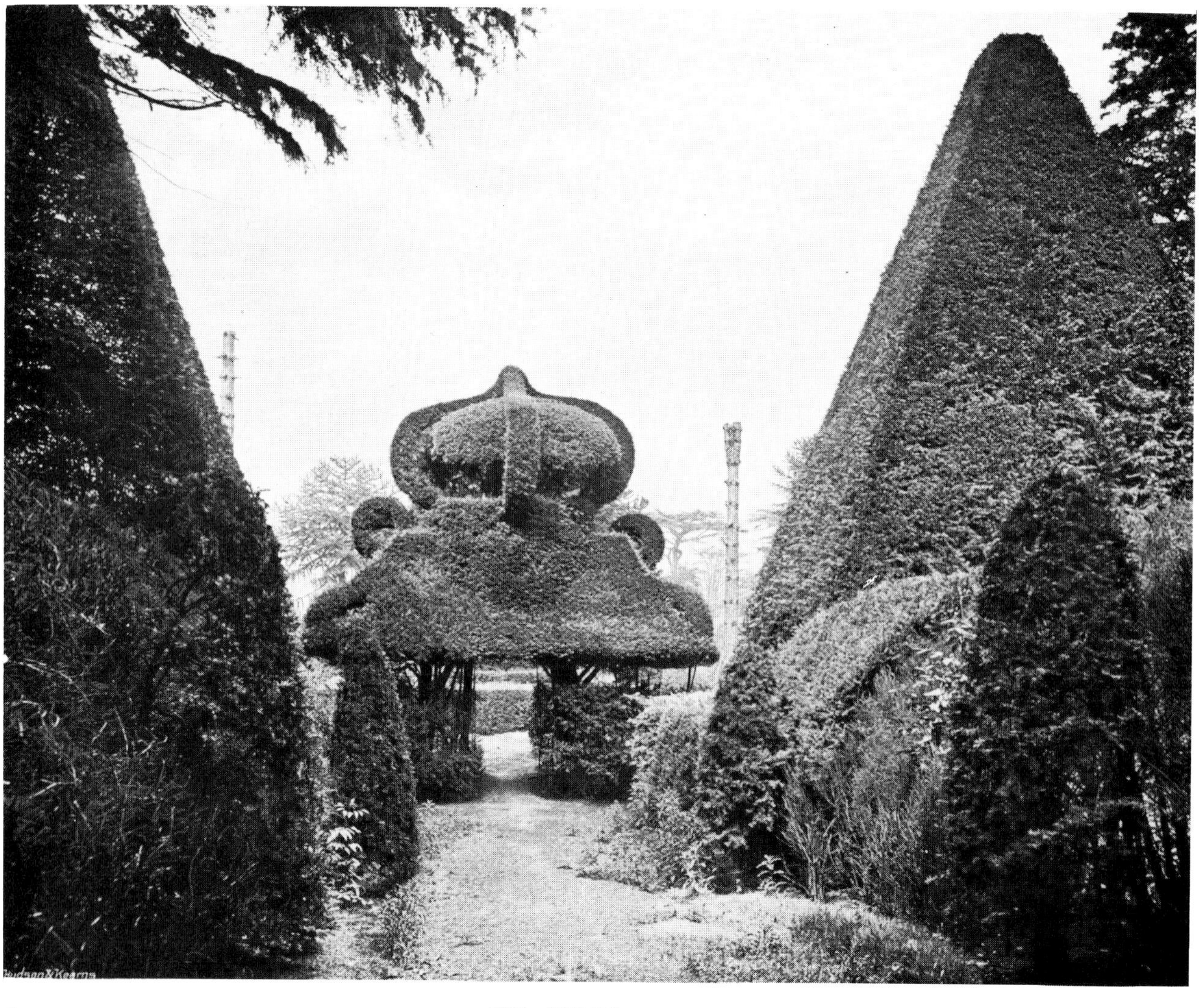

Copyright. THE MOORS' ARCH. *"Country Life."*

"TONSILE EVERGREENS SHAPED INTO A VARIETY OF FORMS."—*PLINY.*

glowing flower-beds, contrasted with the dark shade of "midnight yews." The *topiarius* was, as we have said, an a cient figure, known in the Rome of the Cæsars; he put Nature in duresse in mediæval gardens; he was skilled in the "antike work" of Tudor pleasaunces; alleys of yew and pleached arbours of hornbeam were his care in Stuart and later times. Bacon's ideal garden, it will be remembered, had a green in front, and a heath or "desert" for contrast on the other side, alleys on either hand, and a stately hedge to enclose it. It was not to be "too busie or full of work" within, and, as for "images cut in juniper or other garden stuffs," he did not like them—"they are for children." Yet, in moderate degree, and for the merit of a great deal of quaintness, Bacon admitted the topiary gardener and pleacher to his pleasaunce. It was only when extravagance was reached, with odd figures, that he protested. "They be but toys; you may see as good sights many times in tarts."

Copyright. *"Country Life."*

THE GOLDEN YEWS.

We may gather from his view, which is not lacking in profundity, that topiary gardening is, after all, a question of degree, not of kind. Evelyn himself tells us how they trimmed the hedges of hornbeam, "than which nothing is more graceful," and of that "cradel walk, for the perplexed twining of the trees very observable"—"Queen Mary's Bower," of wych-elm, be it noted, at Hampton Court. He describes how "tonsile hedges," 15ft. or 20ft. high, were to be cut and kept in order, by means of "a scythe of four feet long, and very little falcated, fixed on a long sneed or straight handle."

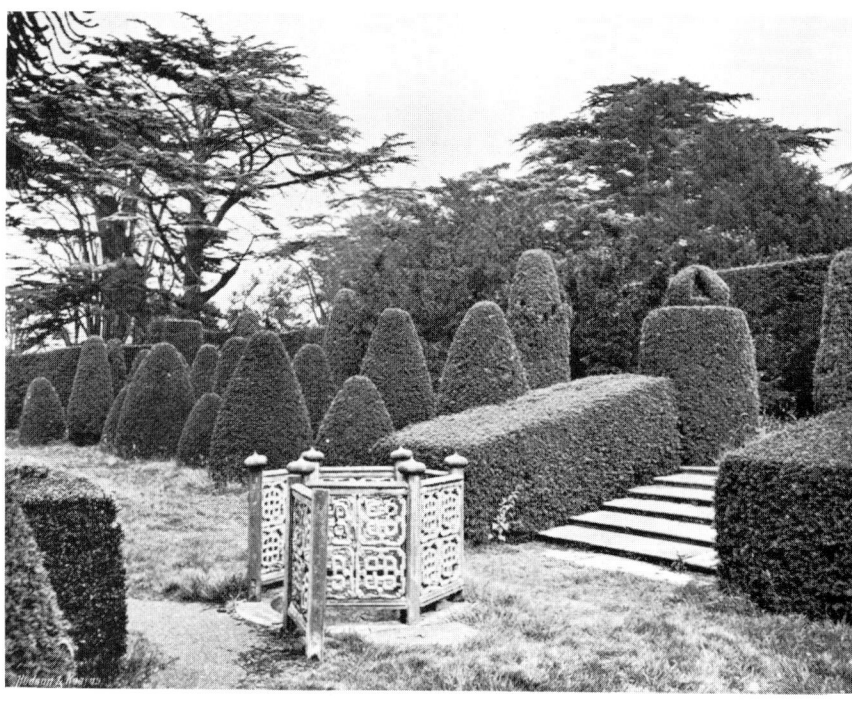

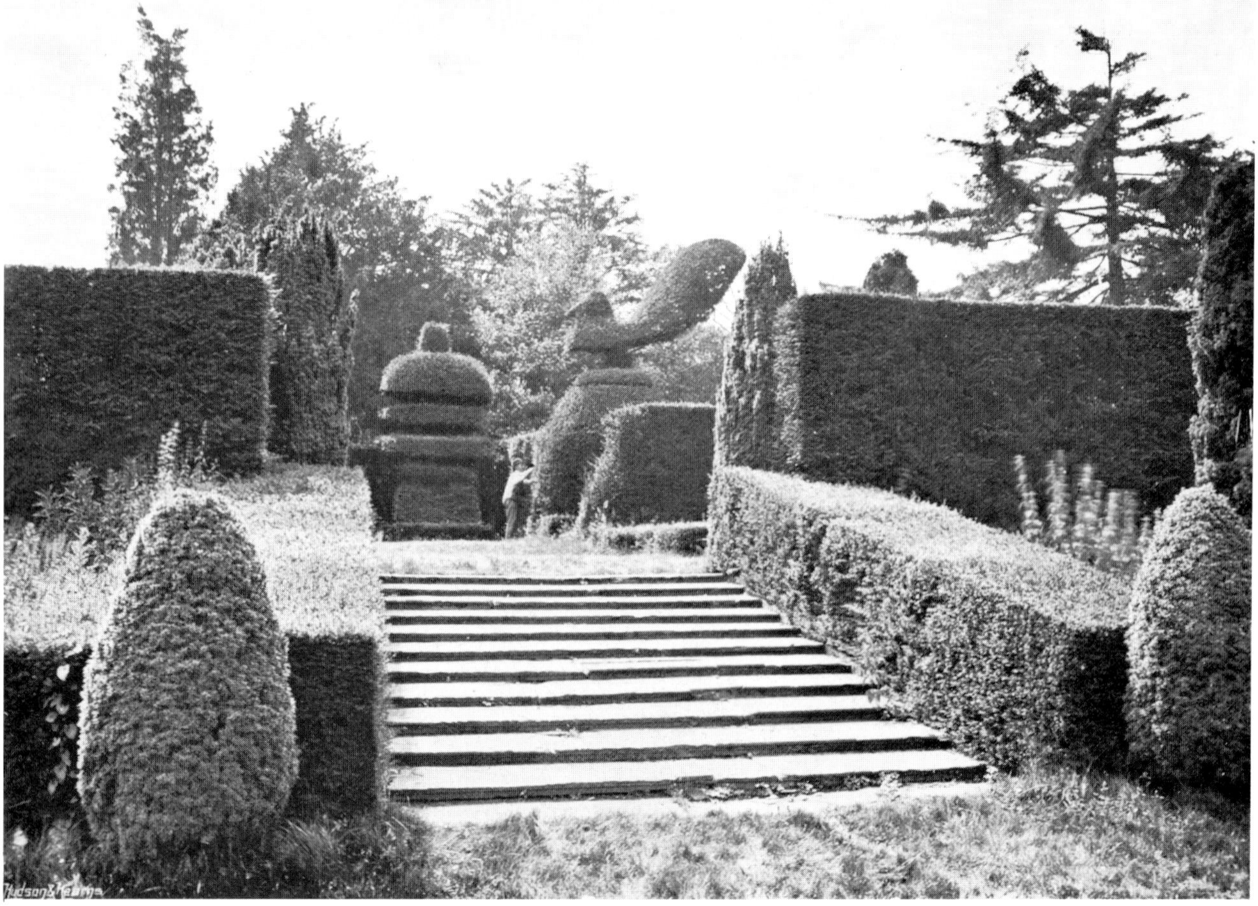

Copyright. *"Country Life."*

THE APPROACH TO THE ITALIAN GARDEN.

THE HOLLOW HEDGE AND ARBOURS.

And he had "four large round Phyllyreas smooth-clipped," at Saye's Court, Deptford. Hentzner, a German who visited Theobalds even in the sixteenth century, spoke of the labyrinths, terraces, trellis walks, bowling greens, geometrical beds, and divers trees clipped into cones, pyramids, and other forms. The most famous early example of a topiary garden in England is Levens, which we have already described, and Heslington Hall, near York, is another very characteristic example. The gardens at Elvaston Castle belong, therefore, to a style of honourable antiquity, and they differ mainly from their congeners in being modern.

Such gardens, of course, as Addison says, do not humour Nature ; rather they deviate from it profoundly. But the essayist recognised many kinds of gardening as of poetry : "Your makers of parterres and flower gardens are epigrammatists and sonneteeers in this art ; contrivers of bowers and grottos, treillages and cascades, are romance writers ; Wise and London are our heroic poets." This is a spirit of eclecticism that should lead us to recognise the merits of Elvaston, though Addison himself, who lived in a time when a profound change had begun, did not like to see trees rising in cones, globes, and pyramids, and to discover the marks of the scissors upon every plant and bush, but preferred to "look upon a tree in all its luxuriancy and diffusion of boughs and branches." *Quot homines, tot sententiæ.* It was a question of taste. Addison did not know whether he was singular in his opinion. Certain it is that only the extravagancies and vagaries of the topiary gardener brought him into discredit. The feeling of taste, to which Bacon had given expression long before, was aroused against his fantastic creations. Gardens about London, said Mr. Lambert, writing to the "Linnean Transactions"

THE "TOPIARIUS" AT HIS WORK.

THE ALHAMBRA GARDEN.

in 1712, were remarkable for fine cut greens, and clipped yews in the shape of birds, dogs, men, ships, etc. Pope was scathing in his sarcasm. His famous gibes set a vogue in garden criticism, and a loud outcry was raised for the natural in the gardener's art, such as some may echo when they see these pictures of Elvaston. It was the sarcasm of the wits that did much to dethrone the sculptor of trees, and his more quaint brother, the pleacher.

Yet it was easy to run into another extreme. Shenstone's dictum, that "Art should never be allowed to set foot in the province of Nature," becomes an absurdity when we remember that without art there can be no gardening, and that essentially there is no difference in principle between the cutting of grass and the clipping of a hedge or tree. The

"Temple of Venus," the "Egyptian Pyramid," the "Ruined Arch," the "Hermit's Cave," the "Saxon Temple," and the oft-recurring grotto, frequent features when the boundaries of the inclosed garden had been broken down, were every bit as absurd as the verdant monstrosities of the grove. The efforts of the *topiarius* were, perhaps, even less to be deprecated than those of the landscape gardener, for the former was content quaintly, and in a conventional spirit, to imitate, while the latter often deliberately set to work to make places and things appear to be what they were not.

It is not, indeed, difficult to understand the prayer expressed by Knight ("The Landscape," second edition, 1795), when he, with many heart-pangs, turned from some destruction brought about by Kent or Brown—

"Again the moss-grown terraces to raise,
And spread the labyrinth's perplexing maze;
Replace in even lines the ductile yew,
And plant again the ancient avenue.
Some features then, at least, we should obtain
To mark this flat, insipid, waving plain;
Some vary'd tints and forms would intervene
To break this uniform, eternal green."

Happily the best of our gardens are flower gardens, and avoid one extreme and the other, and the truest guide in forming any garden must be the hand of taste educated by the comparison of many examples. The Elvaston gardens, which have rarely been illustrated, are a remarkably fine example of the particular form of art they embody. So much all will concede, even

THE BIRD COTTAGE.

though they do not appreciate the characteristic features evolved. Rarely, if ever, has greater skill been evinced, not only in the cutting, but in the transplanting, of trees. These gardens are, therefore, exceedingly interesting, and their very great quaintness and many curious features do indeed make them attractive to the gatherer of gardening lore. To create a garden like this, enthusiasm and knowledge were necessary, not less than skill in the handling of trees, and all these were available. The situation of Elvaston is not picturesque, and had no features of landscape character, whence probably the genesis of its curious gardens.

They might never, indeed, have been created exactly as they are but for the unpicturesque situation they occupy, which offers, it would appear, few opportunities to the landscape gardener. Even that man of fame, "Capability" Brown, seems to have shrunk from the work of laying out the grounds, for he bluntly wrote to the fourth Earl of Harrington, who invited him to undertake the task, that "it was all well, and he would let well alone." Whereupon the Earl demanded the reason for so strange a retort, and Brown replied, "Because the place is so flat, and there is such a want of capability in it." When, therefore, landscape gardeners look upon the topiary work of Elvaston they must be content, since not even the capability of Brown himself, perhaps the greatest exponent of the landscape gardening style, sufficed to give the gardens the character they might wish. He presented, however, to the Earl of Harrington six cedars of Lebanon, which were planted on the east side of the house, and grew into fine and handsome trees.

THE PAVILION AND TERRACE STEPS.

It seems difficult to believe that these quaint and curious shapes at Elvaston, clipped out of trees of fine and luxuriant growth, are really modern. The history of the garden exhibits a triumph. Something akin to genius was needed for its creation. The infinite capacity for taking pains, at all events, was there. Before the Bird Cottage, the Alhambra Garden, the Moors' Arch, and other strange features could be fashioned, the trees must be planted, and England has no more remarkable example of tree-planting. Large sums of money were expended by Charles, Earl of Harrington, in bringing numbers of trees, many of them fully grown, from a distance. In March, 1830, he called William Barron to his aid, who became

A VISTA IN THE DOMAIN OF QUAINTNESS.

famous for his skill in the work of transplanting, and remained in the Earl's service until his Lordship's death, a period of something like twenty years. Mr. Barron thoroughly drained the ground and formed large kitchen gardens, and under his direction hot-houses were built and the transplanting of old trees began. Three cedars, ranging in height from 28ft. to

ON THE TERRACE.

32ft., were removed from near the vicarage to the east avenue, and shortly afterwards a cedar, 43ft. high, with a 2ft. trunk, and spread of branches of 48ft., was removed from the front of the house. Glorious old yews were brought upwards of thirty miles after being raised by means of remarkable tree-lifting appliances and devices which Barron did much to improve. Very large pleasure grounds were also laid out, at one time covering eighty acres, and the artificial lake with its curious surroundings is another work of the time.

No expense was spared to perfect the gardens, and the rarest and finest specimens of conifers, at that time far less common than now, were obtained. As an illustration of the enthusiasm that inspired the creator of Elvaston, it is interesting to note that the first specimen in England of Nordmann's silver fir (Picea Nordmanniana) was planted by the Earl of Harrington, and that some of the yews brought from other places were centuries old, thus making Elvaston truly a link between the past and the present.

The garden is particularly rich in splendid golden yews. Among other trees are the Douglas fir; the Chili pine, or "Monkey Puzzle" (Araucaria imbricata); the Deodar (Picea nobilis), splendid in sombre blue-green colouring; the Spanish silver fir (Picea pinsapo), now a well-known tree; the black Austrian pine (Pinus austriaca); the Swiss pine (Pinus cembra); and the glorious Corsican pine (Pinus laricio). This last may be recommended to all who intend to plant pine woods, being of comparatively quick growth, tall, straight, finely-coloured in the trunk, very hardy, and succeeding well in almost all kinds of soil.

To describe the particular features of the gardens of Elvaston Castle is perhaps unnecessary. They are well illustrated in our pictures, and, as an example and a contrast, can scarcely fail to interest very many. Of the surroundings and islands of the artificial lake, which, at least, is a landscape feature, though scarcely an effective one, the Duke of Wellington is said to have declared that this was "the most natural artificial rock" he had ever seen. It must not be supposed that the coniferous growths and curious shapes of these lordly gardens are dissociated from flowers. The contrary is, in fact, the case, and the hot-houses are stored with very choice plants.

As a pleasant mark of the changed times, and of the far larger extent to which those into whose coffers the streamlets of Pactolus pour admit others to participate in such enjoyments as are to be derived from the contemplation of beautiful gardens, it is interesting to note that Elvaston was closed to the public in the days of the garden-making Earl. He is said to have instructed Barron that, if the Queen came, she was to be shown round, but that no one else was to be admitted. Nowadays there are few great gardens that are not open, on at least one day in the week, for the pleasure and profit of many.

The fourth Earl of Harrington died in 1851, and was succeeded in the title and estate by his brother, Colonel Leicester Stanhope, C.B., who thought it desirable to reduce the large staff of eighty men then maintained. At the same period trees from the reserve nursery, and some others, which could be dispensed with without great loss to the place, were disposed of, a specimen of Picea nobilis going to Osborne for the Prince Consort, while the Crystal Palace grounds were embellished with not a few of the Elvaston trees. Yet how many beautiful trees remain, however, in these splendid Derbyshire gardens the reader will learn from our numerous pictures. These have been taken specially to illustrate the little-known topiary character of the place. Assiduous care is necessary for the maintenance in perfection of such shapes as we depict, and old servants well

SUMMER SHELTERS.

experienced in the work maintain the traditions of the place. Perhaps we ought not to conclude this account of Elvaston without a word of praise for the splendid fruit grown there. Those who visit the great fruit shows have often remarked that many of the richest prizes go to the grapes, peaches, and other dainty productions from this garden.

GARDENS OLD & NEW

ROUS LENCH COURT, WORCESTERSHIRE, . .
THE SEAT OF . . . . .
REV. W. K. W. CHAFY, D.D.

A T Rous Lench Court the garden aspect is generally of the older time. The mossy terrace flecked by the sunlight through overhanging trees, the quaint yew hedges clipped by the patient and judicious skill of the topiary hand—working in the restraint of art, and not developing its extravagance—and the ascending flights of the successive upper terraces, are all cast in the mould of a former time. Yet there is subtle development in the character, and the inclusion of many things that are new. It is this blending of the new with the old which is the chiefest charm of some of our English houses and gardens, and it is the one thing about them which cannot be imitated. As for the making of our lawns is given the heart-breaking recipe, " First we mows them, and then we rolls them for hundreds of years," so of our houses it may be said that first we build them in pleasant sur-roundings, and then we develop them into perfection, or rather leave them to develop themselves by slow process of evolution.

Our present garden is found in a somewhat remark-able part of England. Clustered about the last spurs of the Clent Hills, just where they die away into the Vale of Evesham, are several old villages, all distinguished by the generic name of "Lench." The most important of these sequestered places is Rous Lench, apparently known before the Conquest as "Biscopslenz," or Bishop's Lench, because it belonged to the See of Worcester, and afterwards of Lench Radulphi. It took its present name from a family of great note which long owned it.

The house is one of the true old English character. They would build in the old times of stone, where stone was not difficult to quarry ; but in the forest lands, where stout timber was easy in the getting, the knight or squire would raise a wooden dwelling, with stories and windows that overhung, and numerous picturesque gables. Many such, like Rous Lench Court, are scattered through-out the land ; but few have had its good fortune, for it has descended through careful hands, and certainly is now in the possession of those who know how to value it. The family of Rouse built the present half-timbered house, probably early in Tudor times, halfway up the slope. There were ancient yews there already ; but evidently planting very soon began, and it is delightful to find that both house and garden are preserved with the aspect of ancient days. Here, it is said, Cromwell slept on the night before the battle of Worcester, for the Rouses were his chief supporters

A GRASS-COVERED WALK.

"Country Life."

hereabout, and partly ruined themselves in the Parliament's cause. From them the estate devolved twice through female heirs upon representatives of other families, and in 1876 Sir Charles Henry Rouse-Broughton, Bart., sold the estate to the Rev. W. K. W. Chafy, who was already the owner of Sheriff's Lench, and

       THE SOUTH "AISLE."

where the kitchen gardens are neighboured by a lofty tower. It is a pure delight to linger upon these lovely terraces, where the very spirit of old time seems enshrined. We are in a frame of mind to agree with old Nash that the true glory of this place is, indeed, in its ancient garden. The many forms of yew seem endless as we

thus united the Lenches mostly under one head, a condition they had not held since the days of William de Beauchamp, soon after the Conquest.

Owing to the steepness of the slope the gardens possess a very quaint character, being formed in ten terraces, with mossy flights of steps, beautiful terrace walls, and wonderful yew hedges as we ascend, enclosing delightful gardens and lawns. The yew arbour in the lower pleasaunce has a charm that is almost unique, and the pleacher and cutter of yew has never done more satisfactory work than that we see as we look up the long flights that lead up through the "tunnel" and between the hedges to the top of the hill,

proceed. In addition to the central ascent we have alluded to, there are glorious "aisles" of yew climbing the hill both on the north and the south. The yew walk beside the house has grown into a stately avenue, now widened, lengthened, and duly cared for, and it has scarcely a peer in England, though we do not forget the famous example at Haddon. It is said to have been planted about the year 1480. The long vistas between the solemn yews, shadowed deeply, but flecked with light where the sun penetrates the gloom, are lovely in their sequestered calm. Here we feel the absolute appropriateness of the character, the subtle and satisfying influence of the right surroundings. But we see also that there is no necessary

       THE NORTH "AISLE."

ROUS LENCH COURT FROM THE NORTH.

THE   LOWER   TERRACE.

antagonism between this dear old-world character and the radiant charms of the flower world, which are happily united at Rous Lench Court.

Dr. Chafy has greatly extended the garden, and introduced various forms of verdant adornment. Where the second quadrangle was, there is now a delightful formal garden with a fountain in the midst, the noble terraced path leading up the hill, and another at right angles bringing us into other realms of yew. A pinetum stretches below to the park, and a rosary, with another fountain, and a stone balustrade, leads us down by a great stone stairway to the lowest lawn. Altogether the house and garden, thus placed on the hill, have

THE   LOWER   YEW   AVENUE.

THE HOUSE AND TERRACES.

FROM THE ARBOUR, LOOKING TOWARDS THE TUNNEL.

a fascination quite their own, while in front, peeping through the elms, is the little grey church, with fine Norman doorways, and many monuments of the Rouses, some of them very curious, within.

THE LOWER PLEASAUNCE.

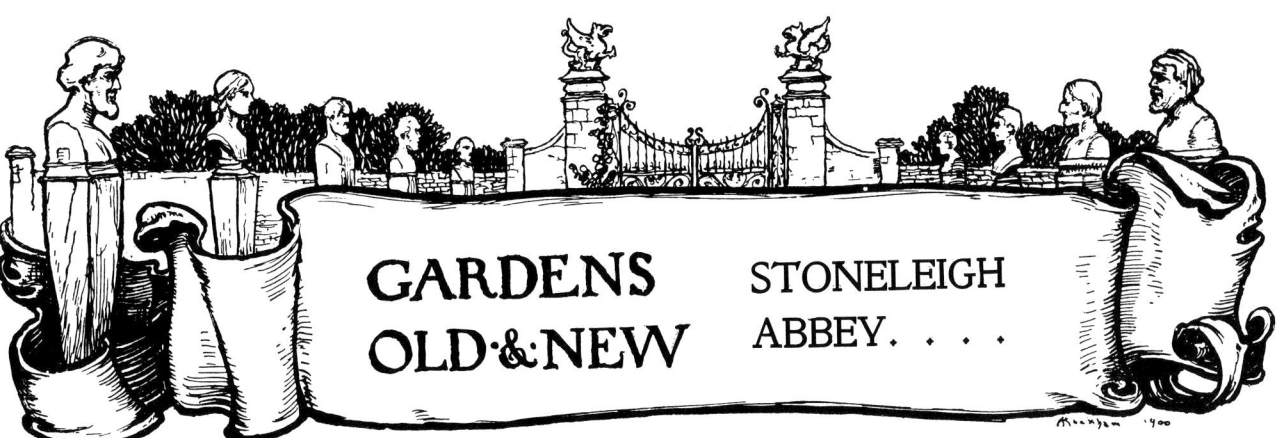

GARDENS OLD·&·NEW   STONELEIGH ABBEY. . . .

A NOTABLE house and a beautiful garden are those at Stoneleigh in Warwickshire. The river Avon, in its course south-westward through the county, glorifies many a great abode, and traverses regions that are famous in our history. It sweeps in broad lakelike stretches through the sylvan park at Stoneleigh, it lingers, as if reluctant to leave, beneath the shadow of romantic Guy's Cliff, it passes by ancient Warwick, where Cæsar's Tower keeps watch upon its waters, it sweeps onward in growing volume to glorious Charlecote and Stratford, and reflects on its broad bosom the scenes that Shakespeare loved, and that are haunted by the splendour of his genius still. It is a region in which the delights of many gardens are found. Here, as he says, we are in the Forest of Arden, that country of the greenwood, where the swineherd tended his grunting troops, crunching the mast of oak and beech. There was feeding, says Dugdale, for 2,000 hogs in the King's woods at Stoneleigh; land, too, where the corn ripened for the sickle, and where the sokemen of the royal demesne, when the day of the lord's "prederepe" came, rode through the fields from dawn to sunset, with the white wand of brief authority in their hands, to make sure that none were defaulting or "laboured idly" in their harvesting for the King. It was ordered that the reapers should eat by themselves, "everyone a little wheaten bread, four eggs and pottage, namely, gruel, without flesh boiled in it, except the lord would afford them other, with cheese and beer sufficient; and after dinner one sitting down with bread and beer; but the sokemen themselves to be served with better diet, according to their degrees." This is a dead-and-gone world, some will say; but reflect how like it is to ours—the reapers stretched at length beneath some shadowy hedge or spreading tree, eating their bread and cheese, and quaffing foaming ale in the heat of the summer day.

"Country Life."

THE WEST FRONT.

A VIEW OVER THE AVON.

The Cistercian monks came to Stoneleigh in the days of Henry II., and the ideals of the world they knew seem embodied in the ancient features of the abbey and the village church, the Norman doorways and columns, and in that glorious gatehouse, which is one of the many gems of the place. But look at the long lines of the great classic mansion

THE GRECIAN GARDEN.

A VIEW FROM THE TERRACE.

of Lord Leigh, and you are in another world entirely. Here all is the stately splendour born of new ideals—great lines of windows, tall Ionic pilasters, supporting the deep cornice and long balustrade. The monks had their herb garden by the cloister, where simples and old-world flowers grew. Now at Stoneleigh we find a stately terrace flanking the majestic pile and overlooking the river, with gardens planned and adorned in the taste of Italy and France, smooth-shaven lawns adorned with the trees of many climes, and umbrageous native woodlands full in the view. In the neighbourhood of the house the garden has rightly assumed its character.

The imposing mansion was built by Edward, Lord Leigh, and the gardens were laid out about the year 1720. The site of the abbey had been granted in 1539 to Charles Brandon, Duke of Suffolk, and after passing through the hands of several members of his family, had fallen to William Cavendish, who sold it to Sir Rowland Hill and Sir Thomas Leigh, aldermen of London. Sir Thomas Leigh was Lord Mayor when Elizabeth came to the throne, and rode before her when she entered the City to be proclaimed at St. Paul's. His wife was the niece of Sir Rowland Hill, his patron, and when he grew wealthy, as a merchant adventurer, drawing profit from beyond the seas, he secured Stoneleigh for his own, and the remains of the abbey were embodied in a building of Tudor and Stuart times that was very picturesque and attractive. Another Sir Thomas Leigh, great-grandson of the first, was loyal to the Royal cause, and received Charles I.

THE GREEK VASE.

"with right plenteous and hospitable entertainment," when the unfortunate monarch, with 6,000 horse, was marching to Nottingham, and found the gates of Coventry closed against him.

The changes that have passed over Stoneleigh since that time, its development into a palatial house of classic form, and the taste of successive owners, have dictated the character of the terrace gardens. The beautiful Avon, broadening out into a lake-like expanse just before the house, implied the arrangement.

Horace Walpole inveighed against the terrace, and the balustrades that "defended these precipitate and dangerous

THE ITALIAN GARDEN.

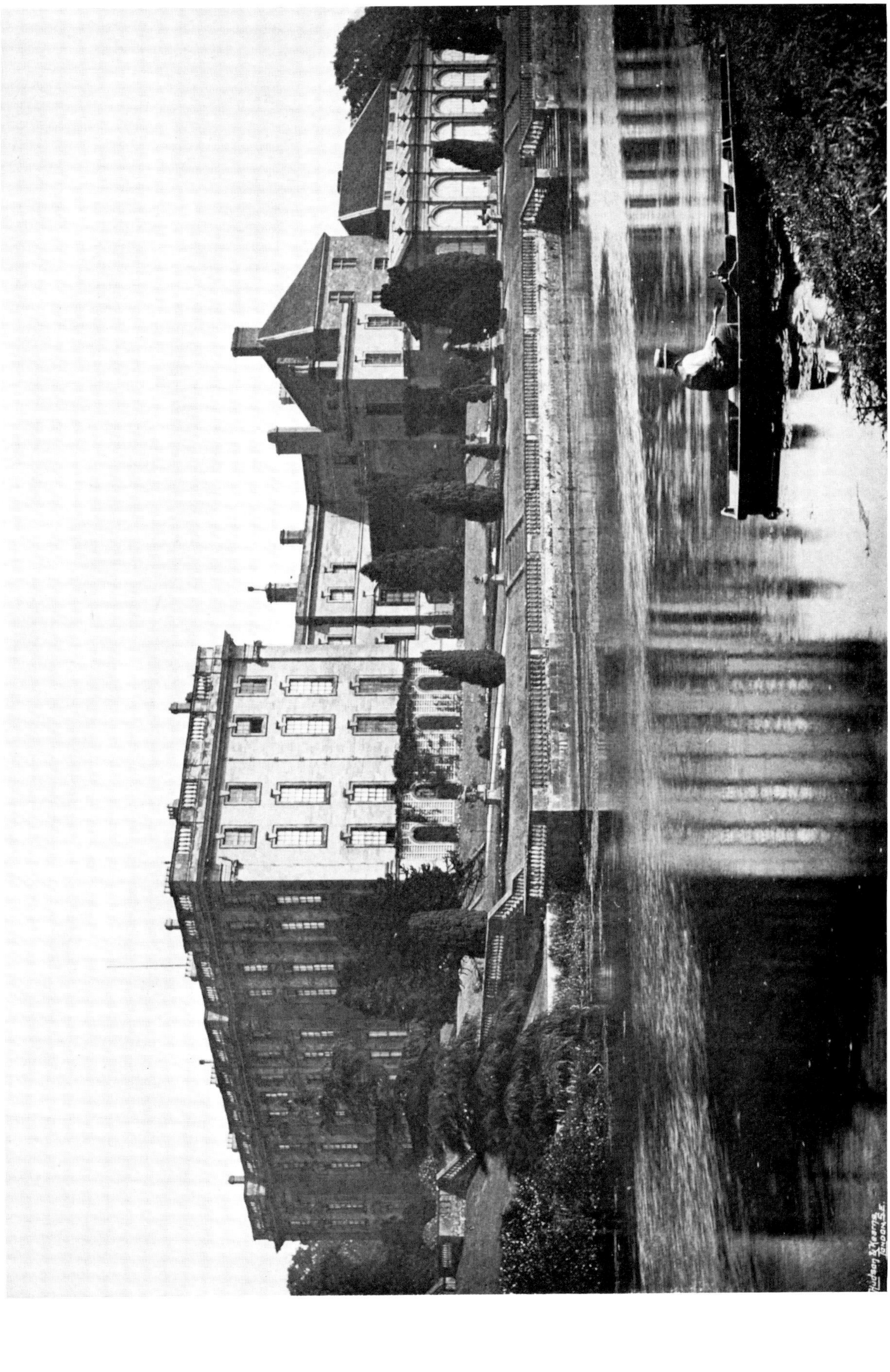

STONELEIGH ABBEY FROM THE RIVER AVON.

Copyright "Country Life."

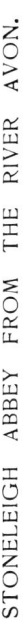

THE ANCIENT ABBEY GATEHOUSE.

elevations," as against the vases and statuary that adorned them, but here at least he would have been content to see no canal " measured by the line," but the mirror-like expanse of the river leading the eye to the "subjacent flats," where the garden melts into the landscape. Here is no featureless garden, no mere landscape conception, but such a picture as we might find in a painting by Claude. The strong points in the foreground, both of form and colour, make by their emphasis a fine contrast with what lies beyond, and the effect is enhanced by the arrangement. The outlook from the terrace is, indeed, wholly satisfying to the eye, for beyond the

river is a broad prospect of the well-wooded park, the trees diversifying the slopes, and forming a rich feast of changing colour in the seasons' change.

And the foreground is radiant with garden beauty, for the terrace itself is beautifully laid out in its "Italian" and "Greek" gardens. These are merely designations, but the character is formal, with quaint box edgings outlining the designs, and the treasures of the flower world are here in much splendour, with effect markedly beautiful. It is not only the tender summer exotics that make this brave display, but the old-fashioned perennials, too, flourishing in abundance, and the

homely flowers of the border adding to the charm, while the fragrant rose is cultivated in great profusion. Dark yews form points of interest to enforce character ; there is a fine old hawthorn planted in 1818 ; and the vases and garden accessories are charming and excellent in form. Particularly interesting trees are pointed out, as, for example, a Wellingtonia and an oak planted by the Queen and the Prince Consort when they visited Stoneleigh in 1858. Very charming features, again, are the ivy-covered walks, bowers, or arbours, which are of great extent, each being not less than 200ft. in length, 8ft. in height, and 10ft. in width. These were planted in 1818, a period when much was done to improve the garden, and lead away from the summer-house, which has open sides, and commands a lovely view of the river and park. On the other side of the mansion, and between

THE WEST GARDEN.

THE WATER TERRACE AT STONELEIGH ABBEY.

it and the old gatehouse, is a fine expanse of turf, with excellent specimen trees about it—grand evergreen oaks, a fine old cork tree, deciduous cypresses, and others.

We do not go far at Stoneleigh without finding something to admire in the garden architecture and accessories — the terrace walls and balustrades, the vases, the fine gate-posts and flights of steps, and perhaps more than all in the excellent character of much of the ironwork. It is all good garden architecture, carrying the spirit of the mansion into its surroundings, and the vases are particularly excellent. Fine ironwork, in gates and clairvoyées, adds infinitely to the interest and attraction of stately gardens, and gives them a character of individuality which they might otherwise lack. The craftsman in stone, iron, and lead is, indeed, a powerful auxiliary, and many examples of skill are to be found at Stoneleigh. And, as might be expected at such a notable place, there is everywhere the evidence of the high state in which the garden is maintained, and the lavish care bestowed upon it.

THE GARDEN GATES.

that the umbrageous beauties and pleasures of Stoneleigh park are accounted for. But this would only be partially correct. The soil is suitable for the growth of trees, but it has been the care of successive owners which has invested the place with its charm. The trees have been planted judiciously for their broad effect, and the variety of hue and contour is very charming.

Indeed the visitor, before reaching the mansion, has already had a foretaste of the glories of the surroundings. The abbey is often approached from the west lodge, known as Glasshouse Lodge. The road hence traverses the home park by a fine avenue, and crosses the Avon by a handsome stone bridge designed by Rennie and erected in 1809. Here are many noble forest trees, but the deer park is even more beautiful. The whole country-side is much diversified, and the slopes are dotted with splendid trees, sometimes singly and sometimes in groups, or even woods, some of them in their prime, others the gnarled and mighty giants of a former day. If these ancient monarchs of the glade could speak, if there were "tongues in trees," what stories they might unfold! Near the abbey is a huge pollard oak, 33ft. in girth, and legend says that Shakespeare wove his fancies beneath an oak in the deer park. Other grand old trees cast their broad shade by the north lodge. Close to the keeper's lodge there are the remains of a fourteenth century cross; Stare Bridge, on the way to Stoneleigh village, is a picturesque structure of many arches, narrow, with recesses in the parapet, built by the monks at the same date; from the higher ground you may discern the three spires of Coventry rising far away to the north, and there is a great and rich district all around, famous for natural

It is not possible to stand on the terrace without desiring to explore the sylvan beauties of the famous park. We cannot forget that "This is the Forest of Arden." We are on the fringe of it, perhaps, but its character is upon the land. For Arden was never a forest in the legal sense—a place set apart for the preservation of game for the sovereign or some great subject, with its officers and courts for the repression of forest offences. The legal forest was not necessarily, nor, perhaps, usually a country of woodland. It often included great expanses of moor and heath, and was a region given up to the chase, where the way of transgressors was hard. But the Forest of Arden, made

famous by Shakespeare, was, even in the modern sense, a well-wooded district of glades and thickets, lying mostly north of the Avon, and distinguished from the Feldon, or more open country to the south. In his "Origins of English History," Elton said, indeed, that a squirrel might leap from tree to tree nearly the whole length of Warwickshire.

In a certain sense, therefore, it may be held

beauties and rich in historical associations, making a fine framework for the special charms of Stoneleigh. Park and garden are indeed glorious, and the abbey itself, with its varied features of many dates, and the great art collections with which it is adorned, is truly one of the noblest mansions in the land. Of its history a good deal might have been said; its many beauties, here suggested, would be hard adequately to describe.

THE WORK OF THE GARDEN CRAFTSMEN AT STONELEIGH.

GARDENS OLD & NEW

WILTON HOUSE, SALISBURY, . . .
THE SEAT OF THE EARL OF
Pembroke & Montgomery.

GREAT are the memories that move, and far does the imagination soar, when we speak the name of classic Wilton—

> "Pembroke's princely dome, where mimic Art
> Decks with a magic hand the dazzling bowers."

Here in stately form is enshrined much that Englishmen prize— the memory of men of lofty ideals, of statesmen and soldiers, of those of chivalrous heart, of poets, painters, thinkers—we scarcely know what lofty thoughts the name of Wilton may not inspire.

The hand of Holbein in its earlier architecture; Shakespeare acting here with his troupe; kings often within its walls; Ben Jonson and Massinger associated with it; Philip Sidney walking in the groves as he conceived and wrote "Arcadia"; George Herbert piously meditating in its halls;

famous treasures of art by fine judgment and liberal patronage brought here together—of all these things do we think when we visit Wilton.

And the gardens, too, are among the most famous in the land. Classic calm reigns over them; they are the home, we think, of contemplation, in the shadow of cypress and yew; they have beauties and varieties such as few gardens can display. In the time of Charles II., who "did love Wilton above all places," the house was altered by a Gascon, Solomon de Caus, and the grounds appear to have been designed by his son, Isaac de Caus, who described and figured them as "Hortus Penbrochianus." One Adrian Gilbert had a great part in the work. Thus does Taylor, the "Water Poet," speak of his achievement: "Amongst the rest, the pains and industry of an ancient gentleman, Mr. Adrian Gilbert, must

HOUSE AND GARDEN—A HAPPY GROUPING.

"PEMBROKE'S PRINCELY DOME."

FOUNTAIN AND STATUARY.

THE PALLADIAN BRIDGE.

not be forgotten; for there hath he (much to my Lord's cost and his own pains) used such a deal of intricate setting, grafting, planting, inoculating, railing, hedging, plashing, turning, winding, returning, circular, triangular, quadrangular, orbicular, oval, and every way curiously and chargeably conceited; there hath he made walks, hedges and arbours, of all manner of most delicate fruit trees, planting and placing them in such admirable art-like fashions, resembling both divine and moral remembrances, as three arbours standing in a triangle, having each a recourse to a greater arbour in the midst, resemble three in one and one in three; and he hath there planted certain walks and arbours all with fruit trees, so pleasing and ravishing to the sense, that he calls it ' Paradise,' in which he plays the part of a true Adamist, continually toiling and tilling.

"Moreover, he hath made his walks most rarely round and spacious, one walk without another (as the rinds of an onion are greatest without, and less towards the centre), and withal, the hedges betwixt each walk are so thickly set that one cannot see through from one walk who walks in the other; that, in conclusion, the work seems endless; and I think that in England it is not to be fellowed, or in haste will be followed."

Plainly there was at Wilton a rare example of the work of the old garden-fashioner, with all its hedged enclosures, its maze, its quaint conceits, and its verdant allegories. Perhaps there is a timid vein of sarcasm in the Water Poet's description of its extravagance. Evelyn, who visited Wilton in July, 1654, was not, apparently, so much impressed. He describes the garden, "heretofore esteemed the noblest in England," as "a large handsome plain," with a grotto and waterworks, which might have been made more pleasant if the river that passed through had been cleansed and raised, for all was effected by "mere force." "It has a flower garden not inelegant," he says. "But, after all, that which renders the seat delightful is its being so near the downs and noble plains about the country contiguous to it. The stables are well ordered, and yield a graceful front, by reason of the walks of lime trees, with the court and fountains of the stables adorned with Cæsars' heads."

Many changes have passed over the gardens at Wilton since those times, and, perhaps, few of the special characters described by

THE ITALIAN GARDENS.

Taylor can now be found there. We do not now trace the touch of ancient Adrian Gilbert's quaint fancy and curious hand there. Yet old yews are in the gardens which probably belong to those early times of classic Wilton, and, lingering in "the yew tree's shade," it is pleasant to remember how the cutter and pleacher of trees worked out his picturesque fancies there of yore. He did not enjoy the advantages of these days, for the florist, with his new charms, has tempted the gardener, we may say, out into the fuller sunshine.

It has always been the happy fortune of Wilton to remain in the hands of those who have valued it. The Herberts have been the patrons and lovers of everything good in art, so that the choicest adornments have been chosen to beautify their home. Judicious planting, the laying out of broad stretches of turf, the addition of architectural features and of appropriate statuary, and a fine conception of what gardens should be, have contributed to make the surroundings of the house peculiarly satisfactory.

The country tends to be flat, but there is the charm

as the reader will anticipate, the features are all Italian. There are gay masses of colour in these beds, with stone edgings and green margins, ranged about the fountain; there is the contrast of rich and glorious foliage; there are the terrace walls and statues of the style, all conceived in the finest taste, without a jarring note to break the classic spell. Then, on the south side, with equal dignity, we find green stretches of lawn, with stone-edged flower-beds at the nearer margin, to set off the stateliness of the splendid pile.

Amid the many aspects of formal and natural gardening that grace this princely abode, the leading characters will be discerned in the rich greensward and masses of trees which enframe or relieve the rest. One particularly noble feature is the group of ancient cedars of Lebanon, planted about the year 1631, and older even than the monarchs of Warwick and Goodwood. They were, in fact, probably the earliest cedars planted in England; and thus we linger, with pleasant thoughts of those who dowered us with these beautiful trees, beneath their sombre shade. Of course the storms

"Country Life."

THE ANCIENT CEDARS.

of water, for the rivers Nadder and Wily—of which one bounds the park, and the other separates the pleasure grounds from the kitchen gardens—add grace to the scene. How the opportunity has been seized of throwing a classic character over the place, may be seen in the picture of the fine Palladian arcaded bridge, designed by Inigo Jones, which was built by Henry, Earl of Pembroke, for the crossing of the Nadder.

Successive hands have, indeed, enriched the surroundings of Wilton with new attractions. The place owes much to the taste and judgment of Catherine, Countess of Pembroke, daughter of Count Woronzow, who died in 1856, and whose noble monument is in that surprisingly beautiful Lombardic church at Wilton, a vision, as it were, of the Renaissance of Northern Italy, erected by Lord Herbert of Lea, her son. This lady, in the changes she effected in the gardens, was guided much by the advice of Sir Richard Westmacott.

There are several styles of gardening at Wilton, giving variety and character to the grounds. Near the house,

of years have thinned the venerable growth of these monarchs, but others have been planted to bear them company and to maintain the history of the pioneer cedars of Wilton.

Here is a lesson that should be learned—to think of the future, and where, in forest or copse, the decay of Nature sets in, to plant the vigorous shoots that shall speak to later generations of the character and beauty of the things we are now delighted to behold.

From the Italian garden we may pass along a pleasant walk between lofty yews, relics of the old garden of Isaac de Caus and Adrian Gilbert, to the building known as Holbein's Porch, a stone structure which formed part of the old house. Sir Richard Westmacott had much to do with the planting of the shrub groups, and there is a broad walk running at right angles to the east front, 300ft. long, and terminating in a stone seat clustered with yew, which also was his. Wherever we go, however, something will please us, and it is much, indeed, to view the noble spire of Salisbury from the gardens of classic Wilton.

GARDENS OLD·&·NEW

MONTACUTE, SOMERSET, . .
THE SEAT OF . . .
Mr. W. R. PHELIPS

"Through this wide-opening gate
None come too early, none
return too late."

SO reads the hospitable legend over the principal portal of
Montacute—a place gracious to enter, and that tempts
the visitor to linger long. Rarely may the radiant
summer awaken greater glories than in venerable
Montacute. Where can spring be more delicious or
autumn more fruitful than here? To sit with book in hand in
that lovely garden-house is paradise indeed. Thence to look
along that many-windowed façade, to conjure up visions of
past times, while witnessing the stately pleasures of these—who
does not feel ravished at the thought? But failing the actual
presence of Montacute, these pictures are enough to suggest its
charms. Here is a Somerset garden filled with the best spirit
of its time, embodying all that is good in the character of the
old garden world, and a valuable examplar of the sunny glories
of the ancient pleasaunce to those who may have felt repelled
by the formal severity sometimes associated with the venerable
yew. Floral grace and garden fancy are happily mated in
plant life and stone at glorious Montacute.

So many gardens in this volume are entered from the
houses they adorn, that it may not be unsuitable to approach
Montacute House from its surroundings, recording the fact that
it lies some four miles only from the pleasant town of Yeovil.
One very beautiful way of reaching Montacute is through the
old village of Montacute—this being the most beautiful, indeed,
of all the four approaches. Leaving behind us quaint cottages
and rustic adornments we reach the lodge on the south side,
embowered in roses, and giving a foretaste of what is to come.
Once there grew hard by a glorious wistaria, which had
attached itself, with unfamiliar friendship, to a box tree, but a
gale swept by, and, as if envious of the delightful effect
produced by the lilac wistaria flowers flung in profusion over
the dark green shrub, broke the quaint association by sweeping
it away. It is a delightful drive or walk from hence to

Copyright.   *"Country Life."*

THE ENTRANCE.

the place where the beautiful structure bursts upon the view amid its gracious surroundings. and as we approach, midway in the drive, a romantic prospect over the country is disclosed, the landscape stretching into the distance, with the church neighbouring the priory ruins, and the wooded hill behind.

The approach from the east is also most attractive, and brings the visitor through the well-timbered park, where oaks and elms abound, to where the house stands nobly, its celebrated façade rising with imposing effect. A number of the older trees on this side bear conspicuous marks of the ravages of time and the elements, but the rich woodland of Montacute has been well cared for, and a great many young trees have been planted within recent years. The north entrance is near the vicarage, a valley intervening between the public road and the house, and is straight, with a broad

is disclosed. To the south you look over the hills of Dorsetshire towards Lyme ; to the west lie the heights below Minehead and Blackdown ; north-westward the Quantocks, the Bristol Channel, and the Coast of Wales ; to the north the Mendips and Glastonbury Tor ; and, sweeping round to the east, many a pleasant prospect beside.

The glorious old house has the advantage of being built of beautiful oolitic sandstone from the neighbouring quarries of Hamhill. Its builder was Sir Edward Phelips, successively Queen's Sergeant, Master of the Rolls, and Speaker of the House of Commons, and it was raised between 1580 and 1601, upon a simple plan—a main block, with projecting wings, so that it takes the shape of a stunted letter H.

The west front is very beautiful, much enriched, and with a gorgeous screen, said to have been brought from Clifton

THE ENCLOSED GARDEN.

stretch of greensward on each side, the background being formed by a long row of solemn Irish yews ; beyond which, again, are deciduous and evergreen trees, such as oaks, elms, cedars, and Weymouth and various other pines. Recently large numbers of flowering trees and shrubs have been planted in this part of the grounds, and, in their season, these will lend new brightness and beauty to the approach.

Montacute is a house of Elizabeth's days, with all the character, and filled with the picturesque beauty, of Tudor times, lying in a chosen part of Somerset, with hill and hollow, wood and field, picturesque villages and rural lanes, for its neighbours—beautiful seats, too, and pleasant houses in the land. About the house are these delightful surroundings, rich and diversified, all dominated by the hill—there are really two— pyramidal and wooded to its summit : the *Mons acutus* that gave the place its name, and from the height a splendid view

Maubank. The east side is equally fine, and its imposing wall, with the three ranges of splendid windows, and statues of Roman soldiers in niches between those of the upper story, looks over the beautiful garden below. This, indeed, is a region well filled with architectural interest, for, as if Montacute House were not enough, there are glorious fragments of the priory, and the village has features of unusual note.

Within, the mansion has many beauties for those privileged to explore. The hall is a noble apartment, with a fine minstrel's gallery, and the customary screen, richly wrought. The upper story is occupied almost wholly by a single chamber, of very great and imposing dimensions. An unusual feature is the winding stone staircase that conducts the visitor to the drawing-room, which he finds a most beautiful apartment, with rich and elaborate ceiling and much fine woodwork. But the delightful features of Montacute

THE TERRACE AND ITS TEMPLE.

are many, and are not to be described here. Neither can anything more be said of the history of the famous house, save that, in the Civil Wars, it was held for the King, and sacked by the Parliament men.

It will be observed that architecture does not end with the house. It has its due place in the garden also, for Montacute has an enclosed garden of terraces, and very charmingly are the walls and other features made a part of the design. The terrace walls on either side of the east garden, extending from the house outward, are simple in character, but adorned with obelisks to the piers, and in the midst, on each side, is a temple of stone, its six columns supporting a circular stone roof, with pro-

THE YEW TREE WALK.

jecting cornice, from which spring three ribs, forming a cupola, crowned with an open ball shaped by two intersecting circles of stone. The garden-houses will speak for themselves. Here, indeed, are most charming conceptions in stone, which group delightfully with the surroundings. The mullioned windows, projecting as semi-circular bays, the angle pillars, the embattlements, the chimney, and roof are singularly picturesque. Such buildings as these, with mossy walls and quaint aspect, are worth, in an English garden, many a classic statue, animated bust, or monumental urn, though each in its place forms a fine garden feature, nevertheless.

The garden or banqueting house is a feature that has distinguished many an old garden. There were four in the Countess of Bedford's seventeenth century garden at Moor Park, in Hertfordshire—two at each end of the terrace walk, and two at the ends of the arcades which extended outward from the

house to enclose the parterre. The arrangement was thus analogous to that at Montacute, and was dear to the old Englishman, whose garden, as Bacon says, was "best to be square," but, in all cases, was in some measure to be retired from the world, yet a place into which the life of the house might be carried. Hence came the banqueting house in the garden, of which many instances might be cited, there being a notable example at Hampton Court. Bacon himself would have had "some fine banqueting house, with some chimneys neatly cast, and without too much glass." The fashion grew more abroad than at home, where the seasons did not always encourage outdoor life. Thus, in the times of Louis Quatorze, the French would often extend their houses into their gardens by building dining and drawing-rooms in the open air, and creating *salons, salles de bal, cabinets de verdure*, and theatres amid the groves where the masques of Molière were enacted at

THE   FOUNTAIN.

THE GARDEN-HOUSE—A GARDEN TRIUMPH IN STONE.

many a brilliant *fete*. The solitude of the old English garden was not found in such places, but it is obvious that the garden-house gave rare opportunities to the garden architect, and it may be doubted if there are in England any better examples of his skill than the charming creations we depict at Montacute. The delicacy and appropriateness of character and the unity of design are most satisfactory, and may well be an inspiration to modern builders. Here is no cold formality, seeming to reject the caresses of the green things that cling fondly to garden architecture, but a distinctive aspect in buildings that rightly fall into the sweet picture, and are vested with many flowering climbers. The Roman soldiers of the long eastern front thus look out over an interesting garden from their lofty stations in the niches, and over fine balustrades, curious temples, and supremely delightful garden-houses. The garden is arranged as an enclosed court, and its aspect is very sunny and beautiful as you walk along the terraces. At equal distances on three sides, and about 20ft. from the walls, you find Irish yews of fine growth. Clematis Flammula wreathes the pillars, making a beautiful picture when in bloom. On one of the walls is a splendid specimen of Garrya elliptica—

call for fuller treatment than is possible here. Certainly in aspect and character, both the house and garden must rank very high, and Montacute, with Longleat and several more, is indeed a notable glory of the West.

The walls of the house on the north side are clothed with that familiar climber, the clinging Virginia creeper (Ampelopsis Veitchi), of which alike the tender green in spring and the reds and crimsons of autumn have a charming effect upon the grey Hamhill stone. On this side is the quaint Dutch garden —a terrace with a wall about 6ft. high all round—and on the north and west sides of the house are closely-clipped yew hedges, about 15ft. in height, making a very fine feature. But yews in many forms are made much of at Montacute, and give character to the place.

Beyond this characteristic court of the enclosed garden is a large square expanse of turf used for croquet, and in few places can the game be played amid such pleasant surroundings On the side adjoining the kitchen garden there is another yew hedge, with a walk at one end, which must yet become a very remarkable feature of the garden at Montacute ; and when, in the course of time, the tops meet, a covered yew

"*Country Life*"

THE MANY-WINDOWED WALL.

that fine winter-flowering shrub which is never happy except upon a wall, unless it be in the sunny gardens of Devon and Cornwall.

It is not surprising to find this Somersetshire garden partly formal in character. It is an example both interesting and elaborate, as we have seen, and should be visited by all who desire to find a splendid illustration of this period or form of the gardener's art. Here walled courts or terraces command extensive views of the romantic surrounding country. We walk among glorious clipped yews, which are one of the chief distinctions of the place, and add a great deal to its interest. They are clipped indeed, but no topiary monstrosity is thus produced, and quaintness and not aggressive surprise is the result.

But the terraces of Montacute chiefly contribute to the fine effect. The great terrace overlooking the west garden is 45ft. wide—a truly noble feature. The walled terrace on the east side has the special beauties alluded to, and many others that the reader will conceive, in flowering bushes and many radiant beds. Grass slopes and terraces lead down to other gardens, and some other features of Montacute might

walk will be formed. Arcaded walks were a favourite, if not a common, feature in old gardens, and the most famous yet remaining is that strange " cradel walk, for the perplexed twining of the trees very observable," as Evelyn describes Queen Mary's Bower of wych elm at Hampton Court. Neighbouring the yew walk at Montacute is a fine specimen of the blue Atlantic cedar (Cedrus atlantica glauca), between 40ft. and 50ft. high, of which the blue-green colouring is very charming and distinctive.

But the effect of yews and cedars is sombre and imposing rather than attractive. They lend, however, rare character to Montacute—though we believe their number has been reduced in recent years—and give fine relief by their contrast to borders of hardy flowers. Roses flourish on their own roots, and, in one favoured situation, upwards of a hundred vigorous bushes of the most beautiful kinds fill the place with fragrance, and furnish many bowlfuls for the house in the summer. But Montacute is equally beautiful in the spring when the trees put forth their green, and when a thousand bulbous plants shoot up through the grass, or in autumn, which gives it a richer charm.

GARDENS OLD & NEW

ST. CATHERINE'S COURT. . . . . . BATH. . . . . .

AMONG the many beautiful houses that adorn, and the radiant gardens that gladden, the county of Somerset, few possess a sweeter charm than St. Catherine's Court, near Bath, long the residence of the late Hon. Mrs. Charlotte Olivia Drummond. The church, a very ancient structure, rebuilt by Abbot Cantlow, of Bath, about the year 1499, immediately faces the house, which once was a grange, or cell of Bath Abbey. Of the sacred edifice nothing shall be said here, save that the quaint structure falls admirably into the landscape on that beautiful declivity of the Down. The configuration of the ground gives character both to the house and the garden, and the effect is admirable. Some parts of the mansion go back to pre-Reformation times, and the observer will note the older character of the side looking down the declivity. Extremely picturesque is the whole structure, built upon those varied levels, with its high gables, its beautiful windows, and its many features bespeaking the style of Tudor and Jacobean times. The singularly beautiful porch, with the chamber above, dates from the days of Charles I. There is dainty picturesqueness in the classic pillars and arch, the unusual niches at the angles, and the open sides with the quaint balustrades.

The house at one time belonged to John Harington, the father, by his second wife, of Sir John Harington, that witty knight whose epigrams and sallies were the amusement of the Court of Elizabeth. Sir John was the Queen's godson. He was knighted in Ireland by Essex, to her great anger, for she resented this exercise of power,

THE TERRACED STEEP.

and, when Haring-ton presented himself at Court, she sent him away with a buffet, swearing loudly, "By God's Son, I am no queen; this man is above me." It was Harington who shocked the Royal modesty by translating a licentious part of "Orlando Furioso," and was punished for so doing by being made to translate the rest. However, the gay knight, "that saucy poet, my godson," was Elizabeth's favourite, and she visited him in Somersetshire in 1591. So much, however, must

THE PORCH AND TERRACE.

strictly formal is combined with the freely natural, and the plants are arranged without any very fixed or precise order, such as we meet in the pure Italian style. It will be agreed that the effect is extremely successful, and that the surroundings are an appropriate setting for the lovely house, which, be it observed, is itself clad here and there with creepers, but nowhere to the obscuring of its architectural character. The situation is delightful, with bold hills enhancing the

suffice concerning the personal interests of St. Catherine's Court. It afterwards passed through many hands, with varying fortunes; and our illustrations show in what a state of perfection the interesting old house now stands.

The character of the gardens is derived from the steepness of the ground. Successive terraces, with grass slopes and balustrades, approached by fine flights of steps, which have a remarkably picturesque effect, are the leading features. They are united with quaintness of design, and an unusual mixture of styles, in a manner we wish to enforce here. The

effect of the garden work, and tall trees making a beautiful tracery against the sky.

In the garden, foliage and flowers are everywhere. Here stand trees and shrubs taking their natural shape; neighbouring them very remarkable clipped yews; close by masses of perennials glowing each in season from early spring until the frosts of winter begin. But, again, with excellent taste, the trees do not obtrude upon the house, which stands, impressing us with the sense of repose, supported and enhanced in its engaging beauty by all the things that surround it. Let it be

THE HOUSE FROM THE LOWER TERRACE.

"Country Life."

GARDEN ART AND NATURAL CHARACTER AT ST. CATHERINE'S COURT.

A VIEW FROM THE UPPER GARDEN.

noticed how effectively the Agapanthus umbellatus, or African lily, is used in large pots near the mansion on each side of the porch. This is just the place for the bold application of tub-gardening, and the simple effects we point out illustrate how satisfactory is the result. There is much scope in this kind of gardening, and the Agapanthus funkia, heliotrope, orange, and many other shrubby plants, which merely call for protection from frost, may, by planting them in tubs, be made to import a charming air of new colour and fresh-ness into our summer gardens. The special character of the gardens at St. Catherine's Court, which has been alluded to, is well seen as the visitor stands by the porch of the house and looks up that long series of flights of steps by which the sylvan crest of the hill is reached. The old stonework, the terraces, balus-trades and urns, the grass slopes, the wealth of foliage, the flowers imparting colour, and the ferns their delicate green in many a sheltered nook, all contribute to make a garden-picture which would be hard to excel.

Then again, from the foot of the lower steps, overshadowed by that beautiful tree, what a delightful prospect does the old gabled house, with its oriel, make as we look up at the grey gables rising from the sylvan framework, and see the ancient walls against that green and beautiful background. Or we may stand at the west corner, upon the terrace looking over towards the distant trees, with a garden foreground in which quaint yew-forms rise up from amid boldly planted shrubs and masses of flowers. Rarely will such huge clipped yews be seen as those giant sentinels of irregular conical form which flank the approach to that upper garden. It has been by bold plant-ing that the fine effects have been gained. And, simple as the arrangement is, all the available space is well utilised, and it is delightful to pass from level to level upon the hill, discovering succes-sive charms.

Then the formal garden is quaintness itself. Walls, gates, and charming grilles of iron, with trees, shrubs, and flowers in abundance, in-vest it with indi-vidual charm at every season of the year.

A CHARMING OUTLOOK.

THE GRASS STAIRWAY AT ST. CATHERINE'S COURT.

BLICKLING, . .
NORFOLK, . . .
THE SEAT OF THE . .
MARQUIS OF LOTHIAN, K.T.

BLICKLING is a place of many-sided interest. We cannot forget that it has been the home of several notable figures in history. To look at the house, or at the counterfeit presentments of it here, you recognise it at once as a famous example of architecture. You are no less apprised that it stands very high as possessing one of the fairest gardens in the land. And you see, too—unlike some old places, where moats are choked and weed-grown, where envious grass invades the pathways, and where black, damp moss clings to mouldering balustrade and urn—that this is a place which it is a pleasure to maintain, where graceful minds have conceived new beauties, and where loving hands labour pleasantly at their garden toil. Let us endeavour, as it were, to walk in the scented pathways, to linger in fragrant bowers, to sit where the blossoms are showering, to explore the sylvan glades, and admire the noble trees of Blickling.

But it were a churlish thing not first to rest in the house awhile. Its very frontal challenges us as we knock. There are heraldic memorials of Hobarts, and reminders of unfortunate Boleyns. But before either Hobarts came or Boleyns went, there had been famous men in the older house of Blickling. Here dwelt heroic, hoary Erpingham—

"Good morrow, old Sir Thomas Erpingham:
A good soft pillow for that good white head
Were better than a churlish tu.f of France."

Then came, to own, if not to dwell at Blickling—for his home was Caistor Castle, some miles distant—Sir John Fastolfe, who, from the threatening field of Patay,

"Before we met, or that a stroke was given,
Like to a trusty squire, did run away."

It was the craven knight that sold Blickling to Sir Geoffrey Boleyn, whose great-grand-daughter was the unfortunate Anne. They say she was born at Blickling, but that it was at Hever, in Kent, she cast the tendrils of her charms about the fickle heart of the King. The Norfolk house of the Boleyns has long been swept away, and Sir Henry Hobart, Lord Chief Justice, to whom the place came, and whose portrait, in judicial robes, with cap, tippet, and chain of SS, hangs in the house, built the present Hall.

"Country Life."

THE WEST FRONT.

THE GREAT FORMAL GARDEN.

Its character is disclosed by the pictures. In the red brick walls, lofty windows, cupola-crowned turrets, and twisted gables, there is exceeding charm and very great interest. The moat is dry, but spanned by a beautiful bridge, and the hollow below is clothed with turf, and made bright and gay with summer flowers. This is part of the scheme of colour adornment that beautifies the whole surroundings of this sumptuous abode. Within, the apartments are of noble proportions, flooded with light through the storied panes of lofty transomed windows, richly panelled with oak, hung with tapestry and fine portraits, adorned with marvellous ceilings, and furnished in the finest taste. It is from their windows that we look over the great gardens and the park. It is a realm of ordered delight, delectable to look upon through these mullioned windows, and doubly pleasant when we think of the long line of Englishmen and Englishwomen who have found their pleasure in beautiful gardens here before. Blomefield, the Norfolk historian, speaks of an "elegant wilderness" as

or, more truly, created, the remarkably attractive garden we depict—a garden eminently successful in its kind. There are the close-clipped hedges, topiary features of unexaggerated form, yews standing like sentinels at regular stations, busts, urns, and basins of the classic school. Such a disposition of the garden is manifestly appropriate. But, formal though the garden is, its formality is not that of stiffness. There is now no character of a "wilderness," and the features are all such as attract, without disturbing the pleasant artistic calm. The lovely trees of varied foliage and growth that rise behind, and the delightful shrubberies, impart a special charm to the gardens. Nor does the extreme form of precise and yet fanciful carpet bedding here find any illustration. We see at Blickling merely the strongly marked character that is required to give distinction and effect, imparted by a master hand.

The principal flower garden, which is about an acre and a-half in extent, was begun by the eighth Marquess of Lothian

THE EAST FRONT.

having been among the attractions of Blickling in his time. But the place, after ripening for 200 years, has reached fruition in these days, and it is impossible to imagine anything more beautiful than the gorgeous feasts of colour spread out beneath these venerable walls. Recent years have seen vast improvements made. The eighth Marquess of Lothian was an enthusiastic lover of the garden, and did much to beautify the surroundings of his fair and winsome abode, and his widow, Constance, Marchioness of Lothian, carried on the delightful work he began.

It is a happy circumstance, to be observed in relation to Blickling, that the gardens and house are in perfect accord. We find the same in the case of all the beautiful gardens we describe. In no other way can satisfaction be achieved, and the judicious hand at Blickling, recognising the need for enclosure, cherishing all the charms of the flower world, realising the value of the umbrageous background, and welcoming the adornments of the architect and sculptor, developed,

and completed by his widow. It is in a sheltered situation, and great labour was expended upon its formation, the ground being excavated, and a terrace wall raised to surround it. The judicious lady who carried on the work is an ardent admirer of hardy flowers, and her taste in the decorative use of them never wavered in the times when formal bedding was at its height. The result is that the garden is filled with colour and fragrance, and that roses, pinks, carnations, lilies, bulbous flowers, and a host of other beautiful things, bloom in rich profusion. The design is bold and picturesque. Beds of simple character, disposed for broad effects, have been chosen, and the principal purpose has evidently been to give lavish effects of colour. The surrounding terraces are very fine, and command most attractive and interesting views both within and without. The fountain-basin and some of the statues in the garden were brought from the stately Elizabethan mansion of Oxnead Hall, in the vicinity, now a ruin, its principal portions having been pulled down long ago. Oxnead was the home of the Pastons, and was built in 1598 by Sir Clement Paston, described as the "champion" of Henry VIII., the "soldier" of the Protector Somerset, the "seaman" of Mary, and the "father" of Elizabeth.

The Poet Laureate has said in one of his garden volumes that a true garden should always be filled with flowers. There should be no dull month in which all has faded. To make every month a June is, nevertheless, impossible, but the gardeners at Blickling contrive to leave no period in which the garden is without interest. Here is undoubtedly a great and desirable art, and the excellent management of the shrubberies, with their many varied colours, is a powerful factor in the matter. The ground rises, and a broad path has been formed up to the temple-like arbour at the top. The path is broken by flights of steps, and the classical features are sphinxes and urns, with terminal busts, a quiet sequestered charm, as of learned leisure, being imparted to the whole place. On either side of the paths are the shrubberies, in which conifers, evergreens, and other trees form a setting of richest green to the glowing beds nearer the house. Lilies, hollyhocks, sunflowers, and a hundred others dear to the Nature-lover are seen richly grouped and massed at Blickling. Let it be noted that grass is the invariable surrounding of the beds, and will always form an unrivalled framework for masses of flowers.

Another feature of Blickling to be particularly observed is that the locality of the flowers is not restricted. They are, in

" Country Life."

THE TERRACE STEPS.

fact, everywhere, and, whether they are the glory of a bed, or light up with colour a mossy urn, the unfelt hand of Art, working in the spirit of Nature, has produced the subtle charm.

In winter a practice is made of filling the beds with evergreen shrubs, so that the garden has interests at all seasons, and never presents that empty aspect so frequently seen when the time of flowers is over. Winter has, indeed, its sober

" Country Life."

THE YEW HEDGES.

attractions, for the foliage of the evergreens, which is the chief note of the picture, is never so rich as then. Thuias and the welcome junipers are planted with excellent effect, and, in association with them, the beautiful variegated maple (Acer Negundo) in the form of low standards—a tree of great charm, but needing to be used with caution by reason of its pronounced leafage ; here, indeed, looking splendid, with the scarlet lobelia beneath it, which is beautiful both in leaf and flower-colouring, and will add much to the attractions of any garden in the early autumn where it is planted freely and boldly.

The west front is very different. Here the lawn creeps up towards the sunken ditch of the moat and the house, of which the view is unobstructed, and thus presents itself with very imposing effect. Ivy clusters upon the walls and terraces, giving colour and character, but without hiding

one place there are a couple of magnificent Oriental planes, neighbouring one another, but sufficiently far apart to allow room enough for each. The branches of these hoary monsters are about 16yds. in length, and, hanging with pendulous grace, have kissed the mother earth with such affection that some of them have taken new root therein, and, growing aloft once more, have added much to the mighty majesty of the parent tree. Then we are charmed by a noble Scotch fir, on the south side, which is about 15ft. in girth at 4ft. from the ground, and a huge oak, with a girth of 14ft. and an umbrageous spread of 86ft. A silver fir, too, 120ft. in height and 16ft. in girth, claims attention, and we notice many fine beeches and birches. There are pollard limes of notable aspect, also, fringing the offices at the approach to the house, and, withdrawn from gaze at a distance from it, the mausoleum of John, Earl of

WHERE THE MOAT WASHED THE WALLS.

the structure. But wherever you go at Blickling you find variety. Much is due, undoubtedly, to the productiveness of the region The trees are abundant, varied, and of fine growth, and the extensive park is traversed by venerable avenues of oak and chestnut, possessing great distinction of character.

The sylvan scenery accordingly is very beautiful. There are nodding narcissi and daffodils shooting up through the grass beneath the trees, and forming fragrant groups by the margin of the lake, which is a sheet of water about a mile in length, and 40coyds. wide at its broadest part, taking the form of a crescent, sweeping round delightful parkland, and margined by delicious foliage. There are splendid limes and noble oaks, with great masses of rhododendrons, which flourish in the kindly soil and hold a rich festival of flowers in the early summer. Some individual trees are of special interest. In

Buckinghamshire, enclosed by dark spruce firs and gloomy sepulchral yews. But once again we turn, this time to the fruit garden, to observe how abundantly the trees and bushes are bearing their treasures of the golden time. Yet we cannot exhaust the delights of historic and instructive Blickling.

Not only are the house, gardens, and park with its lake, beautiful, but the stables and dairy are all that could be wished. Here may be seen a special herd of white polled cattle, short legged and straight backed, with black muzzles, ears, and hoofs, representative of some of the wild cattle of Britain in early times. The cows are far from rivalling Jerseys as milk-givers, but they are not maintained for profit. They are a well-known feature in the park, and add to the many interests of this picturesque and attractive dwelling.

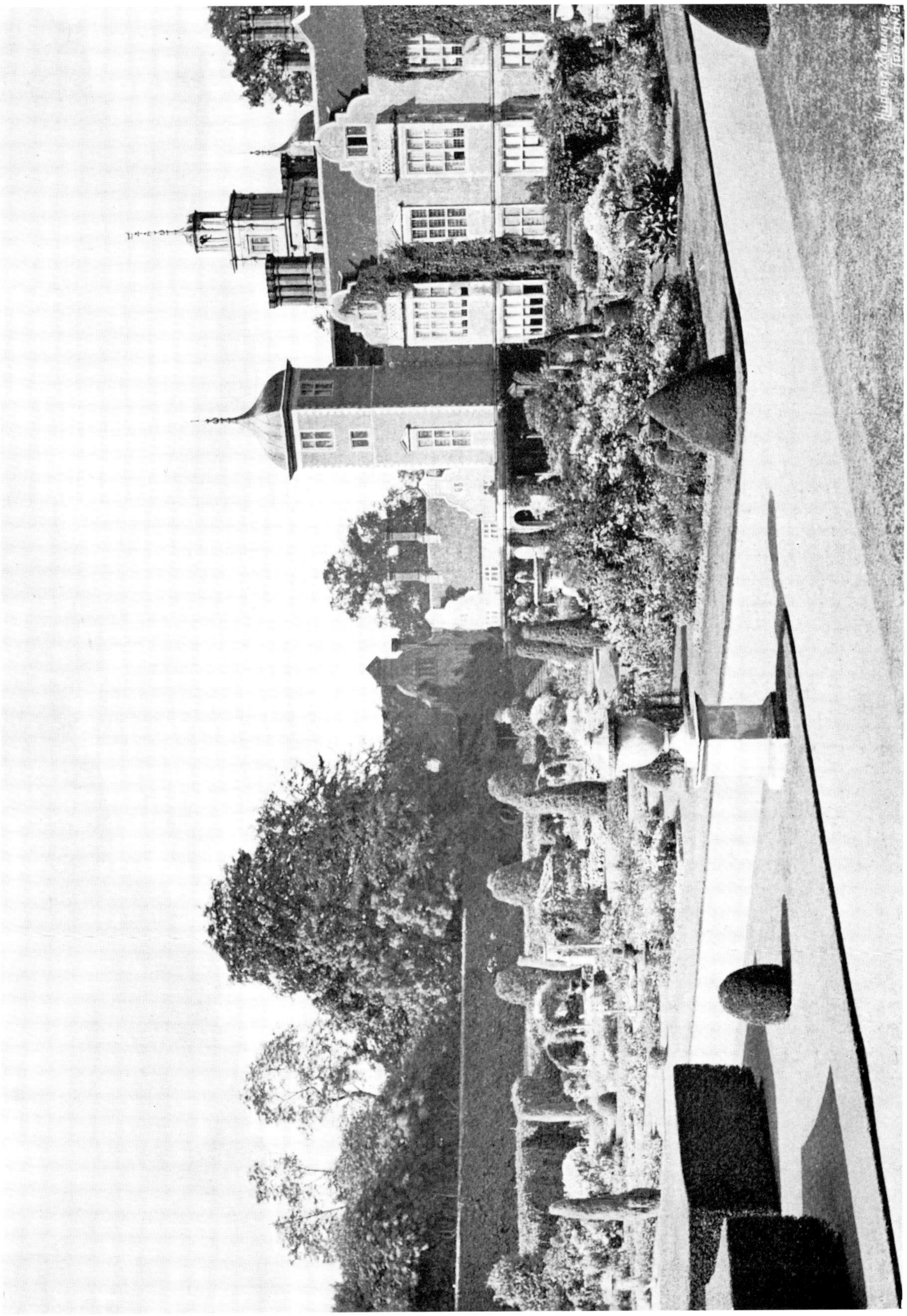

"Country Life."

THE HOUSE FROM THE GARDEN.

Copyright.

GARDENS OLD & NEW

GREAT TANGLEY MANOR, SURREY, ... THE RESIDENCE OF . . MR. WICKHAM FLOWER.

GREAT TANGLEY MANOR HOUSE, lying about three miles south-east of Guildford, and a mile away from the high road thence by Wonersh to Cranleigh, is a triumph of art, and a very notable example of garden construction. It should appeal to Englishmen by its truly English picturesqueness and beauty, by its delightful gardens, and, as the writer trusts, because it is a goodly mansion recovered from decay, restored to its ancient state from the lowly condition of a rustic farmhouse, and brought to the condition in which we see it by the exercise of taste and skill, and by the care of its owner's hand. It was no small achievement to regenerate Great Tangley Manor from its recent uses, and to replace its surroundings of kitchen gardens, stables, cow-sheds, piggeries, and barns by the beautiful and wholly appropriate pleasure grounds which now adorn it. Here, we think, is a notable work in the domain of country life. Wherever we go we meet, with a frequency that begets indifference, such evidences of decay in the shires—deserted mansions, ruined gateways, weed-grown moats, and other marks of the changed conditions of modern times—that it is a real pleasure to find an old manor house that has been recovered from obscurity.

May the example of Mr. Wickham Flower be the inspiration of many. England is full even now of the dwelling-places of former times, wherein the rustic housewife kindles her fire on the hearth of the forgotten lord. Something there

THE MANOR HOUSE AND ITS ADORNMENTS.

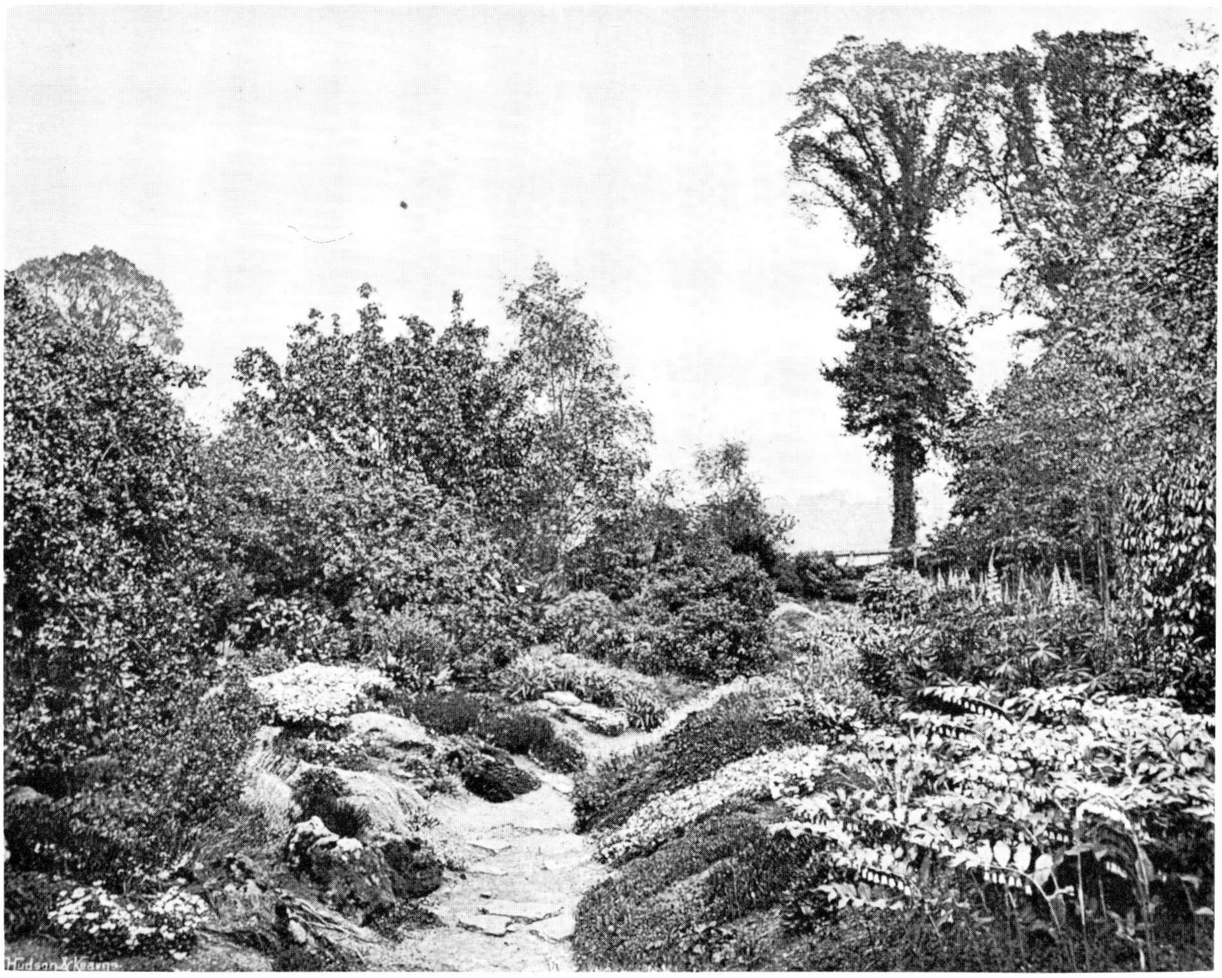

Copyright. "Country Life."

THE ALPINE GARDEN.

is in the panelling, or aloft in the plaster perhaps, of his ancient heraldry, with many a sentence carved in a strange, unfamiliar tongue. She has bedaubed the oaken wainscot with whitewash, clothes from the washing are hung on the rail of the minstrels' gallery, and broad sheets of glass fill the place of beautiful latticed panes. But the old builders were men whose pegged and jointed oak, whose solid stonework, and whose mellow brick will long defy the blasts of time, and such places are not seldom capable of being regenerated from decay. Can there be anything more satisfactory to the lover of country life than such work as that Mr. Flower has so successfully accomplished at Tangley?

Great Tangley is a place of known antiquity. King John, according to the country people, had a hunting lodge on the site. The place passed from the Crown in 1173, when John granted it to John de Fay, and it descended from parent to child until the year 1572, through the great families of Braose, Mowbray, and Howard. Shortly before the execution of Thomas Howard, fourth Duke of Norfolk, Lord High Treasurer and Earl-Marshal, in that year, the manor was sold to John Caryl, who altered it considerably, and added the beautiful half-timbered front in 1582. From the descendants of Caryl the Manor of Tangley passed in the last century to Sir Fletcher Norton, Speaker of the House of Commons, and from the Speaker's descendant, Lord Grantley, Mr. Wickham Flower bought the decayed manor house and farm in the year 1884.

The principal structural alterations made by the new owner were the addition of a building at the west end, and the quaint covered way, in 1886, and of the library and the rooms over it, in the year 1897. The architect was Mr. Philip Webb, who, inspired by the spirit of the old builders, has designed features excellently in consonance with the older

Copyright. "Country Life."

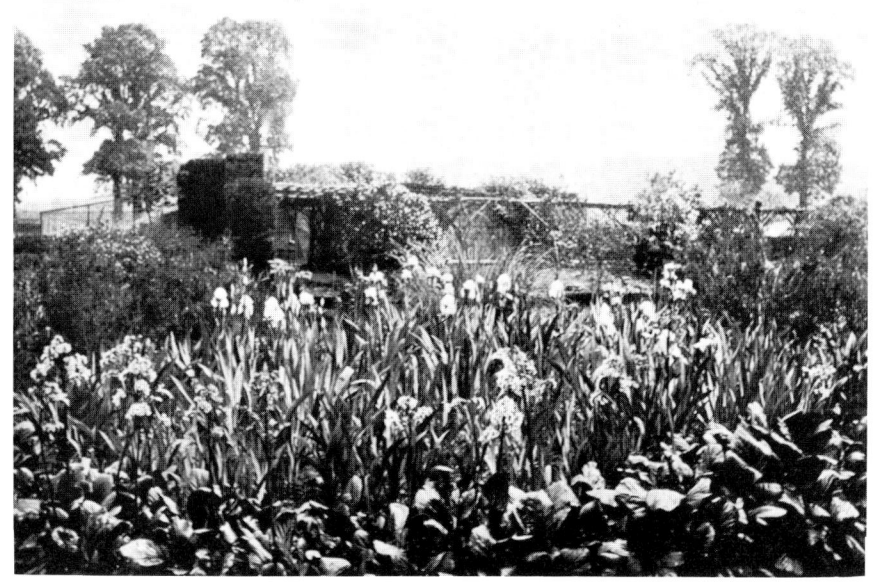

AN IRIS GROUP.

portions of the manor house.

The gardens and grounds are in most happy relation with the structure, and cover a space of between six and seven acres, with fine light alluvial soil. The foliage of chestnut, poplar, and elm falls naturally into the scheme, and the moat, with its quaint bridges, the yew hedges, and the enclosed court are wholly satisfactory and charming. The formation of these gardens and grounds was

THE PERGOLA WALK.

The first work undertaken was the complete excavation of the moat, and the earth removed was thrown up so as to level the adjoining land, while the water of a pond which is fed by a stream passing through the valley of the Tillingbourne was admitted at the north end, and flows towards the Wey from the northwest corner. Additions have been made from time to time upon the same system, but no

conducted chiefly in the autumn and winter of 1884, shortly after Mr. Flower had purchased the place. At that time there existed no ornamental gardens or grounds whatever. With the exception of the old orchard within the moat, and the great elms that border the lane from Wonersh Common, all the trees and shrubs and the yew and beech hedges have been planted in and since 1885. A body of about eighteen labouring men worked under directions given to them week by week, and the gardens and grounds were completed within a period of about six months. The leading idea was evidently to produce a natural arrangement in proper keeping of character and quaintness with the house.

formal plan has been laid down, and no written direction given. Great Tangley gardens have thus a delightfully spontaneous character, but their features have been dictated by good judgment and experienced taste. On the north and west sides the space between the moat and the house is occupied by the old orchard, and on the south front there is a square enclosed court, planted as a flower garden and lawn. The enclosing walls are very old, the parts on the southern and eastern sides being of the time of Queen Elizabeth. They are of Bargate stone, and are loopholed, perhaps for purposes of defence in lawless times. These walls are of great thickness and strength, and when Mr. Flower bought

THE COVERED WAY.

the place an apple tree, apparently self-planted, was growing out of them.

Although the gardens and grounds have followed no formal plan as they grew out of chaos, and although spontaneity is the keynote of the whole arrangement, and infinite variety of beauty the unquestioned outcome, there are fixed and valuable principles underlying the complete result, and these are the same imperishable principles which go to the making of all beautiful gardens, small and great. To be brief, they are completely appropriate in character. If he who would fain create a perfect garden in the widest sense of the word desires success in the end, there is no need to formulate any precise and comprehensive plan at the outset. Indeed it may be wiser to permit the various points of beauty to grow, as it were, naturally one out of another, and out of the character of the place. The first principle is to follow the lead of Nature as much as possible, to seek

THE MOAT.

and ensue that kind of beauty of flowers and foliage which she offers to you most readily. Water gardens and bog gardens are choiceworthy when water is present and available ; rock gardens are admirably placed amidst the surroundings of Surrey scenery. Ideas, such as that of a pergola, may be imported from many countries as freely and as boldly as plants themselves. Unless one is hampered by a cast-iron plan in advance, one need not fear that this or that result will be incongruous or out of harmony. But it is a sin against Nature and against Art alike to attempt the impossible or to persist in trying to grow that which will not thrive, but will at best be poor, stunted, and insignificant. The capacities of a place must be considered thoughtfully, else will the resu t be certain failure.

Let us attempt to give some idea of the wonderful result of the application of such principles during a comparatively short period. As you look towards the back of the house you perceive that the walls themselves partake of the nature of a garden. Thyme and arabis, wallflowers, and the " golddusted snapdragon " that Matthew Arnold loved, have invaded the crevices of the very chimneys, which are bright with fragrant flowers. Man cannot make a garden of that kind ; but he can mar it. There are gardeners whose sense of

discipline is so strong that they cannot tolerate that which springs up into beauty of its own free will and without their command. Such gardeners produce ugly gardens. From this haunt of the self-sown sun-loving plants to the grass slopes and to the yew hedge beyond leads a modest lane with trim box hedges cut low on either side. For the yew hedge, it is a thing of beauty, as such hedges are when they can be grown to perfection.

One of the most pleasant features of the Tangley gardens is the Court, which is entered by the covered way, cool and shady On the walls is a prodigal wealth of climbers, rose. vine, clematis, and what you will, and great care and thought have clearly been bestowed upon the selection of the flowers for this cherished retreat. Daffodils are there, but only those of the choicest and most beautiful kinds. In the early spring days of February and March the deep purple and orange flowers of Iris reticulata bloom profusely, and sometimes they may be seen to great advantage rising over a carpet of pure snow. Myrtle flourishes there, and rosemary, for remembrance, in great bushes ; Iris pumila in many colours gladdens the eye in the early part of the year ; downcast fritillaries, hepaticas, asphodels, yellow and grey, tulips, white and yellow, roses full of fragrant grace, and gorgeous pæonies show their beauty in due season. Not only are the vines which clothe the walls of great age, not only are jasmine, white and yellow, and wistaria, trailing its purple clusters, present in thriving splendour, but the trees of guelder roses are themselves pressed into service as creepers, and the effect is both novel and pleasing.

The visitor to Tangley Manor is almost bewildered by the variety of beautiful scenes that meet his eye. He has admired the court garden ; let us take him also into the little garden, girt about with yew hedges on every side, in which most cherished plants are tended. Inside that protecting bulwark tall lilies and irises, the best of the larkspurs, some of them of the tenderest blue conceivable, and Japanese anemones find a sanctuary and thrive amazingly. Then, come again to the back of the house. Cross the moat and walk upon the broad terrace, 150yds. long, that borders the lawn. That terrace ends in a pergola, happiest of importations

THE ROCK GARDEN.

from the sunny South, covered with vines. Remember, as you note the yew hedge parting the lawn from the meadows, that although it stands 10ft. high now, it is the result of trees which were but 18in. high when they were planted in the winter of 1884 —only sixteen years ago, after all. Through the pergola you reach the orchard, standing on the south-

THE ANCIENT PART OF THE MANOR HOUSE.

of the terrace and you shall visit the bog garden, one of the most beautiful and successful of its kind in England. In the soil, a mixture of the local earth with finely-chopped peat, there is nothing mysterious or unattainable. But the position is admirably chosen, and it has not been less cunningly used, for the bog garden is a few feet lower than the level

western side of the grounds, and hard by Wonersh Common. It is but twelve years old, and it is a thing of beauty, particularly in the fresh spring-time, before "The cuckoo's parting cry, 'The bloom has gone, and with the bloom go I.'"

In nothing has Mr. Flower been more triumphantly successful than in his treatment of the ancient moat, not merely as a thing of beauty in itself, but as a source of new beauties elsewhere. Sixteen years ago the moat was a waterless eyesore, and the water from the pond above was wasted; now the moat is full, and its surplus waters are turned to the greatest advantage. Come to the north-east end

of the moat, so that it can be flooded at will. Yet it is well drained, so that the water is never stagnant, and the manner in which the water is introduced is artistic in the extreme. One is loth to leave the bog garden, crowded with interesting plants; but another feature is hard by—the small lake, fringed with a variety of water-loving flowers. Then the ground rises, and one enters a rock garden, not large, but perfect in detail, and a thousand alpine flowers cover the earth with rich carpets of blossom. Take Tangley Manor for all in all, it is certainly one of the most beautiful pleasaunces in England, and a true work of natural art.

THE   FLOWER-MARGINED   LAKE.

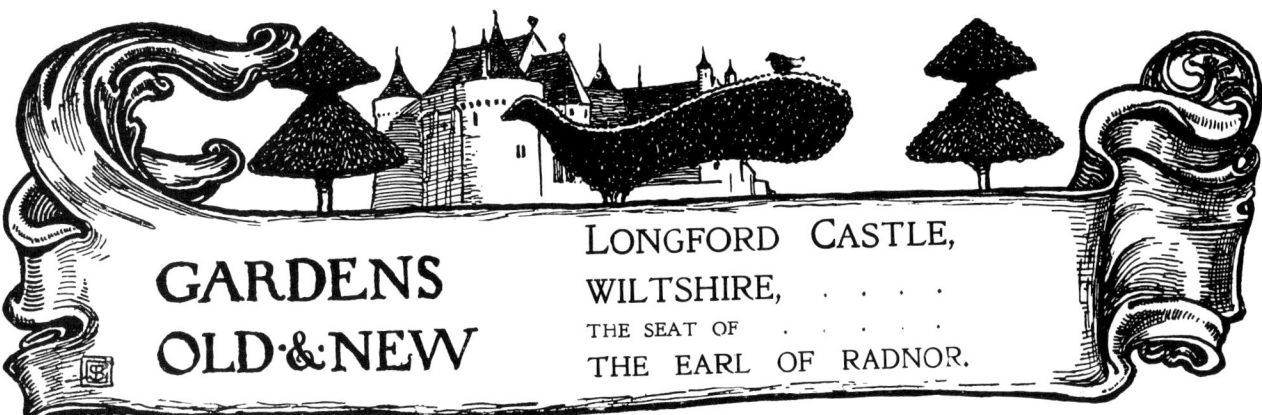

GARDENS OLD & NEW

LONGFORD CASTLE, WILTSHIRE, ... THE SEAT OF . . . . THE EARL OF RADNOR.

"I SHALL be at Longford House to-morrow night, if God please," wrote Cromwell, marching towards Devonshire, where Fairfax had his army, on October 16th, 1645. The iron soldier was not bent, as we are, on the pleasant business of glancing at the famous abode and of lingering in its superb gardens, but on the sterner matter of bidding the defenders march forth under pain of fire and sword. He had the satisfaction of arriving there, as he said, fresh from the famous forcing of Basing, accomplishing his purpose at Longford also. The house he saw was greatly different from that we now behold. It had been built more than half a century before by Sir Thomas Gorges, and the architect had been the celebrated Thomas Thorpe. This "Castle of Amphialeus," as Sidney called it, had been built upon the triangular plan of the Castle of Oranienbaum, which Tycho Brahe had designed. It was an odd idea, but the good knight had been over-persuaded by his wife, Helena Schnachenberg,

a Danish lady, who came here in the suite of Cecelia, daughter of Eric of Sweden. At her sweet behest he put his fortune below ground in driving piles to support his structure, which had never been reared but for the downright defeat of the Dons. There came ashore in 1588, near his command of Hurst Castle, a Spanish galleon, whereof, with woman's wit, his wife beseeched the Queen for the hull. It was a request readily granted, and the silver and other treasures that were discovered in the wreck afterwards sufficed for the building of Longford. The place has since been greatly changed. It came by purchase to the family of the present noble owner in 1717, and remains a splendid mansion of very remarkable character, with abundant classic features, and details rich to elaboration, grafted upon the older style, flanked by five noble towers, and famous for its pictures among all the mansions of England. It has the advantage of lying in a very fine country, and of overlooking a noble English park, in which beech, oak,

THE FORMAL GARDEN.

and many other trees are seen, relieved by the sombre greens of conifers and pines. Eastward the ground inclines to be flat, but rises abruptly, and foliage makes a beautiful framework for the neighbouring landscape, where the village spire of Alderbury rises from amid the trees. On the other side the scene is different. There the ground undulates, and is beautified by groups of chestnuts, while the beech is seen in splendid beauty, and a lover of the pine would notice, too, specimens of Pinus insignis and the deciduous cypress. Here, too, in the distance may be seen the " silent finger " of Salisbury's glorious and world-famed spire.

Few gardens in Wiltshire are more interesting than those of Longford, and their charms are principally due to the zeal, taste, and knowledge of the Earl and Countess of Radnor. To create such a garden, knowledge and love of Nature must combine. The surrounding country is generally flat, or merely undulating, but judicious planting has given relief. Nothing, moreover, has been done that could in any way mar the effect of the splendid mansion. As we have many a time said, the house and its garden cannot be dissociated. They are parts of a whole, and Longford is an example of judicious arrangement. Tall trees do not shut it in, and climbers are not allowed to hide the cool grey stone. Those which we see are there to add the needed touch of colour.

Copyright.   "Country Life."

LONGFORD CASTLE.

During recent years the gardens of Longford have been greatly beautified, and the floral wealth of the garden has been vastly increased. There is, for example, a feature of interest to lovers of hardy flowers in the two mixed borders, each about a hundred yards long, and presenting their pleasing aspect almost throughout the year. Such hardy plants are even used

charming vases and balls along the terraces and their grey-green walls, and the delightful landscape beyond, with its water and rustic bridge. The classic spirit is enshrined in the termination of that splendid garden, where the goddess looks out from beneath her crested temple over a vision of stately beauty, in company with the sages and syrens of old. We are transported in thought to the scented gardens of the South, and as if in the Ludovisi, Medici, Doria Pamphili, or some other garden of Italy, we breathe an air heavy with the fragrance of the land. A choice example of classic garden architecture and sculpture is presented here ; and mark how glorious is the contrast and harmony with the umbrageous region beyond. The urns and vases, radiant with their floral denizens, or vested with fragrant climbers, the terminal figures, and all other like features, and the temple itself, are fine examples of an imposing garden style imported from southern climes to our land.

But the charms of Longford are not all classic, nor do they end or begin with the noble Italian garden. There are terrace walks of the true old English character, and many places of quiet sequestered charm. In wandering about the grounds we reach one very interesting spot. It is an old garden near the Rapids, where the waters of the Avon and Etele meet, and is protected by lofty trees, except on the north-east side. Greensward greets the eye, and moss and other roses bloom here more freely, perhaps, than in the formal parts of the gardens. Here, too, the fair white lily and finely-coloured irises are found, while an old Judas tree (Cercis siliquastrum)—on one of whose

Copyright.   "Country Lif ."

THE PARK FROM THE TERRACE.

to some extent in the principal flower garden at Longford, which is splendidly shown in one of the illustrations. The design is stately and formal, and reminds us of like arrangements at Belton, Castle Ashby, and elsewhere. It is composed of geometrical beds, in which are pansies and many other old-fashioned flowers. The quaint yew hedges will be observed, with their arches — a rare feature—the semi-circular end, with the mossy temple and figure, the classic busts, the

kind old men say did Judas Iscariot hang—will attract attention. Howsoever it be in regard to this shadowy, ill-omened history, certainly we say that the tree itself is more picturesque in growth than many, and more interesting in flower, too, when bunches of purple blossoms are seated on its yet leafless limbs.

There are hardy ferneries, again, at Longford, to remind us how beautiful is the fern when rightly used. Its rich green fronds are cool in colour, rich and beautiful alike in form and

THE END OF THE FORMAL GARDEN.

hue, throughout the summer. Landscape gardeners will some-times forget that shady places become beautiful through the planting of shrubs, flowers, and ferns that demand scarcely a filtering of sunshine for their encourage-ment. The visitor will notice, too, a particular summer-house on a greensward, without any sides, but with a

A   CORNER   OF   THE   TERRACE.

and other choice plants, and it worthily main-tains its position among the finest fruit gardens in Eng-land. Often in visiting the great flower and fruit exhibitions are the splendid products of these gardens found making new triumphs. There are also pines in much abundance under glass—in these days a somewhat un-common feature, since the rapid

heather-thatched roof, supported by oaken pillars, around which roses and clematis are twined. Here a curious and probably unique device is adopted to add colour to the roof, the plan being to insert small pots of crocus and snowdrop bulbs below the rims, whereby pretty bits of spring colouring and effect are secured. Passing by beds of hardy flowers we reach another summer-house, built so long ago as the memorable year 1745 ; and still another, built of brick, attracts attention. It has a handsome oaken table, and its tiled roof is overhung by a splendid yew, which is conspicuous in the grounds—a sombre companion, some may say, in solitude, but always noble and picturesque.

Longford is rich also in houses filled with decorative

transport of West Indian pines now brings them in splendid condition and cheaply to our tables. Grapes are sumptuous, indeed, in the vineries ; and garden walls, to the length of about a mile, are covered with choice peaches, Morello cherries, and other fruits usually thus cultivated in Britain. The figs, again, are remarkable. There are noble trees of the well-known Brown Turkey variety, and a specimen of the kind named the Brunswick covers a space of not less than 300ft.

In adding very much to the beauties of Longford, the Earl and Countess have done an excellent work, a real labour of love, and it may be hoped that they will long continue to enjoy and bestow the pleasures of their noble domain.

THE   TEMPLE   AND   DIAL.

GARDENS OLD·&·NEW

LILLESHALL, SHROPSHIRE. .
THE SEAT OF . . .
The Duke of Sutherland.

THE glorious districts of middle England, which are rich in country homes and monastic remains, have not many places that can vie with Lilleshall. There are finer mansions, it is true, but we have goodly satisfaction in the magnificent prospects, noble trees, and glorious gardens of this Shropshire home. It is unnecessary to compare it with Trentham, the Duke of Sutherland's other and still more stately abode not so far away. There is this distinction, however, to be observed between them—that Trentham lies low in the valley, while Lilleshall is raised aloft on the hill, and surveys from its terrace garden the lovely country through many a fading mile, until, far off, the mountains of Wales are lifted into view. That is something, indeed, to add to the delight of a garden foreground. Nearer at hand, the mouldering walls of the Augustinian Abbey of Lilleshall lie full in view, lending their antique cloistered calm. A glorious feature, we say, is this for England to bestow. Times have vastly changed since the Abbot complained that the neighbouring Watling Street impoverished him by bringing too many hungry mouths to his door. When the Dissolution eased his house of its burden of charity, as of the revenues that had made its bounty flow, the place came to James Leveson, Esq., and from him descended to the Gowers, and so to the ducal house of Sutherland. The old mansion of the Levesons has gone, but the fine modern structure, composite of various mediæval styles, with its remarkable arcaded terrace, has risen worthily in its stead. It carries with it the features of appropriate garden architecture in terrace walls, stairways, and arcades.

The spacious pleasure grounds, with which we are concerned, were laid out when the house was built, that is, about 1839. Including the comparatively small kitchen garden, they cover about twenty-eight acres, and are the foreground and gem of a great panorama. We experience certainly a reminiscence of Trentham as we survey from the terrace the rich maze of the great flower garden,

THE APPLE WALK OR PERGOLA.

THE ENTRANCE TO THE ROSE GARDEN.

THE FORMAL GARDEN AND PARK, FROM THE HOUSE.

THE TERRACE AND ARCADE.

and the leafy pleasure ground beyond, with the vista of more distant charms. The trees are glorious in size and contour, and some of them cast upon the mead a vast expanse of shade.

The arrangement of the great bedded garden is circular and unusual, and the blaze of colour is attained by boldly contrasting various hues to secure rich effect. Dark colours are opposed to light, and zonal pelargoniums, calceolarias, and tuberous begonias are amongst the most important plants employed. The circular garden itself is a contrast, for, as our picture shows, it derives part of its effect from the presence of the rich groups of trees behind. The calceolarias and begonias thrive wonderfully, and the success of the former is the more noteworthy because disease has attacked this once favourite flower within recent years, throwing it partly out of cultivation in many places.

It is worth while remarking that the tuberous begonia is now used in all our great gardens, and that few plants are so well adapted for creating fine colour effects. The hybridiser has much improved the begonia's habit of growth. It is now dwarf and compact, and the flowers are thrown well above the leaves —pure white, orange scarlet, buff, intense crimson, and lovely shades of uncommon tints, all characteristic of the plant, and all produced faithfully from seed. It will be seen from the picture that standard roses neighbour the circular parterre, and that fine oaks, cedars, and other trees are near.

On the south-west side of the house are other noble trees and sloping grass terraces, very green and beautiful, leading down to the lovely setting of sward and woodland. These charms are common to many gardens, but Lilleshall has a very distinctive feature in the glorious apple walk, which is 570ft. in length, and we believe the longest such walk in England. The illustration shows it flecked and barred with sunlight, reproducing very well its delightful character of brightness and predominating shade. The names of the varieties of apple which form the screen have unfortunately been lost, but their sturdy branches bespeak their age, and they bear plenteous crops of well-flavoured fruit.

We are reminded here of the trellised pergola of Italy and other southern climes, which affords grateful shade from the fierce sunlight by giving support to the rose, clematis, wistaria, vine, and other climbing plants.

In this more temperate region we need no such elaborate arrangements as are frequent in Italy, but who can forget that we, too, sometimes seek the shade, and that a simple pergola must sometimes be a welcome retreat. That at Lilleshall, while providing shelter from the fiercer blaze of summer, furnishes also its autumn harvest. It is beautiful in spring, when thousands of blossoms colour the bare branches, not less so in leafy June, and most of all, perhaps, when the fruit

FROM THE SOUTH-WEST.

changes colour and ripens for the gathering. Pergolas may be built of stone, as sometimes in Italy, but here something lighter, as of wood, for example, seems much more appropriate.

It is pleasant, indeed, to pass from the Lilleshall apple walk to the rose garden, which is not only of large extent, but filled with choice varieties, mostly in the bush form, which is generally most richly dowered, while the standard, more especially of the tea-scented kinds, is often killed in severe winters. In the Lilleshall garden upwards of nineteen large beds are filled with such lovely kinds as Alfred Colomb, Baroness Rothschild, Beauty of Waltham, Captain Christy, Margaret Dickson, Mrs. John Laing, Merveille de Lyon, La France, Lady Helen Stewart, and Lord Macaulay. Some of the more hardy tea roses, such as Rêve d'Or, are very successful. Climbing roses of many kinds clothe the walls, including such old favourites as the Garland, Félicité Perpetuée, and the Dundee Rambler, and even the recent and somewhat garish Crimson Rambler,

THE TERRACE STAIRWAY.

than which few roses are more brilliant.

Here is one of those gardens which charm by their very simplicity. The one bold feature of the bedded parterre is the foil to the green surroundings, and adds its effect to the landscape features beyond, with their far vistas, and the umbrageous depths of their woodland. Little more of description is required of the glowing and fragrant garden of Lilleshall. It is not one of those pleasaunces arranged upon a definite architectural or formal plan, but the garden designer has happily succeeded in investing his creations with a character of radiant and ravishing charm not easy to define.

If we had dwelt at all upon the mansion itself, or the venerable abbey that is its neighbour, the space at our disposal would not have sufficed to do any justice to the theme. Therefore, with a glance at the old sundial, dated 1630, a memorial brought from the garden of Lilleshall Old Hall, we leave this beautiful domain.

THE DUCHESS'S ROSE GARDEN.

A VIEW OVER THE PARK.

GARDENS OLD·&·NEW

SYDENHAM HOUSE, DEVONSHIRE,
THE SEAT OF . .
MR. JOHN TREMAYNE.

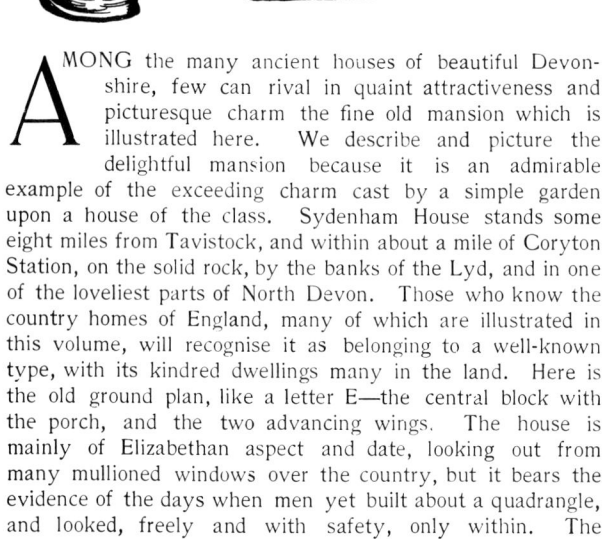

AMONG the many ancient houses of beautiful Devonshire, few can rival in quaint attractiveness and picturesque charm the fine old mansion which is illustrated here. We describe and picture the delightful mansion because it is an admirable example of the exceeding charm cast by a simple garden upon a house of the class. Sydenham House stands some eight miles from Tavistock, and within about a mile of Coryton Station, on the solid rock, by the banks of the Lyd, and in one of the loveliest parts of North Devon. Those who know the country homes of England, many of which are illustrated in this volume, will recognise it as belonging to a well-known type, with its kindred dwellings many in the land. Here is the old ground plan, like a letter E—the central block with the porch, and the two advancing wings. The house is mainly of Elizabethan aspect and date, looking out from many mullioned windows over the country, but it bears the evidence of the days when men yet built about a quadrangle, and looked, freely and with safety, only within. The sturdy men of Devon, who went out to conquer a New World, and wrought such sounding deeds in the Old, came from just such places as this. Mark the richness of effect in the various rectangular, rounded, and lozenge windows, the rare or unique feature of cylindrical mullions of granite, the fine character of the porch; above all, the unusual

elaboration of effect arising from the bold gabled structures that turn inward from the advancing wings, and the fine play of light and shade that results. Nothing better could be wished than such a combination, and the house and garden together form a truly attractive domain. Note, moreover. how the house seems to rise out of its surroundings, and how lovely must be the effect of the many climbers which invest it in contrast with the cool hue of the stone. The slope might have suggested formal terracing, but Sydenham is a notable instance of the variety of character which may be found or developed in like situations.

The house was built by Sir Thomas Wise, who was knighted at the coronation of James I., but his structure arose where an older mansion had stood, of which portions are embodied, for his family had obtained Sydenham, described as Sidraham in the time of the Conqueror, with the hand of the heiress of the Sydenhams in the days of Henry IV. The three chevronels ermine, upon a sable field, of the Wises still remain in their mansion, with portraits hanging in the panelled chambers. Like many other country houses, Sydenham suffered in the Civil War. It was garrisoned for King Charles, and taken by the Parliamentary troops under Colonel Holbourn in January, 1645, and appears to have suffered much. However, when the war was over, it was restored, and it has remained in careful hands ever since. On

THE WEST SIDE.

VIEW FROM THE PORCH.

the death of Sir Thomas Wise in 1675, his daughter and heiress, who had married Edward Tremayne, of Collacombe, in Lamerton parish, carried Sydenham to the family that now possesses it. "Squire Tremayne," as his neighbours call the present owner, is very popular in North Devon, and it is delightful to find how much he and the Hon. Mrs. Tremayne cherish this beautiful mansion, and with what simple and delightful character they have invested its gardens.

Within and without, as our pictures disclose, it is wholly satisfactory. The noble dining-room, with the great fireplace dating from 1656, the many oak wainscoted chambers, and the magnificent staircase, hung with numerous family portraits, and lighted through those glorious windows, all maintain the beautiful aspect of their earlier day, and it is pleasant to watch the pigeons fluttering in through the open windows of the dining-room, encouraged to enter for their food, or to hear them cooing from the chimneys and gables above.

Copyright. FEEDING THE PIGEONS. "Country Life."

The gardens of Sydenham House are indeed in happy harmony with the mansion, and they owe much to Squire Tremayne. Approaching them from the direction of Coryton, we are impressed with the extraordinary beauty of the country. We pass through fine woodlands, and by emerald meadows and cottages wreathed in foliage and flowers, to find the landscape growing in sylvan beauty, a sombre fir here and there enhancing the effect of the tender greens of beech and oak, with their undergrowth of ferns, hollies, and rhododendrons.

At our feet the river pursues its course, and we cross a bridge to the gardener's cottage, almost hidden among

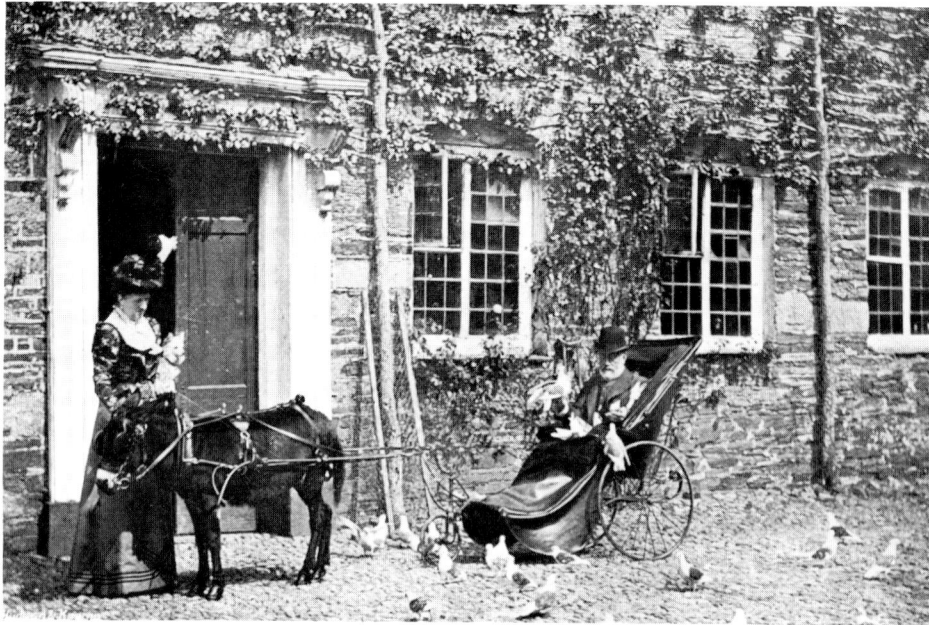

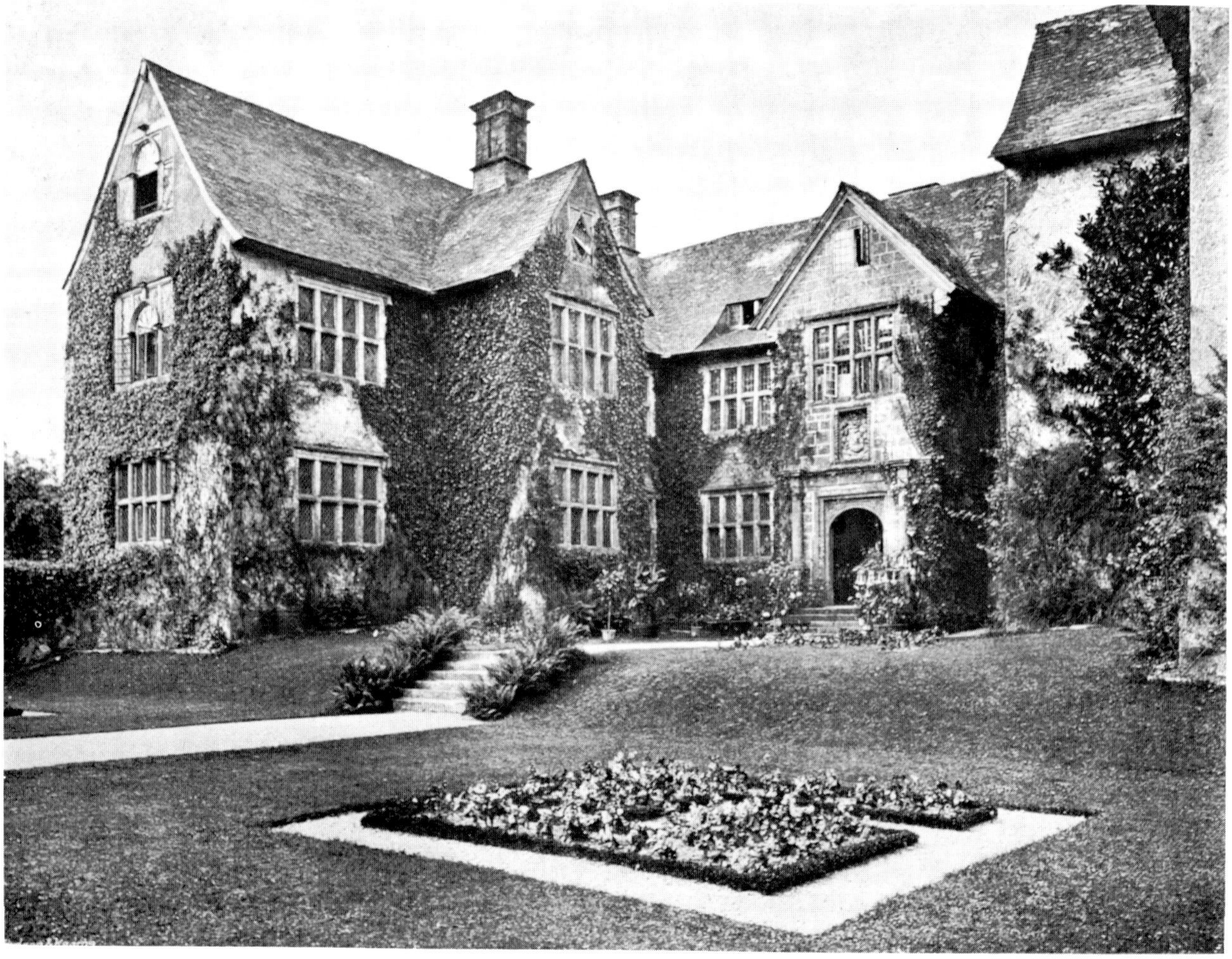

Copyright. MANY-MULLIONED WINDOWS. "Country Life."

trees and embowered in roses and white jasmine. The garden gate of Sydenham House, reached by an avenue of beautiful trees, is a delightful specimen of seventeenth century ironwork, now unfortunately falling to decay, and a pleasing introduction, indeed, to the beautiful scenes beyond.

The house is covered with climbing plants, of which several have grown to large proportions, especially on the south-west side, where the old walls are veritable gardens of flowers. Climbers of all kinds struggle for supremacy. Here is the fiery thorn (Cratægus Pyracantha), in company with the Gloire de Dijon or with old cluster roses, whilst Kerria Japonica makes a cloud of rich orange blossom for many weeks in the year. The door is embosomed in climbers, including noble wistaria, the tender escallonia, and the Pyrus Japonica, a galaxy, indeed, of precious things. The south-east wall is interesting from the fact that it is covered with the spreading branches of two pear trees, trained horizontally, of which one is the "Swan's Egg," a very old English variety.

The garden itself has an old-world aspect and fascinating charm, in keeping with the house and the beautiful scenery surrounding it. There is no attempt to introduce elaborate formal designs, but we have a square, of about an acre and a-half, with a high wall surrounding it. The design is simple, and flowers have their rightful place. A fine border of hardy flowers is near the house, and is beautiful throughout the year, from the time of the blossoming of the Christmas rose until the last starwort has faded. Roses of dwarf growth fill the beds, and are under-planted with fragrant heliotrope, box being used as an edging. Pleasing, too, are the sloping terrace, and the little streamlet, with plants by its side. There is a glorious border also by the fruit-tree-covered garden walls. Box again forms an edging, and flowers of all kinds have been planted— anemones, pæonies, bell-flowers, golden rods, starworts, columbines, and large quantities of other perennials.

The principal garden is skirted on the north-east by park-land, through which runs a tributary of the Lyd. Upon the well-kept sloping lawn are fine shrubs, and in the centre is a long rectangular pond, with Pampas and other grasses at the margin, and noble examples of the Royal fern (Osmunda regalis), which have attained large proportions, and show what beautiful effects may be created by this plant when in suitable soil and in full health.

The visitor to Sydenham will notice near the main entrance a pleasure ground nearly three acres in extent, and separated from the house by a public road. This garden is called the Turtle Grove. Formerly it was an orchard, but

some years since was laid out by Mr. Tremayne as a pleasure garden, in which many flowers thrive, whilst in the spring a glorious wealth of colour is provided by splendid hardy azaleas and rhododendrons. Here, too, are many interesting, trees, especially the cedar of Lebanon, now between 40ft. and 50ft. high, raised from seed gathered by Mr. Tremayne upon Mount Lebanon, and planted in 1847. A number of other interesting trees have been planted, including Scotch fir, scarlet oak, red cedar, and lime. The picturesque and attractive farmyard is near at hand.

It is interesting to know that at another residence of

THE PORCH.

Mr. Tremayne's—Heligan, in Cornwall—there is a famous avenue of the strawberry tree (Benthamia fragifera). We believe Mr. Tremayne's father was the first to introduce this distinct tree into England, but it is necessary to have a warm climate for its growth. Its large strawberry-like fruits are interesting. Mr. and the Hon. Mrs. Tremayne are great gardeners, to whom the rearing and care of the plants are evidently a work of love, and their beautiful gardens show how most pleasing and satisfactory effects may be reached by the simplest means judiciously and lovingly applied. This is indeed a valuable lesson of the pleasant West Country mansion of Sydenham.

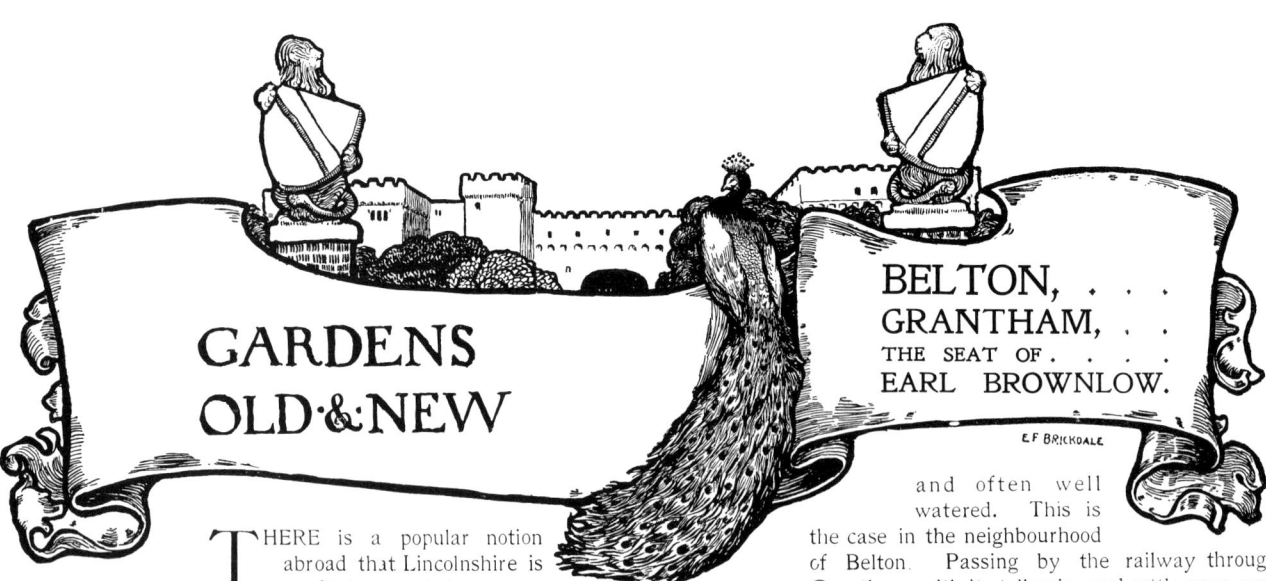

GARDENS OLD·&·NEW

BELTON, . . . GRANTHAM, . . . THE SEAT OF . . . . EARL BROWNLOW.

E.F BRICKDALE

THERE is a popular notion abroad that Lincolnshire is a flat, unpicturesque county, to which the tourist does seldom resort. It is as level, you are apt to think, as your hand, a shire of broad acres, much of it ancient waste, "stubb'd," perhaps, like "Thurnaby waäste" by the old "Northern Farmer," and no longer "nowt at all but bracken and fuzz," but very flat and unattractive all the same. This is a mistake. Putting aside the real beauties of fen country, and the charm that belongs to great over-arching skies, there is abundance of picturesque scenery in Lincolnshire, and in some parts the land is magnificently wooded, and often well watered. This is the case in the neighbourhood of Belton. Passing by the railway through Grantham, with its tall spire and cattle-pens, you do not suspect that a romantic pile like Belvoir is on one hand, and a beautiful seat like Belton on the other. Lord Brownlow has another fine seat at Ashridge, in Hertfordshire, to which some of his art treasures have been removed, but Belton House is very splendid, its park most beautiful, and its gardens superb. It is simply delightful to find the sweet village of Belton on the verge of the park, a place quite typical of the charms of rural life. How deeply Lord and Lady Brownlow are interested in home arts and village industries all the world knows, and Belton has profited very greatly by their love for

FROM THE NORTH STEPS.

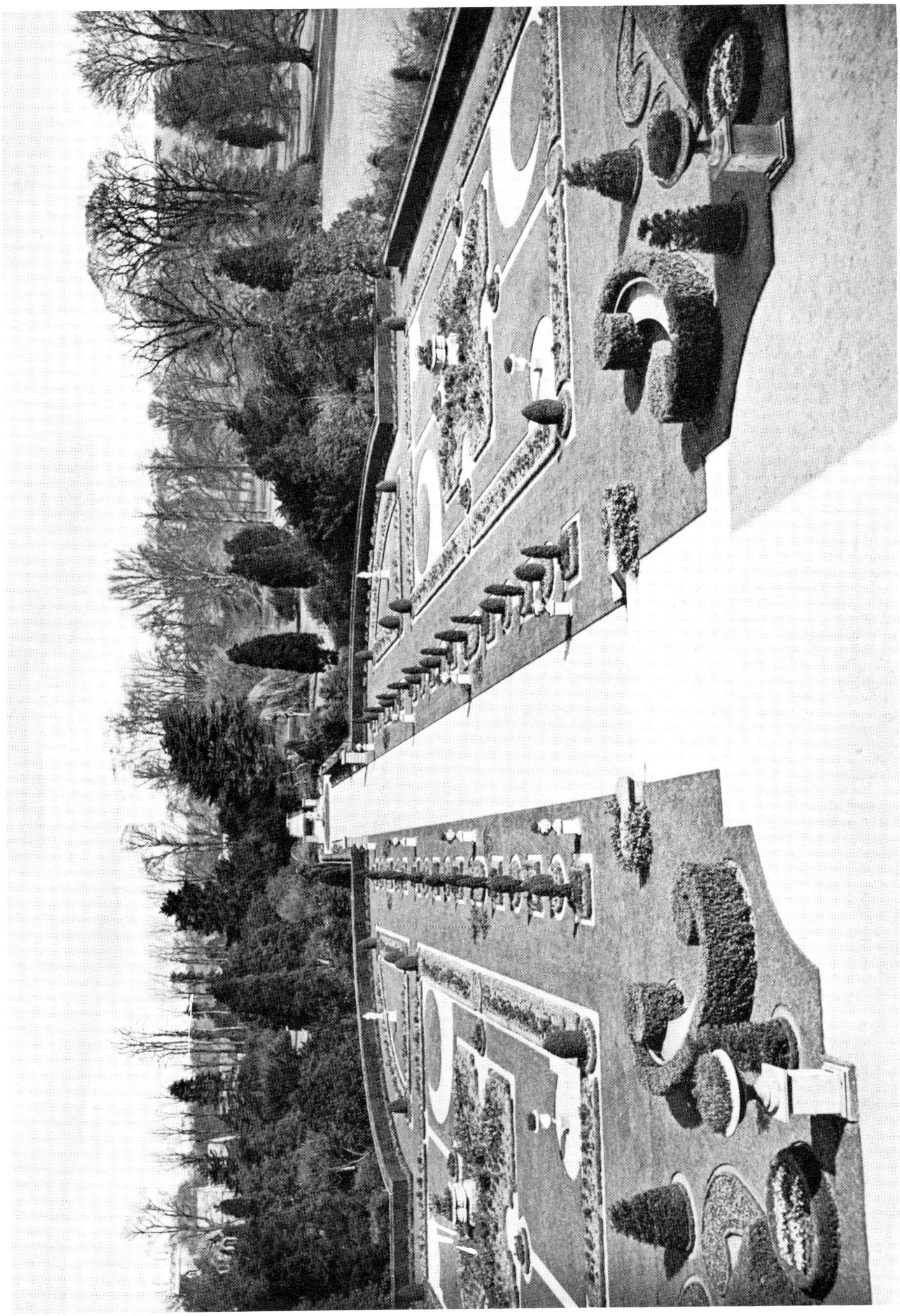

Copyright. THE ITALIAN GARDEN. "Country Life."

THE   COURTYARD.

BELTON   CHURCH,   FROM   THE   ITALIAN   GARDEN.

WATERFALL   IN   WILDERNESS.

rural pursuits. Although the neighbouring village of Sysson is said to be the original of "Willingham," Belton might well have been that village in which Jeannie Deans, on her long walk to London, discovered "one of those beautiful scenes so often found in merry England, where the cottages, instead of being built in two straight lines on each side of a dusty high road, stand in detached groups, interspersed not only with oaks and elms, but with fruit trees."

The older house of Belton, and the surrounding estate, were bought from the trustees of the Pakenham and another family by Richard Brownlow, Esq., Prothonotary of the Common Pleas in the times of Elizabeth and James. Apparently, succeeding owners added to the estate, and it was not until 1690 that Sir John Brownlow, fourth Baronet, the Prothonotary's great-grandson, procured licence to enclose, in Belton, Londonthorpe, and Telthorpe, a park, about which he built a wall some five miles in circumference. Within it stands the house we depict, which was erected between 1685 and 1689, Sir Christopher Wren being the architect. It is in the somewhat familiar form of the letter H—a central block with bold transverse wings. In the high roofs and many windows there is a strong mark of the French style of the time, which was reproduced so much in Holland, but Belton House bears also the evidences of another famous hand, that of Wyatt, who did good work at the place nearly a hundred years later. William III., during his Northern progress after the death of Queen Mary, visited Sir John Brownlow at Belton. The Baronet had planted very largely and judiciously, but there seems to be little knowledge of the gardens he had laid out about his mansion, though, doubtless, they were in the formal taste of his time.

A later Sir John Brownlow, created Viscount Tyrconnel in 1718, made many improvements at Belton, began the fine library, and laid out gardens of great extent and magnificence. These no longer remain, a natural treatment of the land having replaced most of the trim yew hedges, straight alleys, and formal grass plats. The fine brick triumphal arch near the eastern gate, known as the Belmont Tower, which affords a magnificent view from its crest, was built in 1750. Four years later Belton passed to Sir John Cust, Speaker of the House of Commons, in the right of his mother, who was the sister and heiress of Lord Tyrconnel, and Sir Brownlow Cust, who succeeded, was created Lord Brownlow shortly after his father's death. It was he who employed James Wyatt to alter and improve the house. The cupola and balustrade were removed, the drawing-room was made much more lofty, and other improvements were carried out. At about the same time alterations were effected in the pleasure grounds, into which the landscape spirit was more largely infused, and smiling wood and hill replaced some arrangements of the bygone time. But Belton owed much to the foresight of its earlier possessors, for it was they who had so richly planted, and the sylvan beauties of the landscape responded readily to the touch of the later hand.

Thus it will be seen that the development of this estate can be traced through the modifications of successive owners. The excellent character of the house, the charming picturesqueness of the courtyard, the lavish beauty of the iron grilles and gates, the elm avenue with its delightful vista, the various features of the pleasure grounds, the venerable trees, all bespeak the loving care and discriminating taste of generations. Thus are the charms and allurements of country life preserved in England. At Belton we

THE CONSERVATORY.

has passed out to the world—to the college quadrangle, to the camp, the legislature, or the bar—has accomplished his task, and his tenantry follow him to the grave. All this you feel at Belton, because in that pretty village church, with its fine Early English tower and its massive Norman arcade, there are monuments of many lords of Belton, including those of Sir John Brownlow, Viscount Tyrconnel, of Sir John Cust, the Speaker, of the first Lord Brownlow by Westmacott, and of the first Earl and his Countess by Marochetti and Canova, with others.

The gardens, which are among the most important in

THE DUTCH GARDEN ON THE NORTH FRONT.

are, indeed, in the heart of the land. The venerable tower of the village church rises near the house, and it is but a pleasant walk across the garden from the dwelling of the lords of Belton to the place where their ashes lie.

Here is the rounding of the nobleman's and country gentleman's life. The child prattling in the garden paths

Lincolnshire, resemble little, as we have said, the formal pleasure grounds of Dutch trimness which Sir John Brownlow, Viscount Tyrconnel, improved and partly formed about his house early in the last century, though a certain stately formality rightly belongs to them. Yet, except that the splendid Italian garden is as a jewel set in its green surroundings, it is chiefly natural landscape, with picturesque-ness of character, and floral wealth that we discover. That pretty village of Belton, which has been alluded to for its rural charms, lies on the north, while the many-acred park, rich in umbrageous glories, and roamed over by herds of deer, is upon the south side. The woodland character most attracts us here, with many a glade for our delight, many a cloud of bluebells in the spring, many a primrose bank, and many a ferny hollow.

The house may be approached by several ways, but the principal entrance is by a conspicuously straight road on the south side, which has a glorious avenue of elms, one of the finest, indeed, in the kingdom. On the same side, but more towards the east, is the notable Belmont Tower, already referred to, which is approached by a very beautiful avenue of limes, upwards of a mile in length. The other side of the park, where the character of the land is different, is skirted by the river Witham, which flows through part of the gay pleasure grounds near the mansion, adding a very distinct and natural charm to the place. It is, happily, unspoiled and pellucid, so that in dry weather water for the house can be obtained from it.

The landscape features of Belton have been suggested. They consist in the enhancing of the natural character of the land, of wood and water, by judicious treatment, careful planting, and the variegation of foliage, combined with the effect of noble avenues, and rich groups of trees and shrubs. Some features dear to the old landscape gardener may also be discovered, as in the picturesque cottage known as the "Villa," with a broad sheet of water hard by, and in others near the course of the Witham. These, like the grottoes, temples, pagodas, and other varied adornments

represented, and, judging by the growth, soil and climate must be well suited to leafy evergreen shrubs. These may be particularly noticed in that part of the grounds known as the Wilderness, where the Witham pursues its course, and the yew and box make luxuriant growth. Spiræa ariæfolia, the big summer plumy spiræa, is very handsome in this place, and near a rustic bridge, clothed with clematis Jackmanni, honeysuckles, and other creepers and climbers, are some

THE SUNDIAL.

weeping beeches, very pleasing and distinct trees in the landscape.

But all, as we have said, is not landscape gardening at Belton, and as our picture of the principal flower garden reveals. Here is one of those splendid areas of green turf and colour, enclosed by hedges cut like walls, which are seen, with some varying characters, in many great English gardens. The well-gravelled straight paths, the green, close-cropped grass, the yews standing like sentinels as you walk, each in its bed, square or round, and radiant with flowers, the urns and statuary, all enclosed by the hedge, are inviting, indeed, in the evenings of summer, when the shadows lengthen in the sun. You feel that this is the rich jewel set in the land when you turn to the pleasant prospect beyond of wood and hill. It is a stately pleasaunce of happy effect, harmonising with the house, and yet strong in its own classic character. By contrast it enhances the beauty of the woodland, and itself derives much from the presence of its leafy neighbours. We have often re-marked that the garden must be appro-priate to the house, and if not every mansion demands such a noble Italian garden as this, it cannot be questioned that the splendid enclosure is wholly suitable to the house at Belton.

The formality does not by any means imply the exclusion of flower beauty in prodigal profusion. As at Belvoir, a few miles distant, spring flowers are greatly used in the flower garden. Thousands of pansies, aubrietias, wallflowers, primroses, and other blooms gladden the eye, and fill with fragrance the air in the opening of the garden year. Bulbous plants are there, too, in great numbers in the grass, making the spring-time truly enjoyable at Belton. The brilliant hues in the beds, the nodding daffodils, the countless

of the gardenage of what may be called the middle period of garden design, add points of interest to the grounds. It is not necessary to insist upon the attraction of fine trees and shrubs. Oaks, planes, elms, and beeches are conspicuous, with groups of evergreen and flowering bushes freely planted. These add greatly to the beauty of the place, with a changing charm, at every period of the year. As in many other fine English gardens, box and yew are thoroughly well

THE WILDERNESS GATE.

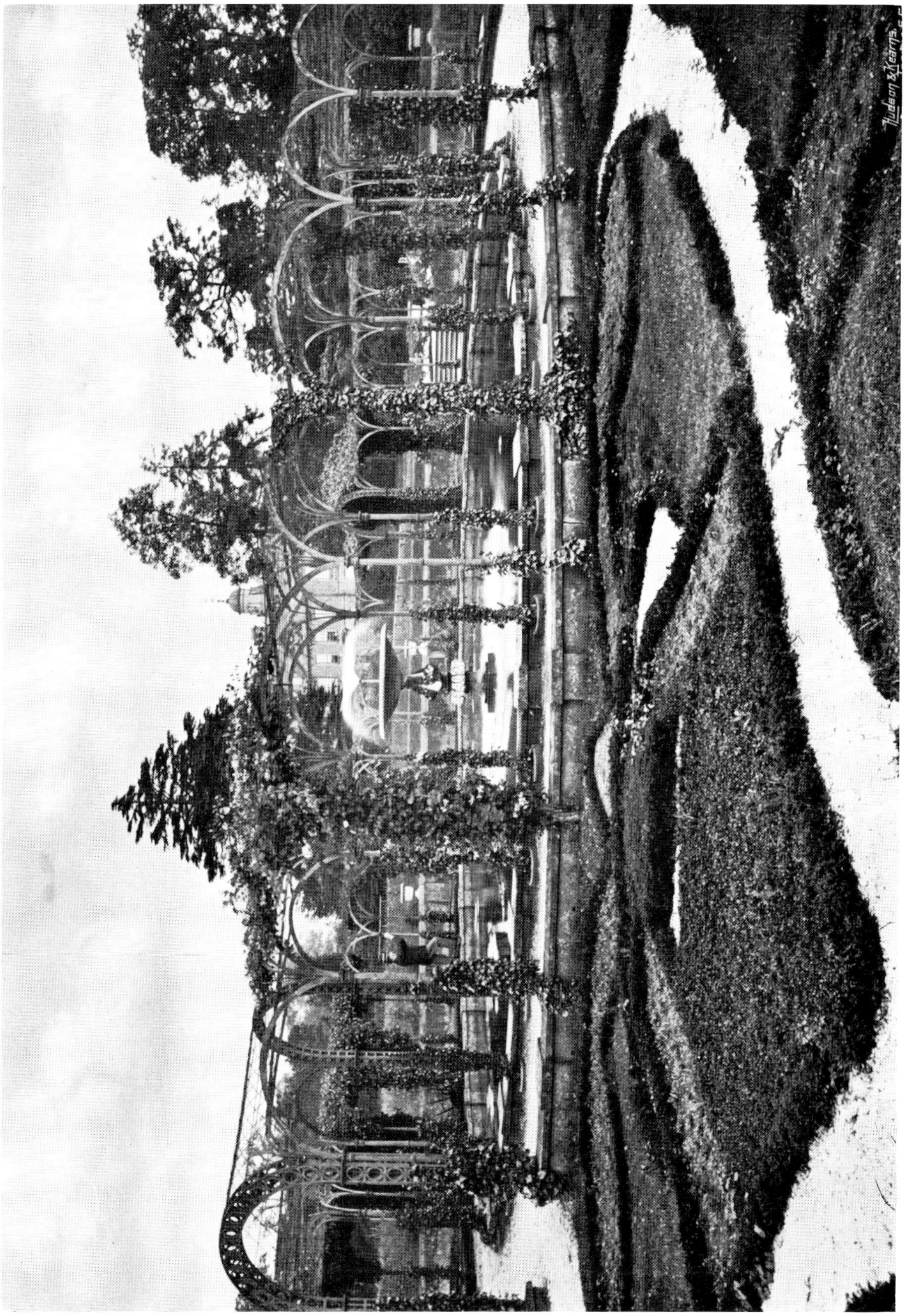

THE FOUNTAIN IN THE ITALIAN GARDEN.

Copyright. "Country Life."

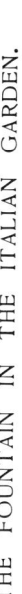

bright and fragrant varieties of flowers, are all delightful in their time. The pansy is a great feature. Nowadays there are so many varieties of the plant in cultivation that new beauties have been attained in diversified and pretty blossoms, all very gay and bold. The improvement in the group is, indeed, quite remarkable, and the "tufted" kinds are particularly noticeable, as being closer in habit of growth and less unruly than the older varieties. These are cultivated in great numbers, and in favourable circumstances, at Belton, and it is satisfactory to know that spring gardening is there considered as much as the more radiant gardening of the summer. But to make a catalogue of the charms of the floral world which have been gathered at Belton would neither be possible nor desirable.

Our fine illustrations show sufficiently the broad character of the place, and imagination will readily supply the rest. There is sound garden architecture to study at this noble seat also; but here, again, the camera comes to our aid, and calls before us the visible presentment of things more clearly than could be the case with any description from the pen. Let us therefore draw to a conclusion.

The very fine conservatory which stands near the house, of good architectural character, wherein all the favourite flowers are grown in multitudes, must, however, be alluded to. A fountain garden, with ivy-grown arches, roses, lilies, and abundant other flowers, is there also. But enough has now been said. Wherever we go, in fact, we find good gardening reflected in each part of the pleasure grounds of Belton House.

Copyright.   RUINS   IN   THE   WILDERNESS.   *" Country Life."*

Copyright.   THE ITALIAN GARDEN AND CONSERVATORY.   *" Country Life."*

ASHRIDGE PARK,
GREAT BERKHAMPSTEAD,
THE SEAT OF . . .
EARL BROWNLOW.

HAROLD
NELSON

THIS great domain lies upon those fair borders of Hertfordshire and Buckingham which are so rich in the seats of the noble, and it is famous among the beautiful places in the land for its rare beauty, its palatial grandeur, and its many memories. The two counties might well strive for the possession of such a place. If Buckingham has the house, the stables and a large part of that umbrageous park belong to Hertfordshire. It was a region of open forest tracts once, where the porkers chewed the beech mast while the swineherd sat in the shade, and is full of green and umbrageous richness still. Ancient men are yet, or a few years ago were, alive who would tell the wayfarer that in their youth the only way to Dunstable was, at will, by the meadows or over the downs. But famous makers of roads and canals have possessed Ashridge—no other than the Egertons, Earls and Dukes of Bridgewater. Through many changes it had come down to them from ancient days. Edmund Crouchback, Earl of Cornwall, son of Robert, King of the Romans, seems to have won Ashridge from the wild. There

he lived, and died in 1300, having founded, near his mansion, a goodly house for the brethren of the "Bonshommes," whom he endowed, not only with wealth, but with a portion of the "holy blood" of Hayles, in Gloucestershire, which brought many pilgrims to the country shrine. Ten years before Edmund died, Edward I. kept his Christmas sadly at Ashridge, for Eleanor had passed away but a few weeks before, and he held a parliament there, to the discomfort of the natives, who were called upon for supplies.

When the Dissolution came, and revenues fell from monastic hands into royal or noble coffers, the Bonshommes went the way of their brethren, and Edward VI. installed his sister Elizabeth at Ashridge. There she was sleeping, and feigning to be ill, as many believed, when the officers of Queen Mary broke in upon her privacy, and in the royal litter bore her off to the Tower. Then Ashridge passed to the celebrated Lord Chancellor Egerton, Earl of Ellesmere, and from him to his son John Egerton, first Earl of Bridgewater, of whom his monument, in the church of delightful Little Gaddesden, outside

"Country Life."

A PARTERRE.

THE FOUNTAIN GARDEN.

the park gates, says that " Art and Nature did strive which might contribute most to make him a most accomplished gentleman." The second Earl of Bridgewater was a liberal patron of learning, and once was a friend of Milton. It was said that upon the circumstance of his losing his way, with his sister, in a wood at Harefield, some miles from Ashridge, the plot of " Comus " was founded. But when Milton published his " Pro Populo Anglicano Defensio," Bridgewater wrote upon the title of his copy, " Liber igne, auctor furcâ dignissimi." Much concerning Ashridge and its old possessors may be read in Todd's "History of the College of Bonshommes at Ashridge," 1823.

Earl Brownlow holds Ashridge by female descent from the House of Egerton, Earls and Dukes of Bridgewater. Their monuments are in the church at Little Gaddesden, with epitaphs so magnificent as to inspire a belief, as one writer said, that we of this later age are but very degenerate individuals. The monument of the last Duke, the father of inland navigation, the suitor, too, of one of the " beautiful Miss Gunnings," he who could see no use in rivers except as feeders of navigable canals, is among them. It was the Duke's misfortune that the beauties of life did not appeal to him. Perhaps they were all swallowed up in the supreme beauty of Miss Gunning, in whose honour he remained a bachelor to the end of his days. Women never waited upon him, and things that were merely ornamental he despised. Once, it is recorded, on returning from London to his Lancashire house at Worsley, finding some flowers had been planted there, he " whipped their heads off and ordered them to be rooted up." When, therefore, he died in 1803, leaving Ashridge to his cousin and successor in the Earldom, General Edward Egerton, his work at his fine

THE MONKS' WALK.

THE MONKS' GARDEN.

Hertfordshire estate must mainly have been destructive, and certainly the gardens cannot have prospered under his hand.

The last Earl of Bridgewater, an eccentric old gentlemen, died in his house, the Hôtel Egerton, in the Rue Saint Honoré, in 1829. His carriage, with three gold-laced lackeys hanging on behind, was well known to Parisians. They used to collect about the hotel to see the steps let down, and the Earl's dogs march out, dressed, if gossip be true, as human beings, returned from their airing in the Bois. The Earl himself remained at home, solacing his feeble days with the "sport" of shooting tame rabbits, and partridges with clipped wings, in his garden. It was a

Photo.   THE EAST FRONT.   J. T. Newman.

reminiscence of his days of youthful prowess in covert and over the stubble. He was a wayward testator, who attached impossible conditions to his will, pledging the legatee to become Duke or Marquis of Bridgewater within a period, and thus he well-nigh shipwrecked the estate in Chancery.

So much for the interesting possessors of Ashridge, all men in whom the spark of talent or the love of literature shone. The house and gardens were very fair and tasteful. The Lord Chancellor had done much for the place, and it had been "a stately house" in Elizabeth's time, though the collegiate church was then destroyed. So the house had remained, with many a change, doubtless, until the year 1800, when the last Duke of Bridgewater, the canal maker, in the height of his wealth, razed it to the ground, great hall and cloisters together, leaving nothing of antiquity save the crypt.

The present splendid mansion was commenced on the old site in 1808 from the designs of Wyatt, and completed by Sir

Jeffrey Wyatville, his son, in 1814. It is a great and imposing pile, splendid in conception and details, elaborate in its character and rich in its internal fittings, now happily maintained by the excellent taste and love for true art of its noble possessor and his Countess. The principal front is 1,000ft. in length, and the great range of buildings presents, as may be seen, a wonderfully varied and picturesque aspect, with towers and battlements, a splendid porch, machicolations above, mullioned windows, arched doorways, and whatever else the Wyatts could fitly wrest from the beauties of mediæval architecture.

But to describe Ashridge House is not the purpose here. Let the pictures speak for themselves. It lies amid beautiful surroundings, for the counties of Buckingham and Hertford, as all the world knows, are famous for their woods. The long avenues of stately trees in the park, the noble groups and single specimens, the broad stretches of turf, the multitudes

"Country Life."
THE SKATING POND.

THE GARDEN FRONT AND CHURCH.

of deer, all contribute to make the finest pictures. One of these avenues, nearly two miles long, leads to a lofty monument erected on a height in honour of the last Duke of Bridgewater. There are splendid beech trees—towering giants, lifting their grey, pillared trunks to enormous heights, where the birds are happy in the greenery among the slender branches stretched towards the sky, while moss and lichen gather about their feet. Then there are majestic limes near the house, planted, as men say, by Elizabeth herself, but really known to have begun their budding when Charles II. was king. Many another splendid tree is here also, and looking round, you say that in this place have lived men who loved and knew the beauties of the sylvan world, and planted that others might enjoy.

THE SUNDIAL.

The reader will already have divined that the gardens are of equal beauty and interest in that fair setting. Several styles of gardening will be discovered, and it is pleasant to find a character preserved in keeping with the old English aspect of the house, as for example in the Monks' Garden, reminiscent of the Bonshommes of former times. Here, therefore, is to be learned the lesson of appropriateness. Then we come to a quaint enclosed parterre surrounded by trees, which lend additional character to it, where rhododendrons are used with moderate freedom. A certain distinctive character is discerned in the conifer hedge, and we say to ourselves that the good box-edgings have very marked value, and that the creepers vesting the stone pillar add a feature that we like to find in gardens. A verdure-clad pillar, an old dial, or mossy urn filled with flowers, standing, perhaps, in the open, or flecked with sunlight through the trees, is far more appropriate in some situations than a gleaming statue or sculptured marble vase. But, just as the old eclectics chose their principles from the teaching of many schools, so can the modern gardener select his features from the best characters of many styles. Ashridge,

for example, has its Italian garden, lying on the east side of the house, very gay with many blossoms, and including delightful borders of hardy flowers also.

One great feature of the place is in its cloister-like alleys, or corridors—if such a word may be applied to a garden—which lead from one part to another, and are cool retreats from hot summer suns. They are clothed, of course, with climbers, and have quite a character of their own.

Then, again, as in so many English gardens, we find the yew a very conspicuous and handsome feature. There are noble specimens near the house, and certainly no tree is more impressive than some ancient yew—its gnarled trunk twisted, as it were, in its warfare with a hundred storms, from which it has emerged a sturdy veteran to delight us with its dense growth and character, and the deep shadows it casts upon the turf. Leaving the "yew tree's shade," we meet the same tree in another form round the skating-pond at Ashridge. Here it forms a fine hedge, well kept, dense, even, and extending for a considerable distance. The lawns, again, are delightful. Now a great glory of many of our best gardens, envied by those who visit them from other lands, is in those stretches of velvety turf, which set off the house to such advantage, and which in many cases have a most attractive effect, enhancing the value of everything else by investing the whole with simplicity and dignity of character.

Another particularly charming feature of Ashridge is the fern glade, leading to the grotto, where ferns luxuriate in prodigal profusion, making a fairy bower, leafy, cool, and satisfying. Ashridge in short, is full of interest for the lover of gardening, who will feel the charm of its varied garden features, its ancient trees and clipped yews, and its many other beauties. The Earl and Countess Brownlow are both interested in the charms of the garden, the arts of the home, and the things that are the beauty of country life, and Ashridge has gained very much under their care.

THE FERNERY.

GARDENS OLD & NEW

CONDOVER, SHROPSHIRE, THE SEAT OF MR. R. H. CHOLMONDELEY.

FROM such a house as this at Condover, in the goodly county of Salop, we enter the gardens with expectancy, and are not disappointed. Few counties in England can boast so many fine seats and families of ancient lineage as Shropshire. Go where you will, some old castle or castellated fragment, some mansion of early time, some example of the timber structures which were so notable a feature of Middle England, or some stout dwelling-place of stone, will attract your attention; and if you enquire, you are as likely as not to find your village resting-place well filled with history. Condover and, in a measure, its formal garden are very typical of Tudor times. The house bears plainly the character of its age, and in the main front there is no small resemblance to Charlecote in Warwickshire, where the old Knight dwelt whom Shakespeare satirised for all time as Justice Shallow. There is the same central block, with its gables and projecting porch; on each side project the same wings, with similar windows, cresting, and chimneys; the grouping is thus about a hollow square, and the front, if you include the porch, is somewhat upon the plan of a letter E. It is certainly a massing of structure that lends itself exceedingly well to the best effects of light and shade, to the artistic picturesqueness of sky-line, and to all those features which we are wont to associate with Tudor and Jacobean times. As we know, there are solid comforts within such goodly dwelling-places as this, and often fine gardens about them.

If you look, too, at the other side of Condover, you will remark a species of corridor or arcade, opening upon the terrace and overlooking the grass slopes, which may remind you in some degree of Hatfield, and you recognise that here should be a garden of distinction and character. The park at Condover is one of rich umbrageous beauties and broad green expanses, and it is somewhat noteworthy that the line between the formal gardens and their natural surroundings is not strongly drawn; the character of enclosure is absent. The rival schools of gardening—the natural and artificial—have had many a battleground, but the conflict has not been waged, and will not be, over the delights of old Condover. Here certainly is nothing of the extremely fantastic, such as you will find at Levens and Elvaston, but merely the cutting of trees to prim forms, analogous to beehives and cylinders, and the natural

THE SOUTH-WEST VIEW.

life of the garden is not overshadowed by the neighbourhood of arboreal curiosities.

But before we enter the garden, let us say something about the spacious and beautiful house. What manner of dwelling was here when the Parliament of Edward I. sat at Acton Burnell hard by—the nobles in the castle, and the commons in a barn—to pass the famous "Statutum de Mercatoribus," we do not know. The estate was purchased in the reign of Henry VIII. by Thomas Owen, who appears to have built the house itself in or about 1598, to be completed by his son. Camden says of him that he was "a great lover of learning, who, being dead, left behind him a son, Sir Roger, an excellent scholar, and worthy of so excellent a father." Thomas Owen was native of Condover, and a gentleman of the law, who rose to be Queen's Sergeant in 1593, and a Justice of the Common Pleas in the following year. He died in 1598, and is buried in Westminster Abbey, where his fine monument may be seen.

Sir William Owen, of Condover, was a wary gentleman in the Civil Wars, who contrived, with a certain agility, to be now on one side of the hedge and now on the other. He

still survives among the beautiful houses of the land. The Owens continued to live at Condover for many years after that critical period in the fortunes of their house, until by marriage the mansion and estate came to the family of Cholmondeley, and it has recently passed to the hands of its present possessor.

The house within is beautiful, spacious, and abundantly interesting, though not to be described here. Fine panelling, rich ceilings and mantels, old portraits, and plenishings of the richest kind, add to its old-world charm, and through mullioned windows there are delightful views over the gardens and park.

Rare and beautiful, with a subtle charm, these gardens are. The principal flower garden is on the south side, where the pictures illustrate the character of the grass terraces with their conical yews, and the noble trees and glades of the park beyond. The arrangement is formal, and quite typical of some gardens of the class. It will be observed that there is nothing elaborate in the design. The slope of the ground lent itself to a terraced arrangement, and there is a simple charm about the varied grass walks, with suggestion, in the character

THE GRASS TERRACES.

was in the Commission of Array, at least, and signed certain warrants, being a supporter of the King, and was in a position of authority at the council house in Shrewsbury. The Parliament Committee afterwards averred in his favour that, when they first "took footing" in the country, and were in the poorest condition, penned up in the garrison of Wem, and there surrounded by the enemy, he held correspondence with them, and offered them possession of his house at Condover, "being a strong stone building within three miles distance of Shrewsbury." Though they were not in a position to garrison it, the circumstance led them to the conclusion that his "affections were always right towards the cause of the public," and if he ever acted otherwise this could scarcely proceed from disaffection, but rather "from some passion of timorousness, or the facility of his nature." Not content with this plea in Sir William's favour, the Parliament party asserted that, after the taking of Shrewsbury, he had manifested the best dispositions towards their cause, while his backwardness in contributing mortgages or yielding assistance to the Royalists caused them to threaten to burn his house. Fortunately for himself and for us, too, his noble mansion escaped the fury of the Royalists he had disappointed, and

of the pleasaunce, for those who do not seek enclosure, but prefer a broad outlook to the charms of a sequestered parterre.

Geometrical gardening marks the west side of the house. There are as fine tall box edgings as you could wish to see, giving character and distinction to the place. Their quaintness is delightful, though to keep edgings in such condition as those at Condover is no easy matter, and with unkempt raggedness the old-world aspect and beauty straightway disappear. The spiral junipers and Irish yews are here an attractive feature. At the end of the garden zinnias, roses, and other lovely flowers fill the beds, and those who enjoy the satisfying shade of a good yew hedge—the glory of many a fine garden—will find a splendid one here, in association with many notable specimens of the golden pyramidal yew.

Something of the character of the beautiful park at Condover will be seen in the pictures. The little river Cound, from which the place takes its name, winds through the pleasant glades overshadowed by very fine trees, and the ground is diversified with hill and hollow. The elms of the park are noble specimens of one of our finest forest trees, and there is a splendid giant on the lawn with branches sweeping the turf.

CONDOVER HALL AND ITS OLD GARDEN ARCHITECTURE.

Fruit and flower gardening go hand in hand at this pleasant abode to an extent rarely seen, and this is not the least interesting feature of the place. The association of the various branches of gardening might often, in truth, be closer than it is, and certainly our fruit and vegetable gardens would gain much in attractiveness by reason of the presence of gayer denizens. The Condover fruit garden may appropriately be described as a reserve flower garden, for great numbers of flowers are cultivated year by year solely for the purpose of cutting for the adornment of the house. Thus is the flower garden proper not ruthlessly despoiled, and its fragrance and beauty are preserved undiminished.

Condover thus has lessons for the garden-lover. There is unfailing charm in a place that possesses noble grass terraces, that is distinguished by its lines of stately yews and glorious hedges, that has

THE GEOMETRICAL GARDEN.

its various levels approached by such stairways as these. A prodigal wealth of flowers scents the gale in this rarely beautiful garden, where once again we find the architect working hand in hand with him under whose care are developed the charms of the sylvan shades, the sentinel yew, and the fragrant parterre. The mossy stonework of old stairways leading up from level to level, united in this garden picture with the green slopes, and with the characteristic yews, is most pleasing. Here is Nature

linked with the other work of man, and thus is Nature, as Schiller says, possessed with a soul and exalted by Art. There are many elements of a liberal education in a good garden; it inspires by its influence and gives the opportunity for expression.

And, in conclusion, it must be said that the modifications of style at Condover, the uniting of old features with something of a new disposition of them, are very charming and suggestive, as affording a fine example of good gardenage.

THE TERRACE STEPS.

A VISTA OF SOMBRE YEWS AND BRIGHT FLOWERS.

GARDENS OLD & NEW

VEN HOUSE, SOMERSET, . .
THE SEAT OF . . .
Sir Edward Bradford Medlycott, Bart.

THE very fine and attractive gardens which we illustrate are the adornment of a notable mansion in the West Country—Ven House, near Milborne Port, on the borders of Dorset and Somerset. This is the head of the gathering ground of the pleasant river Yeo, on the western side of the watershed which separates the basin of the Somerset river from that of the Hampshire Stour. The country is extremely pretty, with much varied natural beauty, and to show that it is interesting it is enough to say that famous old Sherborne, with its enriched and glorious abbey church, is the near neighbour of Ven. At Henstridge Ash, on the hill close by, veracious tradition asserts that Walter Raleigh smoked his first pipe, and was liberally treated with water by the peasants, who thought his clothes were on fire. The country about Ven House is hunted by the celebrated Blackmore Vale Foxhounds, the vale being the wide and fertile level through which the Cale flows southward from Wincanton to the Stour.

The mansion stands close to the little town of Milborne Port, with its fine Norman church and other evidences of a once greater state. An ancestor of the present Baronet began the building of Ven House in 1698, and completed it in 1701. It is a red brick structure of classic simplicity, its front inlaid with stone, and the surface broken by Corinthian pilasters, which run up to a balustrade crested by urns, and its wings are pierced by large archways. The design has been attributed to various architects, and the house was thoroughly restored about sixty years ago. Though far removed from the modern ideals of domestic architecture, it belongs to a period and a style that can never fail to command admiration.

The gardens are in character appropriate to the house, and are well deserving of attention. Near it they have a certain classic formality. At a little distance the regular lines give place to the features of a more picturesque style, and the grounds approach to native simplicity. There is here a happy combination of styles. An enclosed garden with a bordering terrace and classic adornments is the approach to a leafy venue that seems to breathe the grandiose manner of Le Nôtre. Though the mansion is not in a position that gives

THE ENCLOSED GARDEN AND THE ELM AVENUE.

VEN HOUSE AND ITS GARDEN SURROUNDINGS.

THE   GARDEN   AND   GARDEN   ARCHITECTURE.

it extensive views, yet its immediate surroundings are thus attractive enough, and the vicinity is well wooded. A wide avenue of elms extends up a gentle grass slope, which forms the sky-line a mile away, and, on the other side, beyond the garden, a like avenue leads away across many a level meadow. Within the gates are several fine cedars of Lebanon, and a range of beautiful deciduous trees and evergreen shrubs shuts off the neighbouring village from view.

Along the rear of the house, and overlooking the enclosed garden, is a fine broad stone terrace, with balustrade, and urns filled with flowers. Upon this opens a glass arcade, in which are orange trees, palms, and flowering creepers, leading at one

end into a beautiful structure of glass and masonry—a very fine and rich example of Corinthian architecture applied to garden work, which will be seen in the pictures.

Here the principal object of interest is an enormous specimen of the fragrant Datura, which is planted in the centre of the conservatory, and fills the greater part of the space Its trunk is not less than 3ft. in circumference, and it is truly a noble plant, often used with fine effect in the summer garden, where its creamy white odorous blossoms are very handsome. In the house climbing cacti, eucalyptuses, palms, and camellias are its companions.

From this Corinthian garden-house we pass along the broad terrace which has been alluded to, and look over the formal walled garden below, which is rectangular, and an excellent example of the particular style. It will not fail to remind the reader of Sir William Temple's description of the enclosed garden at Moor Park, though it has not the same elaboration of features, and is of quite simple design. Neighbouring Montacute is a more striking example of the character. In the midst of the garden at Ven House is a marble fountain supported by storks, and surrounded by a basin, with water-lilies. From this fountain four broad walks lead away at right angles to the four sides of the garden, one approaching the house, which is reached by a flight of shallow stone steps, and another leading directly away from it to a very beautiful semi-circular marble seat, set in the greenery, and with finely-sculptured figures along the top. The general effect, combined with the excellent standard Portugal laurels, their heads cut into spheres, which line the raised gravel path above and behind the seat, is very striking

THE   BRIDGE   IN   THE   PARK.

and characteristic. Such laurels were in a like situation at Moor Park, a place of uncommon historical interest. The level lawns of this walled garden are studded at equal intervals with standard roses planted in little round beds and surfaced with white tufted pansies. Nearer the walls of the garden are square plots filled with bedding plants, each separated from its neighbour by well-kept box edging, and on the garden walls are trained roses and jasmines, the glorious scarlet Pyrus japonica, and exquisite wistaria, 70ft. in length. At intervals along the pathways stand variegated aloes, quite a feature of the place, in large pots. Terrace walks along and above the sides of this garden enable its many features to be well seen. That opposite to the house and behind the marble seat, and along which the clipped Portugal laurels grow, is approached by fine flights of stone steps at each end, for it is raised some feet above the garden level.

Let it be observed that the garden architect and sculptor have everywhere done admirable work at Ven. Amid a prodigal wealth of garden beauty there is an added charm in the fine balustrades, the richly-carved vases and urns, and the sculptured figures in stone and marble, which give a classic aspect to the place, and carry the spirit of the house into its surroundings. Look at the marble seat in the formal garden, at the figures that flank the ascents, at the fine urns that neighbour the stairways, at the bridge in the park, and at a multitude of other adornments, and you will realise that sound taste has, indeed, ruled the beautifying of this fine garden.

On the left-hand side of the great stone terrace, and opposite to the conservatory, another broad flight of steps leads to the pleasure grounds. It will be agreed that a perfectly beautiful

THE GREAT CONSERVATORY.

picture is formed by this fine mossy stonework, under the shadow of that splendid old walnut tree. Here surely is an ideal place wherein to weave a garden phantasy or conjure up a greenwood romance. We are now in the realm of more natural beauty, and, except for a border of bedding plants at the base of a wall near the flight of steps, no trace of conventionality meets the eye. There are emerald lawns, on which deciduous and evergreen trees flourish. Oaks and elms, tulip trees, copper beeches and their brethren, weeping ashes, yews, laburnums, great aucubas, and a host of other beautiful evergreen and flowering trees and shrubs, diversify the scene. Then, in the changing seasons, we chance upon delightful pictures

THE CLASSIC ASCENT BENEATH THE OLD WALNUT TREE.

and peeps of colour. A colony of pæonies is blooming on a wide lawn, around which low-branched trees have made a rampart: fresh pink monthly roses are clustering round a weathered statue of their goddess Flora ; syringas are shedding their fragrance on the gale ; and Scotch briar roses enter a quiet retreat through a honeysuckle-covered archway.

Further on we discover an octagon summer-house to rest in, built round an ancient apple tree, open to all the winds

VEN HOUSE, FROM THE FURTHER TERRACE.

and strike to the left, where the sound of running water is heard. We emerge then upon the banks of a murmuring brook, an early stream of the Yeo, over-arched by trees, and flowing between fern-covered banks, with many a silent deep and many a babbling shallow, until it passes beneath the span of that graceful bridge amid flag-irises and forget-me-nots. How delightful, we think, to play croquet or tennis on a lawn by such a stream.

Ven House has a garden of woodland and flowers ; almost

of heaven, beloved of birds, and wreathed with climbing roses, honeysuckle, ivy, jasmine, and clematis. Around it are horseshoe-shaped beds of carnations, dwarf roses, and pansies, edged with London pride, and behind these a mixed border, filled with the stronger-growing hardy perennials— giant evening primroses, tall daisy-flowers, delphiniums, phloxes, the old-fashioned double white rockets, and lovely Madonna lilies. But we find, perhaps, a more charming part of the pleasure grounds still if we leave the central vista, flanked by greensward and umbrageous trees, and terminated in the distance by the carven figures of shepherd and shepherdess,

wherever you go the air is filled with fragrance. The centre walks are gay, behind their box edging, with fine arrays of hardy flowers, and you pass beneath many a rose-laden arch. The inner walled garden has the same character. Carnations and daffodils line each side of the centre path, while the rose-arches are masses of bloom, and colonies of lily of the valley hard by produce in due season plenteous harvests of their delicate and odorous blossoms. To convey an idea of such delights is difficult, indeed, but the pictures will enable the reader to realise how really beautiful and characteristic are the gardens of Ven House.

THE ASCENT FROM THE GARDEN.

GARDENS OLD·&·NEW

NORTON CONYERS, YORKSHIRE, . .
THE SEAT OF . . . .
Sir Reginald Graham, Bart

THERE are few places more interesting in Yorkshire than Norton Conyers, that quaint old house which we illustrate. It is pleasantly situated in the valley of the Yore, some four miles north of the city of Ripon, and has a charmingly simple garden, such as its picturesqueness demands. Those who, like Peter Bell, have "trudged through Yorkshire dales," have noticed in their wanderings many places akin to Norton Conyers. Some of them have fallen from their high estate, and the peasant lights his fire upon the hearth about which lords and ladies gathered of yore. Above the mantel their armorial bearings may still remain, with many a device of their ancient heraldry. Sometimes the Royal Arms speak of Stuart days, with such an inscription as "Feare God; Honour the Kinge." Outside at the gates or over the door will be the date and some motto welcoming the guest, or it may be, as in a certain place that the writer knows of, warning those who violate justice that they may not knock thereat. The ghosts of those times still linger in the panelled galleries, and are seen when the moonlight falls through the latticed window, or are heard with silken robes when the wind sighs in the night-time. About them are old gardens, weedy, and sometimes neglected, but often gay with colour and fragrant with sweetness.

Norton Conyers has in many ways been a fortunate place. In that beautiful country of the river Yore, famous for its spreading woods and green pastures, the memory of the Nortons still survives, and the place was long associated with them, as afterwards with the gay and gallant Grahams. There is some difficulty in fixing the exact date when the old house was built, but no doubt can exist that it was standing in the reign of Henry VII. The ancient family of Norton was in possession from very early times, until it was involved in the Rising in the North. A remarkable chapter of English history was that in which those who clung to the old Faith staked their lives for its cause, many perishing, while others, like the Earl of Westmorland, who left historic Raby behind, and ancient Norton, fled to Flanders, and were known in England no more. The story of Norton was taken by Wordsworth as the theme of his "White Doe of Rylstone," in which he accepts the story, as told in the old ballad, of the mission of Earl Percy's "little foot page" to Master Norton. It was a summons he could not resist.

Copyright. "*Country Life.*"

THE ORANGERY AND THE KNEELING SLAVE.

"'Come you hither, my nine
    good sonnes,
  Gallant men I trowe you
    bee;
  How many of you, my chil-
    dren deare,
  Will stand by that good
    erle and me?'

"Eight of them did answer
    make,
  Eight of them spake has-
    tilie,
  'Oh! father, till the day we
    dye,
  We'll stand by that good
    erle and thee!'"

And so went forth ancient Norton with his banner bearing the cross and the five wounds of our Lord. His family was entirely ruined and its estates confiscated, though only one of his sons was executed, while he escaped himself to the Low Countries.

After the attainder of the Nortons, their estates were forfeited to the Crown, and subsequently Norton Conyers passed by a marriage with the Musgraves to the Grahams, descended through "John of the Bright Sword" from the Scottish Earls of Menteith and Strathearn. The first of the Grahams at Norton Conyers was the Royalist Sir Richard Graham, "of the Netherby clan," who had married the daughter and heiress of Thomas

THE OLD CHAPEL.

Musgrave. He was Gentleman of the Horse to James I., was created a Baronet in 1629, and distinguished himself at Edgehill and Marston Moor. The story runs that he fled, desperately wounded, from the latter field, and was followed to Norton by Cromwell, who galloped into the hall and up the staircase, arriving just in time to shake Sir Richard in his bed before he died; and even, as if to confound the incredulous, the print of the horse's hoof is still shown upon the stair. Sir Richard Graham was, indeed, wounded at Marston, but did not die until ten years thereafter.

The exterior of the house has perhaps little claim to architectural beauty, but it falls well into its charming surroundings, and curious, quaint, weird, and picturesque it must ever remain. It is surrounded by trees of great size, and the sycamores are perhaps not surpassed in England. On the northern side is the historic bowling green, on which King Charles I. is said once to have passed five consecutive days in that amusement

THE NORTH FRONT AND BOWLING GREEN.

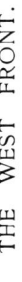

THE WEST FRONT.

THE GARDEN TERRACE.

while waiting for supplies. The garden terrace, and the old gate of hammered iron, hanging between two ball-capped piers, leading to the orangery, with that curious and remarkable sundial and the leaden vases, are features in the midst of a delightful old-fashioned garden, fully appropriate to the venerable house and its green surroundings. Quaintness and old-world charm are everywhere. Look at the kneeling slave, or at the leaden warrior in the glorious park, at the old chapel, at the entrance gates, and linger on the terrace. It is an exceedingly attractive place, with a character quite its own, wherein is no sinning against Nature. We may see here how, without artificiality, and even without marked features, a delightful garden may be created, which is neither a floral wilderness nor a trim parterre. In fact, it is from these old gardens, containing many things which the artist would object to if they stood alone, that we may learn that most excellent lesson of toleration. There are those who speak evil of orangeries, of vases, even of terraces when they stand alone. But, at Norton Conyers, the great artist Time has brought Art and Nature into harmony.

The green lawns, the spreading trees, the borders filled with many a flower in season, and certain adornments of unobtrusive quaintness, are enough, and Norton Conyers is thus a valuable example of the garden art. The green lawns creep up to the house, whose

THE ENTRANCE.

walls are kissed by the rich green of climbing plants. The trees spread their grateful shade, from the house there is a fair outlook over the park, and the grounds have many charms pleasant to explore. The reader will say that there is little here to describe, but will be charmed by the vision of the sweet old-fashioned house and garden we depict.

It is delightful to look out from the windows of Norton Conyers over such beautiful surroundings. Within, the grand old hall covered with ancestral portraits, the broad oak staircase of the legend ascending to the big mullioned window with its many coats of arms, the oak-panelled king's room, occupied by more than one of the Stuart kings, the white-panelled parlour, the library, with its quaint window corners and its Romneys and Zoffanys, are all most charming and beautiful.

Many generations of Grahams had come and gone from the old hall at Norton before the time of the last Sir Bellingham, born 1789, and died 1866—for seventy years a Baronet—a reign of extravagance which sadly encumbered the extensive family estates, inherited by him when but seven years old, on the death of his father (another Sir Bellingham), in 1796. Now Sir Reginald and Lady Graham have for nearly twenty years resided entirely at the home of his ancestors, and in no more fitting hands could this unique possession have fallen.

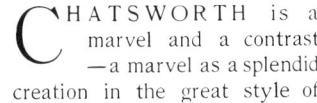

GARDENS OLD & NEW

CHATSWORTH, DERBYSHIRE,

THE SEAT OF HIS GRACE
The Duke of Devonshire, K.G.

CHATSWORTH is a marvel and a contrast —a marvel as a splendid creation in the great style of gardenage, and a contrast to many a less stately domain. We may like better, perhaps, the scented path where lime trees shed their leaves upon some mossy terrace, or to linger in sequestered alleys where the antique dial is companion to the ancient yew, or in some fragrant wilderness with sweetness garlanded; but, whatever be the garden of our choice, we cannot but recognise that England would be poorer if it had no Chatsworth of its own. We may see once again how wide is the world of gardening that can contain characters so diverse, that can give us the simple wayside garden of the rustic cottage, and that can possess places like Chatsworth for its crown. This, indeed, is a great, spacious, stately, and truly ducal domain, with a garden comparable in its kind to any of the splendid gardens of the world, and it is a garden, moreover, in the pleasures of which, through the good will of the Duke of Devonshire, many are freely permitted to share. The situation is superb, for here the Derwent flows between gentle meads beloved of the fallow deer, while the hills rise on either hand in varied height and contour, crowned with a rich woodland of oak, chestnut, beech, and lime to enframe the palatial house, wherein every art finds fitting expression, and where the fruits of learning are plenteously upstored.

Having said this much, there arises the difficulty of choosing how to enter upon this great subject, and how to treat of it within a limited space, for it would be a simple matter to write a volume upon the history of the house and the many rare and splendid things within its walls, and another upon what technical horticulturists call the "lay out" of the grounds and gardens and the glasshouses, which are the most complete example of the genius, perfect in its kind—although it may not commend itself to all tastes—of Sir Joseph Paxton. It was here that this, the most highly honoured of the gardeners of his day—who had entered the service of the then Duke as a gardener at Chiswick, who afterwards became a Member of Parliament, architect of the

THE VIEW FROM THE WEST TERRACE.

THE HOUSE AND THE CLASSIC BRIDGE.

Crystal Palace, and a knight—really enjoyed the opportunity of showing upon an ample canvas, in a supremely beautiful country, and with ample resources at his disposal, what he could do at his best. It is here that his work may be studied to the most advantage.

To describe Chatsworth itself is impossible here. There are many rooms with sombre panelling of carved oak. There are pictures by Holbein, Zucchero, Sir Joshua, Rembrandt,

Luca Giordano, Watteau, Salvator Rosa, Landseer, Verrio, and many others; and they are nearly all famous, and, thanks to the generosity of the Duke in lending them for exhibition, nearly all familiar even to those who have not had the opportunity of visiting their customary resting-place. Who does not know Holbein's "Henry VIII.," Zucchero's "Mary Queen of Scots," Sir Joshua's "Beautiful Duchess," "Bolton Abbey," and so forth? The chapel, with its painting by Verrio, its

THE EMPEROR POND.

THE FRENCH GARDEN.

carving by the unrivalled hand of Grinling Gibbons, is one of the wonders of England; and all England contains no such complete gathering of curious and precious statuary. In a word, or in a sentence, there is an unrivalled collection of art treasures within, just as there is the finest example of the work of a very notable gardener without.

It may be said that Chatsworth is stately, massive, and imposing, rather than exquisitely beautiful, save in point of situation. Yet its very solidity and substance are in harmony with the status of its owner, the owner also of Hardwick Hall, of Bolton Abbey, of Compton Place near Eastbourne, and of Lismore Castle in the County Waterford. It is essentially ducal, and was built by the first Duke, raised to that honour in 1694, and extended

Copyright. THE LOWER WEST GARDEN. "Country Life."

and adorned by the sixth Duke, who succeeded in 1811, and died unmarried in 1858. Of the old Chatsworth and its gardens one of our illustrations will serve to give some idea. Its very quaintness may also cause a feeling of regret that the ancient building and its surroundings have been so completely obliterated. In that ancient Chatsworth Mary Queen of Scots was placed in confinement by Elizabeth. The unhappy prisoner is said to have passed many of her lonesome hours in a garden, called Queen Mary's Bower, on the top of the low square tower or platform which is seen by the visitor amid

the trees as he approaches the house from that classic bridge which Caius Gabriel Cibber, the father of Colley Cibber, adorned with its statues. That tower, indeed, even now, when the creepers have veiled some of its uncompromising outline, is grim and sullen beyond belief. For the rest, we must be content to realise that the Chatsworth of to-day is as different as it is humanly possible for it to be, house, landscape and all, from the Chatsworth in which Mary was immured. The sky is there, and the river, and the lovely and undulating Derbyshire country; but for the rest all is changed.

Copyright. THE SOUTH WALK. "Country Life."

THE ITALIAN GARDEN.

THE ENTRANCE TO THE WEST TERRACE.

Our illustrations serve to give as complete an impression as can be obtained of the remarkable work of that great man Sir Joseph Paxton, the notable and leading exponent of a strong school of gardening, which sought its inspirations and effects in the garden design of classic lands. It were idle to deny that these gardens, generally, leave room for considerable differences of opinion. Indeed, it may well be that the succession of terraces in which the original gardens at Chatsworth were laid out had a special charm of their own, and that, from some points of view, the new garden is less pleasing than the old must have been. That subject, however, is one into which it is unnecessary to enter at any length. Suffice it to say that the gardens, as they stand, are the best and largest example of Paxton's method displayed on the widest and most choiceworthy canvas, that they possess a definite historical value and interest, that they have a distinct quality and character of their own, and that whatsoever may have been lost in natural beauty or garden quaintness has its compensation in the stately and appropriately magnificent scale upon which the whole has been conceived. Let us take as an example that which is perhaps the most characteristic of all the views, that of the South Walk. Here is a broad and white sheet of gravel glowing in the sun, its level raised as it leaves the house by a flight of stone steps, flanked on either side by rhododendrons, which are particularly good at Chatsworth, and by two fine statues—there are more beyond. On either side is a broad belt of lawn, shaven close, and, again, fine forest trees. The whole leads with inexorable and inevitable straightness to Flora's Temple, which is partially shrouded from view by the cascade of the fountain. It is not, perhaps, restful—on a smaller scale it would be intolerable—but in this huge manifestation it is emphatically imposing; and as one looks towards the Temple, with its splendid background of trees, one seems almost to be able to hear the roar and the crash of the failing water.

THE GREAT CONSERVATORY.

THE WELLINGTON ROCK.

The fact is that there is room, and an abundance of it, for every kind of gardening at Chatsworth; room in particular for the line of limes, which were fine trees when Dr. Johnson enjoyed their shade 116 years ago; and beyond the end of this line are three trees of peculiar interest, known as the Royal Trees. Of these, one, an oak, was planted by the Queen when she was Princess Victoria, in 1832. The planter was then twelve or thirteen years old, the tree —unless, indeed, it was a case of sowing an acorn, which is hardly likely—may have been about the same age; and now the planter, held in far more honour than any living man or woman, is well stricken in years, and the tree is in its forest youth. Another, planted on the same day by the Duchess of Kent, is a Spanish chestnut, and the other is a

THE HOUSE FROM THE SOUTH EAST.

sycamore, planted eleven years later by Prince Albert, who had then been Prince Consort for some two years. Room is there also for landscape gardening, and for the arrangement of woods and views and vistas upon a really colossal scale.

The predominant features, we are inclined to say, of Chatsworth are those straight, broad, and uncompromising paths, the statues, and the fountains, of which several views are given. Greatest amongst them is the Emperor Fountain, fed as the others are from the lake 400ft. above, and appearing in our picture as a parallelogram of gleaming water. But the gardens are full of other points of interest also. Look, for

example, at the charming Ring Pond, with its rude boulder in the middle, its lilies in the water, its trim yew hedges, its surrounding sentinels of columnar yews. Or stand by the entrance to the West Terrace, with its ironwork gates, low in height, but of fine workmanship, and note the quaint statues of animals, especially the boy on the lion. Note also the same statues, in the Lower West Garden, from another point of view, and see how fine a view of the distance and of the lawn below is to be obtained from the West Terrace. Observe also the Italian Garden, excellent of its kind; and the French Garden, highly characteristic, with its statues on high pillars, and the pillars themselves wreathed in creepers and

THE CASCADE.

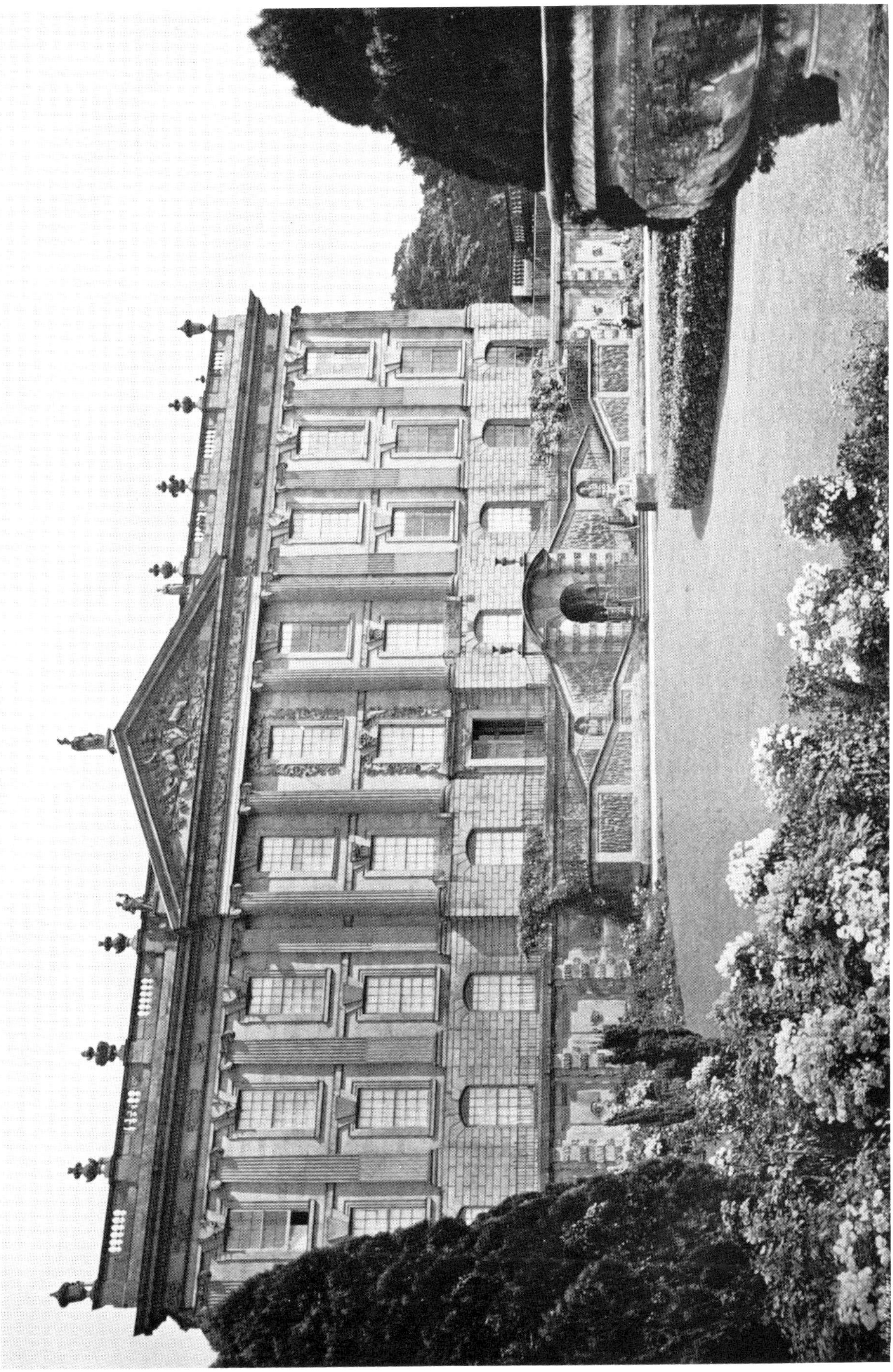

Copyright. "Country Life."

THE WEST TERRACE.

THE RING POND.

roses, and the elaborate centre-pieces. Very beautiful too is the cascade from the living rock, especially on a bright summer's day.

Non cuivis homini contingit adire Corinthum. Not every man, nor every duke even, possesses so princely a domain as Chatsworth, nor the great extent and variety of ground which permits so many kinds of horticultural art to be shown together—this word "shown" is used deliberately, because Chatsworth is emphatically a show place. It would be folly to recommend owners of houses less imposing, and of less abundant space, to imitate the style, with its fountains and its temples, and its French and Italian Gardens. But none the less, taken for all in all, Chatsworth is splendid and unique. We will not say that the formal garden of the past, with its terraces, which Paxton is said to have "destroyed," may not be regretted. But, when all has been said, Chatsworth remains as the most splendid example of Paxton's ideas to be found in England or in Europe, always imposing, valuable as an historical monument, and endowed with a peculiar stateliness of character.

But even now the greatest and most characteristic glory of the gardens remains unchronicled — the pride of Chatsworth and a truly splendid edifice of glass, not very beautiful perhaps from without, but still, on true Ruskinian principles, to be

admired by reason of its absolute and complete suitability to its purpose. It is approached through a rocky ravine, in which everything is done on a grand scale; its dimensions are, like those of the famous house at Kew, almost those of a cathedral, and it is the very temple of tropical gardening. Let the reader consider the picture which is shown, and endeavour to read into it, by effort of imagination, a few significant figures. In length it is 277ft., in width 123ft., in height 67ft. Truly a glorious winter garden, for the heating of which six miles of hot-water pipes are required and used. The carriage drive does not end at the entrance. On the contrary, for a highly-favoured visitor the great doors will open, and the drive may be continued through what is, for all practical purposes, a tropical forest, or the best of many tropical forests combined. The central walk is fringed with bananas, planted, as almost everything is, in the ground and not in pots, and at the north end is a pile of bold rockwork, covered with a luxuriant growth of creeping plants, in which Ficus repens flourishes amazingly, and the euphorbia lends a dash of glowing scarlet.

Behind this rockwork, and screened by it, is a spiral staircase leading to the gallery which goes round the transept, and the memory of the aspect of the conservatory from that gallery is a thing imperishable. Noble examples of palms and

"THE PALACE OF THE PEAK."

tree-ferns, Phœnix dactylifera, Sabal Blackburniana, and a score of varieties beside, reach almost to the lofty roof, and below may be seen the avenue of bananas, the papyrus lifting its willowy stems, caladiums, philodendrons and hedychiums all revelling in the soft moisture. Truly a wonderful sight; and so huge is the scale, so complete the illusion, and so perfect—and it must be added oppressive to Northern lungs—is the atmosphere, that it is quite startling, as well as very pleasant, to emerge from the climate of Africa and South America into the Derbyshire air and to pass through the arboretum into the Old Park.

And when, delighted, the visitor leaves the ducal mansion—favoured, indeed, if

"Country Life."

SOLOMON'S WALK.

it be to cast a line for trout or grayling in the Derwent, the Wye, or the Lathkill—he will not marvel that many have burst into rhapsodies in describing the glories of Chatsworth. The splendours of the park and gardens, the scented pathways, the emerald lawns and lovely trees, the music of the waterfalls, the white-limbed nymphs reflected in pellucid basins, the dancing girls of Canova, the vases of Elfdalen porphyry, the famous waterworks by Grillet, some of them belonging to old Chatsworth, and even the "weeping willow" of copper, which sheds copious streams upon the unwary—all these and many more things have attracted him. From the upper terrace or the "hunting tower" on the hill

he has surveyed the imposing scene, with the palatial house by the Derwent in the midst, and the picturesque model village of Edensor on the wooded hill beyond, and he feels that he leaves behind one of the fairest and richest domains in the land. Certainly no visitor who is privileged to linger in these enchanting scenes at Chatsworth will fail to appreciate the graceful compliment which Marshal Tallard, who was taken prisoner by Marlborough in 1704, paid to the Duke of Devonshire on leaving "The Palace of the Peak": "My Lord Duke, when I compute the days of my captivity in England, I shall omit those I passed at Chatsworth."

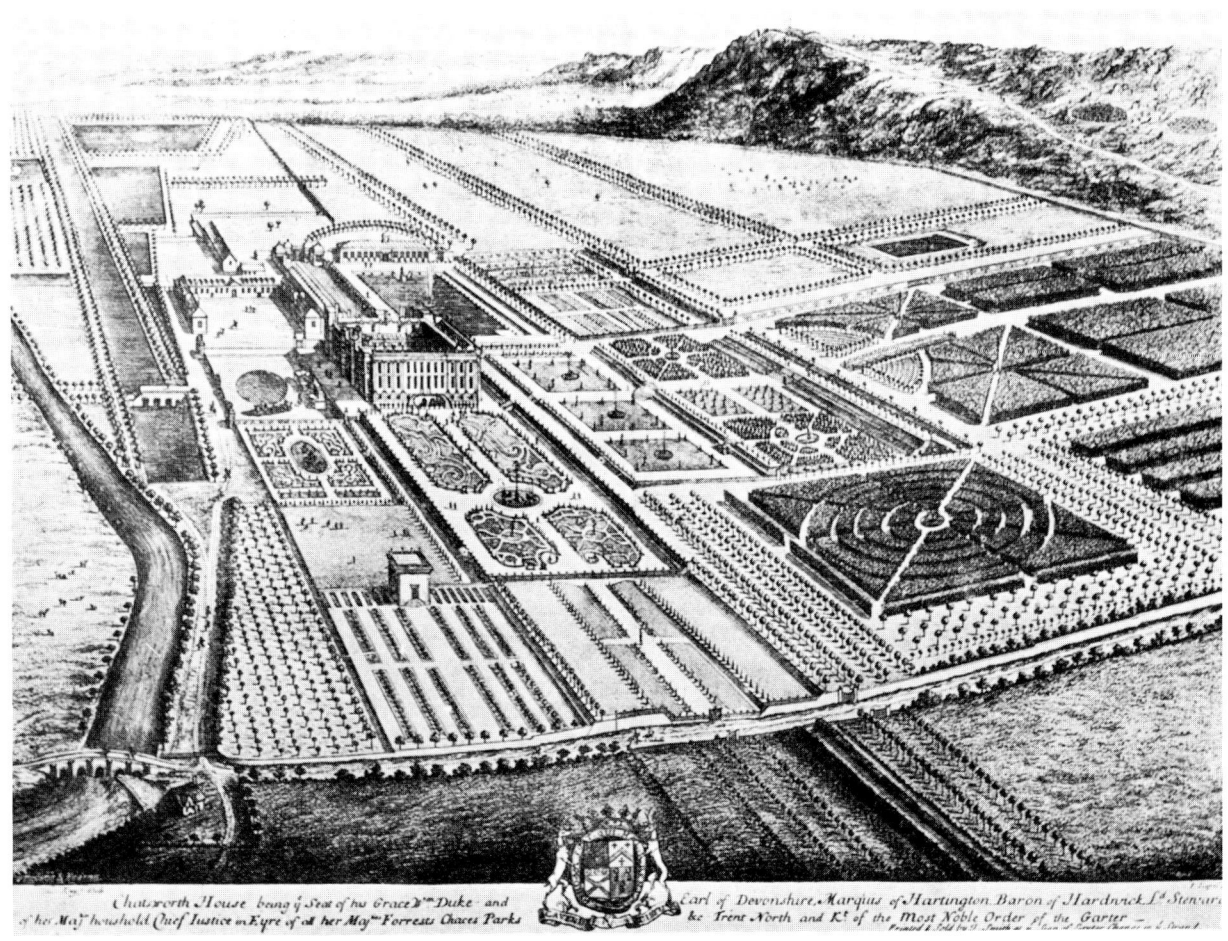

A BIRD'S-EYE VIEW OF THE GARDENS OF OLD CHATSWORTH.

GARDENS OLD & NEW

GUY'S CLIFF, WARWICK, . . THE SEAT OF . . . LORD ALGERNON PERCY.

THE present writer retains a recollection of Guy's Cliff and its gardens that will not be obliterated. It fell to him to visit the place upon a rare evening of early summer, when the hedges were white with the blossom of the scented thorn, the primroses begemming the banks, the bluebells beginning to brighten the shade, and the trees still in their freshest green. Along that beautiful road from Warwick he had journeyed, sometimes under the deep shade of immemorial trees, anon looking out over the country, remembering how the jeering Gascon, Edward's hated favourite, hastily condemned by angry barons in Beauchamp's stronghold at Warwick, had been hurried, accompanied by a hooting crowd, along the very same way, to his beheading on Blacklow Hill.

Neither did he forget the famous Guy, Earl of Warwick, slaughterer of the Dun Cow, who retired to Guy's Cliff long ago ; and, as he approached the scene, the silvery tinkling of bells was heard. They were hanging to the necks of dun kine in the meadows, sleek and beautiful, and possessing none of the terrors of the draconian creature—*monstrum horrendum, informe, ingens*—that fell beneath the blows of heroic Guy. Then there opened a prospect of Guy's Cliff itself, half disclosed at the end of a grandly picturesque avenue of gnarled and twisted old Scotch firs, its front flecked by the evening sunshine. It was a foretaste of what was to come. Down a narrow lane went the wayfarer in quest of the famous mill by the Avon—a place where many have ground their grain ever since Saxon times—picturesqueness, indeed, he said, with that quaint gallery embodied in wood and stone ; and beyond it the footbridge and the meadows, through which you may fare forward to Leamington.

But the mill looks out across a broad expanded sheet of the famous Avon—a lake in extent and character—with water-lilies upon its surface, willow and ash dipping their trembling foliage in the water, and in the deep shadows of the bank green grasses rising from the pools. The slanting sunlight fell athwart

THE HOUSE FROM THE RIVER.

THE FOOTPATH BY THE AVON.

THE SOUTH GARDEN AND AVENUE.

the magic scene, filling the limpid air with radiance, lighting up like a patch of gold the strip of meadow on the further bank, and making splendid the great house rising in the cliff beyond. It is a mansion with a character all its own. You do not here pause to question the architecture, nor to think of the style of the building; you recognise that Guy's Cliff belongs to, and is indeed a part of, the scene you behold; that it grows, if the phrase be permissible, from the rock, in massive grouping, filling the exquisite framework, completely embowered amid noble trees, dignified by lofty elms and by great firs with their rare purple tinge, contrasted with the gay colouring of flower-beds below. It is a place meet for the Muses, a veritable castle of Otranto, seeming as if it might be the home of

romance. Those were the impressions of a visitor who saw Guy's Cliff, as it were, by surprise, and saw it with such conditions of atmosphere and sunlight as Claude or Turner would have desired.

The place is, moreover, one of singular interest, and its legendary history is full of romance. Leland spoke of its predecessor as a "house of pleasure," and the situation attracted the notice of Evelyn. There is, undoubtedly, something of extraordinary attraction about it, and we read without surprise that the famous Guy, who in the light of legend has assumed proportions so heroic, retired to the enchanting margin of the stream to court abstraction from the world. Here for three years he dwelt, unknown and unrecognised by "Fair Phyllis," his wife, though daily he came, clad in the russet garb of a palmer, to solicit food from her bounteous hand. The legend says that not until his end was near did he disclose the rock-bound hiding-place that had been his home. There are caves in the rock upon which Guy's Cliff stands, in which it is certain that anchorites did actually dwell. Near the chapel—dedicated to St. Mary Magdalen, and erected in the time of Henry VI., wherein is a mutilated statue attributed to the hero—are Guy's Well and Guy's Cave, the latter a rude excavation in the rock, now entered between heavy oaken doors. Here a Runic inscription of the tenth century has been discovered, interpreted to embody the prayer of Guhthi, the hermit,

A CORNER OF THE LAWN.

THE OLD AVENUE AND THE HOUSE FROM THE ROAD.

whose occupation of the place may have given rise to the stories of Guy. But the hero is not represented only by his well and cave, for at Warwick Castle they have a wondrous equipment which, it is said, he wore—body and horse armour and a two-handled sword, with a fork, and a prodigious porridge-pot, no doubt used for cooking the rations of soldiers at a later day, as well as "Fair Phyllis's slippers," being really iron slipper-stirrups of the time of Henry VI.

There does not appear to have been any residence of importance at the place in the Middle Ages, but Henry V., who visited it from Warwick, determined to establish a chantry for two priests on the spot. He died, but Richard Beauchamp, Earl of Warwick —the same who founded the exquisite chantry chapel in Warwick Church—carried out his wish, and Rous, the Warwickshire antiquary, was once the chantry priest there. At the Dissolution the place was granted to Sir Andrew Flammock, and afterwards through many hands passed in 1751 to Mr. Samuel Greatheed, who twice represented

THE ENTRANCE.

Coventry in Parliament. Guy's Cliff was at that time an inconsiderable country house, approached by the great fir avenue, which is no longer used as a drive, the lodge entrance being nearer Warwick. The new possessor built the front facing the courtyard— which has partly been excavated out of the rock—and did much else to improve the place, but the character of the house is due to his son, Mr. Bertie Greatheed, who almost entirely rebuilt it from his own plans in 1822. Mr. Greatheed also much improved the grounds and gardens, formed paths, and introduced many adornments, and his work has been carried on by his successors. Through the marriage of his granddaughter, Guy's Cliff passed to the Hon. Charles Bertie Percy, and to the hands of its present possessor. A point of interest associated with the Greatheed family may be noted here. Roger Kemble with his theatrical company was accustomed to perform at Warwick, and Lady Mary Greatheed, attracted by his daughter, the future Mrs. Siddons, was wishful to make a home for her at Guy's Cliff. Her father,

THE LAKE AND LANDING-PLACE.

THE SUNDIAL.

disapproving of her affection for Mr. Siddons, a
member of the troupe, fell
in with the idea, and the
girl was received by Lady
Mary, with whom she
lived for some time. The
attachment was not, how-
ever, broken off, and the
marriage took place at
Coventry in 1773, and the
famous actress—of whom
a bust is in the house—
was afterwards several
times a welcome guest at
Guy's Cliff.

The account which
has been given of the
character of the surround·
ings of the house will suggest to the reader, having
the pictures before him,
how very charming are
the features of the gardens
about Lord Algernon
Percy's stately home. The
situation, which is remarkably picturesque, being
a noble cliff of sandstone
rising by the bank of
the Avon, precluded any
formal arrangement, if
such had been desired.
When Evelyn visited
"Sir Guy's Grot"
from Warwick, he
described it as "a
squalid den made in the
rock, crowned yet with
venerable oaks, and
looking on a goodly
stream, so as it were
improved as it might be,

THE   UNDER   CLIFF.

it were capable of being made a most romantic and pleasant
place." It may be doubted whether the hand of Evelyn
himself could have done better with that marvellous combination of wood, water, rock, and meadow. The ancient trees
are particularly beautiful, and though some of the grand old
firs in the avenue are long past their prime, most judicious
planting has gone forward, and the character of the varied

foliage invests
the grounds with
remarkable
charm. So
beautiful are the
trees growing by
the margin of
the river that it
has the aspect of
a romantic water
avenue. One
cedar is particu-
larly noble, and
is reputed to be
the largest in
the county.

Splendid is
the aspect of
Guy's Cliff from
almost every
point in its sur-
roundings, and
the house itself
is placed in a
particular posi-
tion of vantage

for the enjoyment of the
scenery and gardens.
From the windows of the
drawing-room there is a
succession of enchanting
views of garden, lawn,
wood, and river. The
most romantic of these is
towards the old mill,
across the space of shim-
mering water, enframed
in the glorious foliage,
where it issues from be-
neath the dark arch-
stirred by the slow revolv,
ing of the wheel. The
sombre shadow of elms
and tall firs is relieved
by the bright flower-beds
and the whole combination
of effects would be hard
to excel. It is bright and
beautiful in the sunshine,
and full of varied charm.
The walks are skilfully
contrived to give alternate
shade and brightness, and
those by the margin of
the stream under the wall
of rock are singularly
beautiful. The garden
adornments are both
natural and artificial.
From the Cave of
Despair we emerge to
sunlit spaces, where
radiant flower-beds glow
in the summer. There
are expanses of the
greenest lawn, shadowed
by most handsome trees.
Water-lilies add beauty to
the lake, and irises and

other water-loving plants are thick upon the banks. The
south garden is particularly attractive, with a wealth of many
flowers, and the Kneeling Slave in lead curiously supports a
dial, while a charming vista is opened up through an avenue,
with a meadow rising beyond.

It is not necessary, however, to describe further the garden
attractions of romantic Guy's Cliff. Enough has been said to

indicate that
it possesses a
special character
arising from the
superb situation
it occupies. The
Avon is a
beautiful river
which flows
through en-
chanting scenes,
of which some
have already
been depicted in
these pages, for
Stoneleigh
Abbey is almost
a neighbour of
romantic Guy's
Cliff, which
itself certainly
possesses one
of the fairest
domains in the
whole county of
Warwick.

THE   FERRY.

GARDENS OLD & NEW

CLIFTON HALL, NOTTINGHAM, THE SEAT OF . . . LT.-COL. SIR HERVEY BRUCE.

THOSE who go in quest of the beauties of English gardens, associated with many splendours of architecture and many of the interests of history, will find them in every part of the land. Our survey has taken us north, south, east, and west, and we have found our subjects sometimes on the level plain, sometimes among broken undulating country, occasionally in deep valleys, and not seldom on lofty heights. Each and every situation demands a treatment of its own, and the happy adaptation of the house to the landscape and of the garden to both is the object of the artist's hand, and its delineation is the reason of the present delightful quest. In not a few places have we found the character of the land demanding, or at least suggesting, a terraced formation for the gardens. This is notably the case at Clifton Hall. The terrace has sometimes been found severely formal and classical, at times invested with varied features and much picturesqueness, and occasionally taking the form of an adaptation of the ground itself. This last may be said to be the character of the great grass terraces at Clifton Hall, but they are associated with superb garden architecture, in a most satisfactory way. Of them, however, more anon.

The house stands on an alabaster rock overlooking the wide pastoral valley of the slow-winding Trent, making its way through the greenwood country to the Humber and the

THE OLD CHAPEL AND FOUNTAIN.

THE   WEST   FRONT.

North Sea, and a wide outlook over a far landscape is opened
from the windows and terraces.   The mansion is of late
Jacobean character, belonging to that period or aspect of the
style—if the word style can be used where the features are so
distinct—in which the classic and stately had replaced the
broken and picturesque.   Red brick always falls well into
a garden picture, and Clifton Hall is no exception to the
rule.

The location is ancient, for Clifton is mentioned in
Domesday, and even in the Conqueror's days there was a
house on the site.   The manors of Clifton, Wilford, and
Barton have been held by the family of Clifton ever since
those times, though the estate has now passed through the

female line to the present owner, Lieutenant-Colonel Hervey
Juckes Lloyd Bruce, late Coldstream Guards, whose mother
was the daughter of Sir J. G. Juckes-Clifton, M.P., ninth
Baronet, and sister and heiress of Sir Robert Clifton, the last
Baronet of the line.   She married the Right Hon. Sir Henry
Hervey Bruce of Downhill, Bart., and died in 1891.   The
permanence of English institutions is but the reflection of our
social life, for, great as have been the changes in the descent
of property, it is still possible to find many examples like that
of the long-lineaged family at Clifton Hall in the territorial
records of the land.

The chief features of the grounds at this imposing seat
are those fine grass terraces we have alluded to, of which
there are five, one above the
other, adorned by rows of
magnificent old yew trees, as
well as by some splendid
single specimens.   These
terraces add distinction to the
place, and are amongst the
most notable examples of
their kind in England.   The
gnarled old yew trees, which
give such strong character to
many gardens, enhance the
quaintness of the picture here.
Terraces are of many kinds,
sometimes paved, sometimes
laid with gravel, sometimes
with a balustraded supporting
wall, and sometimes, as at
Clifton, covered with turf,
very beautiful indeed being
these gentle lengths of rich
verdure, overlooking the great
landscape below.

Many notable gardens in
England possess a succession
of terraces.   Those at Chatsworth were for the most
part destroyed in the changes

THE   OLD   BOWLING   GREEN.

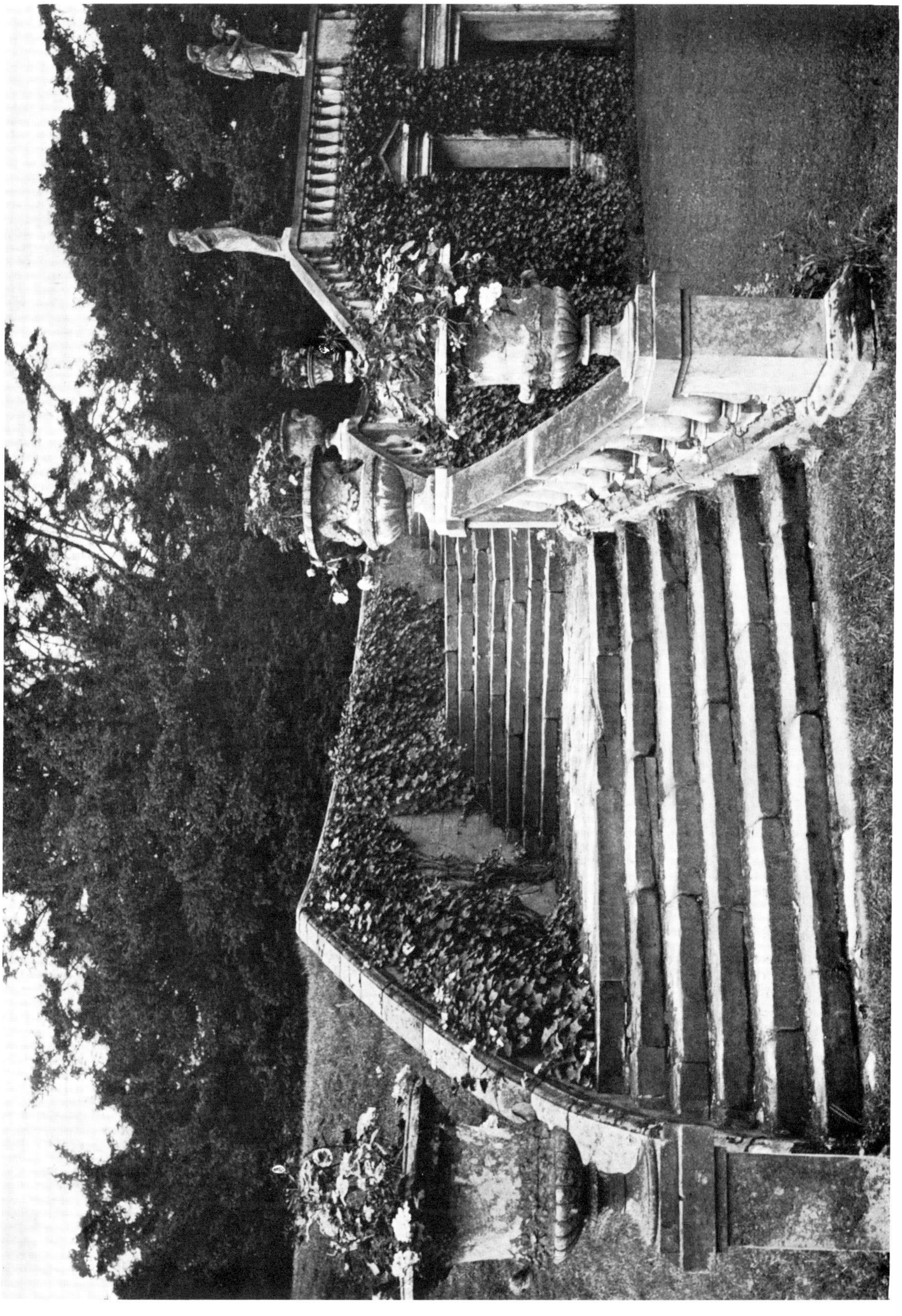

Copyright. A FINE STUDY IN GARDEN ARCHITECTURE. "Country Life."

introduced by Paxton, and at
an earlier date several perished
under the hand of Repton at
Burley-on-the-Hill. At
Haddon Hall the famous terraces form a beautiful feature,
and are well described in
"The Formal Garden in
England," and there, as at
Clifton Hall, the yew casts its
shadow over the turf. The
gardens of Haddon "are laid
out in four main levels; at
the top is a raised walk. . . ,
planted with a double row of
lime trees. About 10ft. below
this is the yew tree terrace,
divided into three plots, about
15yds. square, surrounded by
stone curbs, with yew trees
in each angle. These were
once clipped, but are now
grown into great trees, over-
shadowing the entire terrace.
'Dorothy Vernon's Stairs'
descend on to this yew tree
terrace. A flight of twenty-six
steps led from this terrace to

THE CANOVA LIONS.

a lower garden about 40yds. square, divided into two
grass plots. A walk from this garden skirted round two
sides of a second garden laid out in three levels, and
reached the postern door in the outer garden wall by
seventy-one steps, laid out in seven consecutive flights."
This was an example of garden architecture and design
at their best.

Clifton Hall is also very dignified and beautiful in arrangements of analogous character though different form, for the
grass terraces are adorned with beautiful stonework, and with
classic features scarcely surpassed in English gardens. That
charming grouping of the curved stairways to the terrace by

the old chapel might have been transported from some old
Italian garden of lemon and cypress, of marble stairways and
plashing fountains. Look at the mellow stonework, at the
mosses that clothe the surface, at the ivy that fondly clings,
at the beautiful vases filled with floral wealth; think what it is
to ascend to the green terrace above, and to look out over the
balustrade across that noble basin covered with water-lilies,
and at the gracious scenes around. Then, again, how noteworthy is the quaint and attractive character of the contrasted
semi-circular form of another flight, the convex shape of the
lower steps leading to the concave plan of the upper ascent.
These are instances of imagination leading to a beautiful

THE RIVER-SIDE CIRCLE STAIRWAY.

THE ROSE GARDEN AND PERGOLA.

expression of garden architecture, and the last, though simple in idea, is a delightful garden creation. It is unnecessary to enforce the value of such features, and much has already been said concerning the work of the garden architect.

Conspicuous to the eye of all who look at our pictures is the fact that Clifton Hall possesses prodigal floral wealth—the green lawns that old Englishmen loved, combined with the most radiant galaxy that the modern florist could desire. And yet we discover that the architect, at least in certain parts of the gardens, has freely had his way, and that, hand in hand with his brother sculptor, he has attained a veritable triumph. The haste to secure a luxuriant growth of rare shrubs and splendid flowers has not clouded

the subtle charm that lies in well-ordered design, and there is a sense of fitness in all that has been accomplished. We may trace, in fact, a very keen appreciation at Clifton Hall of the balance of design. A matter worthy of note is the happy manner in which upon the verdant lawns the sky has been captured, as it were, in the reflected glory of the basins. This is a different thing entirely from reflecting a space of sky in basins surrounded by gravel paths. The contrasts, indeed, at this notable place are very many. They range from open lawns and grass plots to the deep shade of woodland, and from stately architecture and sculpture to the radiant sweetness of the fragrant bed and the beautiful border. In short, imagination has invested the place with remarkable character and charm.

The various parts of the grounds at Clifton are very charming. Thus, the Italian garden at the back of the house is remarkably attractive, and commands a superb view. There is a modern rose garden, with beautiful herbaceous borders formed recently, and a pergola. How often do we now see the pergola in English gardens! It has become quite a fashion of late years to create such features. That at Clifton Hall is very delightful, and provides both a grateful shade from hot suns and a place for the growth of beautiful climbing plants, the gloriously coloured vines, the rose, sweet-scented jasmine, honeysuckle, clematis, and many another graceful plant. The word is, of course. Italian, and such places were formed originally of wooden uprights and crosspieces, with stone piers and

THE HALL FROM THE GARDEN.

A PEEP THROUGH THE TREES.

THE LOWER FLOWER LAWN.

A CAPTURED SPACE OF SKY.

pillar supports at the angles. In Italy the vine has been the trailer used to cover these structures, and pergola signifies a variety of vine. But pergolas, if they are new in England, are also old. They were akin at least to the "covert alley upon carpenter's work," beloved of Bacon, through which he would reach other garden pleasures, not willing, in the heat of the day or year, to "buy the shade in the garden by going in the sun through the green" — that delectable place which he proposed with its two pleasures, "the one because nothing is more pleasant to the eye than green grass kept finely shorn; the other because it will give you a fair alley, in the midst, by which you may go in front upon a stately hedge, that is to enclose the garden."

Our ancestors of that time, seeking the welcome shade, would sometimes make pergolas of their own, even without suggestions from sunny Italy, for the pergola sprang from the needs of climate, as the terrace from the necessities of situation.

The roses are very interesting at Clifton Hall, and comprise many choice varieties of the various groups into which the rose family is divided. It is very satisfactory to find how largely the rose has been planted of late years in many gardens. At one time it was confined to the rosery, and trained in the most formal fashion, but since a better gardening spirit has prevailed promoted doubtless by the acquisition of the many beautiful tea-scented kinds, the rose has played a proper part in the adornment of most English gardens. By simple grouping of distinct kinds, keeping each apart, their full value is won, and the tea-scented race flower bountifully until the late autumn, even until winter in mild years.

The woodland surroundings are delightful, and Clifton Grove, a fine avenue of double rows of old elm trees, on which Kirke White wrote a celebrated poem, extends from the Hall to the village of Wilford, a distance of nearly two miles. Clifton Church, which is situated close to the Hall (a private gate opening from the front approach into the churchyard), is of very ancient date, the greater part of it being of the twelfth century.

On the gable at the west end is a stone crucifix, one of the very few remaining in England. It is said to have escaped the hand of the destroyer, owing to its having been overgrown with ivy, in the image-breaking time. The church contains many fine and interesting monuments and brasses to the Clifton family, and its tower is an interesting feature from the gardens.

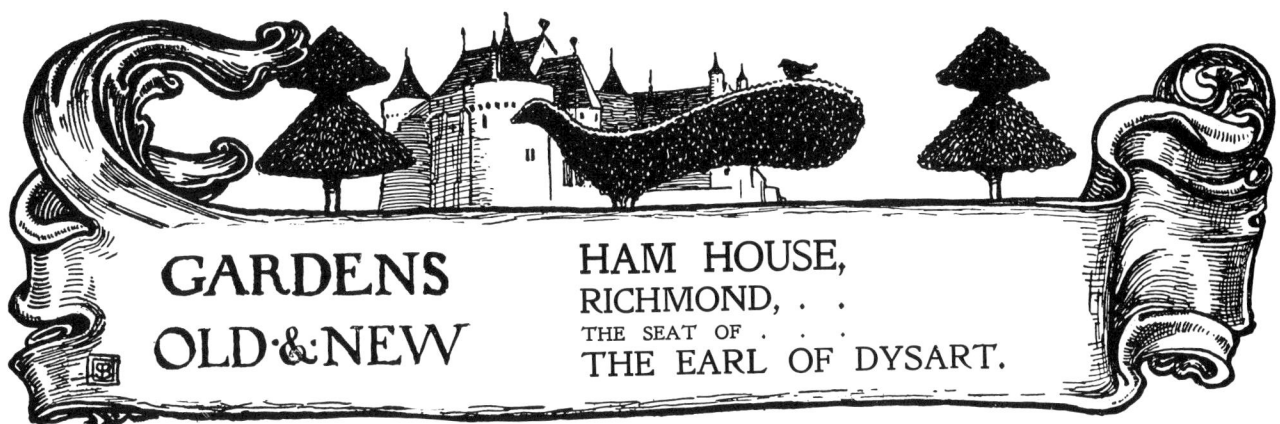

GARDENS OLD & NEW

HAM HOUSE, RICHMOND, . . THE SEAT OF . . . THE EARL OF DYSART.

AFTER dinner I walked to Ham, to see the house and garden of the Duke of Lauderdale, which is indeed inferior to few of the best villas of Italy itself; the house furnished like a great prince's; the parterres, flower gardens, orangeries, groves, avenues, courts, statues, perspectives, fountains, aviaries, and all this at the banks of the sweetest river in the world, must needs be admirable." So wrote John Evelyn of the famous house of Ham, which stands amid ancestral trees, somewhat set back from the river, where Petersham meadows lie at the foot of Richmond Hill on the right bank of the Thames. The house and the region are alike famous, one for its historic interest and rare charms, the other for its noble river and umbrageous beauty, which made it the haunt of Pope, Swift, Gay, and many other *beaux esprits* of their time, and that endear it now to all who find their pleasure by the Thames. "Old trees, the most placid of rivers, Thomson up above you, Pope near you, Cowley himself not far off—I hope here is a nest of repose both material and spiritual of the most Cowleyian and Evelynian sort," says Leigh Hunt.

The great charm of Ham House is its old-world character and seclusion, the "pillared dusk" of its avenues and thickets, the splendour of the trees, and the delight of scented paths and flower borders by the mossy walls. The house itself is severely plain in its quaint character, though deigning to be ornate in its porch, and in the series of busts of famous men in niches in its walls. They look out upon a garden that has scarcely changed since Stuart days, save that the gates are more deeply rusted, and the brick is mellower than of yore. Ham House was built by Sir Thomas Vavasour in 1610, but it soon came into the hands of the Tollemaches, Earls of Dysart. The first Earl was a Murray, but his daughter, who was Countess in her own right, married Sir Lionel Tollemache, and afterwards the Earl of Lauderdale, famous for his share in the Cabal whose members often visited him at Ham.

There are traces of Lauderdale's alterations about the place, but since that time very little has changed. Let it be observed how the house and garden are quaintly associated by the lines of busts in ovals adorning the old brick enclosing walls, which run out from the terrace to the sunk wall that separates

"Country Life."

THE TERRACE AND ENTRANCE.

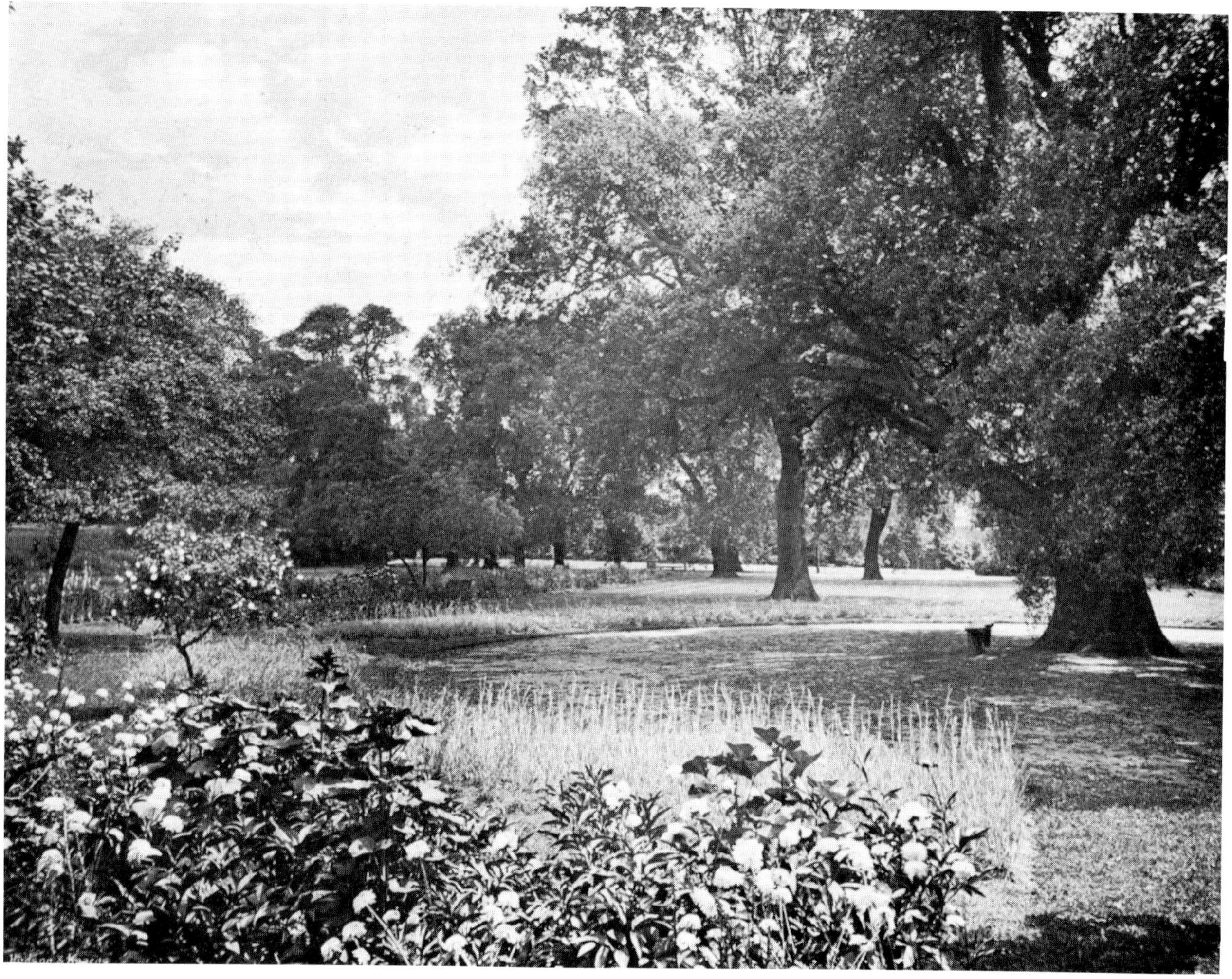

Copyright. "Country Life"

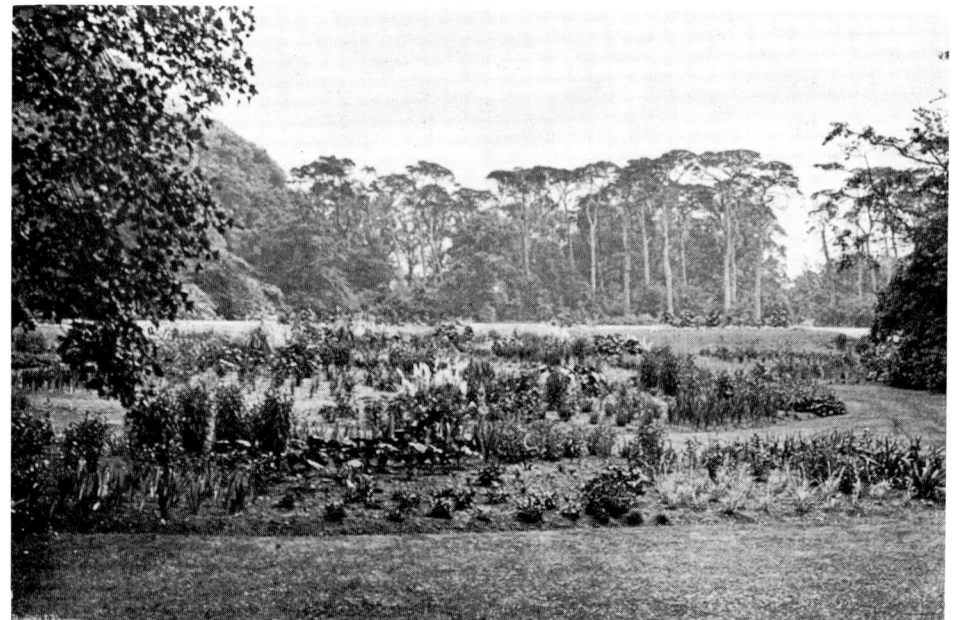

THE WEST GARDEN.

the garden from the meadows. In the midst of the dappled lawn is the recumbent figure of the river god, and beyond, between those mossy urn-crowned piers, hang the famous iron gates. Veneration for the eld has certainly settled upon Ham House, and many a legend is told of how the gates have been opened but once since they were closed on Charles II. When Horace Walpole's niece became Countess of Dysart, the witty scoffer noted the unchanging character of her new abode. Everything was "magnificently ancient," and all his passion for antiquity did not keep him up. "Every minute I expected to see ghosts sweeping by; ghosts I would not give sixpence to see—Lauderdales, Tollemaches, and Maitlands." His nephew was "so religious an observer of the venerable rights of this house that because the gates were never opened by his father but once, for the late Lord Granville, you are locked out and locked in, and, after journeying all round the house, as you do round an old French fortified town, you are at last admitted through the stable-yard to creep along a dark passage by the housekeeper's room, and so by a back door into the great hall."

Copyright. "Country Life."

THE EAST GARDENS.

It is a sweet and characteristic scene that we view from the north terrace, looking across the close-shaven lawn, flanked by beds of hardy flowers and splendid pyramidal bay trees, to the old gates and the noble elms nearer the river. But wherever we go the gardens are in perfect accord with the

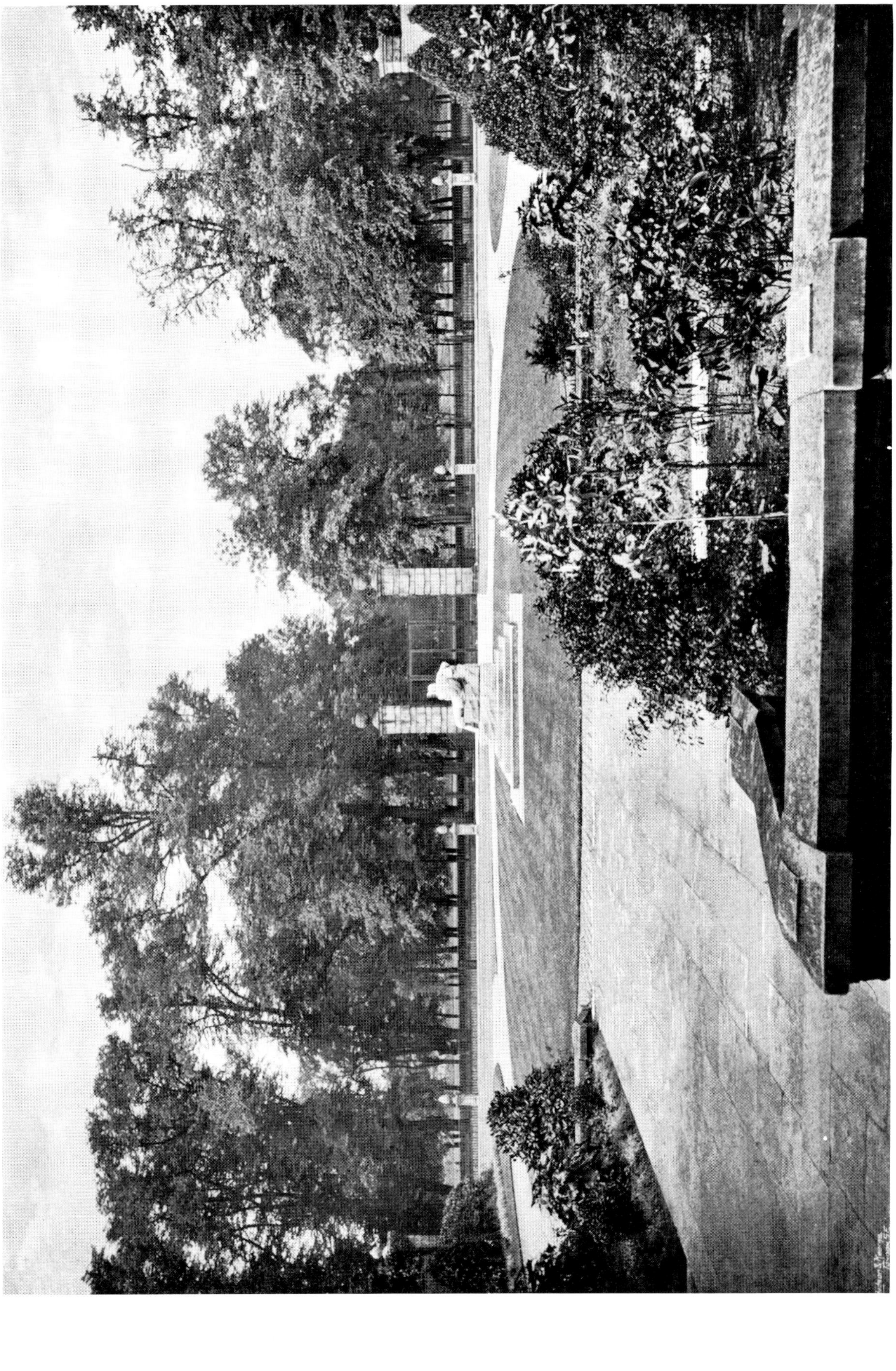

Copyright. THE RIVER GARDEN. "Country Life."

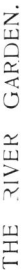

THE NORTH GATE.

quaint old mansion. The hush of ancient times seems to dwell about the Broad Walk as we enter it between those two great pillars, with the beautiful urns on the top, though the glamour of the eld certainly does not imply neglect or decay at Ham House. There are no weedy paths or tangled beds, and, unlike the moated grange of Mariana, where

> "The rusted nails fell from the knots
> That held the pear to the gable-wall,"

everything is kept in perfect order. There is a delightful outlook over the garden from the south front, where the low terrace wall is skirted by a border delightfully planted with masses of flowers. Here in June lovely white lilies and pale blue larkspurs are flowering, followed later by hollyhocks, and such beautiful things as the Alstrœmerias and Galtonia candicans, and there are groups of white Canterbury bells, sea-holly, evening primroses, irises, China roses, and many other favourite flowers. The very walls are green and beautiful with the shrubby growths they shelter. The old house itself, too, is garlanded with many beautiful climbers

FROM THE WEST GARDEN.

THE BROAD WALK.

—such as clematis, fuchsia. magnolia, honeysuckle, and ceanothus—and brightened by the gay orange flowers of Eccremocarpus scaber.

Beyond the border is a well-kept lawn, with groups of rhododendrons and other evergreen and flowering shrubs on either side, thrown into relief by beautiful trees in the background, while a delightful woodland faces us from which noble Scotch firs lift their picturesque branches to the sky.

Leaving the terrace, and turning to the right, the visitor passes through an archway in the ivy-clad wall, and finds himself in another garden, more attractive, perhaps, than the

last, where the lofty red brick walls are vested with roses and other climbers, and the borders are filled with a multitude of gay and fragrant flowers. The lawn here is broken up by rectangular beds, filled with roses and various hardy growths, and several fruit and ornamental trees shadow its surface. It is a perfect lesson drawn from an old book as to the method of forming and maintaining in character a truly English garden. Elsewhere peat-loving plants, such as rhododendrons and azaleas, are intermixed with many ferns in a very charming arrangement. But little further description is necessary. What we find in the gardens of Ham House is a sense of quiet and repose. There is no attempt to impress by sharp contrasts and very brilliant masses of colour. It is simply an old English garden, adorned with many of the beautiful things that these days provide, though possessing all the quaintness of its early time. The garden walls, for instance, are notable examples of good garden architecture. Delightful in their originality are the long walls enshrining the classic busts which have been referred to. The brick coping adds enrichment, and the walls are divided into spaces by buttresses treated as piers, and crested by quaint urns or other carved finials. In some places, as on the north front, the wall is low, and the space between the piers is filled by an iron grille, and sometimes the wall and its coping have a hollow curve rising at the ends to the piers.

As might be expected in such deep soil and upon

THE RIVER FRONT.

so venerable an estate, the trees are particularly fine. Some of the elms are notable, and there is a noble avenue of those trees. The evergreen oaks are also greatly admired, and there is a good tulip tree, while an old red cedar (Juniperus virginiana) is one of the most interesting specimens in England. The whole country, however, is a sylvan paradise, and Richmond Hill forms a noble background to the dear old place.

It would be interesting, indeed, if we could know the history of such a garden. Here and there in old diaries the curious may discover some few references to it. Evelyn, as we have seen, mentions orangeries as existing in his time, but perhaps, as Mr. Blomfield suggests, there were plantations. But the history of the garden of Ham House is reflected in its quaint arrangement and subtle charm, and it is certainly delightful in the summer evenings to linger in its sweet pleasaunces, and with the scent of the flowers, to feel something of the fragrance of the eld.

What Walpole wrote of Ham House is, in a great measure,

THE SUNDIAL IN FORECOURT.

true of it still. "Close to the Thames, in the centre of rich and verdant beauty, it is so blocked up and barricaded with walls, vast trees, and gates, that you think yourself an hundred miles off and an hundred years back." That seclusion which was a reproach in Walpole's days has become a delight in these. Who would wish to see the shadow of change pass over the sequestered charms of Ham? Within the house, too, there has been little alteration since its early times. The splendid galleried hall, paved with black and white marble, the great staircase, the tapestried Cabal Chamber, afterwards called the Queen's Audience Chamber, the Blue and Silver Room, the Duchess of Lauderdale's suite (with her armchair and other articles of personal use), the beautiful Drawing Room, the Chapel, the Long Gallery lined with portraits, the famous Tapestry Room, and the noble Library, have scarcely been touched by the modern hand; and it is from the windows of these historic chambers that the glorious gardens are surveyed.

THE NORTH TERRACE.

GARDENS OLD & NEW

CLEEVE PRIOR MANOR, WORCESTERSHIRE, THE SEAT OF . . . MRS. HOLTUM.

THERE is a feature in the old gardens at Cleeve Prior in Worcestershire that entitles them to a high place in the history of English gardening. They are not, indeed, unique, but they have great claims upon the attention of all who would penetrate the ideas of our ancestors as they were manifested in the externals of domestic life. That famous yew avenue, so fantastically cut, and representing, it is said traditionally, the twelve Apostles and the four Evangelists, is one of the quaintest garden features in all England.

A most quaint idea, indeed, is this attributed to the "Prior's Garden," but it could not be to it alone. Cleeve Prior lies on the borders of Warwickshire, and is actually in the Shakespeare country, within a mile and a-half of Bidford,

which a certain tradition associates with the revelling of the Bard. Now somewhat further north in the same county of Warwick, at Packwood, as Mr. Blomfield and Mr. Thomas tell us in their "Formal Garden in England," the Sermon on the Mount is literally represented in clipped yew. "At the entrance to the 'mount,' at the end of the garden, stand four tall yews 20ft. high for the four evangelists, and six more on either side for the twelve apostles. At the top of the mount is an arbour formed in a great yew tree called the 'pinnacle of the temple,' which was also supposed to represent Christ on the Mount, overlooking the evangelists, apostles, and the multitude below; at least this account of it was given by the old gardener who was pleaching the pinnacle of the temple." The like quaint

THE PORCH.

devotional idea may also be found in the arrangement of windows in a few old houses of 300 years ago.

The middle districts of England are rich in the natural graces of Nature, but they offer many examples also of the manner in which our ancestors fashioned their garden world. In the villages some formal shape will start up from the hedge, confronting us with a strange presentation of bird or animal cut in box or yew. When we remember that the old English idea of a garden was an enclosed place, we begin to see how

A SECTION OF THE YEW AVENUE.   *"Country Life."*

we depict is especially valuable, because it embodies ancient worth, and is the representative of the ideals of a forme time. The moods of the minds of old workers are here ; here is their handicraft ; in this garden they rejoiced. Here they took their pleasure in the quiet life of a less bustling day than ours, and they have left behind them the poetry of their existence.

Cleeve Prior is a sweet place in which to find such a garden. It stands high in the country amid a beautiful range of hills, whose folds it is delightful to trace for their entrancing views and their rare variety. The lofty perpendicular tower of the church of St. Andrew, anciently a possession of the Prior of Worcester, is conspicuous through the surrounding country, and looks down upon a typical village full of the sweetness of rural character. A Norman doorway is below, and there are fine features of Early English buildings, and much else that is interesting in the church. You may notice, too, in the village, the quaint bird cut above the hedge and the beehive yew at the hostel of the King's Head. Then by the rustic way you come to the picturesque entrance to the Manor House, and notice an old *montoir* or mounting-block, from which, in heavier days than these, men got astride their horses, or took their ladies behind them upon the pillion. Trees overhang the way, and rise in massive groups above and behind the house, to which the approach is up the flagged way between the great and lofty avenue of yews. Let all hope, indeed, that these noble relics of a former time may long maintain their vigour and delight generations yet to come. Uncertain tradition says that the monks of Worcester cut and trained the avenue. However that may have been, the sixteen trees are a masterpiece of garden handicraft, cut into their billowy heads and mighty shapes with subtle skill—heavy but not gloomy, for there are transverse sections through which we gain an outlook upon sunlit stretches of grass and radiant banks of flowers, catching sight also of the quaint dovecote in the farmyard. Beautiful is the porch at the end of the

the hedge assumed its importance, what was the function of the terrace, and how necessary was the pleached alley. They afforded shelter from sun and wind, and gave that bounding line which the eye craves, and the terrace by the house looking out over the area below—a pleasant resort at all times. Such gardens as that at Cleeve Prior could not have been unknown to Shakespeare, and we may certainly conceive that he was thinking of Warwickshire and its borderland when he conjured up his visions of quaint garden beauty. A garden like that

pathway, a lofty building of stone, with the motto "Dieu et mon droit," and a chamber over the door, such as we see in many houses of three centuries back. Mullioned windows and lofty chimneys look out over the garden, and the gables group with the splendid trees behind, while the quaint figure that crests the porch peeps out above the yews. On either side of the "Apostles' Garden" we have exemplifications of other styles. The emerald lawn is simply delightful, and makes a pleasant resort, indeed, when the spring

"Country Life."

Copyright.

THE MANOR HOUSE AND THE FAMOUS YEW AVENUE.

touches the yews, and their "gloom is kindled at the tips," and when the roses scent the summer breeze.

There is thus a twofold character of gardening at Cleeve Prior, the ancient and the modern, but both contribute to the aspect of repose. There are some cut trees that aggravate us, as monstrous productions of the topiary art, warring with Nature, but not so the solemn yews in this old garden.

Some forms of modern gardening again are garish and unsatisfactory in their richness and excess, but nothing of this kind is found at Cleeve Prior. The flowers here seem to appeal to us more than in some places where their profusion is greater. There is the sense of repose dominating the whole, and the contrasts of style and colour enhance the effect without harshness or violence of juxtaposition. Then from the lawns and flower beds you may pass into the wild garden, with its tangled growths and its glorious harvesting of sweet and beautiful flowers. From the time, indeed, when you set foot upon those quaint semi-circular steps at the gateway, and traverse the yew avenue, to the moment when you regretfully leave, you find some attraction or interest in all the gardens of Cleeve Prior.

It is unnecessary to dwell further upon garden features, which, save for the Apostles' Garden, are of subdued character, though there are certain points and characters of the place so attractive as to deserve some further notice. The features we allude to are the manifestations of the quaintness, charm, and beauty of country life which we find about this Worcestershire house. The village in its relation to the house, the farm, the dovecotes, the general character of old-world picturesqueness will appeal to many readers. In such places we realise the rural life that has continued for centuries in England with little change in its essential character, we conjure up the impressions of earlier ages, and we feel that the lives of earlier Englishmen are still exemplified among us. At Cleeve Prior we find all this in the house and the garden as well as in the village and the farm.

Even more picturesque than the garden itself is the neighbouring farmyard. Its cart houses, with their lofty gables and external stairways leading to the lofts, have a

AN ANCIENT EXTERNAL STAIRWAY.

singularly pictorial character, while the dovecote is most interesting, and is probably not equalled in England.

In former times detached buildings were frequent in gardens, and garden-houses and dovecotes gave charming opportunities to the garden architect. Sometimes, as we have already seen, there were "banqueting houses" at the ends of terraces, being places where our ancestors were festive in the summer-time, and in "The Formal Garden in England," by Mr. Blomfield and Mr. Inigo Thomas, many examples are given of the exquisite character of such effective structures, which, indeed, at Montacute and many of our great houses are extremely noteworthy.

Aviaries, like that spoken of by Evelyn at Ham House, are now very rarely found in gardens, which may be even a matter for congratulation, since in modern days they have often been crude and inartistic erections. It was otherwise in the sixteenth century, when it was not unusual to find such structures, and the dovecote at Cleeve Prior is a notable example. The authors of "The Formal Garden" remark that these buildings were considered

THE DOVECOTE IN THE FARMYARD.

THE APOSTLES AND EVANGELISTS IN YEW.

indispensable to every country house, though they usually appear to have been placed at some distance, and seldom within the garden walls. At the same time they were often visible from the garden, as at Cleeve Prior, where the tiled roof of the circular building is a picturesque object from the lawn.

"Columbaries," or pigeon-houses, were usually square or octagonal in form, with gabled roofs, and a cupola forming a small open-air dovecote at the top. Circular pigeon-houses like that at Cleeve Prior are less common. There is an example in the rose garden at Rousham, with tiers of nesting-places built in the walls, and in some cases, as at Melton Hall in Norfolk, and at Athelhampton in Dorset, a revolving post stood n a socket in the centre, with a projecting arm to which a ladder was hung. In this way, by turning round the post, access could be had to any part of the structure. The curious interior of the Athelhampton example is illustrated later in this volume. Evelyn mentions a "pigeon-house of

THE MOUNTING-BLOCK.

most laudable ex-
ample" at Godstone
in Surrey. Many old
columbaries, such as
the great square one
at South Stoke, near
Goring, on the
Thames, are, as the
authors of "The
Formal Garden"
say, so exceedingly
picturesque, that
there seems no reason
for excluding them
from the garden—the
greater reason, we
might say, for giving
them a place. The
ordinary barrel dove-
cote or other like
construction upon a
high post was often
erected in old gardens
and may be found in
many places now. In
a garden near South-
water a dovecote
such as this forms
the centre-piece of a
square walled garden,
with straight grass
paths leading up to a
circle in the centre,
and the effect is very
good. Badeslade's
view of Sundridge
Place in Kent (1720),
shows the dovecote
standing in the centre
of the fish-pond. The
water-floor was occu-
pied by the ducks;
above this was a
room, with a balcony
all round, and steps
up from the water;

THE OLD FLOWER GARDEN.

and the upper part
was pierced with holes
and perches for the
pigeons. Again a
large octagonal dove-
cote on a solid wooden
trestle is shown in
Logan's view of St.
John's, Oxford.

Cleeve Prior has,
therefore, a special
claim to attention.
The village is exceed-
ingly picturesque also,
and there again is to
be seen a remarkable
dovecote, though one
in no way compara-
ble to the fine example
at the old Manor
House. But, after all,
the fine and individual
feature of the place is
the great double yew
hedge of the Prior's
Garden. Beyond this
we need scarcely go.
Our ancestors have
left many great illus-
trations of their lives
and ideals; but per-
haps nowhere have
they given us examples
so notable of their
piety and quaint fancy
in practical combina-
tion, as in the few
illustrations we yet
possess of their suc-
cessful efforts to figure
sacred personages in
the green foliage of
the yew. The posses-
sion of such an example
is the distinction of
Cleeve Prior.

THE CART HOVELS.   "Country Life"

THE EAST GABLE AND THE PRIOR'S GARDEN.

GARDENS OLD & NEW

ATHELHAMPTON HALL, DORCHESTER, . .
THE SEAT OF . . . .
MR. A. C. LAFONTAINE.

WITH all candour be it confessed that there are thorns and traps on either side of the path of him who would deal with such a topic as Athelhampton. For Athelhampton as it stands, that wonderful and artistic harmony of house and garden, is truly an "architect's garden," and in the main the work of one who is an architect in the widest sense of the word. Now Mr. William Robinson, whose services to the cause of the beautiful in country life are beyond all price, and many with him, as we have suggested already, cannot tolerate the architect in the garden. " The architect can help us much by building a beautiful house. That is his work. The true architect seeks to go no farther. ' On the other hand, the ambition of the architect—in many ways a noble ambition—knows no limits. He will prescribe for you the plan and outline of the garden over which his windows look, and even, perhaps, the very plants and shrubs which must be grown in the various parts of the garden. Some years ago there was a feud, of that bitterness which appears to be inseparable from literary and artistic controversy, between Mr. Robinson and those who think with him on the one hand, and a group of young and cultivated architects on the other. There is much to be said on both sides. The architect, in designing his house, must think of the work which the gardener has to do afterwards; and the gardener, in his turn, must think of the opportunities which the architect has given to him. In a word, as has several times been said in this volume, the spirit of the house must, if in some indefinable sense, pervade the garden. The ideal situation would be if " the compleat gardener " could work hand in hand with the excellent architect. That kind of combination of talent is, however, possibly rare, and it may happen, especially where an ancient and historic house has to be rehabilitated, that one mind will be called upon to plan, out of existing materials, and subject to present conditions, an harmonious whole. Such was the problem which was placed for solution before Mr. Inigo Thomas at Athelhampton in 1890. How great was his success is shown by our illustrations.

THE FOUNTAIN IN THE CORONET GARDEN.

A VIEW FROM THE TERRACE.

Copyright THE EAST SIDE. "Country Life."

Down in the water-meadows some miles out of Dorchester the clustered gables and battlements of Athelhampton nestle under the spreading boughs of a great cedar, and in the secluded courts there can be heard the gentle coo of pigeons and the conversational patter of falling water. The place was once the home of the Martins, a respectable Dorsetshire family, whose fortunes have long ceased to be connected with the place of its origin and continuance for eight generations. Then the place passed into other hands, and some ten years ago a gentleman from London purchased all of it that money could buy, to enjoy the retirement and old-world charm of the Dorsetshire country, which the magic pen of Thomas Hardy has made so familiar. The prospect before the reconstructor must have been inspiring. A thick forest of larches, no part of any original design, grew up to the very windows of the house; but there were other things far more promising. To start with, a lofty fourteenth century hall, with a roof of carved oak, formed the main block of the building, and from its western end there stood out at an angle a three-storied Tudor wing with chained martens on the gable ends. These two blocks were in good preservation, and could be left intact. From the other end of the hall, and receding from it at right angles, later additions, of no particular character, had been built, and some Elizabethan windows used again in them.

Copyright. THE LILY POND AND LAWN. "Country Life."

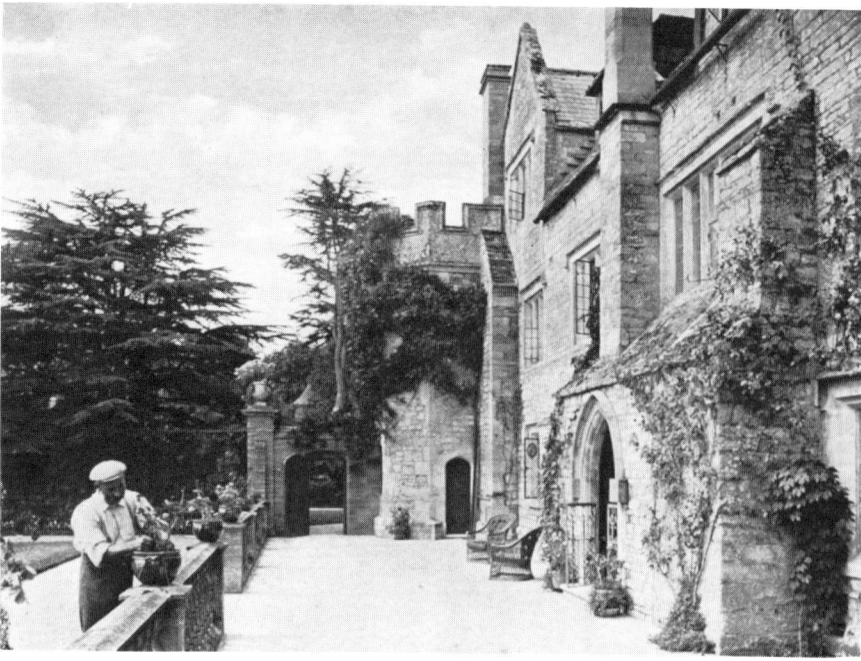

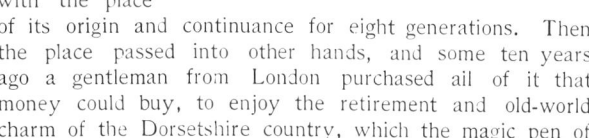

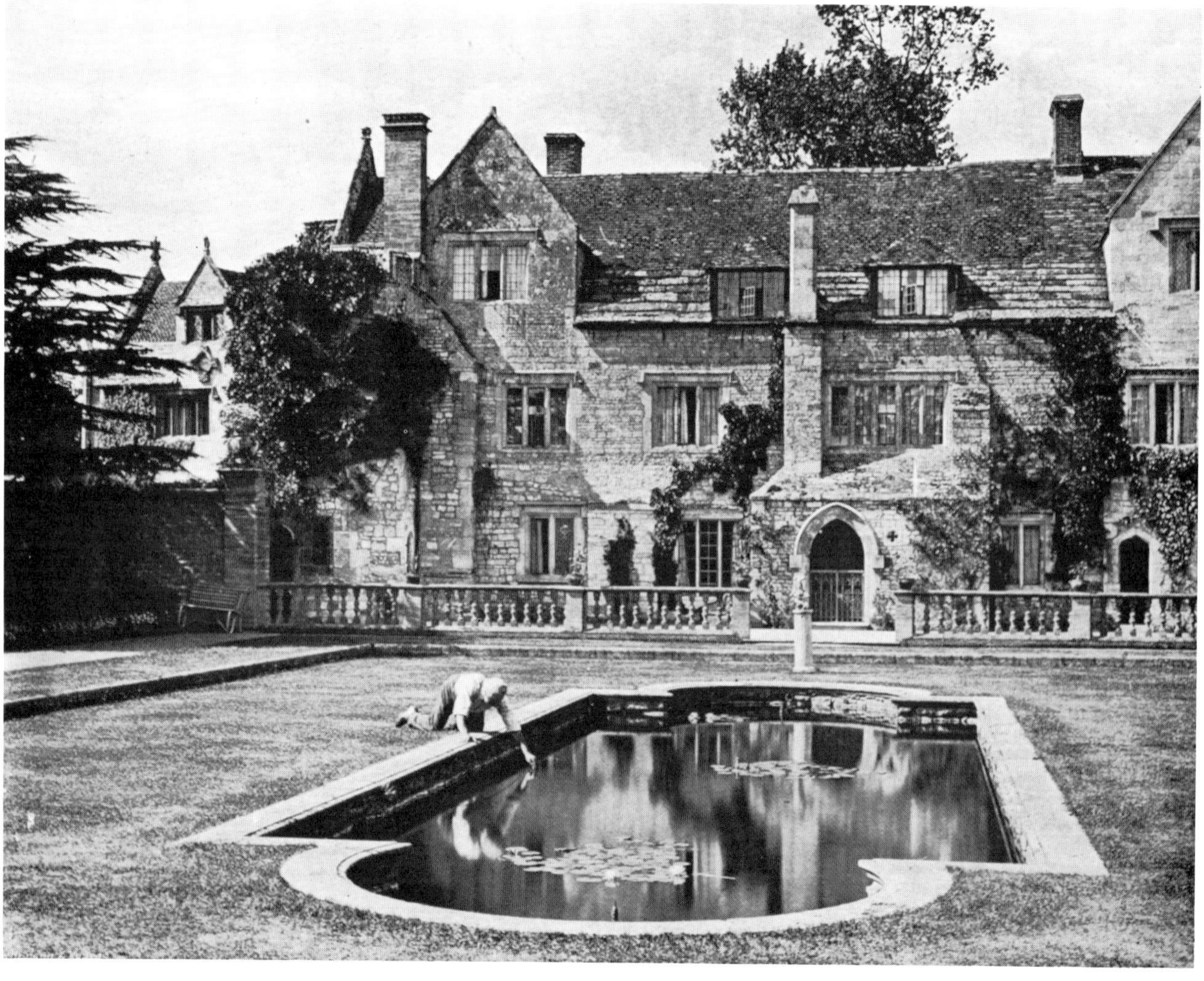

Returning from this, so as to form three sides of a court with the hall, was a still later wing of ruinous brickwork that might have seen eighty summers. Here was abundant material for much hard thinking and planning, and for reconciliation of various ideas and schemes of beauty which seemed at first to be mutually contradictory. But at length the plan shaped itself. It included rebuilding part of these two blocks and connecting the end of the last with the hall by a covered arcade.

So much for the house. And now what could be done in the garden ? There had once been a forecourt with a delightful gatehouse opposite the porch. This was known from old views of the house, and the oriel from the gatehouse still stood in pieces under the great cedar. That was to be rebuilt into the south front. As to the gardens, there were no traces remaining. The larch wood spread past the south front; beyond that was a paddock, then a lane and the road to Blandford. V sions of a sunny court of green on the south front, with a long pool down the centre, seemed to map themselves out on the survey. But the larch wood must go to get it, and the ground be excavated to give a tep down from the doorway. There was a mass of soil to be moved, and the idea took shape of carting it towards the Blandford road to make an upper garden, with raised walks all round and a long terrace beyond, with a pavilion at either end, which would command the whole. Between this and the south court there would be a long, narrow space, a pretty vista from the drawing-room windows when rampant roses and creeping clematis clothed the pinnacles. For in the middle, at the crossing from the upper garden to the south court, some errant fancy dictated a coronet in stone, a circle of pinnacles on ramps, with a sundial in the centre and steps down from the upper garden, with wrought-iron gates and baskets of fruit in stone. Beyond the arcade in the house would

"Country Life."

THE ANCIENT DOVECOTE.

"Country Life."

THE INTERIOR OF THE DOVECOTE.

be the tennis-lawn, and a figure in the yew hedge, reflected in the stream, was to end the vista that would fall through the courtyard, the house, and the south garden.

Another vista, from the seat on the terrace, would cross the upper garden, through the gates and the coronet, to the south court, and, diving into the gloom of a grove beyond, lose itself in the shady recesses of a summerhouse.

Such was the scheme, that called for much in the accomplishing. There were the felling, grubbing, and carting away of trees, the purchase and planting of yew and box, of turf and flowers and creepers. There were tons of gravel, twice sifted, and metalling for the garden paths. For many months waggons laden with russet stone from Ham Hill creaked down the Yeovil road. Rome was not built, nor was Athelhampton rebuilt, in a day. The thousand and one difficulties that attend such undertakings all put in their appearance in due course. But at last the outside work was finished, and the library in the long wing panelled in oak and plastered with a dainty pendant ceiling of iris and Turk's-head lilies.

Eight years have passed since the designer was separated from his offspring, and on the whole Time and Nature seem to have dealt kindly with his work, and to have overlaid the bare form with royal robes of clematis, roses, and honeysuckle, leaving just a hint here and there of architectural form, enough to show its value among growing things. Perhaps some changes in his darling idea might not altogether please him. In the coronet garden a fountain has usurped the place of the sundial. In the sunk garden the formation lacks a centre and the four surrounding figures, and there is a sense of incompleteness from the piers wanting proper finials. But on the whole the gardening seems to have followed the right direction. The paved court with its wicker chairs is the very place in which to bask through a cigarette after lunch; but one would readily

THE GARDEN APPROACH.

banish the glazed pots on the balustrade in favour of good leaden vases with covers for winter. It is interesting to see what eight years' growth will do where things are sheltered by enclosure. In another eight years, or less, the hedges of yew should be as high and as dense as will ever be needed, and the stone has doubtless long since taken the soft lavender lichens that its surface affects and that painters delight in.

The old dovecote in the paddock by the stream is of interest, and is a garden feature also, retaining the revolving ladder hung from a massive post in the centre that helped the collection of squab pigeons from the myriad nesting-places with which the interior is lined, and that does o stil . But in speaking of Cleeve Prior,

we have spoken of dovecotes as garden features, and we need not further elaborate the matter. They are very effective points, like garden-houses and sundials, to be used well by the discriminating hand of Art. What we discover at Athelhampton is that the hand of Art has worked most excellently both in past times and in these. It is most gratifyi g to deal with such a place, because, like some others we might name, Athelhampton is an example of a house regenerated. Like Great Tangley, to name but one, it has been recovered from threatening decay, and it stands amid its pleasant gardens and woods in the picturesque land of Dorsetshire, a fine and characteristic illustration of what ripe judgment and imagination together can make of a good old English dwelling and its surroundings.

THE NORTH PAVILION.

THE WALLED GARDEN.

GARDENS OLD & NEW

IGHTHAM MOTE, KENT, . . .
THE SEAT OF . . .
Mr. T. Colyer-Fergusson.

E.F BRICKDALE

ENGLAND would be poor indeed if it had no such places as Ightham Mote. In this ancient courtyard, with those dear old gables looking down, we have the very type of the houses of former times. We may go to grander places, where the clang of the mailed heel seems yet to echo in stately halls, to more sumptuous chambers, where courtly dames might have seemed, perhaps, more at home ; but in few other places can we find so notable an example of the houses in which the mediæval gentlemen dwelt. It belongs to the days when the times were troubled, and when the knight or squire found it comfortable to live in a house whence, securely through a loophole, the cloth-yard shaft might wing its way, and where it was well sometimes to parley from the gate-tower with the stranger across the moat. There was protection in such houses from the sudden raid, and, at a pinch, with the drawbridge up and the portcullis down, they might even stand a siege. But such measures were only for the turbulent or the unwelcome ; for the friend or the honest stranger the gate was opened wide, and there was English hospitality behind the iron-bound oaken door.

The sun was caught in the courtyard, and was kindly to plant and flower, and such growths as the century knew garlanded gable and chimney, while beyond the bridge the garden lay, all sweet with summer blooms, a gay domain of beauty that many were glad to explore.

Ightham lies in a hollow in a very beautiful part of Kent. The stream running down from the hill supplies its enclosing moat. A pleasant stroll of some four miles from pretty Sevenoaks, through the famous park of Knole, thence along an elevated ridge and by copses and hedgerows, brings the visitor to the point where he looks down upon another world, gazing out upon the tower and gables of ancient Ightham, romantic and beautiful in the valley. Nothing more picturesque can be imagined, whether we look at the quaint old house, with its grey tower and courtyards, its high gables and red-tiled roofs, or turn attention to the luxuriant gardens that add so much to the charm. Here we shall endeavour to do

A CORNER OF THE QUADRANGLE.

THE GREAT TOWER.

A PERGOLA.

both, to catch the spirit of the place in thinking of its history, and to note the characters with which the garden is informed.

The family of De Haut, or Fitz Haut, is said, like many others, to have come over with the Conqueror, and one of its members had a fortified house at Ightham in the time of Henry II. The oldest parts of the existing house go back to

Edward II. or a little earlier, but the greater portion was rebuilt in the reign of Henry VII. and Henry VIII., and a good deal of excellent timber work was added in the times of Elizabeth and James, with the result that, in its varied features of weather-worn stone and picturesque timber, rising from a moat, Ightham is one of the quaintest piles of domestic architecture imaginable. One Richard Fitz Haut of Ightham

THE LAWN AND ORNAMENTAL TREES.

forfeited his heritage and lost his head at Pontefract for joining Buckingham in favour of Richmond, whereupon the Kentish house was granted to Robert Brackenbury, Lieutenant of the Tower. But Brackenbury fell at Bosworth, and when Richmond ascended the throne Edward Haut, son of the dispossessed squire, was installed in possession of the Mote. At this time the tower was raised and the west side rebuilt.

In 1520 the house was sold to Sir Richard Clement, of Milton, in Northamptonshire. It afterwards passed to Sir Christopher Alleyn, Lord Mayor of London, and in 1590 was sold to Sir William Selby, of Branxton, in Northumberland, Warden of the Marches and Governor of Berwick-on-Tweed, a veteran of the Low Countries, whose descendants continued generation after generation at the Mote. The date of the hall

THE FAMOUS COURTYARD OF IGHTHAM.

and crypt is supposed to be about 1340; the chapel, from having Sir Richard Clement's arms and the badge of the Tudors, appears to date from 1520 or thereabouts; the arms of the Selbys in the hall with the motto "Fort et Loyal," and on the tower, also indicate the date of Henry VIII. or later. There still remains in Ightham Church the monument of Dame Dorothy Selby, who died in 1641, and of whom her wondrous epitaph avers that she frustrated Guy Fawkes. Her "curious needle"

"Turned the abused stage
　Of this lewd world into the
　　golden age,"

whilst her nimble wit enabled her to read a veiled letter to Lord Monteagle for the undoing of deluded Guy. And then, as if to confute the doubter, behind Dame Dorothy's head is a carving wherein we see the Pope, in conclave with cardinals, monks, and the devil, instructing the traitor, while ships are discerned making towards England, and the Houses of Parliament are depicted with the faggots, powder-kegs, plotter, and lantern in the cellar.

Even odd conceits and unveracious histories like these add something to the interest of Ightham Mote. Romance undoubtedly belongs of right to the place, as you feel when you traverse the garden and cross the substantial structure which has replaced the drawbridge that of old spanned the water. Here is the embattled and turreted tower with the gateway, and the flanking buildings rising sheer from the moat. Through the archway we are really in another world, with the great windows of the hall and the loveliest of enriched gables and oriels looking upon the sunny space within, while the graces of foliage and blossom

A　GENERAL　VIEW.

cling fondly to the ancient walls, and touch with brighter colour their venerable tones. The hall, the famous domestic chapel, and the apartments are all exceedingly interesting, and from their deeply splayed windows look either into the courtyard or across the glistening moat to the garden and the fair country beyond. In olden times tradition says that 300 horses were stabled in the quaint building opposite to the entrance tower across the moat. These stables and out-buildings form another quadrangle, built entirely of timber in Elizabethan times, and are wondrously picturesque to the eye.

A house such as Ightham Mote must needs have a beautiful garden. If the gardens had been of formal character there would have been nothing unsuitable, but it cannot be gainsaid that the scenes we depict are filled with a sweeter and most appropriate charm. The surrounding moat gives the character,

THE　STABLES　FROM　THE　KITCHEN　GARDEN.

and ferns and water-loving plants flourish, while flowers garland the old walls of the mansion. Someone, indeed, well versed in the character and habits of graceful climbing plants has induced them to grow over the walls that enclose the court, without, however, in any degree concealing the structural character or the architectural details. Here is a lesson not to be overlooked, and the flower masses form a charming contrast to the rich tones of walls and hedges.

How delightful is this wall gardening, with, maybe, an antirrhinum, toadflax, or saxifrage established in the mossy chinks, making tufts of blossom in the summer months. Much of the beauty of an old wall is due to the plants encouraged to send their roots into the chinks and form

A VIEW THROUGH THE GATEWAY.

gardens of precious growth, perpetuated by the natural scattering of seed from year to year.

evening draws in. A delightful resort truly is this for the pleasant old diversion, with the thrush singing in the tree or the cuckoo calling from the hill, and with such a house to return to when the play is over. What a wonderful grouping of buildings is disclosed from the kitchen garden as we look across to the stables. Here the spirit of quaintness is verily embodied in the old timber gables, the high-pitched roof, the clustering ivy, the grey old walls, and the bell-cot lifted aloft. Gladdened with sunlight, and gifted with shadow, rare in the note of mellow colour, and with the bright edging of saxifrage and the rough stone margin in the foreground, this is a scene dear to the artist. The place, moreover, offers a perfect study of the free and luxuriant gardening appropriate to such an abode.

Then, again, we look up the valley, whence the water descends to the hollow, a purling brook that fed the old stew-ponds—where fish were fattened for the table—and the moat; for this, as we have said, is no stagnant water, but a captured expanse of it, that washes the base of the ancient walls, refreshed by the pleasant Kentish stream, which then passes onward rejoicing, with deep and shallow, from its visit to the quaint old place, to other charming scenes beyond. There seems to be no jarring note here, and Ightham is a place where the sweetness of the garden and the country reigns.

THE ENTRANCE TO THE DINING-HALL.

And the gardens themselves are very beautiful, with many a sunny walk and shady retreat, with a pergola under which it is delightful to linger, for the fragrance and beauty of the masses of roses which embower the place, with grassy paths and edgings of saxifrage, gorgeous borders in which lilies and many other splendid denizens of the garden flourish, with noble trees adorning the landscape, and casting their lengthening shadows across the sunny bowling green as the

THE CENTRAL TOWER.

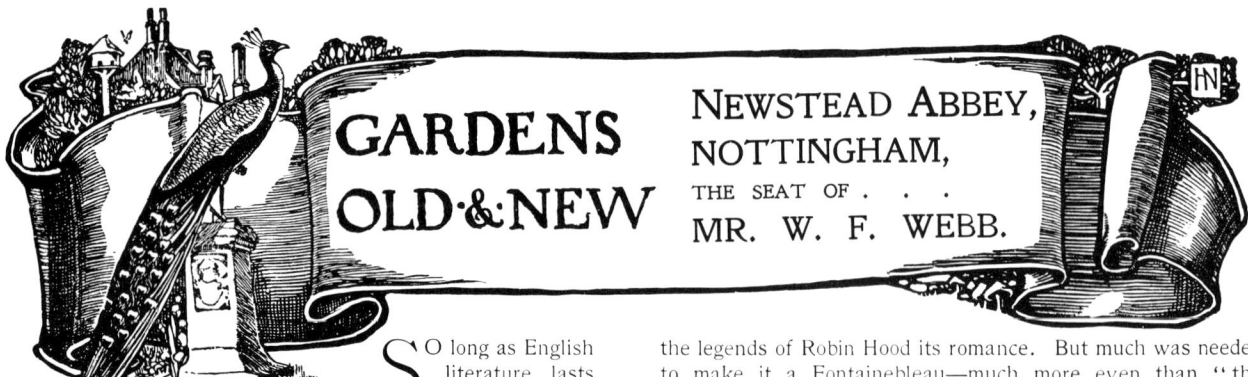

GARDENS OLD·&·NEW

NEWSTEAD ABBEY, NOTTINGHAM,
THE SEAT OF . . .
MR. W. F. WEBB.

SO long as English literature lasts shall the fame of Newstead Abbey endure. Deep'y loved for its charm of the eld, its hoary walls, the deep solitude of its presence, the mystery of its tangled brakes, the legends it cherished, and the dreams of dim romance and high emprise it could evoke, it was the home of the most brilliant poet, and most meteoric genius, perhaps, of modern days.

And Byron never saw its full fruition. Neither the character of his stormy life, nor the means of which he disposed, enabled him to renovate its mouldering walls. His predecessor had left it desolate. The ruined Augustinian house of Newstead, which the Byrons had made their home, had stood a siege in the Civil War, when they fought well for the King.

When Evelyn was at Newstead in 1654, the place reminded him of Fontainebleau. It might be made a noble seat, he said, for it was "accommodated" with brave woods and streams. The oaks of Sherwood were its reverend counsellors, the jewelled banks its adornments, the kine browsing in the meadows and the squirrels leaping in the woods the denizens of its "most living landscape," and

the legends of Robin Hood its romance. But much was needed to make it a Fontainebleau—much more even than "the old Lord's devils," as the country-side called the leaden Fauns which leered at the nymphs and dryads of the grove.

And, looking at Newstead, we ask ourselves whether we should like to see it a Fontainebleau, indeed, whether, for an English country home, those radiant gardens, terraces, landscapes, and varied picturesque features are not on the whole much better?

Horace Walpole visited Newstead in his time. He found "the hall entire, the refectory entire, the cloister untouched, with the ancient cistern of the convent and their arms on it; a private chapel quite perfect." "The park, which is still charming," he wrote, "has not been so much profaned; the present Lord has lost large sums, and paid part in old oaks, £5,000 of which have been cut near the house. In recompense he has built two baby forts, to pay his country in castles for the damage done to the navy, and planted a handful of Scotch firs, that look like ploughboys dressed in family liveries for a public day."

The old lord, returned from his conflicts with the French, had, in fact, raised mimic forts along the margin

THE EAST FRONT.

THE SUNK GARDEN AND MONKS' POND.

of the mere, on whose rippling surface floated a little frigate or other miniature man-of-war.

The poet fitted up a corner of the house for himself, and, adjacent to the chapel, his bedroom remains almost as he left it. But the story of his life at Newstead must not be told here. They whisper that, for his profane revels, he dug up forgotten skulls from monastic graves for the making of drinking cups. But, in other moods and more often, that " glorious remnant of the Gothic pile " — with its ruined fane, its crypt, its great hall, and its cloister — filled him with wondrous thoughts.

THE   CLOISTERS.

> "A mighty window, hollow in the centre,
>   Shorn of its glass of thousand colourings,
>   Through which the deepen'd glories once could enter,
>   Streaming from off the sun like seraph's wings,
>   Now yawns all desolate."

It is, indeed, as we may see, a glorious fragment to this day. The cloisters have a quaintness all their own.

> "Amidst the court a Gothic fountain play'd,
>   Symmetrical, but deck'd with carvings quaint—
>   Strange faces, like to men in masquerade,
>   And here perhaps a monster, there a saint."

The region in which Newstead lies is one of ancient forest; but many an oak of Sherwood had bowed beneath the stroke, and the beautiful woods that grace Newstead in these days were mostly planted by Colonel Wildman, who followed the poet in possession, bringing the decaying house to a condition of domestic charm it had not attained

before, and carrying on a great work in beautifying the surrounding estate. But the final fascination of Newstead has been conferred upon it by Mr. Webb, who, with his daughters, is a true lover of country life, well versed in gardening lore. In such good hands has Byron's abode, with surroundings further altered and adorned, reached a state of splendour which perhaps he could not have forecast. Yet his poetical allusions in " The Dream " are, nevertheless, singularly apt and beautiful. There is a tenderly graceful reference to the " gentle hill," on which he said his last farewell to Miss Chaworth, a hill afterwards ruthlessly shorn by a strange hand of its " peculiar diadem of trees in circular array."

It rises hard by the beautiful lake, to which fine lawns and grassy steeps descend gently from the southern side of the abbey, where many a noble tree graces the slope. Looking on Lake Leman, Byron, writing his lines " To Augusta," bethought him tenderly of the water by which he had often lingered at home.

> " I did remind thee of our own dear lake
>   By the old Hall, which may be mine no more.
>   Leman is fair; but think not I forsake
>   The sweet remembrance of a dearer shore.
>   Sad havoc time must with my memory make
>   Ere that or thou can fade these eyes before."

Many memories of Byron are treasured at Newstead. Here, by the flower garden, is the oak he planted and

THE   TERRACE   ASCENTS.

BOATSWAIN'S GRAVE.

Celebrated in song. Not far away, beneath the shade of a noble cedar, is Boatswain's grave, where his favourite Newfoundland was buried. Many things have happened since he last visited Newstead in 1813. In that generous soil the trees planted after his time have thriven well, and now we behold the beauties that spring from the judicious planter's hand. Mr. Webb has moulded the gardens afresh, and he and his daughters have watched them with judicious care. Thus the fish-pond of the monks has now most beautiful surroundings, and from every point of view new charms are disclosed. Whether we traverse the delightful native English garden, or survey the quaint features of the French parterres, or gather bowlfuls of blossoms in the garden assigned to Spain, or again examine the unfamiliar denizens of the tract of bamboos, or the multitudinous treasures of the rock garden, we feel that true lovers of Nature, possessed with a keen interest in its varied forms and developments, have invested the abbey with its charm.

Newstead is mainly a garden of terraces, gentle grass slopes, and broad mixed borders, in which countless varied blooms have their home. The famous terrace is about 230 yds. long, and is reached by a flight of steps, with

groundwork, for assuredly the box edgings are familiar in the best English gardens, and it cannot be said that the tuberous and other forms of summer begonias, and the many bright flowers that fill the beds, are in any way the monopoly of France.

There is something very quaint and delightful in the Spanish garden, a modern development which is its neighbour, or more truly a part of itself. Here again we find red gravel and box edgings, these last developed into veritable walls, 2ft. high and as many broad. They enframe numerous varieties of bulbous flowers, which give changing colour from spring to autumn, besides lupines, annuals, and a host of familiar flourishing things.

The Devil's Wood is approached from the terrace, but the evil spirit has been exorcised, and instead of a forbidding thicket of dismal yews, we find ornamental specimens of the tribe, well-kept hedges, open spaces of grass, and quite a collection of beautiful crab trees.

Our pleasant journeying at Newstead now brings us to the Eagle Pond, which in character and setting reminds us of a Dutch garden. Its shape imposes a certain formality, which we find in the grass terrace and square flower-beds, and a peculiarly charming feature is

THE   EAGLE   POND.

moss-grown balustrades, and many shadowed seats for those who enjoy its pleasures. You can scarce imagine a more fragrant or entrancing resort than this to linger in when the shadows slowly lengthen, the thrush sings from the apple bough, and the air is rich with the hum of the laden bee. You may make much in your "study of imagination" of a garden terrace—the very place for sober converse, light-hearted laughter, or any delight of the open air—as you survey these gentle grass slopes, broad borders and beds of flowers, and the many features of the garden that lies before.

We have glanced at the grounds on the south side of the house where these emerald lawns, shadowed by spreading trees, fall to the margin of the lake. The gardens on the east side are quite different. The creators of these seem, in a manner, to have ransacked the earth for its treasures. They have captured the garden delights of France and Spain, and even have brought to Newstead the jungled growths of Far Cathay.

But, somehow, these various manners strike no discordant note in the harmonious character of the whole. Here we are in the French garden, and, if there be anything Gallic about it, this must, we think, be in the red gravel

the happy marriage of the finest varieties of rhododendrons with that magnificent flower, the Lilium auratum.

Let us now pass through the tunnel beneath the terrace to the bamboo garden, planted where the old "stew-pond" was, and where these graceful and vigorous grasses lift their feathery stems in fascinating contrast to the dark shade of the yews.

Then we come to the Alpine or rock garden, remodelled and replanted a few years ago, and reflecting the loving care bestowed upon it. Here a thousand starry gems have their home, reminding us of the upland Alpine meadows, where such flowers overspread the ground like some rich carpet. We linger, too, fondly in the rose and carnation garden, where is the sweetest partnership of colour and fragrance in the linking of our two fairest hardy flowers. Go where we may in these gardens, there is something to attract and charm, some delectable prospect, some dainty garden imagining, some enchanting effect of variety. We are led by our surroundings to recall the former dwellers at the abbey, while we revel in the delights created and fostered by their successors. But space is exhausted, and so we conclude our account of the beauties of historic, romantic, and charming Newstead.

GARDENS OLD·&·NEW
FOUNTAINS HALL AND ABBEY, YORKSHIRE. .

FOUNTAINS HALL is a mansion whose stones speak to us loudly of a time long past. The house is Jacobean, and the terraces and hedges of the garden, which are its immediate neighbours, bear the aspect of that picturesque period, but the materials out of which it was built were quarried from the ruins of the house of the great abbot of Fountains. Our minds are carried back, therefore, to the time of the thirteen monks whom Archbishop Thurstan of York took from the Abbey of St. Mary's, and planted in what was then the rugged wilderness by the little river Skell, where they "made the desert smile." These were men with girded loins and the lamp lit, who craved for a stricter rule than prevailed in the Benedictine house at York, for there were roots in the Benedictine soil that thirsted for the water springs found in the silent recesses of Fountain Dale. There had been the same recoil from laxity in the house of Moslesme, from which Abbot Robert had gone out to join with Stephen Harding, the Englishman, in establishing the parent house of the Cistercians at Citeaux. Harding was the master and instructor of the famous Bernard, abbot of Clairvaux, and Thurstan was Bernard's friend, and both had a keen interest in the new house that was to built by the river Skell.

Looking at the smiling scene that greets us in Fountain Dale, we recognise that these monks were the pioneers and exemplars of agricultural development, and of the richness and virtue of country life. To begin with, there was little but the rugged rock and the wilderness to give promise of plenty. They laboured in the making of mats, in tilling the soil, in cutting faggots for their oratory, and such of them as could in that pleasant art of gardening, which, in the years to come, was to cast a new glamour over Fountain Dale. Where the ancients would have found Pan and the Fawns and Dryads, these men discovered the incentives to a higher life. "Your letters smell of the forest," wrote Leo X. to Egidius of Viterbo, "and shed the odour of the shade and of the delightful spot in which your house is reared." And so wrote St. Bernard to Abbot Murdac of Fountains, telling him, out of the fruit of experience, that there was more to be found in the woodland than in books. "Ligna et lapides docebunt te quod a magistris audire non possis."

However much truth, or however little, there may be in the statement that the exquisite message which had sent out the

"*Country Life.*"

THE ENTRANCE GATE.

white - robed workers was forgotten, and that the spirit fled when the form was made perfect, at least it is certain that they entered upon their labour—as is written in the Chronicle of Meaux, ruled over by a monk from Fountains—seeking "their daily bread by the sweat of their brows, planting with their life's blood the vineyard of the Lord of Hosts." Not less certain is it that under their laborious hands the sterile wilderness and impenetrable thicket were brought under cultivation.

Copyright. THE RUSTIC BRIDGE WALK. "Country Life."

Fountains Abbey shall not be described in this place, for it lies mostly outside our scope. It is usual to approach the entrancing scene through the pleasure grounds of Studley Royal, the noble seat of the Marquess of Ripon, from which certain of our illustrations are taken, and few visitors are found to deny that the classical character of those grounds, with the landscape gardening introduced by Mr. Aislabie in the last century, has produced an effect of contrast that is very charming. They are approached by an avenue of splendid limes, and another of noble beeches. The place is full of sweetness, and many hours may be spent amid the delightful woods, in examining the ruins, and in surveying the picturesque beauties of Fountains Hall. Mr. Aislabie's work at Fountains Abbey began about 1720, and he was assisted only by his gardener, William Fisher.

The river Skell was canalised, and caused to open into large ponds, extending between turf-covered terraced banks adorned with statues and bordered by fine hedges of yew, above which rose the natural woodland. Since that time ways have been cut through the wood to the top of the hill, whence

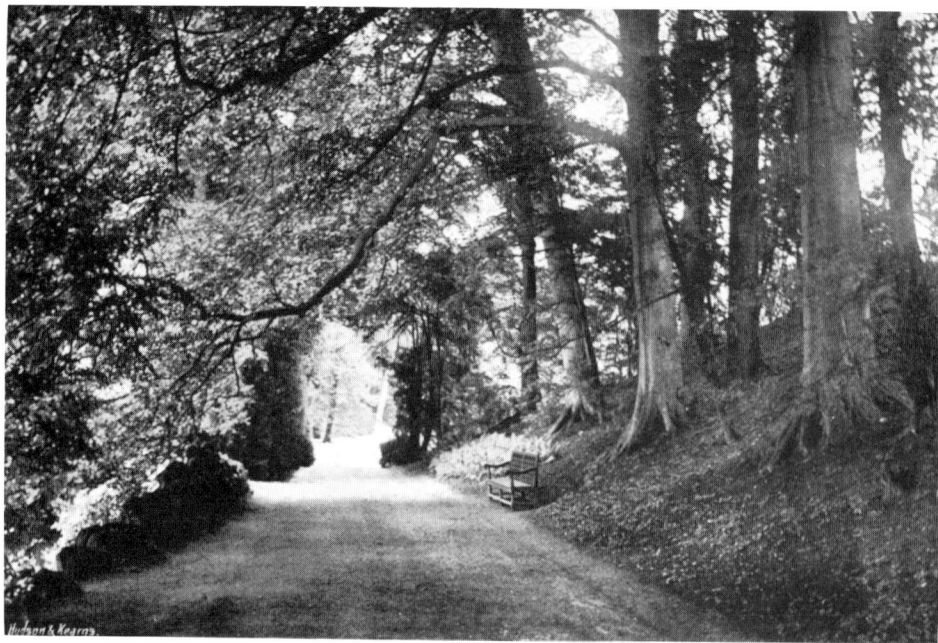

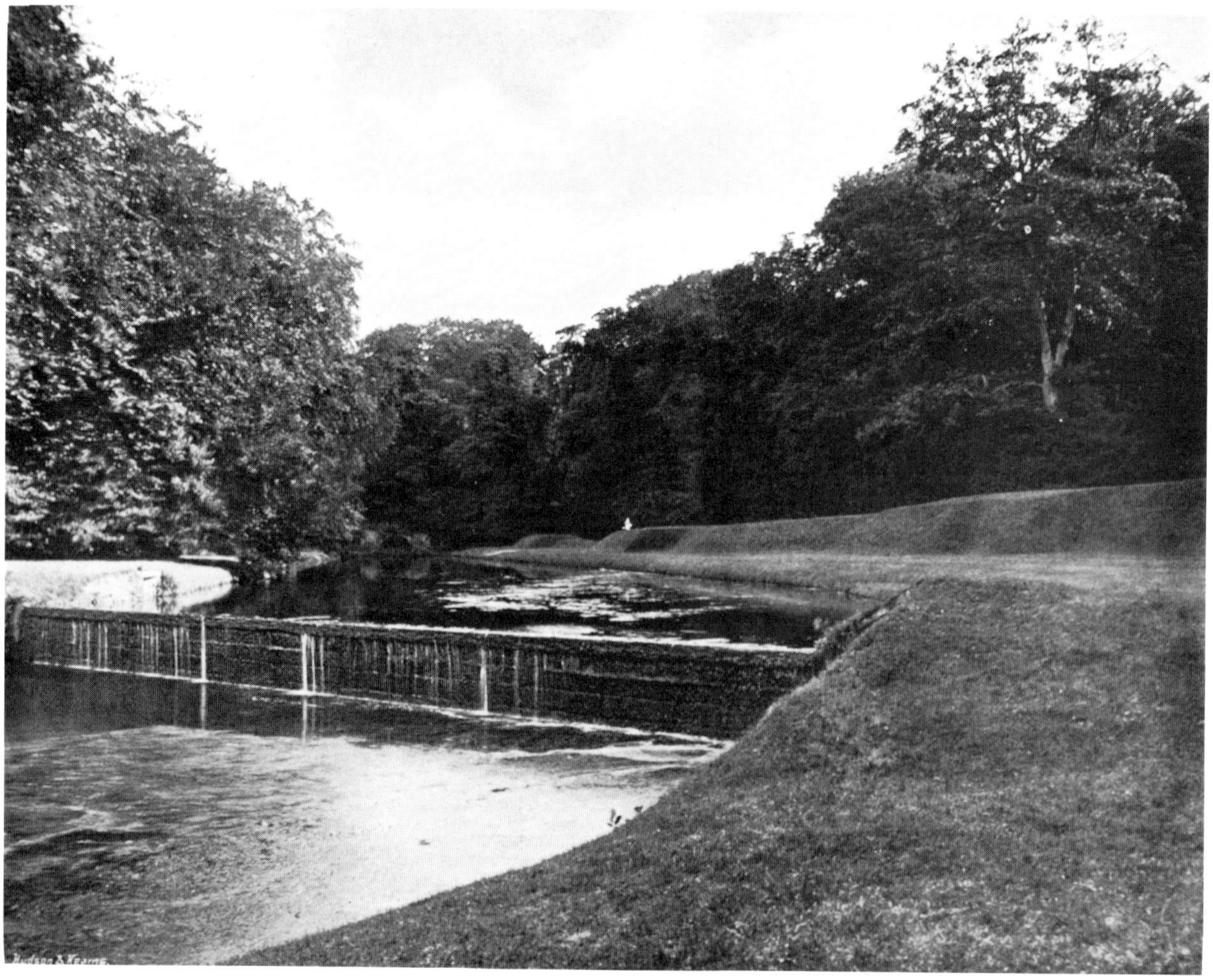

Copyright. THE RIVER SKELL. "Country Life."

THE OLD TERRACE AND GARDEN FRONT.

THE HALF MOON LAKE.

there are charming views of the formal "pleasaunce" below. "The Moon" and "The Crescent" ponds reflect upon their silvery surfaces the forms of classic deities, the Temple of Piety, and the umbrageous woodland. Sometimes the walks pass by the side of the canal, and sometimes through the woods, and are continually opening delightful prospects. There are some exceedingly fine spruce firs and hemlock spruces of great height and girth, with other trees, many of which have been figured by Loudon in his "Arboretum." A particularly beautiful view is from the classical Temple of Piety, beyond which a path through the wood brings the visitor up the hill, and through a tunnel cut in the rock, beyond which the Octagon Tower is reached. It is a point from which there are romantic prospects on every side. The visitor then passes through great woods of noble beech and oak, and reaches Anne Boleyn's seat. Here the doors are flung open, and then is disclosed a prospect scarcely surpassed in England, for the great ruins of Fountains Abbey are seen on a strip of green meadow shut in by the wooded hills.

There is something of pleasant artifice in the manner in which the noble ruin is reached, which does not detract from the impressive and beautiful character of the scene thus

A VIEW FROM THE TERRACE.

THE GARDEN FACADE.

suddenly disclosed, and the visitor lingers to contemplate the great monastic pile. The abbey went through many vicissitudes. Once it was burned by vengeful partisans, but the building went on through the twelfth century. Abbot John, the Yorkshireman, began the choir of the church in 1203. It was nearly completed in 1220, from which time up to 1247 the house was ruled by Abbot John, the Kentishman, to whose taste and energy are due the erection of part of the magnificent cloister, the infirmary, the hospitium, and the exquisite transeptal aisle at the east end, known as the "Nine Altars." The great tower, which is such a conspicuous object in the landscape, was erected by Abbot Huby (1294-1526). The bridge across the Skell belongs to the thirteenth century, and is close to the Abbey Mill, the "Seven Sisters" being near by. These last are no longer seven, but only two, and are venerable yew trees, which have been growing there perhaps from the day when the thirteen monks reached the banks of the Skell, and may even have given them shelter then. From the west gate-house, or porter's lodge, there is a magnificent prospect of the great church with its lofty tower, and the long range of the cloisters and dormitory extending to and across the river Skell. Nowhere in England can the plan of a Cistercian house be so well studied, and the excavations which have been conducted have revealed a vast deal that was formerly hidden. Every style of architecture from Transition-Norman to the Perpendicular is found in perfection in these impressive and beautiful ruins.

The site was granted, in the 32 Henry VIII., to Sir Richard Gresham,

THE PORCH AND ITS SUNDIAL.

and the story of the ruin is a painful and even a terrible one. It is now known that the rich carved woodwork of the choir was torn down and burnt in order to melt the lead taken from the roof, which formed a large item in the accounts of the depredators, and there is good evidence to show that even the graves were rifled in quest of valuables.

In 1597, Sir Richard Gresham's representatives sold the site to Sir Stephen Proctor, who pulled down the abbot's house which had been built over the river Skell at the east end of the conventual building, and used the material to erect the mansion of Fountains Hall. The estate was sold again in 1623, and passed through various hands, until from the Messengers it went by sale in 1768 to Mr. Aislabie, at the price of £18,000. As we have already seen, the Aislabies did

a great deal to beautify and improve the estate, and Fountains Abbey is now well protected and jealously guarded by its proprietor, the Marquess of Ripon.

Fountains Hall, the noble house built by Sir Stephen Proctor, stands a little way beyond the West Gate House of the Abbey, and is a most picturesque example of Jacobean architecture, which has remained unaltered since its completion, and forms an admirable subject for the artist, chiefly because of the very charming grouping of its bay windows, gables, and chimneys. It is approached by broken, weatherworn steps, in the interstices of which the careful hand of the gardener has made green things grow, while a great yew overshadows the way. Then, by a path between well-clipped hedges, we reach the entrance, which is very imposing in its varied character. The round-headed doorway is flanked by fluted Ionic pillars, and adorned with quaint figures and a sundial over the arch. Mullioned windows are on both sides, and a gallery is above for the outlook, with a semi-circular bay and large and beautiful windows set further back. The lofty projecting bays of the structure on either hand, with their gables and embattlements, and their great ranges of mullioned windows, are particularly striking, and the whole composition is of so notable a character that it is scarcely surpassed in England in its kind. Ivy clothes a large part of the façade, and roses and other climbing plants garland the stonework, without, however, concealing its character.

The gardens about the house have a subtle charm all their own. They are distinguished by a simple character in which radiant flowers are contrasted with dark green hedges of yew, and the foliage is particularly fine, the trees being of large size and beautiful growth. The outlook from the terrace over the quaint features of the garden to the meadows is remarkably attractive. Fountains Hall, like Fountains Abbey and the stately gardens of Studley Royal, lies in a singularly beautiful part of the country, within a few miles of the notable city of Ripon, and in a land invested with a character of great natural charm, rich in oak and lime, and often deep in beechen shade. The house is not in itself devoid of any of those elements of attraction which are found in old country houses, and has notable features of broad impressiveness which few others possess, while about it are gardens appropriate to its character, and entirely pleasing, rich, and attractive in themselves.

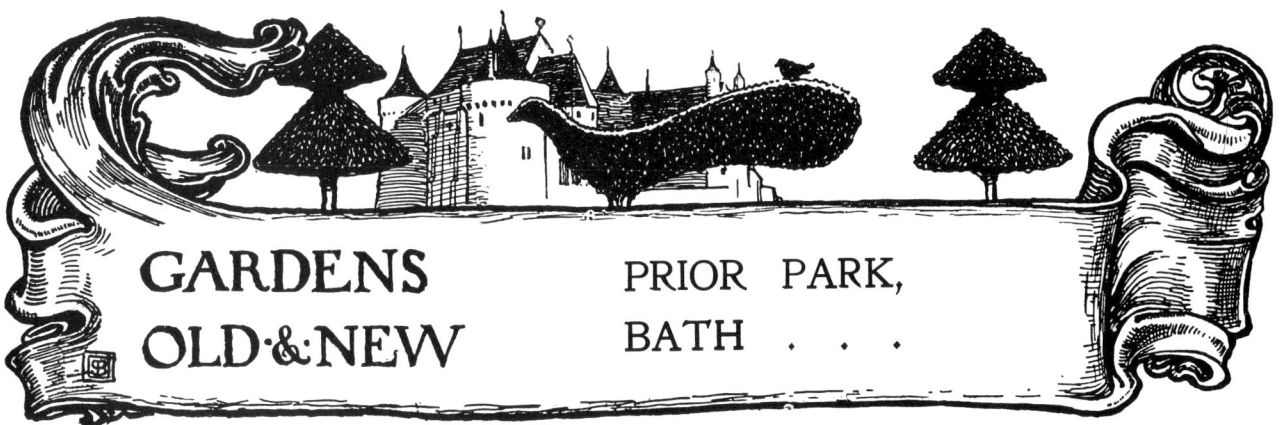

GARDENS OLD·&·NEW

PRIOR PARK, BATH . . .

THE stately mansion and the beautiful gardens we depict constitute one of the most interesting domestic places of comparatively recent date in England. The house was the creation of a very remarkable man, whose personality impressed itself upon the City of Bath, and the pleasure gardens in general date from his time. Ralph Allen died in 1764, and the mansion which he so highly valued is no longer devoted to the purely domestic purposes for which it was built. It has now for a long time been a Roman Catholic College, and nowhere in England are students more magnificently housed, though there may be buildings that seem more adapted to student life, perhaps, and Prior Park has nothing to remind us of the halls and quadrangles of Oxford, or of places like Eton or Winchester. Architecturally, this is a palace, with the great and imposing aspect which we find in such places as Blenheim and other creations of Vanbrugh. To describe it at length is, however, unnecessary. The massive central block, with its vast Corinthian hexastyle portico and pediment, and the balustrade with which the structure is crested, is striking enough, and is connected by arcades with outlying pavilions or wings, now converted into the Colleges of St. Peter and St. Paul.

The situation is superb, and has dictated both the character of the house and the disposition of its glorious park. It stands at the head of the Vale of Widcombe, 100ft. below the level of Combe Down, and 400ft. above the City of Bath, over which there is an imposing prospect, closed by the distant height of Lansdown. Being thus upon a slope, a terraced formation became necessary, and nothing could surpass the excellence of the arrangement, which will be seen in the pictures. The great curved stairways, with their statuary adornments and urns, and their exquisite balustrades, are remarkably good. The place commands the whole range of the beautifully-wooded park below, with the exquisite Palladian bridge crossing the lake as a prominent note in the landscape, and the gardens are very beautiful, though extremely simple, and the whole estate is preserved with traditional care. It may be said here that the house itself is the residence of the President of the College, while the wing pavilions of Mr. Allen's mansion are devoted one to junior students, and the other to those more advanced, and that such as desire to embrace the clerical state pass from the St. Paul's College to the President's School of Theology and Philosophy.

Copyright.   THE GREAT STAIRWAY.   "Country Life."

THE PORTICO AND SOUTHERN WING.

But it is now time to turn to the extraordinary man who built Prior Park. Ralph Allen appears to have been the son of one John Allen, the host of the "Duke William," or the "Old Duke," at St. Blazey, in Cornwall. His grandmother kept the post-office at St. Columb, and it was the good fortune of the boy, while he was staying with her, to attract the attention of a postal inspector, who procured him a place in the post-office at Bath. There young Allen did himself credit, and, by detecting a Jacobite plot, won the favour of General Wade, whose natural daughter he afterwards

LOOKING NORTH.

THE VIEW OVER THE PARK AND THE CITY OF BATH.

THE NORTH COLLEGE.

THE SOUTH COLLEGE.

THE CARRIAGE DRIVE.

married. In 1745 his enthusiasm led him to form a corps of Bath City Volunteers at his own expense. He very soon rose to be Deputy Postmaster, and, having long been convinced of the fatuity of a postal arrangement which might send a letter from Bath to Worcester round by way of London, he set himself to devise a system of cross-country posts, which were officially approved. His scheme was adopted in April, 1720. Allen at once became a "farmer" of these posts, and it is stated that from 1720 up to 1764, when he died, his profits on the business were not less than £12,000 a year. He also turned his attention to the development of the rich mineral resources of Bath, and, by opening quarries at Combe Down, became a great employer of labour, and very popular in the locality. Thus did Ralph Allen make himself so prominent a man in the West of England that he was known as the "Man of Bath." Once he was Mayor of the city; but he seems always to have ruled the affairs of the municipality, and there is a caricature representing him as the "One-headed Corporation."

Ten years after Mr. Allen had introduced his cross-country posts he set about the work of building his splendid mansion out of the stone which he quarried. His lofty ideas confounded the architect, John Wood, to whose taste Bath owes so much, but he was able to carry them out in the form in which we see them to-day. Here he enjoyed his leisure in beautifying the place and in laying out and planting the grounds. He had another house at Bathampton, and he built that picturesque tower known as "Sham Castle," which stands on a hill south-east of Bath.

We have so far seen only one side of Ralph Allen's character—that of the shrewd man of business. But the prosperous postmaster was filled with the spirit of munificence, and he freely disbursed of his plenty for the alleviation of the distressed. It is said that he never expended less than £1,000 a year in charity, and he did much for the Bath Hospital, and encased St. Bartholomew's Hospital in London with stone. He was greatly esteemed by all his contemporaries, and Prior

Park became the resort of many wits and writers of the time. Among those he befriended was Fielding, who has typified his friend for all time as Squire Allworthy in "Tom Jones." In that book he describes Prior Park in glowing terms, speaking of the splendid outlook and the multitudinous trees, omitting the Palladian bridge, but extending his vision beyond the height of Lansdown.

Fielding dedicated "Amelia" to Allen, and after the novelist's death his children were cared for by his benefactor. Pope also was a friend and admirer of Allen, and in the Epilogue to the "Satires of Horace" speaks of him in a couplet which is familiar to every ear:

"Let humble Allen, with awk-
 ward shame,
 Do good by stealth and blush to
 find it fame."

THE MIDDLE STAGE OF THE GREAT STAIRWAY.

The friendship at one time was interrupted, owing, it is said, to the poet's desire to impose Martha Blount upon the family at Prior Park, or, according to another story, to that lady's having demanded Mr. Allen's chariot to convey her to the Catholic Chapel in Bath. Whatever might have been the cause of the breach, it was made good, and Allen continued to shower favours upon Pope and his friends. One of these was Warburton, who married Geraldine Tucker, Allen's favourite niece, and who was appointed by Pitt, it is said at the instance of the philanthropist, Bishop of Salisbury. Pitt was an intimate friend of Allen's, and when the latter died he left the great statesman £1,000, "as the best of friends, as well as

the most upright and ablest of Ministers that have adorned our country." Pitt, Warburton, Hurd, and other writers of the time, all speak of the splendid hospitality, the great natural ability, the simple manners, and the elevated tastes of Allen. When the philanthropist died, in 1764, he left one son, who became Comptroller of the Bye-Letter Office, and of whom comparatively little is known. Such was the man who created Prior Park, and it is excellent testimony to his enlightened taste and classic knowledge, that he chose a fine situation and built a house which stood high among the palatial dwellings of the land, while he disposed the whole of the surroundings with a master hand to contribute to the effect.

THE PALLADIAN BRIDGE.

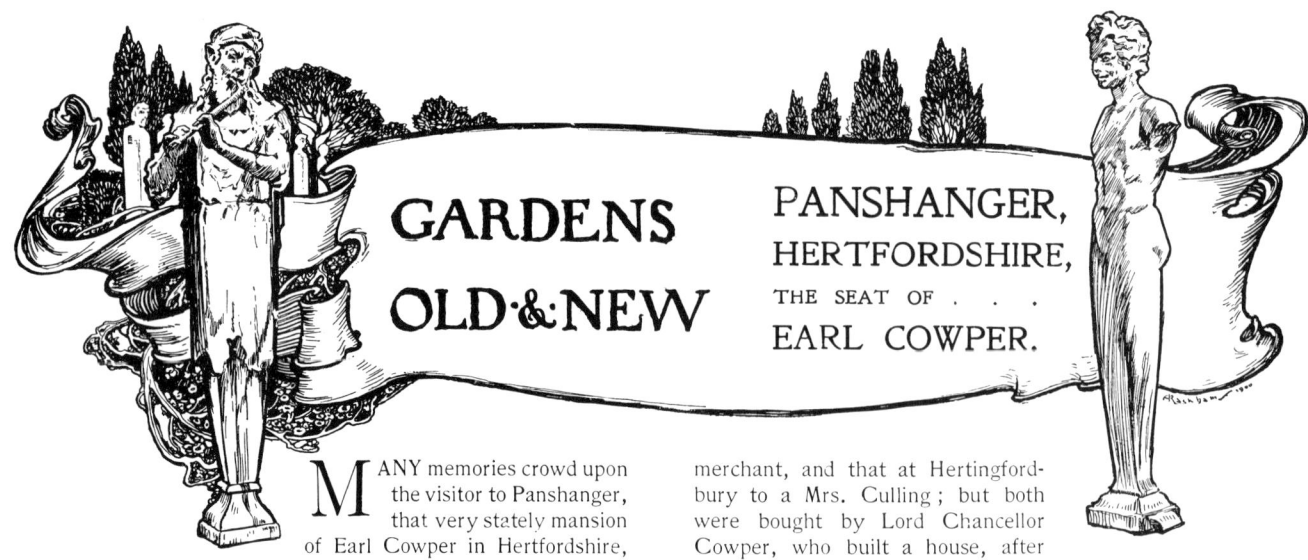

GARDENS OLD·&·NEW

PANSHANGER, HERTFORDSHIRE, THE SEAT OF . . . EARL COWPER.

MANY memories crowd upon the visitor to Panshanger, that very stately mansion of Earl Cowper in Hertfordshire, a place possessing all the characteristic features of a great house, and in particular having a very large and finely-timbered park, with the pretty river Mimram running through the midst of it, and a truly noble garden for its adornment. The house is comparatively modern, and of the Gothic of the beginning of this century—a bad period, unfortunately, for any house to have been built in—and it is very famous for its magnificent collection of pictures. It stands in a fine position on the brow of a hill commanding a prospect of the park, which lies between Cole Green and Hertingfordbury, and of the surrounding country. The Cole Green estate belonged early in the last century to one Elwes, a London merchant, and that at Hertingford-bury to a Mrs. Culling; but both were bought by Lord Chancellor Cowper, who built a house, after the year 1740, in a favourable situation near Cole Green. Later on, when considerable additions had been made to the estate, the fifth Earl Cowper decided to erect the present house on the higher ground. The noble collection of Italian pictures had been made chiefly by the third Earl, who passed a considerable part of his life in Florence.

The present Earl Cowper takes very great interest in the estate and its gardens, and our pictures reveal the condition of perfection in which the latter are maintained. The situation is favourable, for the park is picturesquely undulated and the woodland fine, whilst the mansion presents a most imposing appearance in its setting of varied green.

THE TERRACE GARDEN.

THE NEW FORMAL GARDEN.

In many places the walls are wreathed with climbing plants, and give support to such growths as the splendid Magnolia grandiflora, whilst some of them, as on the north side, are richly mantled with ivy.

There is a character of great stateliness in the noble pleasure grounds at Panshanger. The broad expanses of green lawn, upon which mighty trees cast down their vast domain of shade, combine with the features nearer at hand to compose surpassingly beautiful pictures. It is a goodly prospect, indeed, a region of delectable charms, that we survey, wherein Nature and Art together have worked to produce the glory of the gardens. The formal character prevails largely, though the diversity of treatment leaves room for much that is natural and picturesque. In the first style is the "box garden" at one end of the terrace, where are the arms of Cowper and De Grey grown and cut in well-trimmed box. The Dairy Garden, on the east side of the terrace in front of the great conservatory, a sweet place with a quaintness of its own, is formed in a similar manner. On the other hand, the rock garden, a delightful

A BACCHIC VASE.

retreat, is full of natural charm, and is adorned with many of the plants collected by the Countess Cowper during her travels. Ferns are grown here in great abundance, the British varieties being very prolific. The rose garden, again, is extremely delightful, with pillar, standard, and climbing plants. Everywhere extreme richness characterises the place. The hardy flowers are well planted in clumps for effect, and grow in great numbers, and the splendid woodland forms a fine background for the radiant charms of the flower-beds and the more sober attractions of the lawns. In short, turn which way we may, there is something to satisfy the eye in the pleasure grounds of Panshanger.

To the many pictures accompanying this article must be left the full illustration of the charms of the place. The beauties of the garden do not end with the gay and fragrant things that grow so luxuriantly, for it has architectural accessories of excellent and appropriate character. We should go far, for example, before we found so splendid a garden adornment, of classic aspect, as the great Bacchic vase we depict.

THE ROSE GARDEN.

THE BROAD WALK.

The park is truly magnificent, and an entrancing view is revealed from the terrace. The wide valley of the Mimram opens out beneath the range of hills that give the place its most conspicuous character, and the stream widens below into a lake, which reflects its glorious surroundings. The landscape is beautifully wooded, and the oak, beech, Spanish chestnut, sycamore, and lime prevail. An island in the lake is a delightful resort, threaded by footpaths amid its growth of shrubs and trees, where nodding daffodils and sweet primroses give their glory to the spring. A romantic view of the valley is disclosed from it, and the babbling river may be traced from where it issues from behind the wood to its lower course among the long grass of the meadows.

The extraordinarily beautiful woodland derives a good deal of its character from the care with which planting has been conducted, and the healthy growth that results from attention devoted to the work of thinning. The oaks are splendid, and of the conifer tribe the deodars and the cedar of Lebanon are conspicuous, with the stiffer Wellingtonia gigantea and the Chili pine (Araucaria imbricata). But the pride of the park is certainly the "Panshanger Oak," which for two centuries or more has been famous, though now showing some signs of being past its prime. The tree stands on a broad lawn a little to the west of the house, and was described by Arthur Young in 1709 as the "Great Oak," and in

1719 was estimated to contain 315 cubic feet of timber. A measurement made in 1805 gave 799 cubic feet, and excellent Strutt, who lived for some time at the interesting village of Tewin near by, and loved the tree, which he etched in his great "Sylva Britannica" (1830), has much to say about it. At the present time the dimensions of the trunk are 20ft. 4in. at 5ft. from the ground. The charm of the tree, however, resides not so much in its size as in its superb form. The trunk rises unbroken for a height of about 12ft., and then the giant boughs sweep out on every side, forming a circle 100yds.

THE SOUTH FRONT.

across, while the vast symmetrical mountain of foliage above is tall "as the mast of some great ammiral."

It may be interesting to record what old Strutt says about the tree, which he tells us in his time appeared not to have reached its meridian. "The waving lightness of its feathered branches, dipping down towards its stem, to the very ground, the straightness of its trunk, and the redundancy of its foliage, all give it a character opposite to that of antiquity, and fit it for the cultivated and sequestered pleasure grounds which form part of the domain of Earl Cowper, at Panshanger, in Hertfordshire ; where it stands surrounded with evergreens and lighter shrubs, of which it seems at once the guardian and the pride. It is 19ft. in circumference at 3ft. from the ground, and contains 1,000ft. of timber. On looking at an object at once so graceful and so noble, raising its green head towards the skies, rejoicing in the sunshine, and imbibing the breath of Heaven at every pore, we cannot but feel equal wonder and admiration when we consider the tininess of its origin, the slenderness of its infant state, and the daily unfolding powers of its imperceptible, yet rapid, progress." The good tree-lover begins his book with a description of this monster of the grove, and goes on to quote Evelyn where he says, "So it is that our tree, like man, whose inverted symbol he is, being sown in corruption, rises in glory, and by little and little—ascending into one hard erect stem of comely dimensions, beneath a solid tower, as it were. And that this, which but lately a single ant could easily have borne to his little cavern, should now become capable of resisting the fury and braving the rage of the most impetuous storms—*magni mehercle artificis, clausisse totum in tam exiguo, et horror est consideranti.*"

"Hail old patrician trees !" may we well say with Cowley when we linger in the green gloom of the Panshanger Oak and its hoary brothers, possessing each "its charm peculiar." It has always been the

THE SEAT AND FOUNTAIN.

pride of the English gentleman to love his neighbour trees, and Washington Irving discovered in this the chief characteristic of the good old Englishman. Many a time, alas! have the ancient trunk and the young hamadryad together bowed beneath the stroke of need, or been laid low at the call of some spendthrift necessity. No such storm, most happily, has ever swept through the woods of Panshanger, and long may the mighty oak, in Ovid's words, "tower o'er its subject trees, itself a grove." It is right to remember, in the presence of such a giant, how great a part the oak—" the unwedgeable and gnarled oak "—has played in English national life as "the father of ships." Old Collingwood, dropping acorns into the hedges, was a glorious type of the Englishman, preparing in the embryo

"Those sapling oaks which at Britannia's call
Might heave their trunks mature into the main,
And float the bulwarks of her liberty."

THE DAIRY GARDEN.

All through the land there are oaks which sprang from this patriotic ideal, and therefore as a part of national life is the oak to the Englishman.

The charms of a walk through the park and gardens of Panshanger are many indeed. Everywhere the careful hand of Art, working in the spirit of Nature, has done its unobtrusive work. Look, for example, at the green lawns, with their enclosing trees, and at the delightful vista opened out from the beautiful broad walk. It is pleasant then to stroll to "Cowper's seat"; not that from which the poet surveyed the sylvan scene, but a more modern successor at the same place.

The poet was a nephew of the Lord Chancellor, and loved the simple delights of Panshanger. In 1769 he wrote to Mrs. Cowper: "If the Major make up a small packet of seeds that will make a figure in a garden where we have

Copyright. THE BOX GARDEN. *"Country Life."*

little besides jessamine and honeysuckle, such a packet as one may put in one's fob, I will promise to take care of them, as I ought to value natives of the park."

Cowper loved his garden well, and the woodland and orchard not less. Perhaps he was thinking of the care bestowed at Panshanger when he wrote, with practical knowledge and poetic force, of the "self-sequester'd man":

"Proud of his well-spread walls, he views his trees,
That meet, no barren interval between,
With pleasure more than e'en their fruits afford,
Which, save himself who trains them, none can feel.
These, therefore, are his own peculiar charge;
No meaner hand may discipline the shoots,
None but his steel approach them. What is weak,
Distemper'd, or has lost prolific pow'rs,
Impair'd by age, his unrelenting hand
Dooms to the knife; nor does he spare the soft
And succulent, that feeds its giant growth,
But barren, at th' expense of neighb'ring twigs
Less ostentatious, and yet studded thick
With hopeful gems."

A little to the east of Cowper's seat is a delightful region, where the hawthorn blossoms in the spring, and in the park to the south is a fine avenue of elms and limes. But it would be difficult to exhaust the interests of Panshanger. One notable feature is a magnificent Beaumontia grandiflora superba, for which the place is famous, shoots of its glorious flowers having been shown often before the Royal Horticultural Society.

Lastly, it is interesting to note — and on many estates the same thing might be done—that the river Mimram is "harnessed" for the useful work of pumping up water to the mansion and the fruit and kitchen gardens.

Nature is doing her own work directed by the hand of man, and this is but an extension of the essence of all good gardening. From every point of view, therefore, is Panshanger a place to be admired.

Copyright. A CORNER OF THE SUNKEN GARDEN. *"Country Life."*

GARDENS OLD & NEW

SHIPTON COURT, OXFORD, . . .

THE SEAT OF . . .

Sir George Compton Reade.

SHIPTON COURT is situated in a village of the same name, distinguished from the many Shiptons which are dotted over Oxfordshire as Shipton-under-Wychwood. Years ago, before the Clearing Act of 1850, the forest of Wychwood extended down over the slopes at the foot of which the village lies. But since the disafforesting took place the borders of the forest have gradually receded, until they are at the nearest point some miles from the village itself, and the name alone remains to perplex the casual visitor.

The Court began mainly with the advent of the Stuarts. Part of the house appears to be good work of the sixteenth century, but the main portion of the fabric dates from about the year 1603—the date of Chastleton, near by—and was built by one of the family of Lacey, who held it during most of the century. From them it passed, in 1673, to the Reades, whose monuments remain on the walls of the parish church— Sir Thomas Reade (Clerk of the Green Cloth to George II.)—

Sir John—Sir Compton—Baronet after Baronet—and at the present time it is let to Mrs. David Reid. The house is built of the grey stone of the country, and is another illustration of the fact that the builders of those days understood their art. Placed on the slope of a little valley, the house is a story higher on the east than on the west, and springs so straight and steep from the grass alley at its foot, that its sheer front dominates the terraces and fish-ponds like the keep of a fortress. Thick walls and massive foundations endow it with an air of strength and endurance that are yet only the beginning of its charm, for gable after gable stands out clear-cut against the sky, and on each face and at every corner the outline of the house assumes new picturesqueness, angle overlapping angle in a design perpetually broken and yet never irregular.

And, if one must attempt to analyse the effect of such a building upon the eye, it is found in a beauty that continually claims and holds the attention, that to one pacing below it

THE WEST FRONT.

"Country Life."

THE EAST FRONT AND THE UPPER FISH-POND.

THE LAWN AND ITS FLOWER BORDER.

offers at every step a fresh development of the first plan ; not the beauty of a plain building magnificently ornamented, but the miracle of a living organism, the creation of an art in its very flower.

The great charm of the gardens lies not so much in the variety and rarity of shrub and flower—though there is an abundance of both—but in the perfect way in which they have been adapted to, and harmonise with, the architecture of the house. This is well shown in the illustration where a long grass alley, running the whole length of the garden and flanked by a yew hedge, sweeps one side of the house and on

THE TERRACE WALK.

the other is raised to a terrace, which leads to the entrance door. Unfortunately, the hand of the "improver" was at work here nearly a century ago, with the result that almost all the windows of the first and second stories were then deprived of their mullions, though, fortunately, one side of the house has been spared to vindicate its original beauty and to act as a deterrent to further vandalism.

The best view of the house as a whole is that in the picture taken from the meadow, access to which is obtained from the garden through an iron gate and down a flight of stone steps. The waters of the fish-pond, which hardly appears in this view, are seen lower down. In "Skelton's Oxfordshire" is an engraving which shows the upper pond of the two before the ground above had been raised into a lawn, and when it sloped gradually down to the water's edge ; and at the end of the lower pond, shown in the illustration, the old arrangement still remains.

One of the most conspicuous features of the place are the yew hedges, which form the main lines in the design, and divide off the garden into different parts. The north garden, with the fountain in the centre, is separated by a hedge of this kind, as well as by a wall of goodly dimensions, from the orchard and rose garden below it, and from the west front by a terrace, flanked by another wall and the ubiquitous yew hedge beyond.

From the north garden is obtained the best view of the

older portion of the house. The end window of the dining-room opens upon a flight of stone steps, which lead down to the fountain and the pink and white hawthorns that lend a blaze of brighter colour in the spring to the eternal green and grey around. And here advantage has been taken of the slope of the ground to add very greatly to the privacy of the gardens, for the approach to the kitchens and the basement generally has been led between stone walls, so roofed over in part as to form a terrace above and a quiet covered way below. Thus there is no back to the house, and the gardens encircle it completely.

Another illustration affords a view of the west front, now screened from the road by a mass of yews and boxes. Originally there was nothing between the road and the house but the hedge and a low curtain wall, which appear in the foreground, and a pair of magnificent walnut trees. An excellent view of the unchanged front is to be found in Neale's "Views of Seats," a work which throws valuable light on the state of many country houses at the beginning of the nineteenth century.

Close to the south-west corner of the house are the stables, built in the same manner and as delightfully as the house. They form two sides of a great stable-yard, in one corner of which stands the picturesque dovecote, capable of holding 2,000 pigeons, and standing sentinel over the herbaceous border beneath it. The wall along the line of which

Copyright.   *"Country Life."*

THE TERRACE, LOOKING SOUTH.

it is built is typical of the majesty of design and breadth of conception inspired by which the old builders, undeterred by cost either of labour or of material, carried out their plans; their walls, to be worthy of the name, should be 15ft., and sometimes 20ft., high; their hedges, to be hedges, should be 8ft. thick. Their work, two and three hundred years old, still remains to testify to the care and skill which they lavished upon it.

As the visitor approaches the house under the shadow of one of these monumental walls, and, turning in at the entrance

Copyright.   *"Country Life."*

THE HOUSE FROM THE MEADOW.

THE NORTH FRONT.

gate, looks from the deep shade of the avenue across the road to the sunlight playing on the gables, he is carried back to a time when men built and planned and planted not for themselves, but for their successors and generations to come.

Close to the house, but screened by these stone walls and yew hedges, runs the road from Burford, dipping down here from its bleak or burnt uplands into the shelter and shadows of the valley. In old days, one fancies, men did not hate to see the road from their windows. To the dweller in the country the highway was his link with the world, and with those who passed his gate, either travellers upon their business or the neighbours, rich and poor, who made his society and perhaps followed his leading. Now we must shut out the world, buy up the right-of-way, plant out the railway, in a vain effort to forget that our treasure is in the city, and our hearts turn there also.

But here the road runs by, and beyond it the avenue leads not to the house, but away from it. For directly opposite the gate begins a long straight walk

between tall and close-set limes, which with fields on either hand passes away into a pleasant medley of wood and grass, involuntarily named "The Pleasaunce." Upstairs in the house the middle rooms of the west front look right down this avenue, and it is always with a fresh shock of delighted wonder that the guest, late arrived overnight, throws open his window and, with eyes and ears yet scarcely cleansed from the dust and din of Piccadilly, looks out through the morning sunshine into that long dim tunnel of cool green light. The avenue draws his feet with a gentle insistence. It seems to lead to something different in kind from the stately house and the ordered garden, to a ruin, perhaps, or to the scene of a tragedy. Sometimes it seems a walk designed for meditation; sometimes rather one of the " places which pale passion loves." And at the end of it is nothing strange—only a wilderness of thickly-shaded paths and unexpected waters. For it comes suddenly upon a pond at the foot of a mighty cedar, where the wild duck rise and are away in

THE STABLES FROM THE GARDEN.

FROM THE GRASS WALK.

a moment, and the silence falls again on the wood and the water and the little island in the midst of the water. So the walks lead on, now by the side of a sleepy channel, now at the edge of a meadow, but always under the trees, until the great green cloister is all trodden, and at the end of the vista the sun shines again upon the grey gables of the house.

THE LOWER POND.

GARDENS OLD & NEW

KING'S WESTON, GLOUCESTER,
THE SEAT OF . . MR. R. NAPIER MILES.

THIS volume depicts and describes several gardens in the vicinity of Bath and Bristoı, that favoured land where many people have been attracted to dwell, rich in great houses and beautiful examples of gardenage, where there is a pictorial character in the landscape and a generous richness in the soil that are the chief elements in the beauty of a chosen part of England. King's Weston is a remarkable house, in a fine situation and amid very lovely surroundings, in the neighbourhood of Shirehampton, commanding superb views of the diversified, romantic, and gloriously wooded country. The mansion dates from the year 1711, and has the solid classic qualities of the reign of Queen Anne. The pleasant colour of the old Bath stone, weathered and mossy, lends a charm to the Corinthian pilasters, the pediment, the cornice, and the crowning urns of the structure.

An uncommon feature is found in the design of the house, for the chimneys above are quite unusual in character, and take an architectural form and grouping rare and effective. We do not wonder at the classic proportions and harmonious features of the structure when we learn that it is a work of Vanbrugh. We do not know whether he designed it wholly, but it bears the mark of his hand. The tough fighting man who became an architect and then a dramatist, laid many a heavy load on earth, as his punning epitaph says, but there is some uncertainty as to his actual share in the design of certain buildings. Castle Howard in Yorkshire, Blenheim, and Greenwich Hospital were wholly or partly designed by him. We therefore look at King's Weston with a good deal of interest.

But what will most impress the visitor to the house, and the reader who sees our pictures, will be the extremely peculiar manner in which Nature is tempted and encouraged to invade

THE WEST FRONT.

THE GARDEN-HOUSE.

THE   WATER   GARDEN.

the realm of Art.   Here is a union of the two such as will be seen in very few places.   The " flower in the crannied wall " is familiar.   There is a charm in the weathered brick giving hospitality to a crowd of beautiful things, and crowned with white and red valerian, or snap-dragon, or wallflowers, or with some other radiant thing that finds good rootage where soil and moisture and sun are to its liking.   Such things we may find at King's Weston, as in many West Country gardens ; but what we note as individual here is that flowers are invited to root themselves in the crevices in the steps that lead down from the mansion.   Alpine flowers are flourishing in the stair-way with many gay companions, and giving floral beauty where it is quite uncommon.   There is something fresh and

original in the pleasure of finding flowers garnishing thus the way by which we descend ; something, we may say, especially appropriate to the gentler sex, where Flora attends their coming.   On the other hand, there may be those to whom this plan of cultivating flowers in the hollows of substantial masonry may not seem right.   We are accustomed, perhaps, to regard the vesting of stonework with thick moss and flowers as the proper accompaniment of decay or rough-ness of construction.   What is suitable, some may say, to the old garden wall, to the broken rockery, or to the clefts of the rugged stone support that holds up the higher bank flanking the garden path, and over which we look to the fair denizens of the woodland shade, may not be suitable to the regular masonry of the house and its immediate approaches.   But

King's Weston is a standing witness that this manner of gardening is, or may be, good.   There is harmony in the result where some might expect incongruity, and the investing approach of Nature to the house gives many a clinging plant to clothe the cool stonework.   Yet shall we invite her not only to clothe our house, but, as it were, to enter intimately into the structure ?   *Quot homines, tot sententiæ.*   It is a legitimate matter of opinion, but we may, at least, gather one lesson—that there are many forms of beauty in gardening, each appealing to a particular taste, and that it ill befits a gardener to be a doctrinaire, pinning his faith wholly to this school or that, adopting one manner to set his ban upon another, and rejecting, in his rigid view of his art, a good many beauties that otherwise he

THE   FLORAL   STAIRWAY.

might have used and made others enjoy. The gardener, in short, must be a cosmopolitan. His work is to accept and select, and to invest his garden with character and adornments appropriate to soil and situation, so that it expresses an individuality. So shall the garden, as Schiller says, be Nature invested with a soul and exalted by Art. It shall be the place where the man expresses himself in his own conception of Nature adapted to his needs or his inward likings. Whether it be a walled enclosure, with openings like the gates of a Roman camp, or a great pleasaunce upon a terraced slope, or merely a homely garden, there shall be individuality in it. It may be a place where the strawberry-bed neighbours the roses, and where he wanders among apples, cherries, plums, medlars, and filberts, with a multitude of flowers, small and great, in their company. This would be an individual garden. And so, at this beautiful West Country seat, we find personal character in the floral adornment of the solid masonry.

And we see at King's Weston that this idea of welcoming the garden in the very approaches to the house is not confined to one flight of steps, or to one side of the house, but is borne out in a free and delightful use of plants and flowers in pots and boxes. The care which is devoted everywhere to wall and water gardening is excellent testimony to the love of flowers which has beautified this old place. The rectangular pond garden is gloriously festooned upon its walls, and, in combination with borders of hardy flowers, there is an abundance of moisture-loving plants, of the beautiful things that will grow and flourish in the crannies of walls bordering water, while the water itself is made rich in a plenteous growth of lovely water-lilies. This garden, in fact, is a perfect study in this special class of gardening. Especially charming is the view of the old garden-house, with the ivy-wreathed wall, and the brilliant broom, and the lilies, irises, poppies, and ornamental garden thistles, to name no others, reflected in the glassy sheet. There is a world of beauty in gardening like this, giving radiance and sweetness combined. And such gardening at King's Weston

THE GARDEN STEPS.

is wholly in keeping with the character adopted nearer the dwelling.

The garden dates from the same period as the house.

THE ECHO WALK.

having been formed about the year 1711. The "view garden," we are told, is supposed to occupy the site of an ancient market-place, and the ivy-covered column there is said to be the original market cross. The square walled garden is quite characteristic, and has one wall covered by an old Turkey fig tree, celebrated for its age and for the extraordinary size of its fruit. Two or three trees cover entirely one long wall, and are remarkable for their prolific growth and rich fruitage. Extremely attractive is this quaint and quiet retreat, with the rockery, the curiously cut spindle-shaped yews, the yuccas, and the sequestered character of the place. The walled garden was dear to our ancestors, being but another form of the well-hedged parterre —a place with ample sun, not shadowed by trees, and sheltered well from all the winds that blow.

Then how attractive is the Echo Walk at King's Weston, with the lovely greensward flanking the path, the standard roses adorning it, the glorious masses of flowers on either side, the fine plants in tubs, and the noble elms, pines, and other

THE GARDEN TEMPLE.

ornamental trees. The happiest spirit directed the formation of this wholly beautiful place, and the same spirit maintains it in the perfection which our picture discloses. It affords a contrast of charm and character which is delightful, and opposes a measure of stately formality to the picturesqueness which reigns elsewhere, thus adding a very pleasing and attractive variety to the gardens. The terrace, too, is very beautiful, looking out over the Avonmouth, with the fine balustered wall, a notable example of good garden architecture, comparable with many we have described, the green grass within, and the adorning yuccas and the noble view without, and those grand trees which rise majestically from the park below. It is not necessary to describe King's Weston much further. We have suggested the special character, and our pictures will do the rest.

There are charms both in the classic architecture of the mansion and the garden-houses and in the rare beauty of the garden, and we find special interest in the manner in which the qualities of the two are combined.

THE TERRACE.

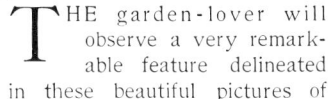

GARDENS OLD & NEW

HENBURY COURT, GLOUCESTERSHIRE,

THE SEAT OF . . . MR. T. J. LENNARD.

THE garden-lover will observe a very remarkable feature delineated in these beautiful pictures of charming Henbury. We have seen yew hedges in many places; we have insisted upon their value very often, for are they not a glory of the English garden, appealing, by their ancient aspect and curious associations, to our sentiments, and wholly satisfactory and pleasing, as a relief and contrast either to gay masses of flowers or to green expanses of turf? "The yew wood, the true wood," is the wood of Old England, the brother-ancient of the hoary oak, companion of the mighty beech, noble where it stands unfettered, and beautiful where it assumes its place in the garden world.

In few places in England are there arches of yew like those at Henbury Court, which, however, have much in common with the arches in the famous yew walk at Cleeve Prior. Their unusual character and the overhanging mushroom-like heads of the yews themselves have a quaint and indefinable charm. They grace a very beautiful house and a charming region of the West Country, for Henbury is a near neighbour of Bristol, being, in fact, only five miles away. There are few who do not know something of the peaceful beauties of that favoured land. The high downs thereabout afford magnificent prospects, extending over the surrounding country and across the Severn to the mountains of Wales, while the valleys are embowered in woodland of surpassing loveliness, and the many fine houses and seats are rich in their attractions of evergreens, flowering banks, and wide lawns. King's Weston, one of Vanbrugh's best designs, surrounded by a singularly beautiful garden, has already been illustrated in these pages, and the view from Weston Ridge, which is covered with the finest turf, towards the Severn and the Avon, is of ravishing beauty.

Henbury Court is its neighbour, and is a house of character quite distinct. It was built in the memorable year of Revolution, 1688, but has gone through various changes, and

THE UPPER LAWN AND THE CHURCH.

now, in its general architectural
features, recalls the houses of an
earlier time.   To describe the
mansion is unnecessary, for its
excellent gables, high roofs, and
mullioned windows, all very
charming, are well seen in the
pictures.   The land hereabout
was monastic property, and the
location bears the evidences of
antiquity.   The road that passes
by is the old pack-horse way
from Bristol to Gloucester, and
many thirsty wayfarers have
doubtless tarried in the village
of Henbury, and recently in
levelling the ground at Henbury
Court a skeleton was discovered,
which seems to point to an
ancient burial-ground having been
here.

The mansion stands in
a fine position, and the
grounds are very appropriate,
with excellent grass slopes
and a most attractive disposition of trees, bushes, and flowers.

At the beginning of the century the ancient yew hedges
were a solid wall of greenery, evidently of great age,
but it was boldly decided to cut them into arches, and the
result was undoubtedly an addition to the attractiveness
of the effect, an enhancing of the form and character.   Such
an operation should of course be entered upon with great
consideration, especially in the case of old hedges, but none
can say that the arch-cutting at Henbury was other than a
conspicuous success.   It is recorded, however, that the yews
were a long time in shooting after the first arch was cut.   It
was as if they resented a little the intrusion of the tree-cutter's
hand.   But the yew is the friend of man; it lends itself to his

THE   SOUTH   FRONT.

taste and his uses, and is kindly in its response to his skill;
and so the lofty hedges of Henbury at length budded anew.   The
two lines of curiously-shaped trees partly enclose a velvet-like
croquet lawn, which is in a situation that could not be bettered,
since it is in close proximity to masses of beautiful flowers,
and there is a landscape outlook that is really superb.
How delightful is the turf of English gardens, how soft and
velvety are our lawns.   The college lawns of England are
doubtless the richest of all.   Thus did Nathaniel Hawthorne
feel their indescribable beauty, shadowed by their ancient
trees, living a quiet life of centuries, nursed and tended with
such care and so sheltered from rude winds that they seemed
the happiest of lawns.   At picturesque Henbury, too, there are

THE   GARDEN   REST.

THE YEWS AT EVENTIDE.

THE OLD FLOWER GARDEN.

the same green lawns and tall ancient trees, heavy masses of foliage, and sunny glimpses beneath green branches and through arches of yew. Altogether the effect is particularly quaint and fascinating, and we see that the hand of good judgment has fashioned the garden in this attractive way.

In this descriptive series, it has several times been remarked that the effect of yew hedges in relation with flower masses is charming. This may again be observed in the picture of the old flower garden at Henbury, where fragrant groups of carnations and other beautiful things in profusion make sweet the air. Gloucester and Somerset are counties famous for their floral charms. The climate, the soil, and the love of such things which the country gentlemen manifest,

conduce to a richness that seems to surpass what one finds elsewhere. Henbury is, indeed, distinguished by its great wealth of blossom, which invests its garden with the twin delights of colour and fragrance.

The church, as is often the case in country villages, is near the house, and its substantial character may be gathered from one of our pictures, where it is disclosed through the quaint arches of green, making a very pleasing picture from the garden. Although old, much of it is modern, for it was enlarged in 1833. One curious feature in it is the great divergence of the chancel to the north of the line of the nave. Slight inclinations of this kind are common, but in few places is the feature so marked as in this structure. The church is generally Early English in style, with Decorated details of excellent character. It contains the monuments of many prominent families of the neighbourhood, and notably those of Sir Robert Southwell, M.P., of King's Weston, Envoy to Portugal, and President of the Royal Society, who died in 1702, and Edward, Lord De Clifford, dating from 1777.

Although Henbury Court has no famous history or associations, it well deserves to be noted as a country house of excellent character, of which much has been made, and which is valued and cared for by those who love its charms, and who know what the delights are of the beautiful region of England in which it is enshrined. The simple character of its gardens, with the few marked features we have alluded to, is chief among its charms.

THE WEST FRONT.

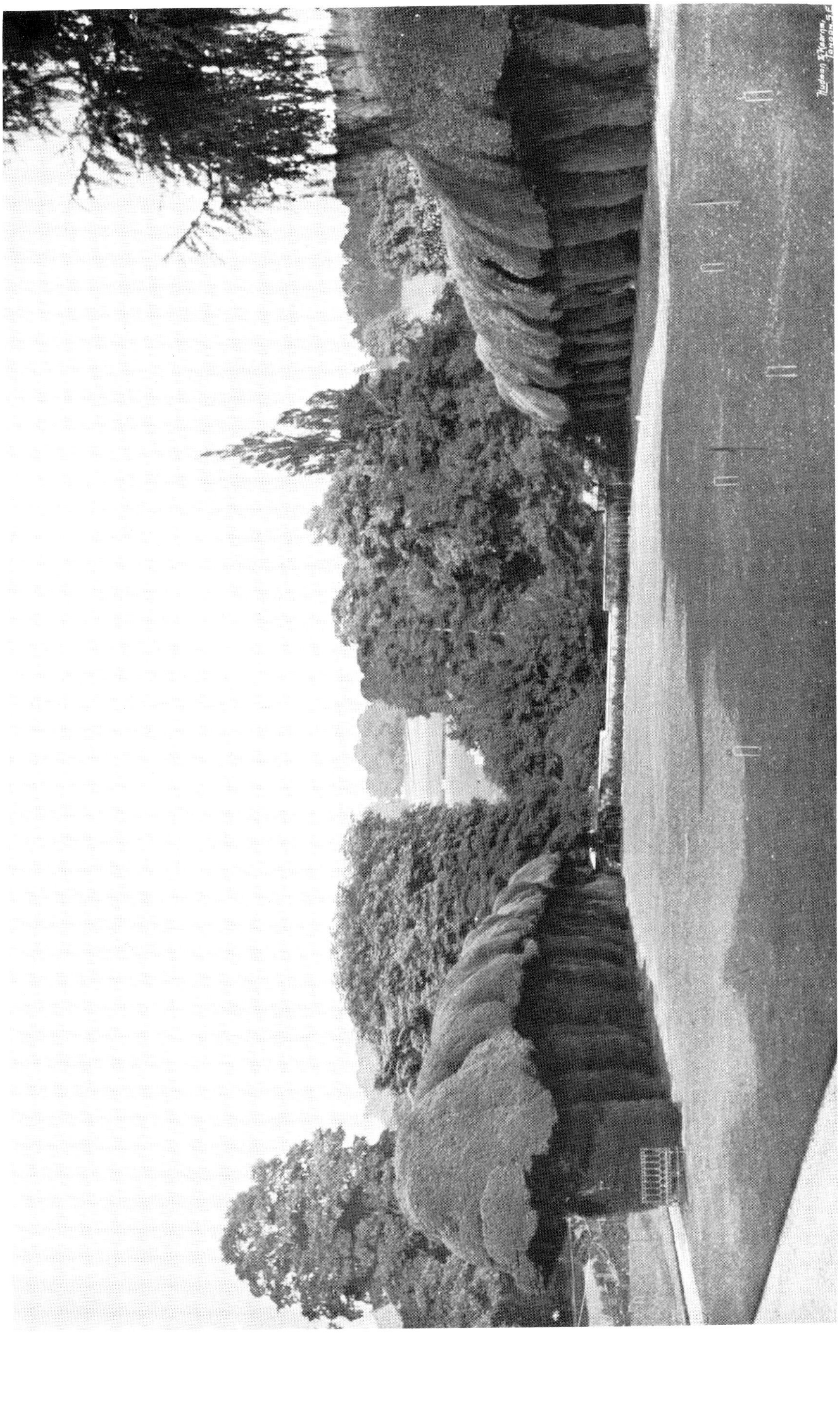

Copyright. THE CROQUET LAWN. "Country Life"

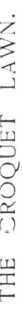

GARDENS OLD·&·NEW

DRAYTON HOUSE, NORTHAMPTON,
THE SEAT OF . . .
Mrs. Stopford-Sackville.

E.F BRICKDALE

"WELL! we hurried away to Drayton an hour before dinner," wrote that inimitable gossip Horace Walpole to George Montague, in July, 1763. "Oh, the dear old place! You would be transported with it! The front is a brave, strong castle wall, embattled and loopholed for defence. Passing the great gate you come to a sumptuous but narrow modern court, behind which rises the old mansion, all towers and turrets. The house is excellent, has a vast hall, ditto dining-room, king's chamber, trunk-gallery at the top of the house, and seven or eight different apartments. Then it is covered with portraits, crammed with old china, furnished richly, and not a rag in it under forty, fifty, or a thousand years old; but not a bed or a chair that has lost a tooth, or got a grey hair, so well are they preserved. I rummaged it from head to foot, examined every spangled bed and enamelled pair of bellows, for such there are; in short, I do not believe the old mansion was ever better pleased with an inhabitant since the days of Walter de Drayton, except when it received its divine old mistress. If one could honour her more than one did before, it would be to see with what religion she keeps up the old dwelling and customs; as well as old servants, who you may imagine do not love her less than other people do. The garden is just as Sir John Germain brought it from Holland; pyramidal yews, treillages, and square cradle walks, with windows clipped in them."

Walpole's description of Drayton House is as good as a photograph, and it is true in every particular to-day. Still

THE INNER COURT AND COLONNADE.

THE BOWLING GREEN.

THE STAIRWAY TO THE UPPER TERRACE.

Drayton to whom Walpo'e refers was a member of the great family of De Vere, Earls of Oxford, who lived in the time of Richard I. The branch of that family which retained Drayton assumed the name, and the estate descended from them, through the marriage of successive heiresses, to the Greens, the Staffords, and the Mordaunts. It was Lewis, third Baron Mordaunt, 1572-1601, who added to the Edwardian structure the noble Tudor front which looks out over the formal pleasaunce, and his arms, with those of his wife, Elizabeth D'Arcy, still remain on the sundial on the low wall dividing the "wilderness" from the principal garden. The famous John Thorpe is said to have been the architect. The fourth Lord Mordaunt, who lay a year in the Tower through supposed complicity in the Gunpowder Plot, was deprived of the custody of his boy by James I. This boy was afterwards created, by Charles I., Earl of Peterborough, but adhered to the Parliament and was General of Ordnance under the Ear of Essex.

there is the brave front, dating from Elizabeth's days, looking out over that delightful garden; there are those wonderful leaden vases and iron gates and *clairvoyees ;* we may see the splendid classic front with lofty Corinthian fluted columns, strangely linked, in bold contrast, without modification or breaking of the style, with the remains of a much earlier day, enclosing the narrow court, exactly as Walpole describes it. Such a house must be abundantly interesting. The Walter de

His successor, Henry, the second Earl, was a very remarkable man. His early sympathies were with the Parliament, but he passed over to the King in 1643, and

THE TERRACE WALL AND BANQUETING-HOUSES.

THE PLEACHED ALLEY AND CRADLE WALK.

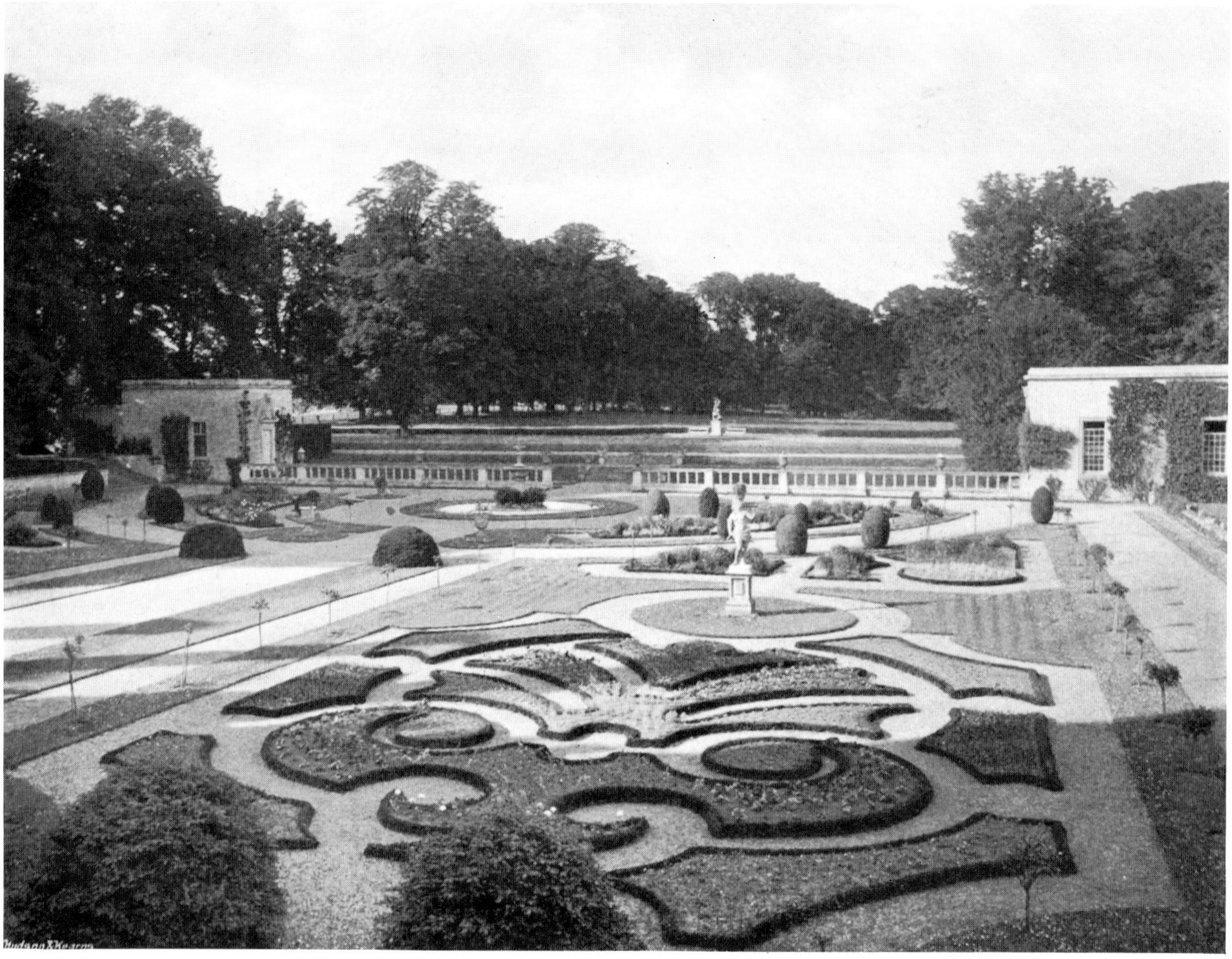

Copyright. "Country Life."

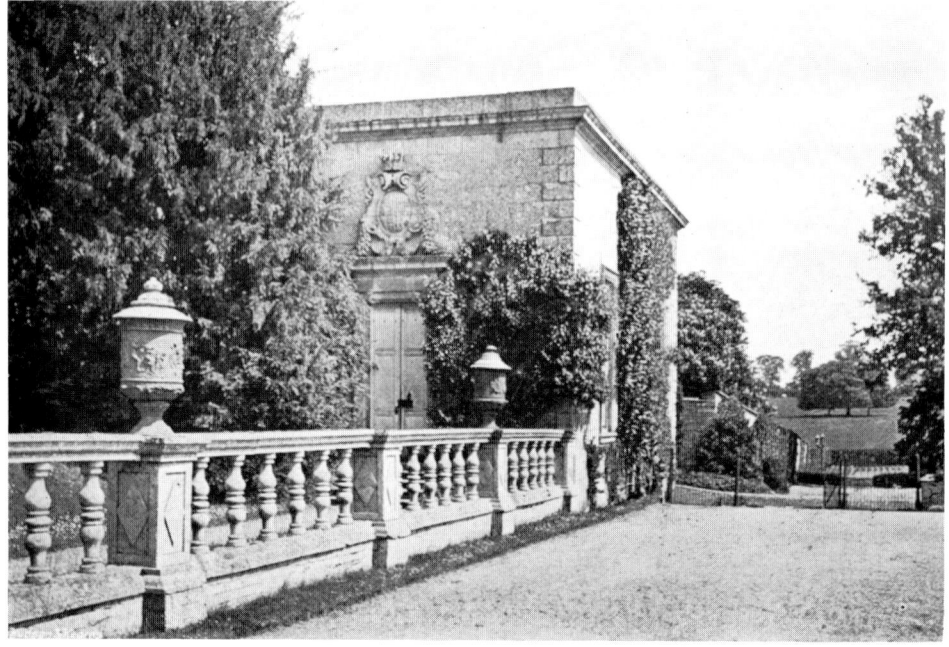

THE FORMAL GARDEN, LOOKING EAST.

fought gallantly at Newbury, being wounded in the arm and thigh, and having his horse shot under him. In 1646 he returned to England and compounded for his estates, but was soon embroiled again, making a last effort for the King, by raising the royal standard at Dorking, with the idea of seizing Reigate. Once more he escaped, wounded, to the Continent, and again compounded, and at the Restoration became Governor of Tangier, afterwards served with the fleet, and was an envoy in the Duke of York's matrimonial affairs. Trouble again visited him, for in 1689 he was impeached for high treason "in defaulting from his allegiance, and being reconciled to the Church of Rome." This Earl did a great deal to Drayton, and, though the general arrangement of the garden is earlier, he certainly improved it greatly. The "banqueting houses," terminating the terrace at the further end, were erected by him, and it is probable that the beautiful terracing and flights of steps may be attributed to his time. To about the same period belong the magnificent leaden vases and statues which are scarcely excelled by any in England.

When the Earl died his title went to his nephew Charles, afterwards the great Earl of Peterborough, that famous seaman and soldier, but the Drayton estate passed to his daughter, Lady Mary, Baroness Mordaunt, who married the Duke of Norfolk. This lady carried on her father's work at Drayton, and the magnificent iron gates and grilles, some of them bearing her monogram, were erected in 1699 and 1700. We are thus able to see how Drayton House became the splendid composite building it is, and how it was adorned with gardens and garden accessories exactly appropriate to

Copyright. "Country Life."

THE BALUSTRADE AND LEADEN VASES.

THE OUTER COURT, GATES, AND CLAIRVOYEE.

it. The lady married, as her second husband, Sir John Germain, a well-known soldier of fortune, who accompanied William III. to England.

Walpole, as we have seen, said that he brought the Drayton garden over with him from Holland, meaning that he imported the Dutch style. The truth evidently is that he grafted something of Dutch quaintness upon similar forms already existing in the garden. The pleached walk will

remind many of that quaint alley known as "Queen Mary's Bower" on the south front of Hampton Court, and it is not a little singular that the colonnade within the court of Drayton should bear a general resemblance in position and aspect to that which Wren erected in the Clock Court of the palace of William III. It was Sir John Germain, William's friend, and, as some say, his half-brother, who raised the colonnade at Drayton. Walpole took a delight in jibing at Sir John. In a

THE GARDEN FRONT.

THE GATE TO THE FORECOURT.

letter to the Countess of Ossory (November 3rd, 1782), written nearly twenty years after his characteristic eulogy of Drayton, he says, "There is a modern colonnade, erected by Sir John Germain, the pillars of which, according to his usual ignorance, were at first, as Lady Suffolk told me, set up with their capitals downward, supposing them pedestals." But Walpole, when he wrote this, was old and afflicted with the spleen, without "philosophy enough to stand stranger servants staring at my broken fingers at dinner," ready to hide himself "like spaniels that creep into a hedge to die," and he wrote to the Countess: "Your new visitor, I hope, Madam, has carried you to Drayton; it is a most venerable heap of ugliness, with many curious bits." "*Omnia mutantur, nos et mutamur in illis,*" may we truly say of decrepit Walpole!

When Sir John Germain's first wife died she left Drayton to him, but it embroiled him in legal difficulties. The Earl of Peterborough tried to dispossess him, and, though the House of Lords decided in his favour, actions were in progress until he died. They were thereupon dropped, because Germain's widow came into possession by will, and the Earl of Peterborough had said that if she received the estate he would relinquish his claim. This lady was the "divine old mistress" extolled by Walpole—Lady Betty Germain—who survived her husband for fifty-one years, dying in 1769, and was a friend and correspondent of Swift, and a famous lady of the last century. She greatly prized her possession, and left it to her cousin, Lord George Sackville, third son of Lionel, first Duke of Dorset, from whom it has descended to its present owner, who prizes and cares for the splendid place as much as Lady Betty ever could have done.

In the passage of all these years it has, of course, gone through various changes, but Mrs. Stopford-Sackville and her late husband made the present arrangement of the formal garden, assisted by Nesfield, in 1846. It was actually a work of resto-

ration, and little is really changed since James I. and his Queen visited the place in August, 1605. We have endeavoured, so far, to suggest the evolution and perfect appropriateness of the gardens. The formal paths, stately terraces, hedges of hornbeam and beech, grass walks, avenues, and pleached arbours are as when the cavaliers and dames of a former day delighted in them. The piece of still water and the great limes are most beautiful, and the antique air truly is about the place. There are three main divisions at three different levels. The first, along the north side of the house, is a spacious lawn bisected by a double row of well-grown lime trees, beyond which again is a large parallelogram divided into four by high palisades of elm, beech, and hornbeam; within these are ancient flower, fruit, and vegetable gardens. Here we find the pleached alley. The whole is surrounded by a high wall,

OLD HAMMERED IRON GATES.

admittance being gained through a pair of fine iron gates. The next level, to which we descend by a flight of steps, is that of the formal garden. The general arrangement goes back to the time of the third Lord Mordaunt (1584); the leaden figures and vases are of rare excellence; and the terrace at the further end, with its terminal banqueting houses bearing the coronet of the second Earl of Peterborough, its flights of steps and splendid urns, is extremely fine, and separates the garden from the mount or raised terrace, which looks over a ha-ha into the park. At a still lower level is a third parallelogram, divided by a single row of lime trees into water and kitchen gardens, and beyond again is the bowling green, with its splendid iron gate bearing the cypher of Mary Duchess of Norfolk.

Our pictures will enable many to appreciate the beauties and interests of Drayton, which was great in Stuart times, was extolled by Horace Walpole in the last century, and of which a modern writer has said that, "if it yields to Burghley in uniform magnificence, and to Althorp in pictorial riches, yet excels them, and all the county houses, in the wealth and subtlety of its artistic and historic charms."

FLEMISH GATES.

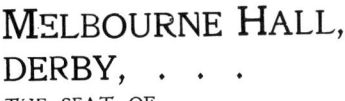

GARDENS OLD·&·NEW

MELBOURNE HALL, DERBY, . . . THE SEAT OF . . EARL COWPER, K.G.

WE have now to describe a place which holds an important position in the history of English gardening. We have surveyed already many gardens that bear the marks of an earlier time—long alleys and shadowy walks beneath sombre yews; quaint courts with their mossy terraces, where peacocks spread their plumes in the sun; the strange and curious cutting of the trees. We have been able to note the growth of new tastes, and the breaking away of barriers, and have glanced at the work of the landscape gardener.

We have seen also the fruitful love of flowers which has filled our modern gardens with splendour and variety that the old gardeners never knew. But this survey has so far given us merely a glimpse of the grand or stately style associated with the name of Le Nôtre. There could, in the nature of things, be comparatively few examples of it, for the creation of great intersecting or radiating avenues formed of forest trees was an achievement not many could contemplate. Not to go abroad to the land from which the new spirit came, we have a classic example in the great gardens and park of Hampton Court, partly arranged by London and Wise under the personal supervision of William III. Here a long water-piece and splendid avenues bespeak the new taste of a remarkable time. It is to this time and this school that the lovely gardens of Melbourne belong, and they may be described as a complete illustration, on a comparatively small scale, of the manner of Le Nôtre as it was developed in England. Be it observed, however, that these noble avenues, dense hedges, and stately lengths of formal water do not preclude—nay, perhaps they demand—the wealth of floral beauty that the modern gardener should know so well how to bestow.

But, before we say anything in detail of the character of this interesting place, it will be well to learn a little of the history of the great house and its former possessors. The

THE LAKE AND BIRDCAGE.

THE FOUNTAIN WALK.

name of Coke deserves to be greatly honoured among lovers of the country and its pursuits, for the Cokes have ever loved both. It was a Coke who wrought a marvel in developing the agricultural possibilities of Norfolk. It was a Coke who created the gardens we are now to survey. The first of the family to be resident at Melbourne was Sir John

Coke, Secretary of State to Charles I., who acquired the place in 1628. He was lessee of the estate under the Bishop of Carlisle, to whom it belonged, and from whom it was purchased by his heirs. Sir John Coke was a man of importance in the royal counsels, and it deserves to be remembered to his credit that he did a great deal to reform the naval administration of his time. It was after his marriage that he retired for a period from the cares of State, and occupied himself in farming at Melbourne until the events of the Civil War called him back, in January, 1643, and he lived and died at his house at Tottenham. His son and successor was another Sir John Coke, also a man who loved the life of the shires. It is noteworthy that in the civil broil he took the popular side, while his brother Thomas remained a Cavalier. In those troublous times, if any men were safe, they were the brothers who thus divided their sympathies, if they could but be true to one another; and the curious will find that there was, in effect, often a brother on either side of the hedge.

The Melbourne correspondence gives a remarkable insight into the country life of the age, upon which it would be pleasant to dwell. The two Sir Johns, father and son, were both devoted

THE HOUSE FROM THE GARDEN.

THE CROW WALK.

to falconry, and the letters contain many allusions to it. Thus writes Sir John the younger: "Mr. Harpur, son of John Harpur of Calke, comes hither (to Melbourne) pretending to see my hawkers fly, but in reality to see my sister." It was a brother's remark; but we may hope that the gentle swain loved to see the lady with the hawk upon her wrist, for it is a sport in which a graceful woman may well look her best, and bring down other game than such as fly.

The house about which these pleasant diversions went on was, of course, not that which we depict. In it Baxter, the Puritan divine, wrote some part of his "Saints' Everlasting Rest," and it was a house of gables and mullioned windows, with an old garden of its own. The present solid and substantial structure may well date from about the year 1700.

Copyright "Country Life."

THE BLACK SLAVE.

The older garden seems to have consisted of a terrace, with two levels below it, and brick walls on either side, a quaint and beautiful arrangement, where the clipped hedges and fragrant flowers would be very charming to view. These pleasaunces, however, were entirely remodelled for Thomas Coke, afterwards Vice-Chamberlain to George I., from designs by the famous Henry Wise. This was between the years 1704 and 1711, a time when the grand style of Le Nôtre, made known largely through the work at Hampton Court, was very popular. Gardens were then necessarily formed upon a larger scale, for the long avenues were

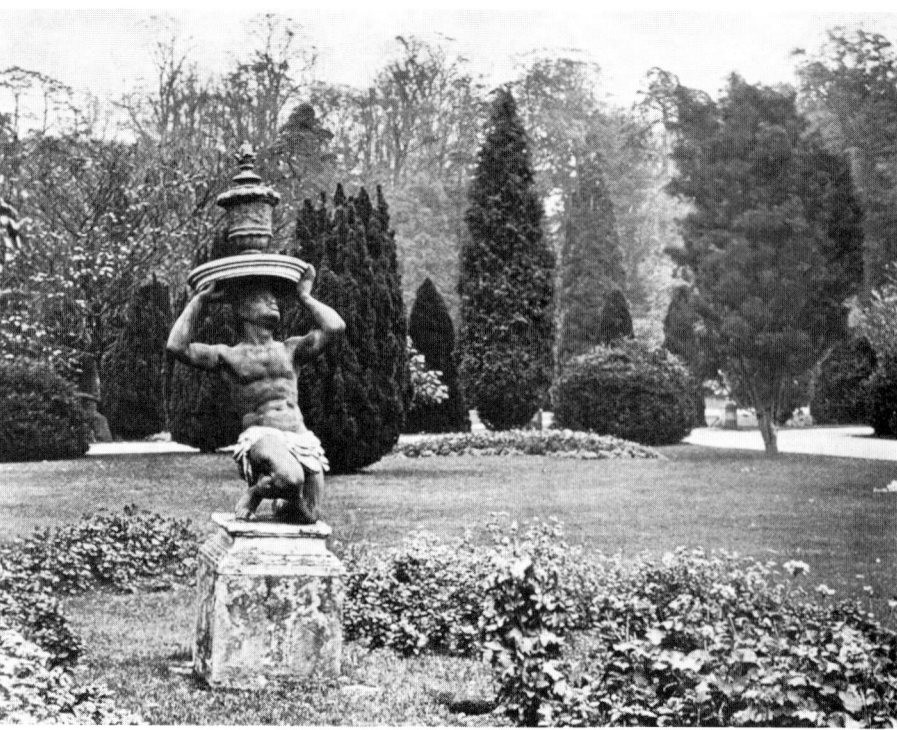

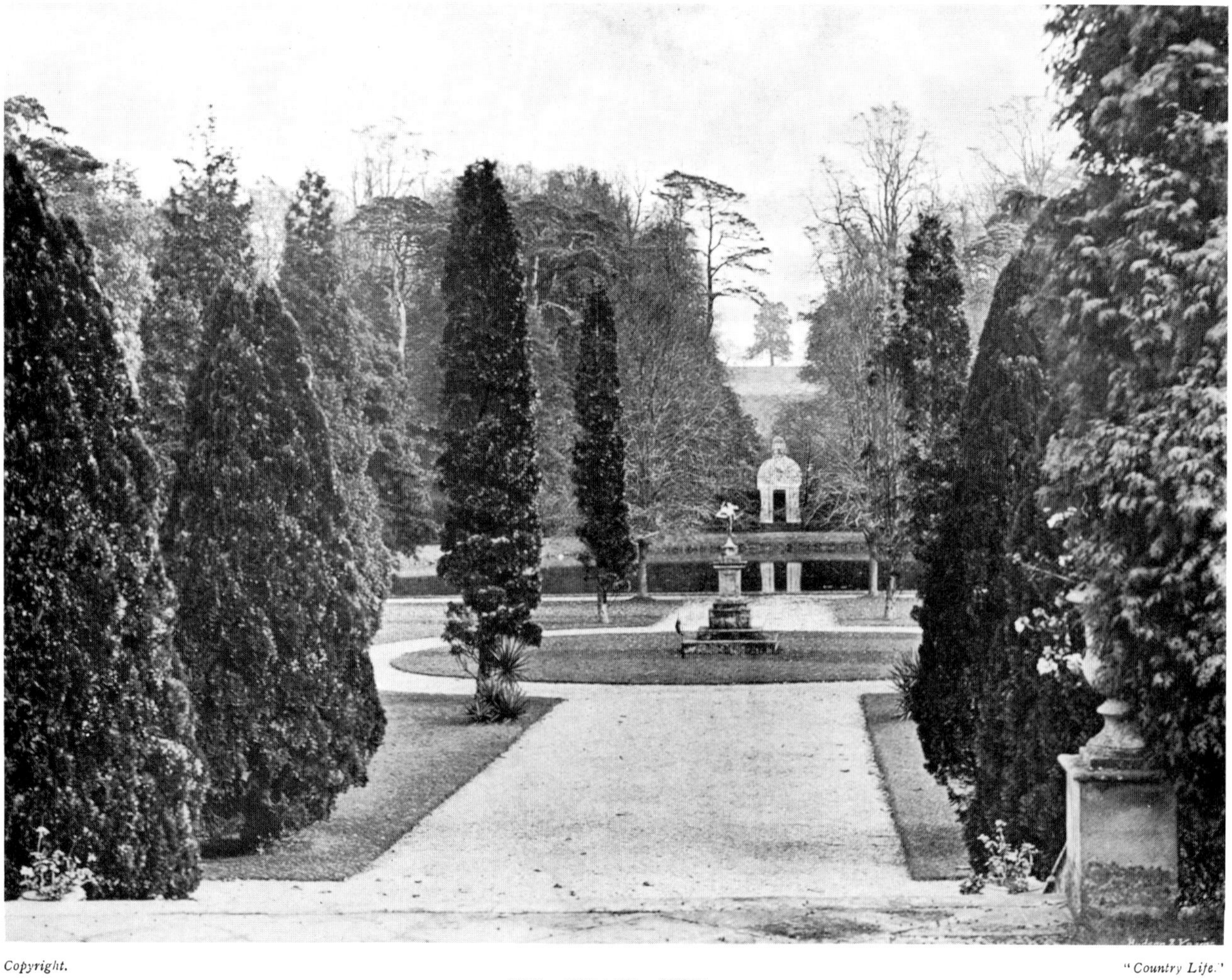

Copyright. "Country Life."

THE UPLAND VISTA.

THE CROSS WALKS.

THE ARCHED YEW WALK.

THE OLD YEW HEDGE.

carried through the parkland, which before had been left in native wildness.

In "The Formal Garden in England," by Mr. Reginald Blomfield and Mr. F. Inigo Thomas, the following account is given of the work of Henry Wise at Melbourne: "The lower wall (of the old garden) was probably removed, and an extensive *bosquet* or grove planted, with a great water-piece and several smaller fountains. Long alleys with palisades of limes were formed, and an amphitheatre of limes with vistas radiating in all directions from a superb lead urn in the centre. The ground is of irregular plan, but the difficulties are met by the design in a most masterly manner. Some alterations were made in the garden about fifty years ago. Otherwise the original design is substantially perfect, and is a very valuable instance of a garden laid out when the French influence was still dominant in England." The book from which this quotation is made is one which can hardly be characterised in terms of excess of praise, for in it Mr. Blomfield and Mr. Inigo Thomas, who have distinct and clear ideas, express their views with rare moderation of tone. The trees have now grown to grand dimensions, and are lovely in form and colour; and the Vice-Chamberlain, if he ever conceived the full effect of his work, must have lamented that he could never see its prime, and to him we owe honour for the pleasures he prepared for posterity.

Our pictures illustrate admirably what is the character of these noble gardens. The great water-piece is particularly fine, and has a somewhat elaborate character. Its formal outline is broken by curves, there being a half quatrefoil on the further side,

THE FLYING MERCURY.   *"Country Life."*

where the curious wrought-iron garden-house or bird-cage is seen. The green verges of grass, the dense hedges of yew, with recesses for seats and statues, the great belt of splendid trees in the background, and the hill rising beyond, combine to create a very remarkable and striking effect.

The leaden statues and adornments of the gardens are among the most characteristic features at Melbourne, and are as important as anything of the kind in England. In the view of the ornamental water, the very notable figure of Perseus will be discovered in its niche in the yew hedge, as well as the most remarkable Flying Mercury on a pedestal nearer the foreground, of which also a larger picture is given.

The Black Slave is extremely fine, and the wrestling Cupids and the other figures and urns are all particularly interesting. White marble is a very lovely material, but it sometimes looks cold under English skies, while the colour of old leadwork belongs as it were to the garden, and has a charm all its own. Bacon, in his time, had some objection to statuary. The princely garden he spoke of, in which no cost was spared, had perhaps no such adornments. There were those, he said, who, taking advice with workmen, instead, perhaps, of seeking that of men like himself, would "set their things together," and sometimes add statues and such things, for state and magnificence, "but nothing to the true pleasure of a garden." Yet statuary is of ancient date in English gardens. At the famous house of the Lord Treasurer Burleigh at Theobalds there was a semi-circular summer-house, with twelve Roman emperors in white marble standing round the curve, as terminal busts, we may suppose, and here in leaden cisterns was water for fish, or for bathing in the summer. No one truly can gainsay that such statues as those at Melbourne are at home amid those lofty groves and stately hedges.

The Fountain Walk, with sparkling showers, and the Crow Walk are two striking illustrations of the rare beauty that belongs to this style. The trees are noble in size and aspect, the yew hedges are grand, and the green turf is delightful to tread. Where there are trees like these, we have beauty alike in the bursting green of the spring, the riper hues of leafy June, again when the foliage turns to red and gold, and still when autumn has blown, and above the great yew hedges the matchless tracery of the trees is lifted against the sky. Very characteristic is the long yew walk—the length from the top to the fountain is about 120 paces and the width is 12ft. inside—which has closely-knitted branches, making an almost impenetrable shade.

Like Queen Mary's Bower of wych elm at Hampton Court, it is, to use Evelyn's words, "for the perplexed twining of the trees very observable." There is, however, something good and characteristic wherever we look at Melbourne. We have dwelt only on the distinctive character and more noteworthy features of the place, but the visitor will find there many other delights drawn from the rich and fragrant storehouse of the gardening world.

GARDENS OLD & NEW

THE HALL, . . BRADFORD-ON-AVON, THE SEAT OF . . . MR. JOHN MOULTON.

IT is not at all surprising that the exquisite example of Jacobean architecture depicted in these pages should have been chosen as the model for the British Pavilion at the Paris Exhibition of 1900. The Hall, Bradford-on-Avon, is, indeed, one of the gems of our domestic architecture. In richness, variety, and originality of treatment it is scarcely excelled. There is in its features the expression of that new love of life, and the things that life could give, that flashed through the world in the great and wonder-working age. For good or ill, men had turned their backs upon all that was ascetic and severe in the former time, and scanned eagerly, in the light of a new sun, the promise of a larger age. Bradford-on-Avon, where this wonder of architecture stands, is a place of historic interests, and still bears the evidences of many changing times. By strange coincidence, it met a stronger rival in the huger Bradford in Yorkshire, which captured its clothing trade. In both places the busy sound of the shuttle speeding through the loom invaded the silent chambers where lute and virginal had made music in the years before, and in many an ancient house amid the hills has the writer seen the beams of old hand-looms hanging still.

This singularly attractive mansion was built by a member of the family of Hall, rich clothiers of Bradford, but the exact date of its erection has not been determined, though we do not doubt that it belongs to the reign of James I. Once it was known as Kingston House, but earlier still had been styled the Hall, a name which was restored to it by the present owner, Mr. John Moulton, in 1894. The mansion derived its second name from the Pierrepoints, Dukes of Kingston, who formerly owned it. Some authorities have surmised that it was erected by that famous John of Padua who was engaged upon the work at Longleat, and it is recorded that the celebrated John Aubrey, in the year 1686, declared it to be "the best house for the quality of a gentleman in Wiltshire."

Kingston House has seen many changes, but it is most famous—or, we might say, notorious—from the fact that the bigamist Duchess of Kingston occasionally resided within its walls, and still the country-folk tell of her eccentricities.

THE TERRACE AND FLOWER BORDER.

THE GRAND APPROACH.

The last Duke bequeathed the property to her for life, but her interests were disputed, and great excitement was caused by her arraignment before the House of Lords in 1785. At her death the property passed to the last Duke's nephew, who became Earl Manvers in 1806. From that time, however, the old Hall fell upon evil days. The beautiful furniture disappeared, and the whole of the building suffered considerably, several of the best rooms being given up to the work of hand-loom weavers, who lived in tenements within the walls. In this state it continued until some fifty years ago, when the property came into the possession of the late Mr. Stephen Moulton, who restored the glorious fabric of the building. His brother and successor in the estate, Mr. John Moulton, has completed the work of beautifying the immediate surroundings and improving the gardens. The site affords little scope, because immediately in front of it, within 50yds. indeed, are india-rubber works, only partially hidden by a belt of trees and by shrubs at

Copyright.   "Country Life."
THE ANCIENT DOVECOTE.

the bottom of the lawn. The grounds are, nevertheless, remarkably secluded. The view from them is not extensive, but the old white gables of Bradford are visible, and, though hidden, the waters of the Avon rushing over the weirs may be heard as they speed through the valley. The scenery in this part of Wiltshire is charmingly picturesque and attractive. As our illustrations reveal, the gardens are formed in terraces, with beautiful enriched walls. A good wall in a garden is a feature to be seized upon, because against it can be planted many beautiful things that will scarcely prosper elsewhere. The upper lawn, devoted to tennis courts, is a pleasant resort, where gay flower borders creep up to the sward, and at the back of the flower border on the upper side are several rows of ornamental shrubs quaintly trained, with elms, pines, and other trees behind.

Some 10ft. below is another lawn, devoted to bowling, the fine old English game that is becoming more popular every

Copyright.   "Country Life."
THE HOUSE AND TERRACE FROM THE WEST.

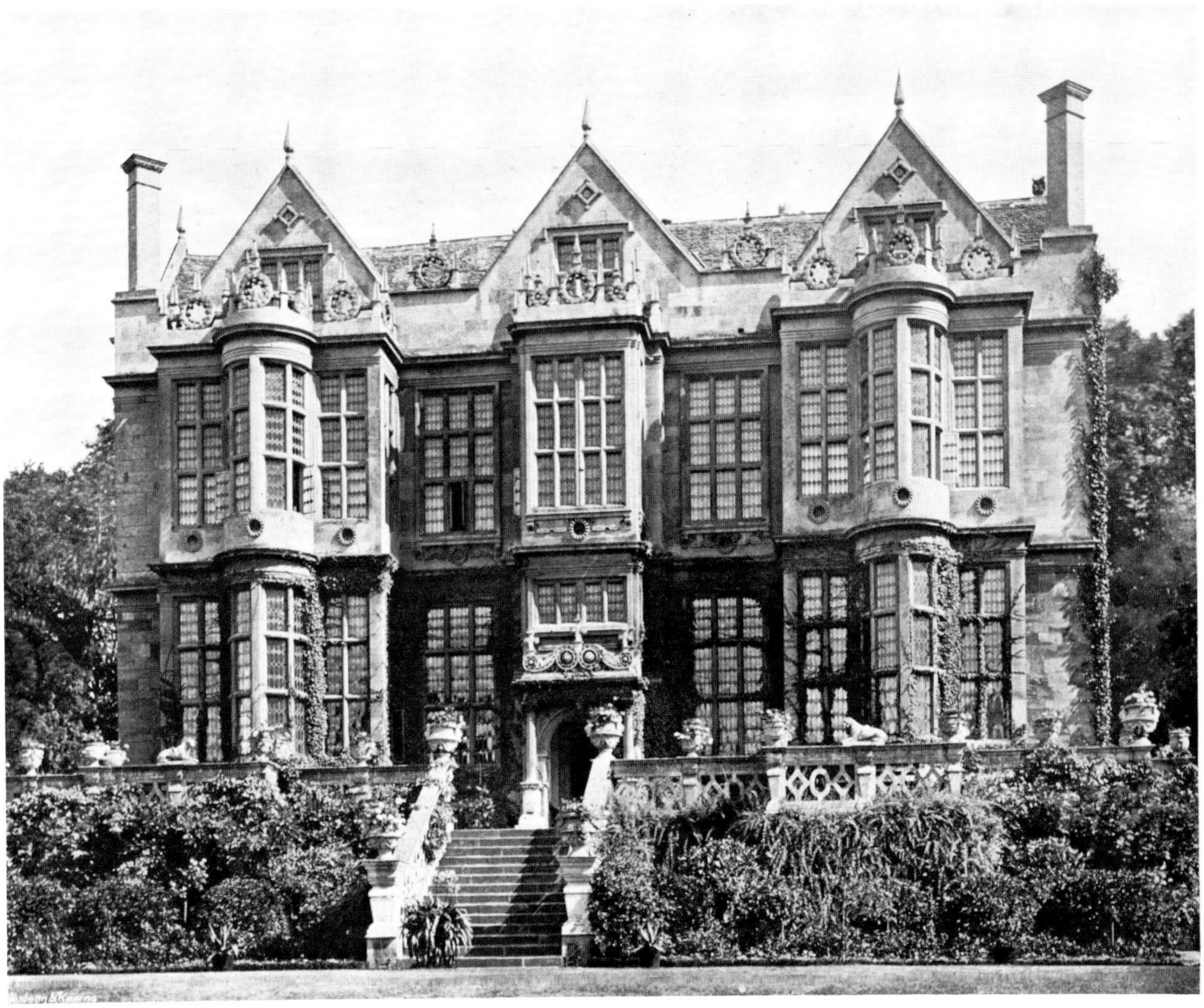

Copyright. "Country Life."

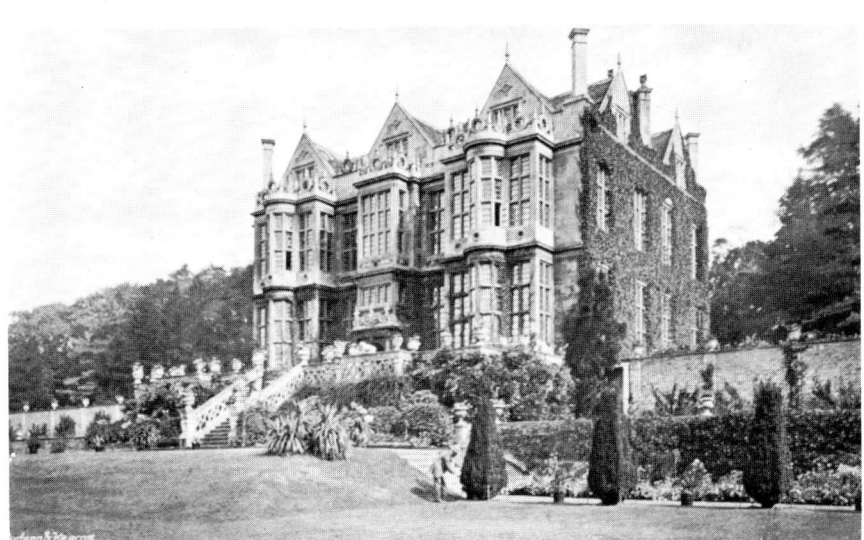

THE GEM OF JACOBEAN ARCHITECTURE.

year. Here the terrace wall is covered with peach trees perfectly trained and in full vigour, and against the lower terrace walls are several noble pear trees horizontally trained. The borders by the lower terrace walls are filled, like the others, with hardy flowers, their brilliant colour in the summer-time relieved by standard and other roses. The walls themselves are architecturally beautiful, and enriched with the addition of vases excellently carved in stone. On the lowest lawn is a fine specimen of the yew, and in the belt of surrounding shrubs many choice kinds of conifers have been recently planted. Along the side of this lawn, next to the terrace, stands a row of beautiful Irish yews, and, near adjoining, there is a small orchard and fruit garden, laid out in squares, planted with standard trees, and surrounded with apples, pears, and other fruits on wire trellis. The whole character is made quainter still by these squares being edged with box, in the bygone manner now revived. On the right hand of the Hall is the slope garden, where are standard apples, plums, etc., and trees trained on trellises, whilst the squares and borders are used for the growth of flowers and vegetables. Leaving this slope garden, we come to a Dutch garden, laid out on the site of an old factory, and only recently completed. It is not often that we see, in these days, such a quaint feature created. There are vineries, peach, orchid, and other plant-houses in these wonderfully compact gardens, which may be classed amongst the most interesting of their kind in England, and show what intelligent and loving care can accomplish, where casual interest and indifferent attention would have achieved very little.

Copyright. "Country Life."

FROM THE EAST.

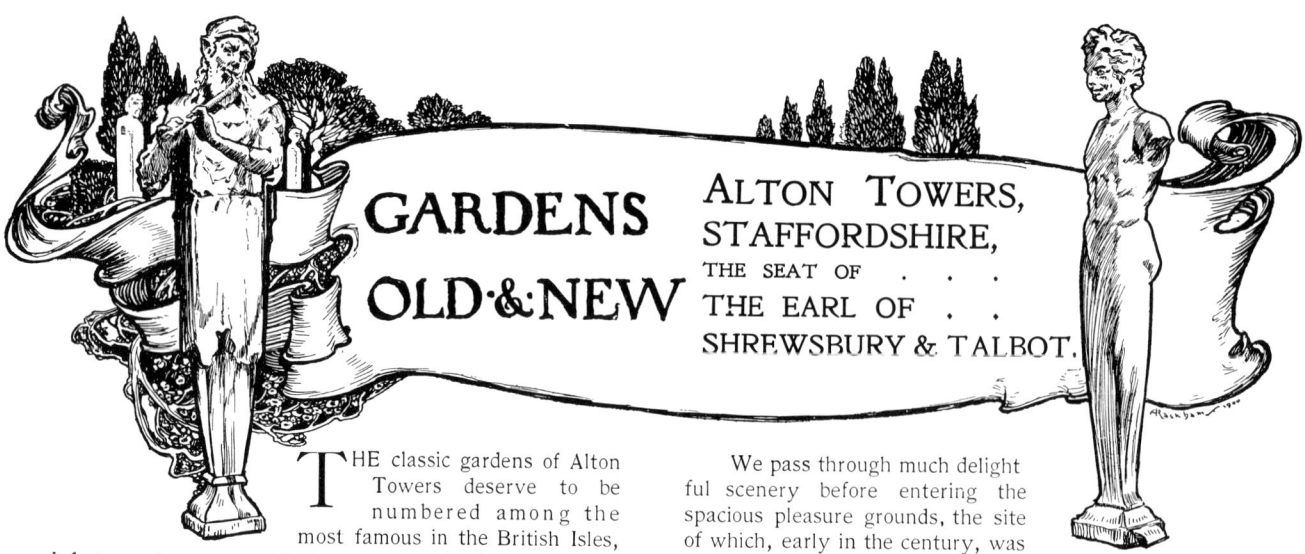

GARDENS OLD & NEW

ALTON TOWERS, STAFFORDSHIRE, THE SEAT OF . . . THE EARL OF . . SHREWSBURY & TALBOT.

THE classic gardens of Alton Towers deserve to be numbered among the most famous in the British Isles, and fortunately we are able to recount their history. It was to Charles, fifteenth Earl of Shrewsbury, that the formation of them was due. Enamoured of the natural beauties of the country, and being an ardent lover of the garden, he determined to surround his abode with a delightful realm of trees and flowers. The presiding characteristics of the Earl's creation, for it was nothing else, were classic grace and luxuriant richness, and in one part of the gardens is a circular temple in the style of the famed monument of the choragus Lysicrates—that exquisite example of the Corinthian style long known as the " Lantern of Demosthenes," which appropriately bears the inscription, " He made the desert smile," in allusion to the creative work of the Earl, a bust of whom it enshrines.

We pass through much delight ful scenery before entering the spacious pleasure grounds, the site of which, early in the century, was a wild woodland, where rabbits gambolled and squirrels were many in the trees ; but all this was changed through the zeal of the noble owner. The scene lent itself to the improvements effected by his hand, and the gardens are now a maze of beautiful flower-gemmed turf walks threading a romantic valley, and from the temple alluded to we command a superb view of the exquisite sylvan scene. Below are these ways through rhododendron and azalea groves, where the leafy bushes with their multitudinous flowers are a source of unfailing delight. Miles of pony drives thread the beautiful place, and attract by reason of the soft and velvety turf with which they are spread.

But let us now pursue the beautiful path that runs down from the circular temple. On our way we pass the arcaded

"LE REFUGE" AND THE FOUNTAIN.

THE YEW ARCHES.

THE   CASCADE   AND   LAKE.

wall, and descend to the ravine, where, in summer months, brilliant masses of colour light up the surroundings The natural configuration of the ground has made terraces a marked feature of the place, and it will be seen how sculpture finds its right use at points where the slope is broken. The same characteristic of the ground opens out many delightful views from various positions. One feature is the Harper's or Swiss Cottage, which is well seen across the valley as we

stand by the great conservatory. Another, in the lower garden, is the terrace of the Muses, which is surrounded by beds of rich and harmonious flowers.

But wherever he goes in the gardens of Alton Towers, the visitor will find something to his mood. If tired of statues and masonry, he will wander through rhododendron groves, and linger in leafy recesses with flowering shrubs for his neighbours. Then he may discover a flight of 172 steps, known as Jacob's Ladder, which conducts down the slope, and may wonder at a fountain like a Chinese pagoda, of quite imposing height.

Alton Towers itself commands, as it should, splendid views of its gardens and surroundings, and it is difficult, if not impossible, to discover on the heights a spot from which a delicious prospect or panorama is not spread out below and around. There are special points to be visited in the gardens. Thus we may go to the Gothic Temple upon its sandstone rock, or climb the flag tower, which looks over mile after mile of romantic scenery to the distant Wrekin itself.

In few gardens can tree-life be more vigorous. Rhododendrons are everywhere, and we tread even upon little seedlings which endeavour to usurp the pathway, so strong and forceful is the growth of this leafy shrub. Many of the

                          THE   LION   FOUNTAIN.

finer kinds have been planted, and hence largely the extreme beauty of the early summer at Alton, when the valley-sides are clouds of varied colour. Hence, too, the green charm of the winter, when other shrubs have cast their leaves. The beech, the sweet chestnut, and the acacia are in rude health in this chosen spot, and there are firs to give relief, by their sombre hue, to the deciduous trees and statuary. These splendid gardens preceded the existing mansion they so lavishly adorn, and have therefore appropriately been first described.

The fifteenth Earl of Shrewsbury, the same who "made the desert smile," turned his attention to gardening as an enthusiast, and began his work in the year 1814. His successor, the "good Earl," was not neglectful of his green heritage, which he greatly improved, but his attention was devoted more particularly to the house, which, by successive alterations, he converted into an imposing pile. Before his time the place had never been known as Alton Towers. Fortunately, in his later life, he made the acquaintance of Pugin, and the two worked hand in hand, the Earl having an inspiring worker, and the famous architect a munificent patron. Between them the mansion grew into what it is, and was stored with historic treasures and works of art ; but, unfortunately for the place, both owner and architect died too soon. Their congenial work did not end with Alton Towers, for, as everyone interested in the later development of our English architecture knows, churches and other buildings sprang up under the liberal hand of the Earl, and through Pugin's loyal truthfulness to style and to mediæval tradition. Those times have gone by, but the work of those two men has left its mark on the land. When Bertram, Earl of Shrewsbury, died, the senior line of the Talbots failed, and, after some litigation, Alton Towers, with the Shrewsbury title, fell to the late Earl Talbot of Ingestre.

The imposing conservatories, 300ft. long, with a central domed house, are architectural also, but here the hand was not that of Pugin, but of Loudon. Their vast size and lofty character cause them to stand out boldly among their beautiful surroundings, but it is unfortunately true that architectural effect, if associated with great size, may mar the object for which conservatories are intended. Few plants can be happy in buildings so large and draughty that the greatest skill can scarcely make them suitable for their inmates.

Some of the architectural features of Alton Towers, which are external to the mansion itself, have already been referred to. The Gothic Temple, "Le Réfuge"—that quiet nook, which we have illustrated, under the hill—the Harper's Cottage, a picturesque building of Swiss aspect, on the opposite height, the Pagoda Fountain, rising strangely amid lovely foliage and reflected in still water where lilies sleep, the Modern Stonehenge, and other features of this great estate all add their points of interest or attractiveness to the domain. Then there is Ina's Rock, where the great King of Wessex is said to have held a parley with Ceolred, the Mercian, after the battle.

From these various features the visitor who is seeking out the garden and sylvan beauties of Alton Towers may return to the old quarry near the mansion, which in the happiest fashion has been made rich in conifers. Here, indeed,

they succeed beyond expectation. The Deodar cedar, Pinus Cembra, P. insignis, Abies Douglasi, and A. Menziesi are amongst the most flourishing of the tribe in the quarry.

Before we leave Alton Towers, it is pleasant to linger a while in the private garden of sweet-smelling flowers, also near the house. Here a crowd of roses, honeysuckles, and other beautiful plants exhale their welcome perfume. Hence, too, a quiet walk leads to the private chapel or oratory of a late Countess of Shrewsbury of the old line, and is entered by an iron gate, surmounted by a cross.

Pleasant it is, too, having enjoyed the charms of the ornamental grounds, to glance at the indoor plants and at the fruit quarters, where many a fine English pear is as luxuriant as the rhododendrons in the woodland, or the gay denizens of the parterres. The illustrations depict better than words can describe the character and some of the beauties of this truly famous garden. Our country may well be proud of such places. Here the mossy trunk, the still pool, the green wall, the radiant parterre, and the silent glade are the outward tokens of the subtle glamour

"Country Life."

THE PAGODA FOUNTAIN.

of such surroundings. Silent, did we say ? Not so, indeed, for here is a pleasure-land beloved of birds.

> "This guest of summer,
> The temple-haunting martlet, doth approve,
> By his bold mansionry, that the heaven's breath
> Smells wooingly here."

So may we well say, in a place filled with song, and whose every path and glade is fragrant with the breath of the country summer. Not that the gardens at Alton Towers are summer gardens only. The varied foliage makes them delightful at every season of the year, whether it be in the bursting of the bud, the leafy triumph of June, the mellow charms of autumn, or the chill days of winter, when lovely branch-tracery extends against the sky, and silver glitters on the dark greens of rhododendron, cedar, and yew. But now no more may be said, and the writer is content to remember an inscription on a pillar of one of the conservatory vestibules at Alton Towers : "The speech of flowers exceeds all flowers of speech."

GARDENS OLD·&·NEW

HOLME LACY, HEREFORD, . .
THE SEAT OF . . .
The Earl of Chesterfield.

THERE are many beautiful seats in the romantic valley of the Wye, and among them stands Holme Lacy in a fine situation, surveying a glorious prospect of hill and wood, about four miles south-east of Hereford. It is a very lovely country, famous for many charms, and hard to surpass for its prospects of the far-winding stream. The landscape, composed of hills in endless variety, descending to the glorious river, is rich in its luxuriance, and full of English charm.

Here, centuries ago, the great family of Scudamore held sway, the lands by the Wye coming to it through a marriage with the heiress of De Lacy. Knights and squires, men famous in the court and the field, were these, and one of them, Sir James, was a patron of Edmund Spenser, and the type of " Sir Scudamore " in the " Faery Queen." His son, who was at one time ambassador in France, became a Baronet in 1620, and was created Viscount Scudamore and Baron Dromore in 1628.

Holme Lacy was the principal seat of the family, and the present house was largely built by the third and last Viscount, the friend of Pope, who died in 1716, and whose daughter and heiress married, as her second husband, Colonel Fitzroy, who assumed the name of Scudamore. Their only daughter was the wife of Charles, eleventh Duke of Norfolk, but she died childless in 1820, and Holme Lacy devolved upon Captain Sir Edwyn Stanhope, Bart., R.N., whose son succeeded in 1883 as ninth Earl of Chesterfield. The house is beautiful in its simplicity, and has a charming outlook on each of its three fronts. Within, it has some splendid apartments, notably the saloon, with much wonderful carving over the chimney-piece from the chisel of Gibbons, whose work exists also in other parts of the house.

The character of the very charming gardens at Holme Lacy will be discerned in the accompanying pictures. In very few places are various styles so satisfactorily blended and contrasted, and, as is usual where effects are pleasing, the materials employed are simple and good. The house is seen from the park beyond a broad lawn rising from the lakeside, amid a wealth of foliage, everything enhancing the effect. It is a happy framing of greenery for the structure, which is cast in a plain half-classic style, with advancing bays, a long balustrade, and characteristic roofs ; and the union of mansion, park, and pleasure grounds is excellent in character. Nearer the house we have the well kept gardens, of which that on the south side is

Copyright.

"Country Life."

A STUDY OF YEWS.

THE CONTRAST OF FLOWERS AND YEWS.

said to have been formed in the style of the gardens at Hampton Court.

"What of the yew?" asks Dr. Conan Doyle in another relation. "The yew was grown in England!" Much, indeed, in our shires have we of the dark ancestral yew, the yew that "changes not in any gale," and yet, its dark steadfastness notwithstanding, whereof the poet exclaims, "Thy gloom is kindled at the tips!" Yes, the careful watcher of the yew will discern the seasons' change in that dark foliage, and we have observed, too, in this series of garden studies, how this "ductile yew," though rising often in its native grandeur and ruggedness, is yet subdued with endless variety as the handmaid of architecture. At Holme Lacy, the ancient sentinels of the park, seared and dark with the branding of many a summer sun, seem scarce akin to the trim hedges that neighbour the mansion. They stretch forth their arms in sturdy freedom; these are shaped by the cunning

garden beauty, and no better illustration of what we have said can be found than in the gardens at Holme Lacy. Here the deep colour and protecting shade of the hedges are in the happiest union with gay beds of herbaceous flowers. A forest of foxgloves, delphiniums, and other tall plants send up their glorious spires of blossom from the mixed borders, and their effect is wonderfully intensified by the colour of the background. Thus we mark how the character is strengthened with good and distinctive effect.

Note how the dense hedge separates the long garden of hardy flowers from the more formal garden of ribbon and other bedding. There is no gainsaying the fact that this "bedded-out" garden is remarkably beautiful in situation, colour, and special features; and it is certainly most interesting to find the two great families of plants growing side by side—in one garden the geraniums and other bright summer flowers dear to many gardeners, and possessing a

THE   GREAT   YEW   HEDGE

hand of art, to subserve the gardener's need. There are many splendid yew hedges in England; we have seen not a few in these pages; but we may go far before we find any to surpass in beauty and variety the yew hedges of Holme Lacy. Some idea may be formed of the extent of them if we say that two men are occupied six weeks in cutting them once. Several of them are of great height and thickness, and all are remarkably dense and of fine colour. The greater hedges, moreover, have that quaint billowy aspect which adds so much to their charm.

We have marked two great uses for a yew hedge in a garden apart from the inestimable value of the hedge as such—the shelter it will give to tender growths or open flower gardens, enabling many beautiful things to flourish in situations where they could not succeed without shelter, and the value of the hedge, by colour and form, as the background to flowers, enhancing and enforcing their beauties of hue and growth. We have often found the yew hedge playing this part in

very real attractiveness of their own, and in the other the sweet and homely perennials thrown into relief by their sombre background. Such striking effects of contrast are found in very few places. The yew hedge has its great value also in increasing the effectiveness of the sweet rose garden.

The foliage at Holme Lacy is remarkably fine. The visitor discovers this at the very entrance gate, where great elms and other trees overhang the way. It is a sylvan land, and many varieties of forest trees are found in the park; and the contrasting tones of oak, elm, ash, beech, and cedar, and of not a few fine coniferous trees are remarkably beautiful.

The noble old yews have already been alluded to. The splendid "Monarch Oak" on the ridge of the park has a circumference of 21ft. 10in. at 5ft. from the ground, and the "Trysting Tree" is grander still. The undulating character of the ground and the rich green of the turf complete a picture

THE ROSE GARDEN.

THE TWO STYLES OF GARDENING.

that car be better imagined than described, and the harmony of the effect is un-obtrusive evidence of the taste that has ruled the planting and laying out of the park and gardens. Richness, too, is to be observed as charac-teristic of the place, and the orangery, clustered with magnolia, and many other features might be described.

As the visitor would expect, fruit is grown with great success here. Hereford is a famous county for fruit culture, and the favourable conditions are taken much advantage of in this charming place. Holme Lacy, indeed, has an honoured record in the development of Hereford-shire fruit growing and agriculture. The first Lord Scudamore, who entertained Charles I. at this house in 1645, did much to improve the local orchards and breeds of cattle. He paid great attention to the growth of the cider apple, and a local poet wrote thus of his success:

> " Yes, let her to the Redstreak yield, that once
> Was of the sylvan kind, uncivilis'd,
> Of no regard, till Scudamore's skilful hand
> Improved her, and by courtly discipline
> Taught her the savage nature to forget;
> Hence styl'd the Scudamorean plant; whose wine
> Whoever tastes, let him with grateful heart
> Respect that ancient loyal house."

THE TERRACE WALK.

But the pear is not less successful here than the apple. Near the vicarage house stands a famous specimen, an orchard in itself. There is authority for saying that in 1776 it yielded from 14 to 16 hogsheads of perry of 100 gallons each. It appears that a large branch was broken down by the wind, and, though still adhering to the trunk, its head fell to the ground. There, in course of time, it rooted, and the vicar had other layers made in the same way. Thus an interesting place in many ways is this pleasant country house, whose beautiful features are well depicted in the accompanying illustrations.

THE LAWN.

GARDENS OLD & NEW

OLD PLACE, LINDFIELD, . .
THE SEAT OF . . .
MR. CHARLES E. KEMPE.

THE village of Lindfield, between Cuckfield and Horsted Keynes, is one of the most interesting to the artist and the antiquary in the whole county of Sussex, which is a very great thing to say. Few of those who pass through Hayward's Heath on the way to Brighton are aware that a place so charming lies near. It is a lovely wooded country, from which many views are gained of the distant South Downs, with picturesque and rustic scenes such as we are familiar with in the paintings of Constable. From the earliest times there has been an important residential district in this part of Sussex, and on both sides of the South Downs are numerous great mansions or the remains of them, not seldom turned into farmhouses. The wayfarer will constantly come across quaint bits of timber architecture hereabout, with a rustic beauty possessng a special charm of its own, and Lindfield itself still possesses many houses of timber in its ancient street, of which several are very deserving of notice.

The ancient gentry have departed, but several of their houses remain. There is Pax Hill, an Elizabethan house of stone, built in 1606, and very picturesque. Kenwardes was once the seat of the old Sussex family of Chaloner, of whom Colonel Chaloner was a supporter of the Commonwealth and a Justice of the Peace, who is recorded to have celebrated lay marriages in his house under an ordinance of the Parliament; and Lunt and East Mascalls are other notable houses in the vicinity of Lindfield. Happily the architectural treasures of the region have not been overlooked, and a new sun of prosperity has shone upon some few places that had fallen into decay, leading to achievements in the domain of country life which are very noteworthy indeed.

The Old Place, a mansion originally built about the year 1590, is a notable illustration of the fact. Here has the skill of modern hands recovered the spirit of the eld in the regeneration of the house, and thus created a jewel well befitting that beautiful land. Mr. Kempe, who loves his garden well, was also his own architect. This is a house of a class found in many parts of England besides this district of Sussex, but few examples of it are so satisfactory in their varied features. Look at those wonderful gables, in their picturesque grouping, at the lofty chimneys, at the mullioned windows with their storied panes. Ask yourself, then, if anything can be more English in character than the

THE SUNDIAL.

"Country Life."

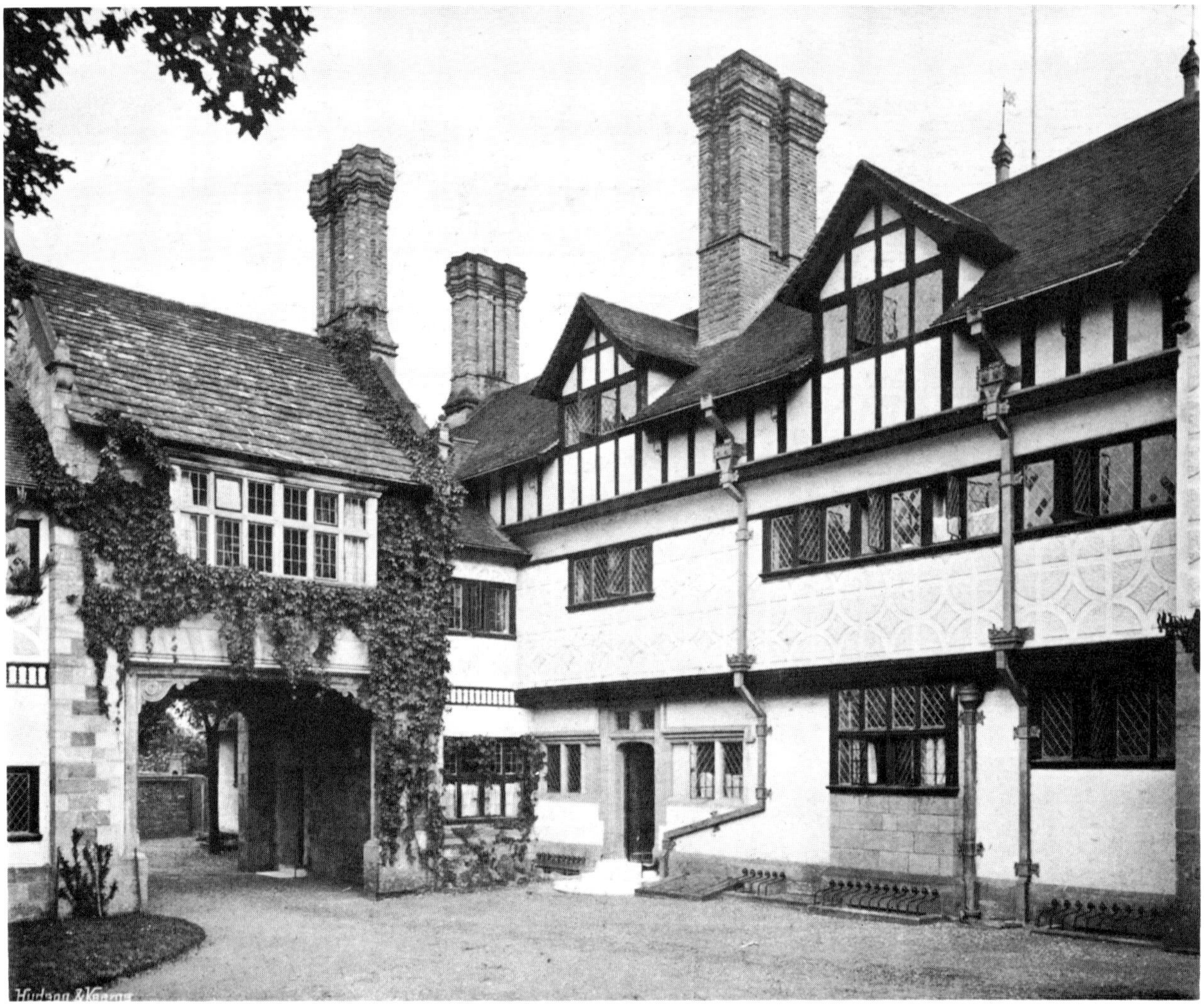

Copyright. *"Country Life."*

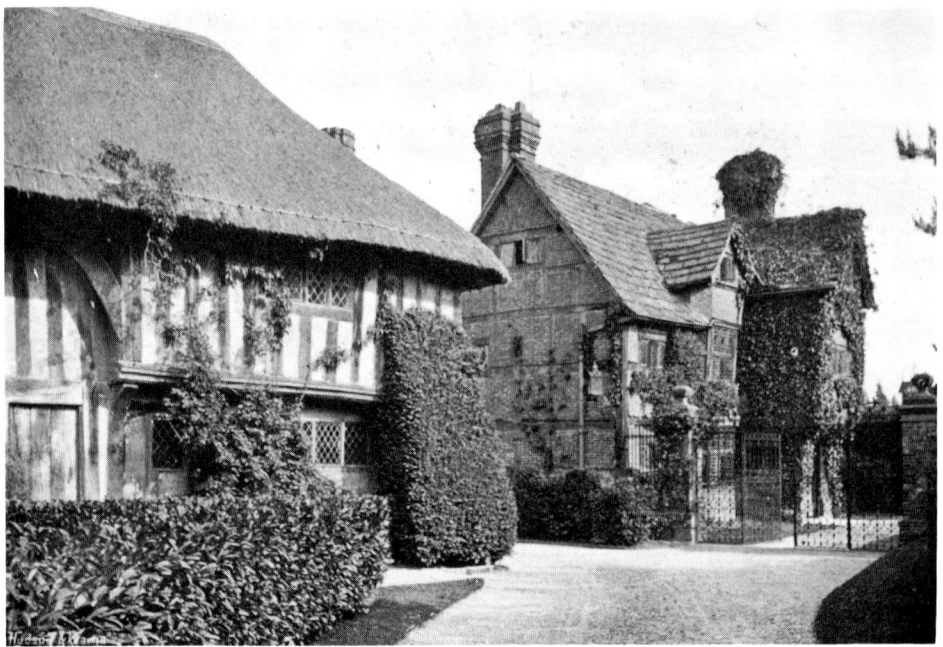

THE COURTYARD.

Old Place. Harmonious contrasts of colour are found in the varied hues of its brick, wood, and stone, of its mossy tiles, and the rare greens of the ivy and flowering climbers that vest its structure. There is rich detail in the mansion, yet all in the simple style, developed from simple materials. Never, surely, did the ancient worker produce a more subtle charm than we find in its many features. The splendidly-carved barge-boards, the armorial adornments of the porch, the slender vanes, the quaint forms of the pargeting and chiselled wood-work within the court, all mark the rare hand of an artist. Moreover, whatever is new here is own brother to the old—to the rugged time-worn timbers, and to the thick thatch of straw, beneath which nestle the diamond panes well sheltered from wind and sun.

And, if we would seek a feature of distinction, and a rare adornment for a garden, do we not find it in that splendid dial with its faces lifted aloft upon the twisted pillar, that speaks of the fleeting hours? This garden monitor of the life passed joyously or sorrowfully in the pleasaunce or in the outer world, might well be an exemplar for many. It is a delightful garden creation. *Nunc sol; nunc umbra* — so is it true of the garden as of the world. And above the dial, in bronze, is the pelican "in her piety"—the desert bird "whose beak unlocks her bosom's stream," feeding her young with her blood. Could we grace a garden with a fairer adornment than this?

Copyright. *"Country Life."*

THE ENTRANCE DRIVE.

THE GARDEN FRONT.

Could we seek a more fitting centre about which a garden should grow? Where, compared to such an object, are the mouldering temples, fabricated ruins, or anchorites' cells of another age than this? Perish they from the sweet domain, where labour the conjoined hands of Nature and Art —those presences dwelling in the garden world!

Copyright. "Country Life.

THE GREEN ALLEY.

But the added charms of the Old Place do not end here. There is the sweetest fancy to be found displayed in all the gates and surroundings of the mansion. Look, now, at the marvellous grouping of the house, where many gables rise from overhanging stories, where rarely-leaded windows give their picturesque charm, where the barge-boards are a masterpiece of the craftsman's skill, and where the chimneys and vanes rise up to the over-arching sky. Mark how the shadows fall on this glorious frontage; how an air of sweet mystery seems to cling to the wood and brick; how the imag'nation is tempted to seek new beauties in all those nooks and shadows, wherein clinging clematis bestows its starry charm. What a pleasure, then, is it to pass down from that Tudor porch along the green alley to the garden realm without, with the delight of flowers and of yew.

Then the garden-house! What can we say of this fascinating resort save that it is a supreme triumph of garden architecture in subtle harmony with the surroundings,

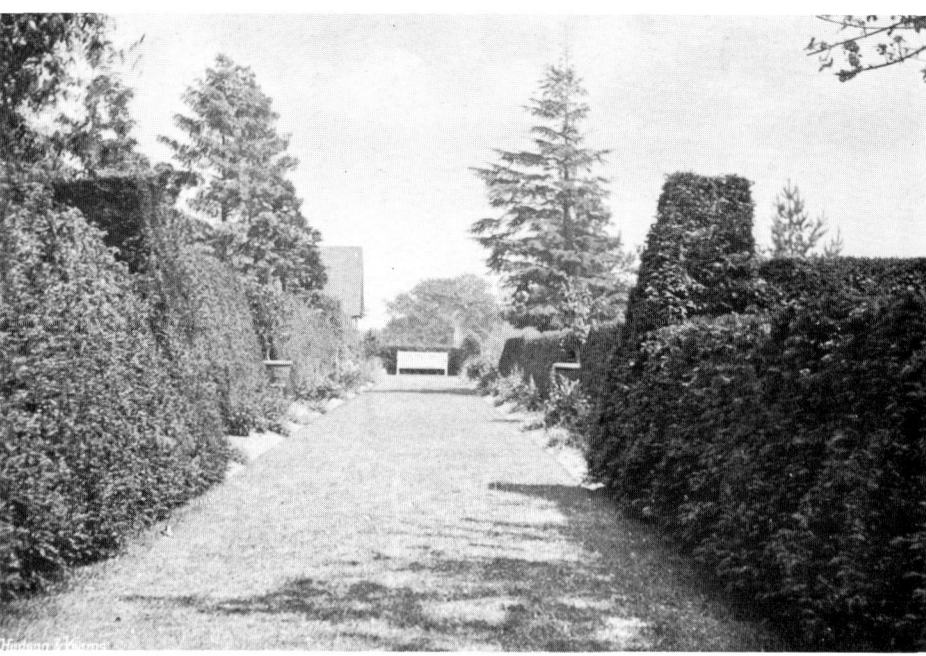

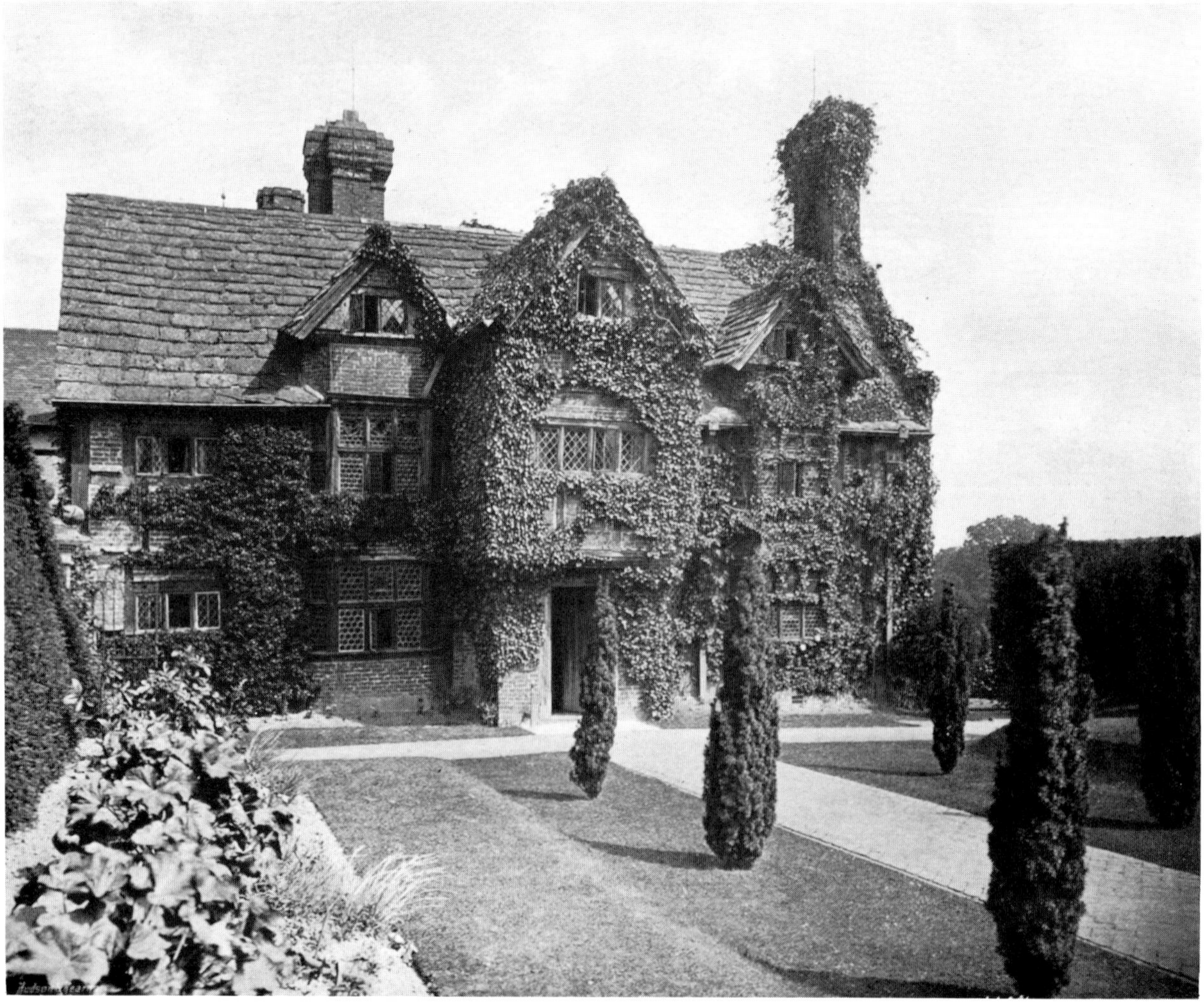

Copyright. "Country Life."

THE WEST END.

THE FORMAL GARDEN.

THE HOUSE FROM THE GARDEN.

and carrying the spirit of the house into the green pleasaunce without? Here is picturesqueness truly embodied. And from those windows ranged along the length what a realm of beauty do we not survey? Look at that wondrous double hedge of yew, buttressed and strengthened, as it were, in its curious and unfamiliar shape to flank and enclose the way. We do not know another hedge exactly like this, for, if the expression may be pardoned, the hedge is architectural too, and possesses the same spirit that we find in the house itself.

And this yew walk is flanked by sweet and fragrant gardens, wherein are abundant floral treasures. *Tantus amor florum*—such is the love of flowers indeed. Hence is nothing banished but what would be garish or would obtrude. Simple blooms are these that neighbour the standard laurels garnished with ivy. It is a character the pictures disclose, but that the pen can scarcely convey.

Yet it is evident that the hand of knowledge has guided the formation of these pleasure grounds, and it would seem that there has been an admirable system—the good old system described by T. James in " The Carthusian ' —" of terraces and angled walks, and clipt yew hedges, against whose dark and rich verdure the bright, old-fashioned flowers glitter in the sun." There has certainly been a surpassing love of flowers, and hence does the garden prosper. "You have heard it

THE SIMPLE GARDEN.

said," wrote Ruskin, in "Sesame and Lilies," " (and I believe there is more than fancy even in the saying, but let it pass for a fanciful one), that flowers only flourish rightly in the garden of someone who loves them. I know you would like that to be true ; you would think it a pleasant magic if you could flush your flowers into brighter bloom by a kind look upon them ; nay, more, if your look had the power, not only to cheer, but to guard—if you could bid the black blight turn away, and the knotted caterpillar spare—if you could bid the dew fall upon them in the drought, and say to the south wind in frost, 'Come, thou south, and breathe upon my

BISHOP'S GATE.

"*Country Li e.*

THE EAST END.

THE GARDEN PAVILION.

garden, that the spices of it may flow out.' This you would think a great thing." Many a time might these words be quoted by the garden-lover. Without pursuing Ruskin's magic words to their deep human significance, we may say that they have an objective truth also—that they imply the effect of the love of a garden upon its outcome, as the *causa causans* of its perfection. Such, we think, must have been—and, indeed, manifestly has been—the origin of the perfection of the gardens at the Old Place, which, to paraphrase the words of William Morris, in his "Hopes and Fears for Art," are both orderly and rich, well-fenced from the outside world, stored with floral charms, but not with the "mighty strong colour" of glowing masses, and yet not imitating either the wilfulness or wildness of Nature.

Then, again, we must notice the pleached avenue of the stately limes that margin and adorn the straight path to the interesting church, with ever a view as we proceed of architecture and garden combined that would be hard to excel. Yews of many shapes and kinds are here to invest the place with the solemn character that they alone can impart—a solemnity that wins us to sweet garden melancholy, as it were, irradiated with a beauty and a joy that otherwise we might never experience in our pleasaunces. The tall-growing lilies and irises, the branching roses, and all the sweet galaxy of the garden, find their foil and contrast in the lines of these deep hedges and of the sentinel yews that neighbour them. Thus is the character of enclosure given to the garden, but of enclosure brightened by open lawns like velvet to the tread, and by many a distant view of the hills and meadows of that delightful Sussex land. Therefore is the Old Place at Lindfield a most artistic and interesting abode.

To create, or re-create, such a place as this is a very notable thing, and to make all harmonious in house and garden is an artistic triumph. Here we have an admirable exemplar of what it is within the compass, not, indeed, of many, to accomplish, but of a favoured few. These will find both suggestion and encouragement in our pictures. Simplicity, quaintness, and occasional elaboration will be noticed, and no more than this happy association, in the adornment of the garden with foliage and flowers, is needed to produce a charm which all may admire.

THE PLEACHED WALK.

GARDENS OLD & NEW

BROUGHTON CASTLE, BANBURY, . . .

THE RESIDENCE OF . .

Lord Algernon Gordon Lennox.

A FEW years ago, Broughton Castle being in the market, its noble character and many beauties commended it to Lord and Lady Algernon Gordon Lennox, into whose hands it passed, and the latter became its presiding genius. None, even among the most stately homes of England, could afford a subject more absolutely appropriate for this volume than this, for in Broughton Castle as it stands now, after five years or thereabouts of loving care, there is an unrivalled example of the triumphant results which may be achieved by cultivated modern taste in dealing with an ancient edifice and its surroundings. The fabric—it stands before the reader's eye in many aspects—is in part, at any rate, nearly six centuries old ; the gardens have been but four years in the making. Yet the whole is a harmony.

Something of architectural history, a measure of allusion to the part which Broughton and its inmates have played in the nation's story, must needs be written in connection with a house of character so unique. Broughton, regarding a large portion of its structure, is among the earliest examples of considerable domestic architecture in England which still house great families. It is in three distinct periods, and to the earliest of these, which can all but claim to be of the thirteenth century, belongs a large and interesting part of the present structure. It was in the interval between 1301 and 1307 that John de Broughton built the original castle. Of his early fourteenth century work much still remains, and may be studied in our pictures. His was the groined passage, graceful and lofty, leading to and from the Hall. The chapel with its stone altar and five consecration crosses, still in position, the dining-room, the newel staircase, the priest's room, the armoury, and the hospital, with its beautiful Early English windows, were all his work. But Broughton was not to remain in the hands of the De Broughtons for any long time. In 1369, it was bought by William of Wykeham, father of our public schools, and prince of artists in architecture. The very object of the purchase is an example of Wykeham's magnificence.

THE GREAT SUNDIAL.

Not for his own use, not for a present to the King, did the founder of Winchester and of New College acquire this stately house. He bought it with a view of settling it upon his sister Agnes and her family, and in that family, directly first and indirectly later, it has remained ever since. Thomas Wickham, grandson of Agnes, obtained from Henry IV. in 1406 a licence to "crenellate his house at Broughton," by which licence, in all proba-

bility, the house was raised to the dignity of a castle. The said Thomas, like many another good man and true of those stirring days, when the lives of men were often cut short, left an heiress, whom William, second Lord Saye and Sele, espoused. And from the hands of that family Broughton has not departed. Changes have been made in the fabric, of course. The embattled part of the building, early fifteenth century, speaks of the licence "to crenellate" se-

cured by Thomas Wickham. The Tudor windows of the north front were added in 1544, and the ceiling of the great hall and the oak-panelled drawing-room are of the same period.

In the days immediately preceding the Civil War Broughton witnessed the beginnings of a great movement. William, second Baron Saye, was "the godfather of the Puritan Party" in the days of Charles I., and in his house took place many a secret meeting of those who were dissatisfied with the King's government. Hampden would come thither,

and Pym, St. John, Lord Brooke, the Earls of Bedford, Warwick, and Essex, Lord Holland, and Nathaniel Fiennes. Under the roof, too, is a great space, known as the Barracks, where Lord Saye and Sele's regiment of 1,200 men passed the night before Edge Hill ; and on the following day Broughton fell into the hands of the King.

And now for the gardens, the beautiful framework in which this antique architectural jewel is set. The subject is particularly pleasant, because this is one of those rare cases in which the evolution of a garden may be followed, and the all-pervading influence of dainty and cultivated taste may be traced. Of the present occupants of Broughton it may be said that they entered upon their tenancy in circumstances demanding great creative skill. They had to face desolation ; the space appropriate to gardens had been absolutely neglected, and a rough pasture-field ran up to the walls

of the house under the drawing-room windows. The best that could be said of the situation was that it offered free scope to the artistic imagination ; but the task to be achieved was stupendous, the problem was of infinite complication. Nevertheless, in a few short years, and with the aid of but four gardeners and a boy or two, great things have been achieved, and a long series of beautiful scenes has been created. In some cases—for example, in that of the pergola, which the roses have not yet clothed completely—it is plain that the beauties of the future will surely excel those of the present ; but

ONE SUMMER'S DAY.   "Country Life."

"Country Life.'
THE SOUTH-WEST CORNER.

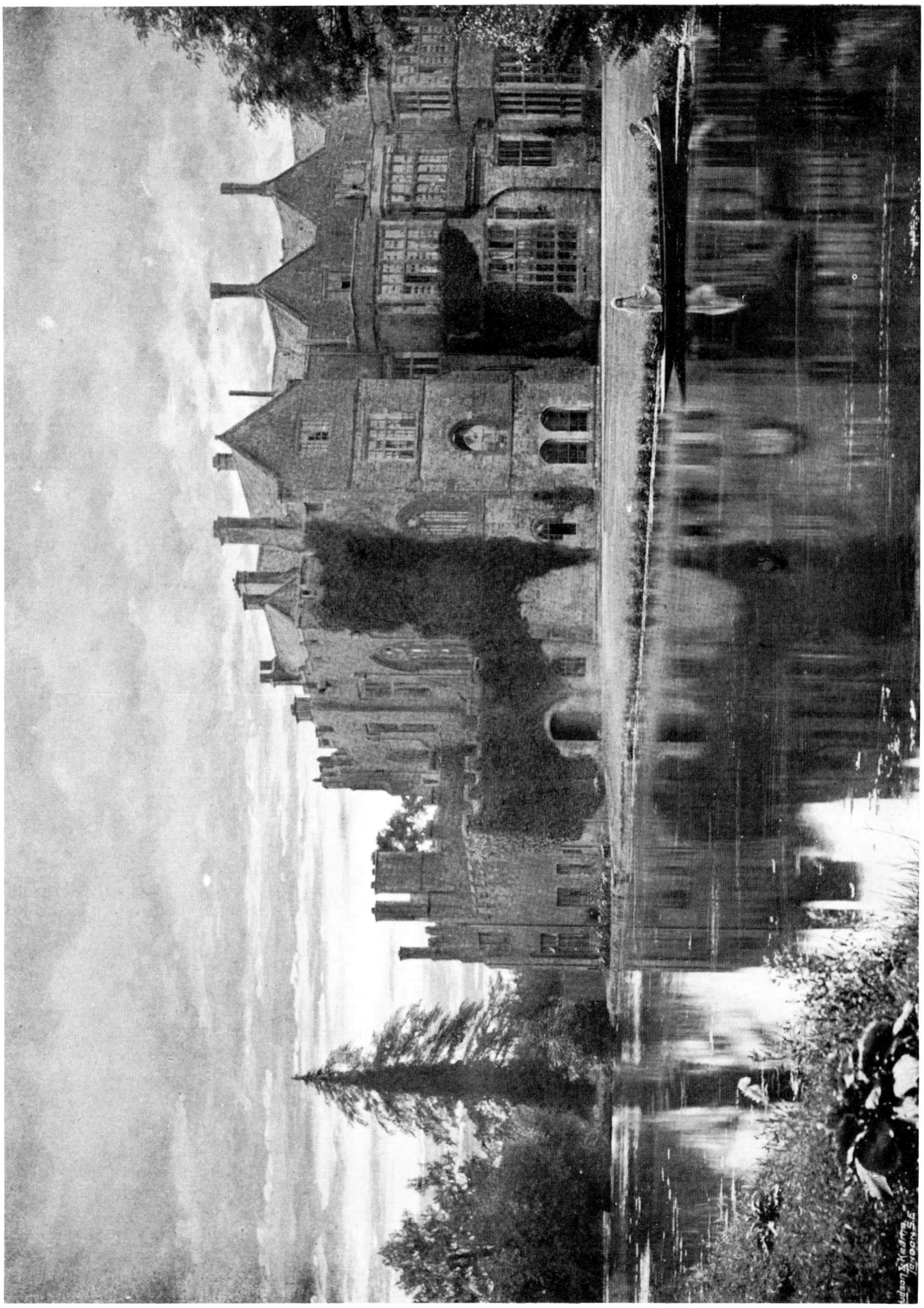

Copyright. "Country Life."

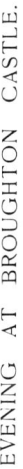

EVENING AT BROUGHTON CASTLE.

our pictures, taken as a whole, make it abundantly plain that the thought, and the taste, and the loving care which have been devoted to these gardens have been richly rewarded.

What is the principle animating the makers of the gardens which has produced so admirable a result. To our mind, pondering on the gardens as a whole, or in detail, it is deliciously, deliberately, and definitely indefinite. No hard and fast rules have been followed; no external authority, no matter how eminent, has been allowed to dictate rules of taste. In the spirit of willing desire to recognise beauty in many systems, in the wise determination to borrow good ideas from many sources, and with set purpose to devote attention principally to those plants and flowers which should show themselves appreciative of the soil and climate of Broughton, the new master and mistress of Broughton set themselves to work. It is delightful to see the progress which they made, and the readiness with which they assimilated ideas. One of our pictures, for example, represents a curious dial, of which the style is a clipped shrub, while the hours are designated by figures in flowers and foliage set close in a semi-circular bed cut out of the green turf. That pretty conceit was borrowed from the ancient gardens, long ago remodelled and now grown old a second time, of New College, Oxford. Doubly appropriate is this, for Wykeham's name is closely associated with New College as with Broughton. The motto, too, is neat, " Give light to them that sit in darkness, and guide our feet into the way of peace." Roses, again, were indispensable; but of the rose garden proper, as it now stands, there was but the framework in the shape of an old and utterly-neglected walled garden. That it was the best of frames need hardly be said. Now it has a rich herbaceous border running along the wall, and all the central space, cut into beds of somewhat elaborate shapes, is full of roses, which flourish amazingly. Where the terrace now lies

MY LADY'S GARDEN.

beneath the drawing-room windows, where the yews, clipped into dark green spiral form, stand sentinel, was formerly an unsightly pasture, and beyond, a restful spectacle from the windows, is a formal garden. In the west garden, also, great efforts are being made to introduce yew hedges, the trees having been planted at a height of 3ft. 6in., and the chances are they that they will flourish and endure to be a glory of Broughton for ages, and to attain beauty very soon. Fountains have their place, and one of them, shown in a picture, is encircled with a beautiful verse from Fitzgerald's " Omar," and the reader may exercise his or her imagination in selecting the most appropriate quatrain; for there is a fountain, and it is in a rose garden (of China roses, by the way), and Omar can find a quatrain appropriate to either or to both. A pergola also is there, of rustic boughs cunningly built together, and something stark in outline at present. But the roses grow at its foot; they give sure promise of rich clothing of leaf and blossom, and the picture serves our purpose of showing the gardens of Broughton as they grow in beauty year by year. Even now the most peculiar and essential feature of the gardens remains unsung. To few persons, indeed, is it given to enjoy so unmatched an opportunity of creating a garden of the water and the water-side as that which the moat at Broughton affords. Its still and gleaming waters are the home of many a beautiful water plant, and the Marliac lilies, the most beautiful of them all, grow there in great perfection. And on the far side of the moat, in the deep, moist soil, is an attractive half-wild garden of the Marish plants. Here Iris Germanica, Sibirica, and the common yellow flag thrive in strong colonies, and Iris Kæmpferi displays its wealth of glorious colour. Here Arundo Donax, Gunnera Mannicata with its grand leaves, and the common bulrush, grow in lush luxuriance, and form already a beautiful picture. So we part from Broughton, presuming to say that never in its long history of nearly six centuries has it presented so fair a spectacle, and that the aspect of it will grow in beauty year by year.

THE ROSE GARDEN.

THE GATE TOWER AND CASTLE FROM THE NORTH.

GARDENS OLD & NEW

TRENTHAM, STAFFORDSHIRE, THE SEAT OF . . . The Duke of Sutherland.

AMONG the great houses and great gardens of England very few indeed can vie with Trentham. The Saxon swineherds, whose grunting porkers ate the beech-mast and acorns beneath the trees of that little "ham" by the Trent, would have opened wide their eyes to witness the triumphs and spendours that these days disclose. Then, the classic conventions of architecture and the glowing glories of spreading gardens no English mind had conceived; then, no mighty smelting furnaces cast alternate gloom and flame athwart the sky; then, no Wedgwood had filled the Potteries with a busy hive of men. But the pioneers had begun their work. There was a little priory by the Trent, presided over at one time by St. Werbergh, sister of King Ethelred, refounded at a later date, as some say by Ranulph, Earl of Chester, as a house of Augustinian canons.

Cattle, wool, and hides were carried to the markets of the country towns, and the tenants brought their plenteous grain to grind at the priory mill. The sounding politics of mediæval England awoke their echoes at Trentham, but of the priory little is known, until it shared the fate of other houses, and was suppressed by Henry VIII. It thereupon became a possession of Charles Brandon, Duke of Suffolk, who had married Henry's sister, the widow of Louis of France. But the place did not long remain in the Duke's hands, for presently we find it in the possession of the Levesons, an old family of Willenhall, in Staffordshire. of whom Nicholas Leveson was Lord Mayor of London in 1539.

It was the Lord Mayor's descendant, Sir Richard Leveson, who built old Trentham. His was just such a house as was beloved by country gentlemen in Stuart times. There was

A TERRACE WALK.

THE LAKE TERRACE AND THE GARDEN.

the central block, with its porch, flanked by two projecting wings, as at Hatfield and Charlecote, and there were twisted gables and many chimneys above, while immediately to the left rose the Perpendicular western tower of Trentham Church. The hollow square formed by the house was completed by a garden wall and balustrade, in front of which was still another court forming the approach, and entered through an ornamental gate. Within these courts were doubtless formal beds appropriate to the situation, with cut yews and, perhaps, a sundial or a basin of water in the midst of each. The parapet of the enclosure had a perforated inscription raised against the sky. It ran thus :

CAROLO BRITANIÆ REGE RICARDVS LEVESON EQVES BALNEI
ÆDES HASCE HIC FIERI VOLVIT.

If the curious in such matters will take from this inscription the letters I, V, L, C, and D, as they follow in sequence, reading them as Roman numerals, and will then add them together, he will arrive at the total of 1633, which was the year of the work of Sir Richard Leveson, Knight of the Bath, at Trentham.

family who married the Leveson heiress, and in 1703 Sir John Leveson-Gower was created Baron Gower of Sittenham. Later descendants added the honours of Viscount Trentham, Earl Gower, and Marquess of Stafford, and, in 1833, the husband of the Countess of Sutherland was raised to the Dukedom of Sutherland.

The house which has been described stood until towards the end of the last century, when a plain structure of Georgian solidity took its place. The tower of the closely neighbouring church was taken down, and a kind of dulness settled upon Trentham, though much was done at the time to beautify the gardens and grounds. The house was surrounded by beautiful woodland, clothing the swelling hills, rare beauties were in its gardens, and a sheet of water, fed by the yet unpolluted Trent, diversified by sylvan islets, extended across the dale. But the second Duke of Sutherland saw greater capabilities in his house, which Sir Charles Barry was employed to beautify and enlarge. At the western end of the southern façade a great conservatory was built out, matched by a projecting dining-room at the other ; the crest of the building was adorned

THE WEST SIDE AND ENTRANCE.

This front of the house, like the principal entrance to Trentham at the present day, faced the west, but the great gardens, as now, were on the south side. Old Plot, in his "Natural History of Staffordshire," shows them very clearly. They had the rectangular character common at the time, and were in the form of two walled enclosures, separated by a division running out from the house at right angles to its southern front. These gardens looked down the valley of the Trent, towards the wooded hills and the fields, but the great lake, which now fills the bottom of the hollow, had not been formed, and Perseus did not yet dominate the scene.

Sir Richard died childless, and his estates descended to his grand-nephew, William Leveson-Gower. The Gowers were an old family of Yorkshire, settled at Sittenham, near Sheriff Hutton, a property which still belongs to the Dukes of Sutherland. Of that place was John Gower, the poet, "moral Gower," the "master" of Chaucer. Another Gower was concerned in the death of Gaveston, and still another in the Wars of the Roses, as standard-bearer to Prince Henry at Tewkesbury, where he was captured by the Yorkists and afterwards beheaded. It was the second Baronet of the Gower

with a balustrade ; and a stately campanile arose behind ; while to the west a semi-circular corridor or loggia, with a noble portico in the middle, was erected as the principal entrance, and, at the other end of the pile, a splendid suite of private apartments arose, extending along the terrace to the east.

This is the Trentham which is depicted in these pages. To describe it in any detail is not the purpose here. Whatever unstinted care, taste, and judgment could achieve has been lavished within and without upon the great ducal abode. Here hospitality presides, and the workers of the Potteries, who are privileged at times to survey the glories of Trentham, have endless delights in its extensive gardens and park. The church, as of old, closely neighbours the house, in its shadowy grove. The corridor entrance is imposing and unique, and leads to the magnificent state apartments of the house. The hall and grand staircase are very splendid and ornate, and are hung with family portraits. Although Trentham is not one of the great "show" places of the country for its pictures, it possesses several choice examples of Romney, Reynolds, Gainsborough, and many more. A noble corridor leads to the

A GLORIOUS GROUND OF COLOUR.

billiard-room, where the table is made from the wood of Kempenfelt's ill-fated "Royal George," and to the great suite along the southern façade—the bright and cheerful drawing-room, the saloon, the library, and the breakfast-room, each noble in proportions, rich in plenishings, and rare in pictures. Then comes the projecting dining-room, entered through a spacious hall, and adorned chiefly with statuary, and beyond lies the new wing with the private apartments, those along the great southern façade having the beautiful family dining-room at one end, and the Duke's study at the other, with the Duchess's boudoir, hung with fine family portraits, and the Venetian Room.

We, however, are content to look out from the noble terrace, over that glorious ground of colour presented by the gardens, to the further terrace, where Benvenuto Cellini's Perseus lifts aloft the head—we think of the great Florentine flinging his dishes and porringers into the furnace to make up the metal for the casting—and to the lake, with its wooded islets and the sylvan thickets that overhang.

it was found possible to maintain the level of the lake by conducting into it various sources of supply from the hills. But the work of diverting the Trent was one of very great labour, though all difficulties were overcome, and the river now joins a culvert underground, being thus conveyed through the grounds and out into its own channel lower down, and away from the surroundings of the house. Needless to say, Trentham, by this great work, has been made almost a different place, and it is an illustration of the loving care bestowed upon the domain, as well as of what can be done to avert such dangers as threaten some fair place in the garden world. Among other improvements recently brought about is the rearrangement of the great conservatory.

As the pictures show, the flower garden is of an essentially formal character. This is especially true of the great garden on the south side, but even lovers of landscape gardening will admit that it is in excellent keeping with the house it adorns. From the mansion, on this side, a splendid view is obtained,

THE   FRONT   VIEW.

For Trentham is more famous, perhaps, for its gardens than for itself. The situation is one of especial beauty. Behind the house, indeed, to the north, a few miles higher up the Trent, are those thriving towns of the Potteries, but these do not obtrude upon the fair scene, and notwithstanding their proximity, it is observed that plant life is very robust, and certainly wholly satisfying to behold in its varied forms. The aspect of the gardens and park in summer, and, indeed, throughout the year, is extraordinarily beautiful, and testifies to the care bestowed upon them by the noble owner. The pictures well illustrate their special characteristics and merits. Perhaps no place in England—unless it be Chatsworth—is so sumptuously laid out, and since the present Duke of Sutherland came into possession a great deal has been accomplished in adding further to the beauties of the place. The chief work has been the cleansing and purification of the lake. The Trent had grown foul by reason of the sewage of the great towns above, and it became necessary to supply the water from another source. Happily

the eye being carried over the beautiful formal foreground to the ornamental water, from the margins of which the land rises, clothed with woodland, to form a charming setting to the picture. Especially glorious is this prospect of the Tittensor Hills when autumn clothes the steeps with its resplendent hues.

A stone terrace, with a parapet or balustrade, extends round the house, connected with a gallery, and as the visitor paces this delightful walk, with charming alcoves and classic canopies for statues here and there, he beholds a magnificent panorama of the valley of the Trent. But there is nothing to exceed in beauty the great view from the south terrace, already alluded to, with its acres of flower-beds, its myriads of blooms gloriously massed for their colour, and the lake and the wooded hills beyond.

The flower garden calls for special notice. In its formal character it may be classed as a very fine example of the Italian style. We have, as it were, three stages. First there is the terrace garden, admirably figured in the pictures, with distinctive beds, taking, as will be seen, the form of the letter " S," for Sutherland, where a regular arrangement of vases and precise panelling are the features. Then we come to the Italian garden proper, where there is something of finer conception, and here we find clipped shrubs, trees in tubs, statuary, trim hedges, alcoves, and fountains. The statue of Perseus already alluded to is at the lower end of the great garden, at the edge of the lake, and from this point, looking back over the intervening space, there is a very fine view of the massive house.

The pleasure grounds cover about eighty acres, and adjoin the formal gardens, affording, indeed, a sudden contrast as we pass from one to the other, and awakening, perhaps, in some a pleasant feeling of repose. Here many improvements have been made in recent years. In particular, grassy glades have been opened out where before there was much crowding of bushes, and this work has been conducted with the right purpose of disclosing the beauty of individual shrubs, and doing away with tangled confusion of effect.

Turning to the right, we pass some very fine beech trees, exceedingly handsome in their spreading, leafy growth and bending branches, which sweep the ground, and have in some cases rooted. Pursuing our way further, we pass through very interesting woodland to reach the monument on the knoll at Tittensor, erected to the memory of the first Duke of Sutherland.

Charming then, indeed, are the wooded stretches on the left. Here are groups of choice rhododendrons, which luxuriate in the soil, to delight beholders in the first summer days with their wealth of flowers and varied beauty. In this part of the grounds at Trentham the arrangement is all of the landscape character. The groups of bushes are arranged with natural aspect, the greensward here creeping up to them, and again falling back, and then there is an expanse of simple lawn, followed by other rhododendrons, so that we are pleased with equal charm and variety.

" Country Life."

THE PERSEUS OF BENVENUTO CELLINI.

But rhododendrons are not a predominant feature. There are many very beautiful hollies, fine in their colour effect, such as the Golden Queen, Milkmaid, and Hodgkinsi. Then, again, we have glorious groups of hardy azaleas to diversify the scene. Trentham is rich, too, in Japanese maples, whose colour, varying between bright green and deep crimson, is very handsome. But we might go on noting variety after variety from among the great collection in the gardens and pleasure grounds, while the park is distinguished for splendid trees, singly and in groups, and there are fine cedars of Lebanon near the house.

It is the good fortune of Trentham to be splendidly maintained, and to exhibit alike the highest skill of the gardening art and, in its park of 400 acres, the capable hand of the best woodcraft. The visitor to the place comes away with the thought that he has seen in every department, whether it be of flower, fruit, or ornamental tree, the best the country can produce. In the great conservatory he has found the choicest growths in wonderful perfection. Elsewhere he has set eyes on specimens of the Calville Blanche apple, in pots, brought from Paris at the time of the great Revolution, and yet producing bounteous harvests year by year of this old variety. In the orchid houses he has found a feast of interest and a dream of colour. He has noted on the roof of one house a great white lapageria, which has been known to produce in a single day as many as 3,000 of its waxy, white, bell-shaped flowers. He has walked through acres of glass-houses, and has seen thousands of carnations, chrysanthemums, and other varieties innumerable. The roses have been a feast of delight, and he leaves beautiful Trentham behind with the prayer that the smoke of the Potteries may never gather volume to blight its charm.

" Country Life.

A BRONZE VASE.

BARLBOROUGH HALL, CHESTERFIELD,

THE SEAT OF . . .
MISS DE RODES

HAROLD NELSON

THIS very characteristic and interesting mansion, which ranks high among the architectural gems of Derbyshire, stands in the north-eastern part of that county, close to the Yorkshire border, about eight miles from Chesterfield and eleven from Sheffield. The situation is high and imposing, for, like Hardwick and Bolsover, its neighbours, the place is lifted aloft on a hill. It was built by Francis Rodes, Queen's Sergeant in the time of Elizabeth, who afterwards became one of the Justices of the Common Pleas, and in the mansion he was so proud to build his descendants have lived to the present day. This learned lawyer, who took a great part in the affairs of his county, was the son of John Rodes of Staveley Woodthorpe, Derbyshire, and his family traced its descent from Gerard de Rodes, a prominent baron in the reign of Henry II. He appears to have made a considerable fortune by his practice, and was among the Derbyshire gentlemen who assured the Queen of the peaceable state of the county at the time of the Northern Rising. He was raised to the order of the coif in 1578, and became Queen's Sergeant in 1582—at about which time he began to build his beautiful Derbyshire home—and, after becoming a Justice of the Common Pleas, took part in the trial of Mary, Queen of Scots, at Fotheringhay. He died in the year of the Spanish Armada, at Staveley Woodthorpe, though Barlborough Hall was his principal seat.

The personality of the judge is impressed upon his abode. Over the splendid door on the south front you see his arms and name, and read the inscription " Serviens Dominæ Reginæ ad legem, Anno Domini, 1584," this probably being the date of the completion of the house; and a similar inscription is over a splendidly-carved mantelpiece in the admirable long gallery which runs along the whole eastern face of the mansion, with the judge's arms repeated on two panels, accompanied by some unusual heraldic features. Again, in one of the rooms is a fine four-post bed, hung with blue embroidered cloth, which is said to have been given to him by Queen Elizabeth. That the judge was no ordinary man may be inferred from the legal dignity

"Country Life."

THE STAIRWAY AND AVENUE.

THE PORCH AND GARDEN FRONT.

FROM THE SOUTH-WEST.

to which he rose, and also, we may say, from the suggestive fact that, when Worksop Priory was desecrated, he obtained permission to remove to Barlborough Church, where it may now be seen, the monument of Joan, the daughter and heiress of William, Lord Furnival, who carried vast estates to her husband, Sir Thomas Nevile, and was the mother of another heiress who married the famous John Talbot, the Talbot of Shakespeare, who fell at Chatillon.

Those, therefore, who stood prominent in the sounding times of Elizabeth, lived in this beautiful and dignified mansion, which is a place of many interests besides those which belong to its beautiful gardens. It may be compared with its neighbours, Bolsover and Hardwick, both built by famous "Bess of Hardwick," and seems, as it were, to occupy a place midway between the two, for it has neither the castellated aspect of the former, nor the spacious, lightsome character of the latter. Yet, in a real sense, it typifies its age better than either, for the day of the castle was over, and the influence of modern ideas, which seems manifest in Hardwick, had then in few places exercised a well-marked sway.

It is not in any way surprising to find Barlborough Hall so very remarkable in itself. Here, indeed, is the visible presentment of the time in which it was built. We feel that the modern hand had no right of intrusion in such a place, that it would be something of a sacrilege if aught should break the quaint historic charm. And, as a matter of fact, the house externally has practically been left untouched; it remains as it left the hands of its builders, with ancient features unimpaired. The centuries have passed over it, leaving upon it little mark save that of the kindly hand of Age, which has clothed it with mosses, and touched its grey stone with the tender greens that are the vesture of the eld. Within, however, many changes have been made, especially in the lower part of the structure, and much has been modernised.

If much of ancient Barlborough Hall, therefore, remains untouched, notably the splendid south front, we cannot say the same of some of its surroundings. The utilitarian needs of the coalfields have shadowed that district with features the reverse of beautiful, and the pits that are in the vicinity

THE NORTH-EAST VIEW.

of this ancient place, and the wretched habitations that are their accompaniment, have blotted a fair page of Nature's book. It is as if the hand of the twentieth century were about to knock at the long-closed gate of the sixteenth, and long may its intrusion by the stout warder be repelled.

Look at the features of the impressive frontage. Note how wonderfully varied they are, how interesting in character are the structural elements of the house. You might well believe that the portal would open, and that the people of an earlier day might still descend into their pleasaunce, so unchanged is the character and so untouched the charm. The entrance is itself very remarkable, with its arched door, the double classical pillars that flank it, the shield of arms above, and the triglyphs in the cornice

THE GATEWAY IN FORECOURT.

over it, the shield and the beautiful window still higher, and then the ornamental cresting, and the third shield, all constituting a very striking and characteristic centre-piece for the structure. Nor shall we find in many places anything so notable as the great bays with their many mullioned and transomed windows rising to the turrets above. The effect is, indeed, extremely fine, and quite characteristic, and, in combination with the many other windows of the façade and the lofty and imposing character of the whole structure, is extremely grand. The details, too, are very good, as, for example, in the heads which are found in lunettes in the bays, and carvings in many other parts of the mansion. The architectural character, moreover, is carried out in the

surroundings, as in the enclosing wall of the forecourt, and the " lion spring," in the western court, which is quaintness embodied and makes a remarkable composition with the old structure behind. The excellent iron gates between the pillars, the iron lampholder, and many other features external to the house itself, are most attractive and architecturally valuable. The stone steps on the south front lead down into the principal garden, to which is an approach between stone pillars at either end, although the chief entrance is no longer on that side of the house. Beautiful turf and lines of yews, with tall flowers in clumps and borders, are the features here, and the garden is enclosed by a low stone wall of plain but excellent character. Outside lie the park and other gardens,

THE " LION SPRING."

THE FISH-POND.

all very fair and attractive. The unpromising character of some things in the vicinity of Barlborough Hall has been alluded to. Most happily, however, they do not mar the charm of the gardens or the park. There is no reflection of them in our pictures, and nothing breaks the sweet garden spell. The surroundings, indeed, are very beautiful, as the illustrations sufficiently disclose. There is character in the rows of clipped yews which flank the pathway down the

south forecourt, and the same may be said of the sentinel yews which are found in other parts of that enclosure. These serve to give point and distinction to the place, and by their happy contrast enhance the beauty of their floral surroundings.

In regard to the general disposition of the gardens at Barlborough, it may be said that the house is partly enclosed or surrounded by them. On the eastern side there

THE OLD GARDEN.

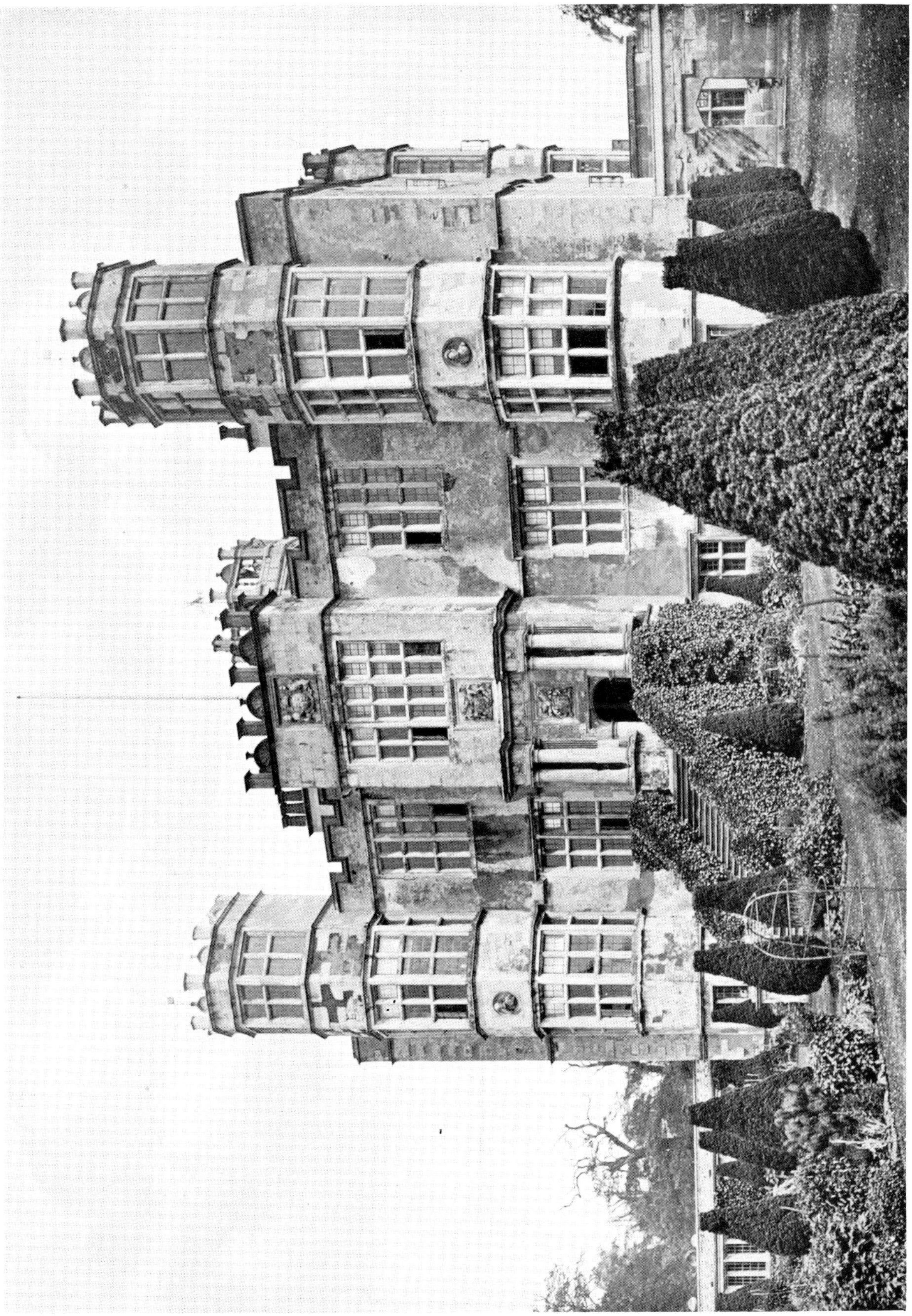

Copyright. BARLBOROUGH HALL FROM THE SOUTH-EAST. "Country Life."

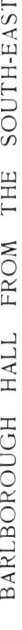

THE ROSE WALK.

ANOTHER VIEW OF THE SOUTH FRONT.

is a pleasant grass plat or lawn, with a large conservatory to the south-east. On the south is the formal enclosed garden, and the attractive forecourt possesses those excellent hammered iron gates which have been alluded to; and on the other side are further interesting portions of the grounds.

The whole arrangement is very satisfactory, and is in absolute harmony with the character of the structure. A prodigal wealth of flowers makes a gay picture from the windows of the front, while beyond extends the park with its magnificent avenue, leading to Barlborough village, and its many fine trees, both groups and individual specimens. It is a spacious outlook, truly, from these windows of the lofty Hall, standing high above the surrounding country in a commanding position on the hill. There is something extremely attractive, too, in the fish-pond and its surroundings, with the well-shaven lawn on one side and the standard roses thickly blossoming on the other, neighboured by those beautiful ornamental trees. Varied foliage plays a large part in the attractions here. The rose garden, again, with its arches, is a place pleasant to rest in, and notably attractive in its wealth of beautiful specimens. But it is unnecessary to describe further these attractive garden features. The illustrations enable us to dispense with that. Let it be said, then, that nothing seems wanting to complete the beauty of this delightful domestic picture, wherein the ancient house looks out upon its pleasant surroundings, and finds itself, we may say, reflected therein, while discovering some floral charms that belong entirely to these days. We began by speaking of the builder of Barlborough, and we may conclude by once more expressing the hope that the place may long continue unchanged, and preserve its features unimpaired. Like many others we have illustrated, it is a great exemplar of the lives of our forefathers, and in its presence we are able to re-create, as it were, the pictures of a long-past age. Barlborough Hall is, indeed, an extremely interesting place, and in itself and its surroundings it forms a remarkably attractive subject of study.

GARDENS OLD & NEW

BROME HALL, NORFOLK, . . THE SEAT OF . . . LADY BATEMAN.

E.F. BRICKDALE

THE counties of Norfolk and Suffolk are rich in country seats and fine estates, and Brome Hall is one of them, with famous Helmingham for its neighbour. It was long the seat of the Cornwallis family, and the cradle of the race which gave to the country many public servants, and among them the famous Marquis Cornwallis and the Admiral who shared with Nelson in the final compression of the French.

The house itself is picturesque and good, though modern, and preserving only a fragment of the older mansion, which seems to have been built by Sir Thomas Cornwallis, who died in 1590. Brome has the picturesque attraction of enriched gables and embattlements, good windows, and boldly-massed features, but it does not rival some of the great architectural treasures of East Anglia. The Cornwallis title became extinct in 1823, and Brome subsequently passed to Sir Edward Clarence Kerrison, Lady Bateman's father, who died in 1886. In his lifetime much was done to improve and beautify the surroundings of the house, and the special character of variety and formality in the gardens has thus been imparted within comparatively recent years.

To many the surroundings of the Hall may seem more attractive than itself, for here are all the marks of an ancient domain which has been treasured by successive possessors. It is approached by a magnificent avenue of oaks, kingly trees of vigorous growth, sturdy strength, and noble aspect. The whole country is well timbered with old woodland and many plantations, and the park is extensive, with fine groups of trees, broad open stretches of turf, and coverts well stocked with game.

The flower gardens are about ten acres in extent,

THE BOX-EDGED PARTERRES.

WHERE THE WATER-LILIES GROW.

and are comparatively modern. A terrace extends along the south and west fronts of the house, looking over from which, at a depth of about 6ft., another and much larger terrace of gravel is seen. This second terrace is laid out with patches of green turf, and with box beds of geometrical design, dotted with English yews of perfect symmetry, which are always beautiful, and give character and distinction to the garden. The arrangement adopted for the box beds at Brome Hall is peculiar, for the beds are inlaid, as it were, with broken tiles or stones, upon a system once much in vogue both in England and France, with the purpose of introducing colour, the particular scheme chosen consisting mostly of blue, grey, and white. In these days we are more accustomed to find the glories of colour imparted by all that is beautiful in flower life.

It must not be concluded that such garden glories are wanting at Brome Hall. Very far from this, indeed. The terrace walls are adorned with statuary and with vases, about which tea and noisette roses twine their flower-laden stems. All through the summer the place is redolent with the fragrance of the queenly flower, for the rose is there largely cultivated in every form, from the dainty tea varieties to the vigorous climbers, which lift aloft their glowing burdens to the sun.

The south terrace overlooks the tennis lawns, which are surrounded with flower borders, having conifers and flowering shrubs in the background. This is a delightful spot, rich in colour when the lily, larkspur, sunflower, and other bold perennials throw up their sheaves of flowers against the fine background of the deep green shrubs. Amongst these rise graceful bamboos, which we now begin to know more of, with laburnums, the mock-orange, lilacs, spiræas, and Forsythias, those golden-flowered climbers of March.

All this beauty of tree and shrub is heightened by the sombre hue of the purple beech, and relieved again by the beautiful sheen of the silver maple. During the months of spring, when the tints are freshest, this mingling of silver and rich brown in trees and shrubs is not less happy in its effect than the most charming associations of flower colouring.

On the lawn there is a fine specimen of Biota orientalis, about 30ft. in height, while on the western side of this fine green expanse rises a beautiful example of the Magnolia conspicua. This is a Chinese tree, and the present example is about 20ft. in height. Unfortunately it was damaged about three years ago by the fall, during

THE TERRACE WALK.

THE VERDANT ARCHES AND CLIPPED YEWS AT BROME HALL.

Copyright "Country Life."

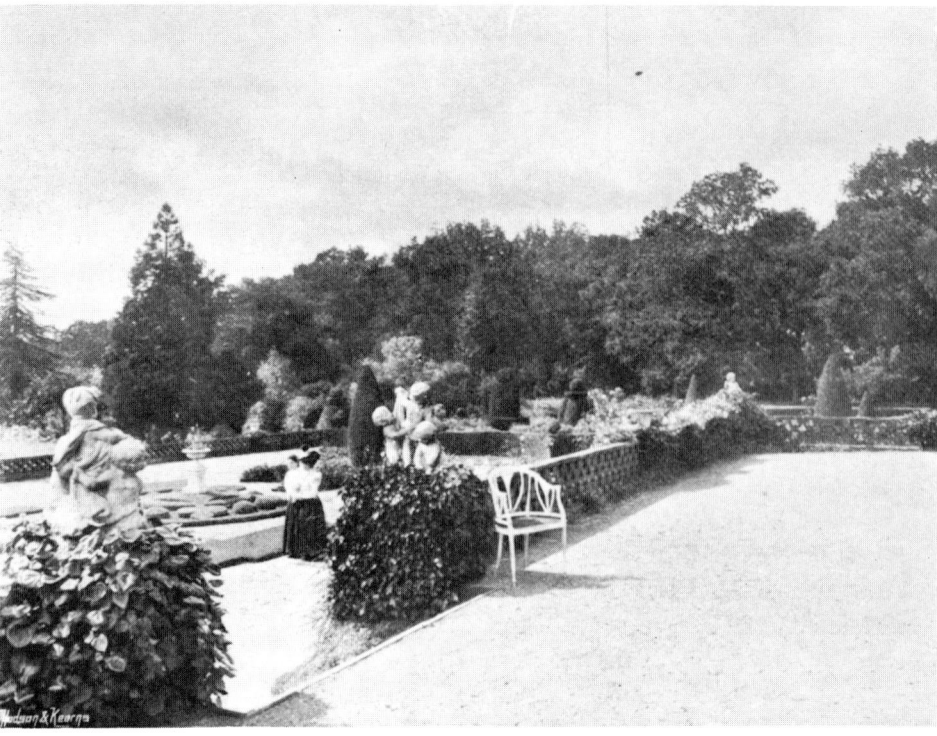

A VIEW FROM THE TERRACE.

a storm, of a neighbouring tree, which carried away part of its branches. In spring, even before the frosts have left us, all who know the lovely magnolia look for its multitudes of great waxen lily-like flowers, which cover every branch, and give it the colloquial name of the lily-tree. Interesting walks intersect the grounds in various directions. One extends the whole length from east to west, and is delightfully picturesque and quaint. The formality of Brome Hall is rarely, if ever, extravagant; but here, as the visitor walks along between the yew fences that flank the way, his attention is attracted by the curious figures formed in the leafy growth—animals, heraldic designs, and other strange devices. Running from this yew walk to the north is another over the turf, known as "The Spong." This delightful way is enriched, as we traverse the velvety turf, by splendid mixed borders on each side backed by flowering trees and shrubs. There is a subtle charm about the place, and all the world knows the beauties of the grass walk, the glory indeed of many gardens. Continuing along the walk, we reach an avenue of well-trained Irish yews, with masses of hybrid perpetual roses in beds between them, and the combination of yews and roses is unusual and striking. There is charm, too, in the walls of this beautiful East Anglian dwelling, to visit which is abundantly pleasing, instructive, and interesting.

Copyright. "Country Life."

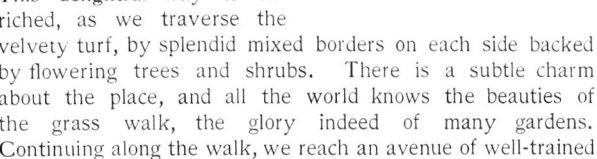

A GROUPING OF VARIOUS GARDEN CHARACTERS.

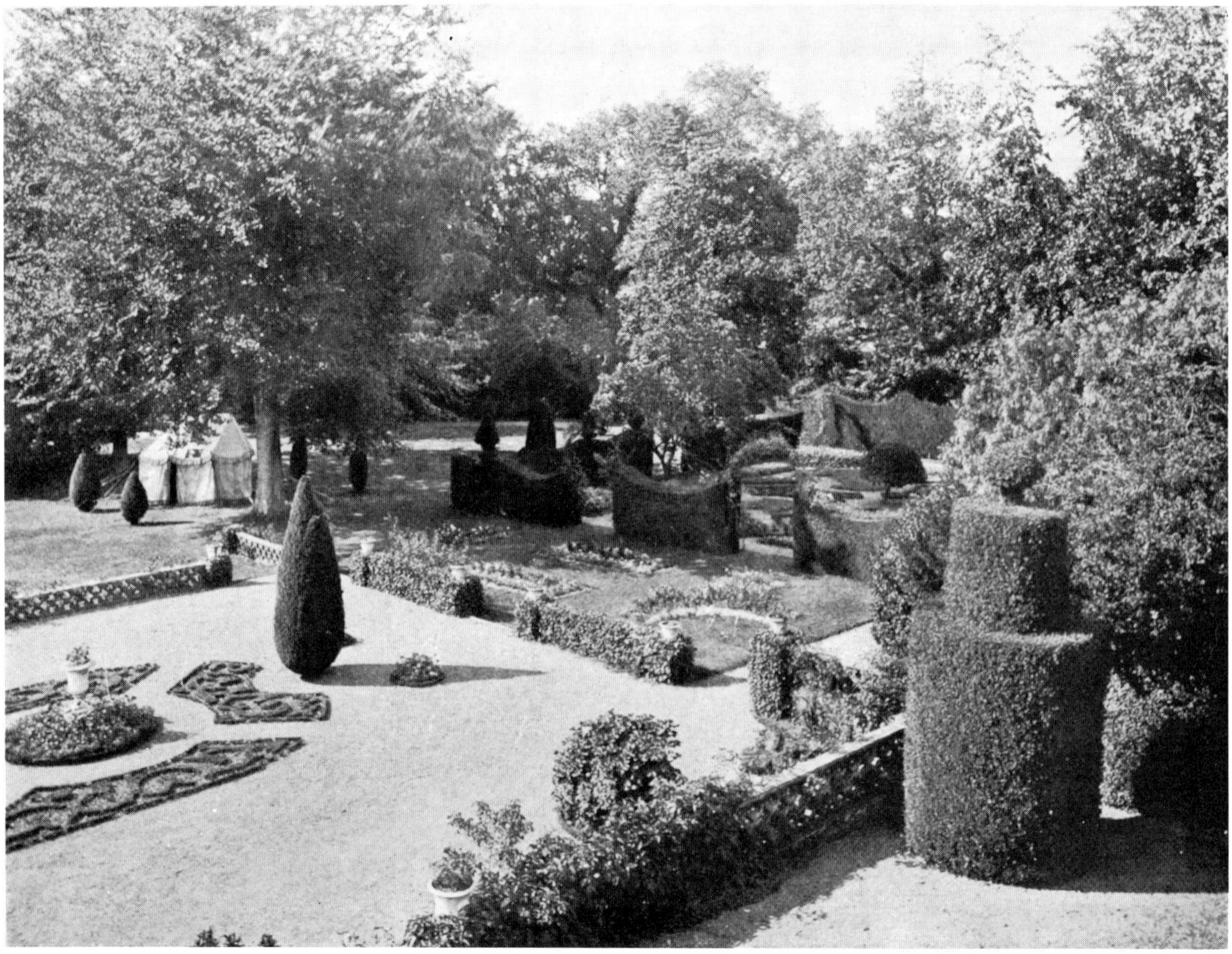

BROME HALL FROM THE SOUTH-WEST.

GARDENS OLD & NEW

BRICKWALL, SUSSEX, . . .
THE SEAT OF . . .
COL. EDWARD FREWEN.

I T would be difficult to discover in the South of England a more attractive sixteenth or early seventeenth century manor house than Brickwall, the Sussex seat of the Frewen family. Here we have one of those quaint country houses which bear the marks of many periods of history, surrounded by gardens which are very pleasant to linger in. They have the attraction which belongs to yew and beech, to old bowling greens and fish-ponds, to trees quaintly shaped, to the stately and the picturesque combined. You enter through a gateway which would not seem out of place even in the splendid gardenage of Hampton Court. There are then the old brick walls touched with green mosses, the time-worn steps and gates, and the trees which add much to the surroundings.

Northiam, the village in which Brickwall is situated, and indeed the entire district which lies between the marshes of Romney and Lydd, and the marshes of Bodiam, seems to have long evaded all modernising influences. The visitor discovers in the heart of what remains of the great Hurstmonceux oak forests a house dating from Tudor days, which remained sequestered completely until, in this year of grace, 1900, the screech and rattle of the locomotive began to be heard, and a railway station was planted in Northiam, awakening the village, as if reluctant, from the sleep of the centuries. The iron horse of the Rother Valley Railway has, indeed, invaded a quiet corner of Arcadia. Upon the village green which slopes down from the church stands a glorious old moribund oak, which is over 24ft. round the trunk at a height of 5ft. from the ground. Queen Elizabeth, who had been staying with Sir Henry Guldeforde at Benenden, lunched

Copyright.   *"Country Life."*

THE TERRACE AND GARDEN FRONT.

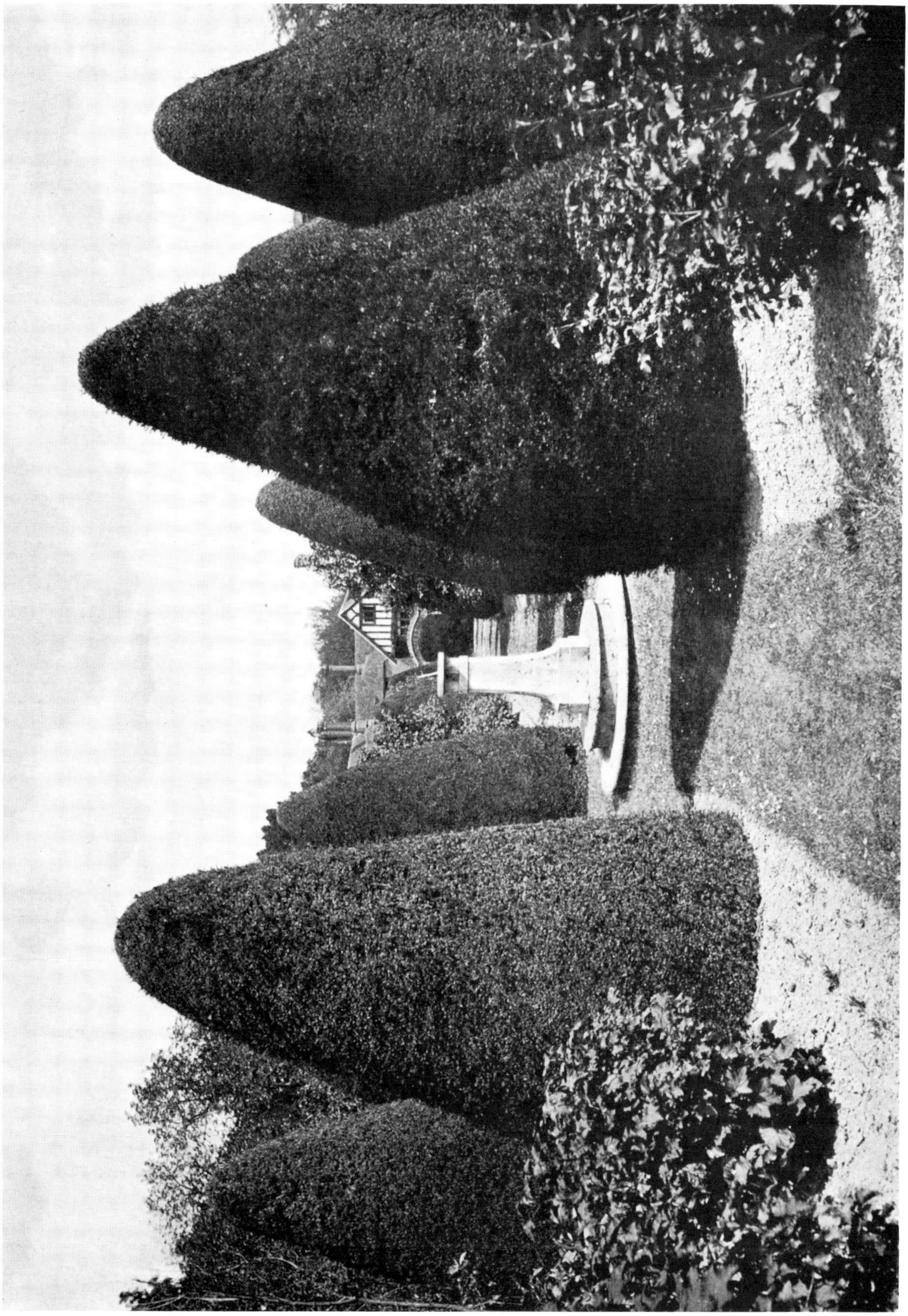

Copyright "Country Life."

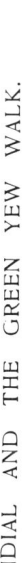

THE SUNDIAL AND THE GREEN YEW WALK.

THE FISH-POND—EVENING.

under the tree in August, 1573, when on her way to Rye. She changed her shoes, which were begged of her tire-women by the villagers as a souvenir of the Royal visitor, and these shoes, of green damask silk with heels, be it noted, 2½in. high, and a sharp toe, are to be seen still in a glass case in Brickwall.

Attached to the church is the beautiful old mortuary chapel of the Frewen family, some of the mural tablets claiming in old-world phraseology almost superhuman virtues for those who sleep in the vaults below.

Brickwall itself was built towards the close of the sixteenth century upon the site of an old house, no portion of which remains; the half-timbered front bears upon its

west gable the date 1617. The house was added to and decorated by Sir Edward Frewen in the reign of James II., the beautiful ceilings in the drawing-room and on the front staircase having been constructed at that time by Italian workmen. There are also in the drawing-room two Chinese lacquer cabinets with pier glasses, concerning which Sir Edward leaves a memorandum to say that he paid for them the extraordinary price of £500, the scarcity of Chinese bric-a-brac at that period, 1690, alone justifying this lavish outlay.

The house contains a fine collection of paintings, for the most part family portraits. There is a good picture, by Mytens, of the Rev. John Frewen, who was born in Queen Mary's reign, and was Rector of Northiam for nearly fifty years. His eldest son, Accepted Frewen, whose picture by Gerard Zoest is also in the drawing-room, was born at Northiam in 1588, and was chaplain to the British Ambassador, Lord Bristol, at Madrid when Prince Charles arrived to be betrothed to the Infanta. The Prince of Wales being at that time much solicited to embrace the Catholic religion, the chaplain preached from the text (1 Kings, xviii., 21), "How long halt ye between two opinions?" Prince Charles professed to be much edified, and presented the preacher with his miniature, which is still at Brickwall. Accepted Frewen was Vice-Chancellor of Oxford University in 1639, and was responsible for the despatch of the

THE HOUSE FROM THE SOUTH-WEST.

University plate to King Charles in 1642. A reward of 1,000 guineas was offered for his person, dead or alive, by Cromwell, but the warrant being made out inadvertently in the name of his brother Stephen, the Vice-Chancellor successfully escaped to France. After the Restoration, he returned, and was consecrated to the See of York, and was interred in York Minster in 1664. He left a very considerable fortune to his brother Stephen, of Brickwall, who is said to have survived two attacks of the great plague of London in 1665. With the Archbishop's legacy Stephen Frewen added to the Northiam estates the quaint old manor of Brede, and 2,000 acres of land adjacent, which he purchased from the ancient house of Oxenbridge.

Amongst other noticeable pictures at Brickwall is a full-length portrait of Louise de Querouaille, Duchess of Portsmouth—a splendid dame, whatever her morals—by Lely, and on the front staircase there is a picture, by Vandyck, of Richard Weston, Lord Portland, the Lord Treasurer who died in 1634. The Hall Chamber bedroom, which is hung with stamped Spanish leather, and is noticed in the inventories at least as far back as William of Orange, is an attractive room.

It is perhaps not unnatural that the owners of this quaint untroubled wilderness of oaks and yews should have been a very long-lived race. It is recorded of Thomas Frewen, whose portrait hangs in the dining-room, the great-

THE BOWLING GREEN.

grandfather of Colonel Edward Frewen, the present owner of Brickwall, that he had frequently gossiped with the old housekeeper at Wollaton, who remembered seeing Cromwell ride up to that house after the battle of Naseby in 1645. Here is a link with the past not unworthy of record at this turn of the century.

The dwellers at Brickwall have looked out, we may be sure, with delight upon the garden which lay before them, and have expended their labour in creating and modifying its character in accordance with the taste of their times. They have walked in the green alleys, and sped their bowls upon that long bowling green—a

THE BOWLING GREEN TERRACE.

delightful place wherein to pass a long evening of summer enjoying the ancient game; and such a place, be it noted, as is within the compass of many to imitate in gardens of their own. Then this garden at Brickwall is another such place as Leonato and Benedick might have walked in, that plea-saunce where the gallantry of men and the wit of women are presented in a manner so masterly upon the wonderful stage—where Hero and Ursula lingered in the pleached alley talking of Benedick, and where was "little Cupid's crafty arrow made." You go down from the house at Brickwall —with its green vesture of climbers, which do not hide its beauty—beneath a curious arch of brick, and through that strange and picturesque laby-rinth of conical yews, by the old sundial, to the bowling green, and beyond it to another world of yew and oak. It is a garden realm of ancient and curious

THE BEECH WALK.

aspect—all quaint and orderly, with the fascination that must always belong to the places where past generations have found their pleasure. In the shape given to the yews a special character will be found. You may linger in the beautiful and retired beech walk, where the well-cut trees make a sequestered shade, or you may sit in that enclosure of yew by the old fish-pond in the sun. But, wherever you go at old Brickwall you will find the subtle charm that belongs to all such places, a charm that is indefinable and cannot well be described, 'but that all can feel, and that the pictures in a large measure convey. There are flowers also in prodigal plenty, as need scarcely be said; but, after all, the great distinction of this place is to be found in its old-world character, which, it may be remarked, accords well with the timber struc-ture, the mullioned windows, and the fretted chimneys of the abode.

THE HOUSE AND THE FISH-POND.

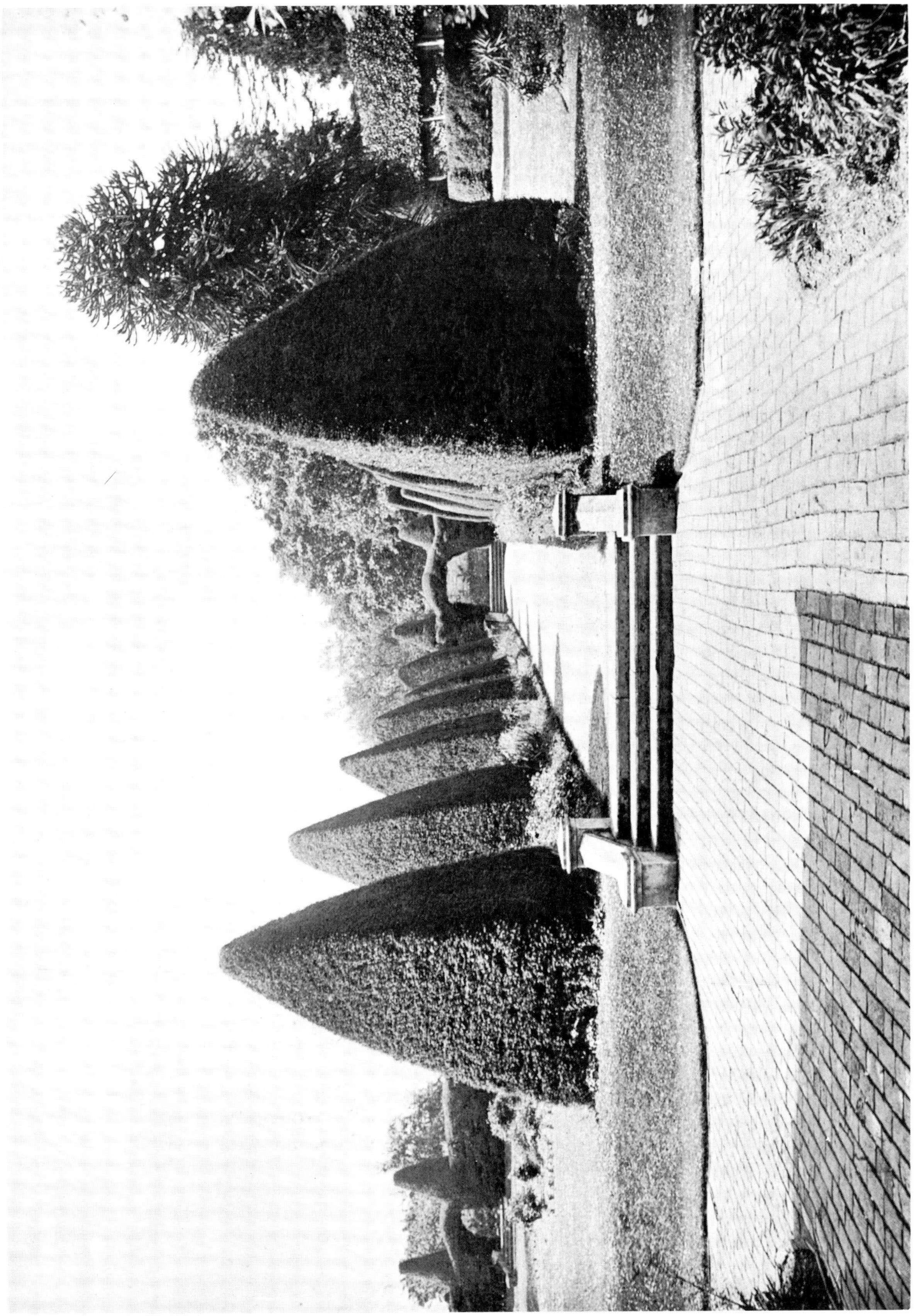

Copyright. "Country Life."

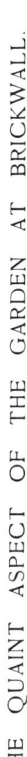

THE QUAINT ASPECT OF THE GARDEN AT BRICKWALL.

GARDENS OLD & NEW

RENISHAW HALL, CHESTERFIELD,
THE SEAT OF . . .
SIR GEORGE R. SITWELL, Bart.

RENISHAW HALL is one of the many great houses that are an ornament of the fine country lying along the borderland of Derbyshire, Yorkshire, and Nottingham. Quaint and beautiful old Barlborough, which is already known to the readers of these pages, is its neighbour, and within a dozen miles or thereabouts to the east and south are Welbeck, Clumber, and Hardwick. Renishaw is in Derbyshire, in the valley of the Rother, there flowing northward to mingle its waters with those of the Don. The whole country is extremely pretty and quite charac-

teristic, and the traveller by the railway to Sheffield is attracted by the prospect of the rich hanging woods of Renishaw, which clothe the hills rising on the left. The natural attractions are many in this region, though in places they are marred by the advances of industry, and the walks are very beautiful, that to Worksop markedly so, by way of the romantic dell of Markland Grips and Cresswell Crag.

There is much that is pleasant in the long lines and the embattled cresting of Renishaw Hall, its pinnacles and bay windows, and the varied play of light upon its frontage, but evidently the modern hand has replaced some things that were old, and Renishaw is now no architectural marvel like its neighbour Barlborough. We are here, however, to look for garden beauties, and how many they are the numerous pictures will sufficiently disclose. What is the character that we find here? That of spaciousness and yet of enclosure in the first place, of broad terrace levels with fine descents, excellent in architectural fitness, of floral wealth, of a great outlook, and, above all, of splendid trees. What more should we seek? There has been no straining after effect. All is simple and natural, and we pass from level to level, attracted now by some sweet and radiant flower-bed, now by the creeping things that clothe the walls, here and there by an appropriate accessory of dial or dovecote, always by the long borders that fringe the terrace walls. We linger in the woodland garden beneath the trees, where the sunlight, falling through the trembling foliage, invades the shadow. We find many a pleasant vista among the woods, and look out through that delightful gateway and iron grille from the garden into the park. We love the ancient limes that rise aloft to unaccustomed height, with the most imposing effect which dignifies the whole garden, and we emerge upon the open lawns, where there is a far outlook to other masses of trees.

A pure and simple effect,

THE AVENUE AND POND.

Copyright.

THE TERRACE WALK AND THE GROVE OF ELM AND LIME.

THE GREAT AVENUE AND FLOWER-BEDS.

we say, that has grown rather than been created, and wherein all is appropriate and beautiful. Other places have charms of their own ; there are greater hedges, terraces more imposing, designs more ambitious, but here we know that all is suited at least to Renishaw. What a vista is that along the terrace walk far into the green depth of the woodland ; and it is worth while to note how effectually trees in tubs are used for further

adornment. The excellent character of the architectural accessories has been alluded to. Good stonework marks the terrace walls, and these are most beautifully margined by the long beds wherein countless tall-growing blooms tempt us to the lower level. The descents are very characteristic, flanked by tall pinnacles, and in one place the steps have an effective semi-circular form. There is a great lawn upon

THE SEMI-CIRCULAR MARBLE STAIRWAY.

THE HALL FROM THE GARDEN.

Copyright. "Country Life."

THE LOWER GARDEN PLAN.

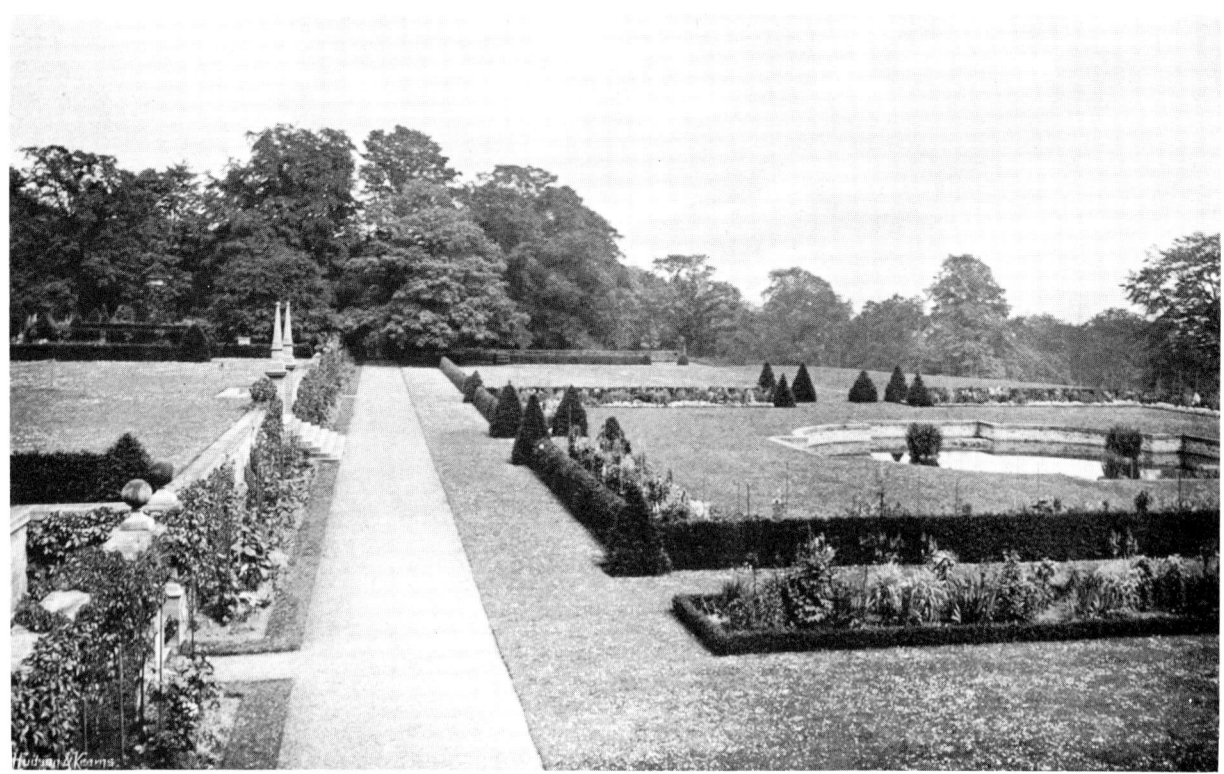

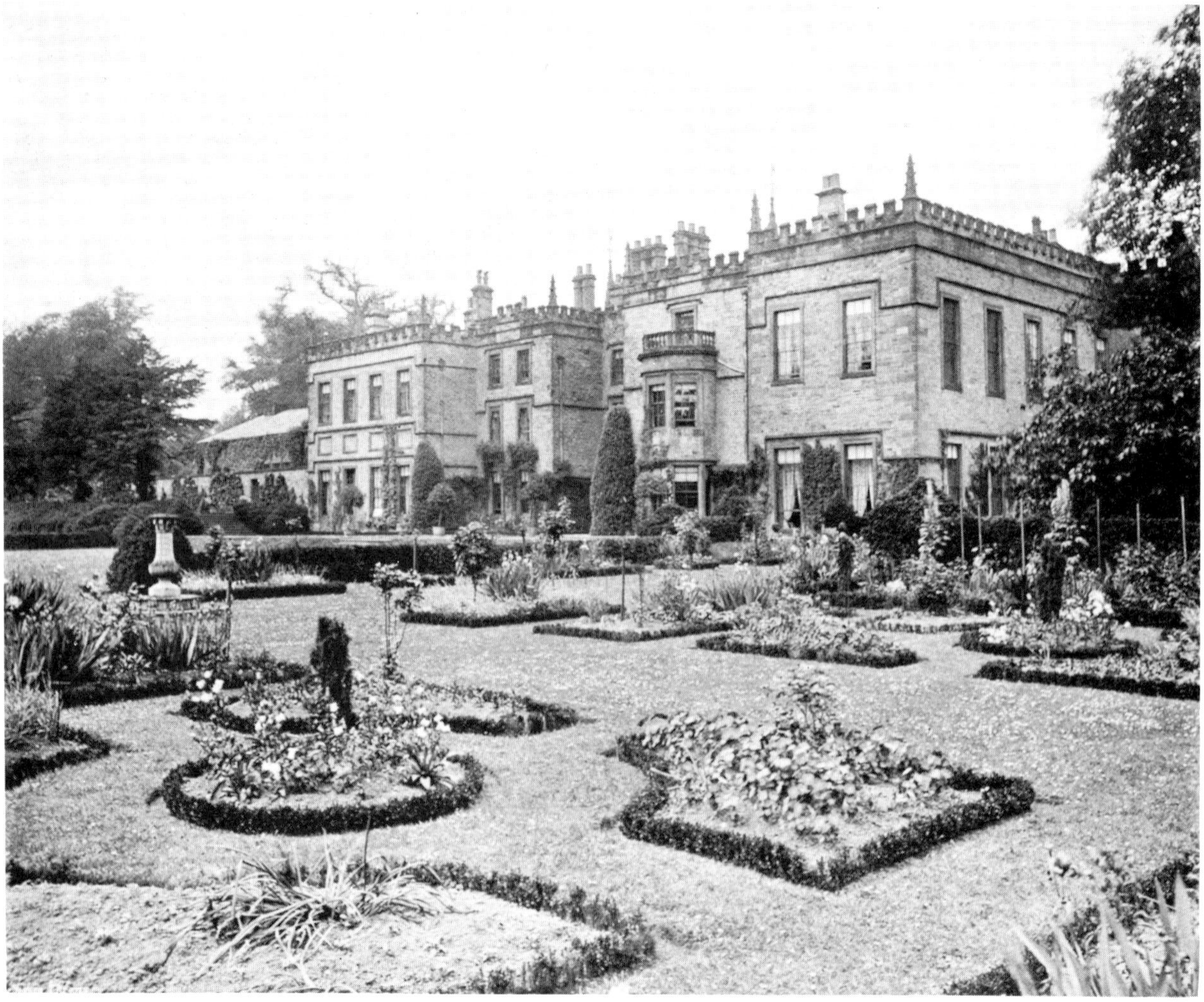

Copyright. "Country Life."

THE TERRACE GARDEN.

the lower area, with a yew-hedged enclosure, and other flower borders, and in the midst an ornamental stone basin. Leaden soldiers of old Rome greet us as we go forward through the wood garden, amid the flowery ways, and the paths are delightful to thread on the hillside.

We know not whether to like most the sweets of the fragrant woodland or the more ordered charms of the broad terrace garden. The hand of good judgment rules everywhere in the disposition of floral charm, and the grass walks between the beds are both pleasant to walk upon and satisfactory in the artistic harmony. An extraordinary wealth of hardy flowers is in these box-edged beds and in the terrace borders. Mark how along the embanked slope under the great row of trees, by trellis and buttress, multitudes of blooms are coaxed to grow. There is a subtle art in discovering the suitable place for every flower, those that love the full sunlight and those whose charms are discovered most beneath the partial shade. Larkspurs and lupines, columbines and foxgloves, cyclamens and snapdragons, and a prodigal host of others, are here.

Copyright. "Country Life."

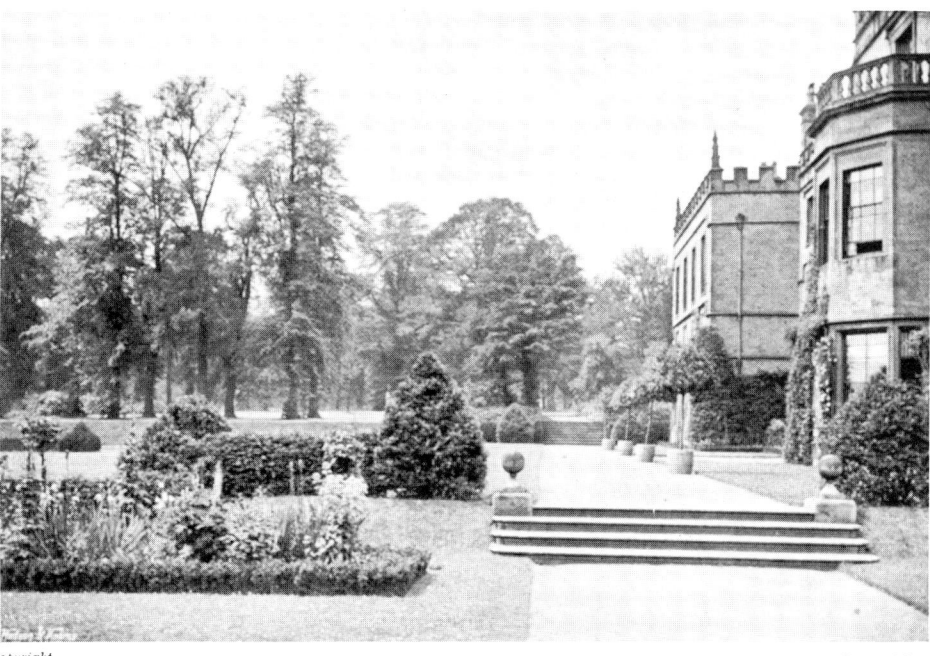

THE TERRACE WALK AND LOFTY LIMES.

Roses, too, of many kinds flourish exceedingly, and ivy and many climbers lend their charm to the house and the terrace walls.

It is, perhaps, unnecessary to attempt to draw lessons from such a garden as that at Renishaw Hall. Much is owing there to the work of the old planters, and we cannot hope to create such

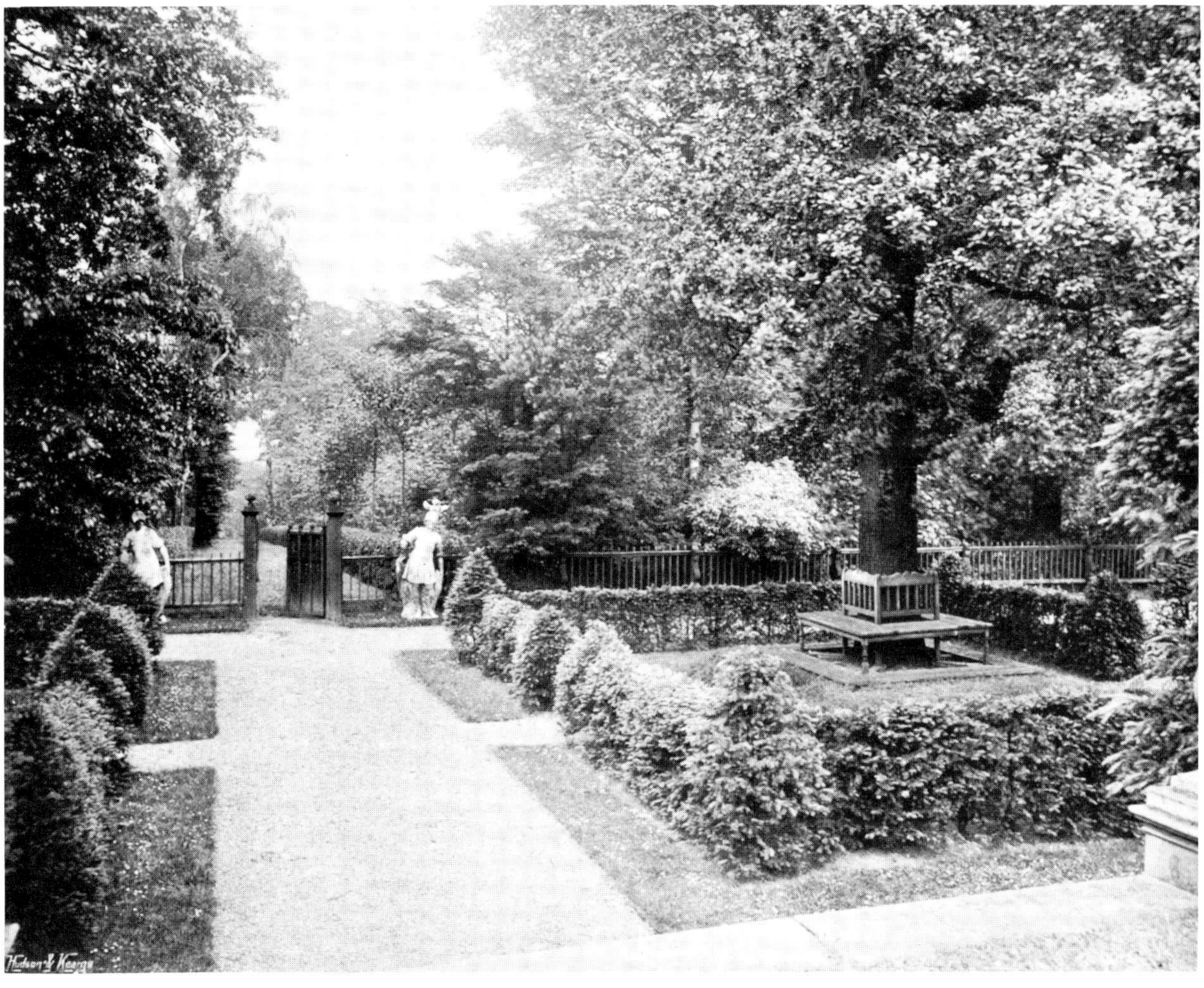

Copyright. "Country Life."

A GARDEN VISTA WITH LEADEN FIGURES.

A WOODLAND GARDEN.

a charm as belongs to ancestral trees. *Tandem fit surculus arbor.* Our saplings may be long before they burgeon into a grove. But meanwhile there is much to be done in forming suitable terraces, narrow on the steep hillside, broad and flower-gemmed on the gentle slopes, as at Renishaw. Let there be well-built walls, hospitable to climbing growths, sheltering flower borders like these. Open out some pleasant prospects, viewed, if it may be, through excellent ironwork such as we see at the terrace end at Renishaw. Construct basins where lilies may float, or where your garden creations may be doubled, or in which a patch of sky shall be brought into your foreground. Add the enforcing features of balls or pinnacles along your terrace walls, or at the flanks of your well-built stairways. These are some of the points that are suggested by a survey of the simple and effective gardens of Renishaw Hall.

THE DOVECOTE AND SUNDIAL.

GARDENS OLD & NEW

KINGSTON LACY, DORSET . . .
THE SEAT OF . . . MR. R. W. BANKES.

THIS beautiful and extremely interesting mansion lies a short two miles north-west of Wimborne in Dorsetshire, on the Blandford road, in the valley of the pleasant River Stour, flowing thence to ancient Christchurch and the sea. The country is attractive with the charm of Nature, and rich in the memorials of history and ancient occupation. Norman lords have added distinctive names to local designations, and Maltravers and Marshall, Glanville and Stourton, and many more whose names are written in the proud Roll of Battle Abbey, have left their mark on the county. The great family of Lacy, Earls of Lincoln, were once lords of Kingston, and so it bears their name to this very day. Now, for many generations, the place has been the possession of the old family of Bankes, whose mansion stands in the midst of a beautifully-wooded park, distinguished by the presence of numbers of noble trees of ancient growth. Sir John Bankes, Attorney-General in 1634, "that exceeds Bacon in eloquence, Chancellor Ellesmore in judgment, and William Noy in law," was the purchaser of Corfe Castle, whose wife so stoutly defended it, during a siege of six weeks, for the King, that the Parliament men drew off and left it unsubdued.

The house at Kingston Lacy was built by Sir Ralph Bankes, and was begun shortly after the Restoration in 1660, as may be inferred from the date 1663 appearing in the pediment of the north front, and doubtless indicating when the work was finished. The influence of Inigo Jones has been attributed to the design, but, since he died in 1652, there can be no certainty as to that. The mansion has since undergone many changes, and everything above the main cornice is modern. The whole of the exterior, which was formerly of red brick with stone quoins, has received a facing of Caen stone, and was embellished with further architectural features and details in the Italian style by the late Sir Charles Barry about the year 1854. How beautiful and spacious it is, our illustrations

THE GARDEN STAIRS ON THE EAST SIDE.

THE TERRACE.

sufficiently reveal. There is in it a character of completeness that is very charming and satisfactory, and the care that has been lavished upon the house has been carried also into the garden, where the architecture and sculpture are superb and extremely rich in character and detail.

Garden architecture, as has more than once been remarked in this volume, has been much neglected in English gardens, but it holds a high place in the function of uniting the house with its surroundings to constitute a pleasing and harmonious whole. As the house is, such is the character of the brick or stone work in the garden. It may be stately and formal,

befitting a classic pile, or it may take a quainter cast and fall into a different picture, with a terrace and a mossy balustrade flecked with sunshine and shadow, and a flight to a lower lawn, seeming wholly appropriate to the battlements, pinnacles, and mullioned windows of Tudor and Stuart days.

A magnificent staircase of Carrara marble, 30ft. wide, leads up from the entrance hall at Kingston Lacy, and the house is full of the finest examples of art drawn from the best collections in Europe by the care of successive hands. The pictures are superb, one room being filled, for example,

BRONZE VASES.

THE HOUSE FROM THE NORTH-EAST.

chiefly with splendid works of the Spanish masters. Sir John Bankes, who from Attorney-General became Lord Chief Justice of the Common Pleas—the purchaser of Corfe Castle —began to fill his gallery there, and several pictures which he admired are now at Kingston Lacy. Successive members of the family have possessed the same fine taste and discriminating judgment, and have been men of well-known attainments, who in extensive foreign travel have gathered many beautiful things for their home.

A perfect unity of character exists between the house and the garden. The terrace is extremely rich and beautiful, and it is supremely delightful to look thence over the lawns, to note the beautiful trees, and feel the fragrance of the flowers. There are beautiful urns of bronze upon highly-wrought pedestals, and upon the south lawn, sheltered by the long, over-hanging limbs of noble cedars of Lebanon, or strewn with the blossoms of venerable limes, are disposed large vases of various forms and rich materials, some

of them of ancient pozzi, and " well-heads " or cisterns brought from the courts of Italian palaces, or fashioned out of the marbles from the parti-coloured quarries in the mountains above Verona. Sculpture by the late Baron Marochetti, too, is here to give further adornment, and the broad terraces and marble steps have dignity and character that is very delightful.

The Kingston Lacy sculptured cisterns are very note-worthy. In many fine English gardens will be found superbly wrought capitals of classic columns, sometimes wrongly described as coming from Venice, where, strange as it may seem, there are no wells, and consequently no " well - heads." The mouths or openings of these cisterns are usually circular, and not infrequently elaborately sculptured. The finest example still remaining is the noble one in the courtyard of the monastery of San Sebastiano, by Sansovino, which has often been copied in various materials, from marble to copper, an admirable receptacle for very large plants. Another

THE FERNERY.

fine example will be found in the Campo San Giovanni e Paulo, richly decorated in the Renaissance style, with sporting *amorini* (cupids) and armorial bearings. Indeed, in many places in Italy are to be found numerous circular and richly-sculptured so-called "weli - heads," originals and copies of which are frequently met with in our more majestic gardens. A few of these have been designed to represent

THE LION AND SERPENT.

immense capitals of classical columns. Such are the two magnificent specimens which adorn with very striking effect the great lawns of Kingston Lacy. These are evidently genuine Venetian cistern-heads belonging to the best period of the Renaissance, of the same class as the beautiful one by Sansovino at San Sebastiano, which is signed by his name.

Fresh drinking water was brought to Venice in former times from the mainland in feluccas, and sold about the streets by women who wore a very curious costume, and carried on their shoulders a yoke, from the ends of which dangled two buckets. Modern improvement has swept them and their calling away, and now ugly leaden pipes of prodigious length,

which run along the railway viaduct, linking Venice to the land, bring thence the supply of drinking water to the Queen of the Adriatic. But the Venetian cisterns still remain, and their often elaborate decoration might easily be reproduced for decorative plant pots, and introduced to break up the monotony of our lawns, even in comparatively homely gardens. They would make indeed admirable garden adornments. All over Italy the capitals of columns will be found converted into flower-pots or

THE OLD SUNDIAL.

pedestals for statues and sundials. An amazing number of ruined temples and monuments have been in past times destroyed, and their materials used up in the decoration of churches and palaces, but the capitals of columns were in many instances preserved, and turned to use as decorations for gardens and courtyards. This occurred at Venice and

THE ARMILLARY SPHERE.

Naples, and in the gardens of both cities beautiful Corinthian and composite capitals will often be noticed employed as flower-pots and sundials. There were some magnificent specimens in the Ludovisi Gardens at Rome, which the cupidity of modern speculation has wantonly destroyed and replaced by streets of hideous buildings. There was nothing in the world to equal the loveliness of these gardens, which were literally the direct successors of those of Sallust, whose site they occupied. They were the delight of poet and painter, who haunted them, to enjoy their manifold beauties, and the glorious views of the Eternal City which they commanded. The wanton and greedy destruction of the Ludovisi Gardens was one of the most monstrous acts of vandalism committed in Italy in this century. But beautiful works of ancient art, such as the cisterns and column caps we have spoken of, though diverted from their original uses, are not, we may say, misapplied in garden adornment, as the examples at Kingston Lacy will show.

Copyright.   A VENETIAN CISTERN.   *" Country Life."*

Another notable feature in the grounds is a large Egyptian sarcophagus of granite, and a still more striking object rising skyward is the tall and stately obelisk of red granite, brought from Philæ by Belzoni in 1819, and erected in its present position at Kingston Lacy. The venerable monolith stands within full view of the house, and in a place chosen by the great Duke of Wellington, who laid the foundation of the pedestal on August 17th, 1827.

The garden at Kingston Lacy has thus a very distinguished character. In spacious dignity, the broad sweep of emerald lawn, the far-spread shadow of noble trees, the attraction of a beautiful park, it has few equals. Quaintness is there, too, with a more wistful charm, perhaps, in the moss-grown sundial and fine armillary sphere ; but wherever we go at this charming seat there is something to appeal to the sense of beauty, and much to satisfy the sense of fitness. We may walk from the stately terrace to pass through the scented avenue of glorious limes, whose boughs sweep the turf, and may linger in the delightful hollow of the cool fernery deep in its welcome shade. There are yew hedges, too, if not so extensive as in some places, and the climbing plants cling to the balustrade, and the garden is full of flowers.

What more shall we ask ? As the years go by we find greater richness and beauty arising in flower effect in our English gardens. New forms are introduced, while the old hardy flowers, improved, still hold their sway. Kingston Lacy is not wanting in any of these. The present owner, who was high sheriff of his county in 1880, is a great lover of the garden, and has recently added a fine range of glass-houses extending over 600yds. He has added much to the charm of the place, and its condition is all that could be desired. A happy union, we repeat, is this of house and garden —a seat ranking high among those in the West of England.

At Kingston Lacy are kept the keys and seal of Corfe Castle, that ancient place so closely connected in its later fortunes with the family of Bankes, and of which Mr. Bankes was the last mayor in 1881. He is also "lay Bishop" of Wimborne Minster, with which his family has many associations. The north porch there was erected to the memory of the late Right Hon. G. Bankes, M.P. for the county, and the beautiful east window of the minster, with its lancet triplet and shafts of Purbeck marble, was filled with old Italian glass by Mr. W. J. Bankes. The present Mr. Bankes of Kingston Lacy is, by royal charter, Lord High Admiral of Purbeck, an office of great antiquity in relation to the defences and privileges of the shore.

Copyright.   A DECORATED CISTERN.   *" Country Life."*

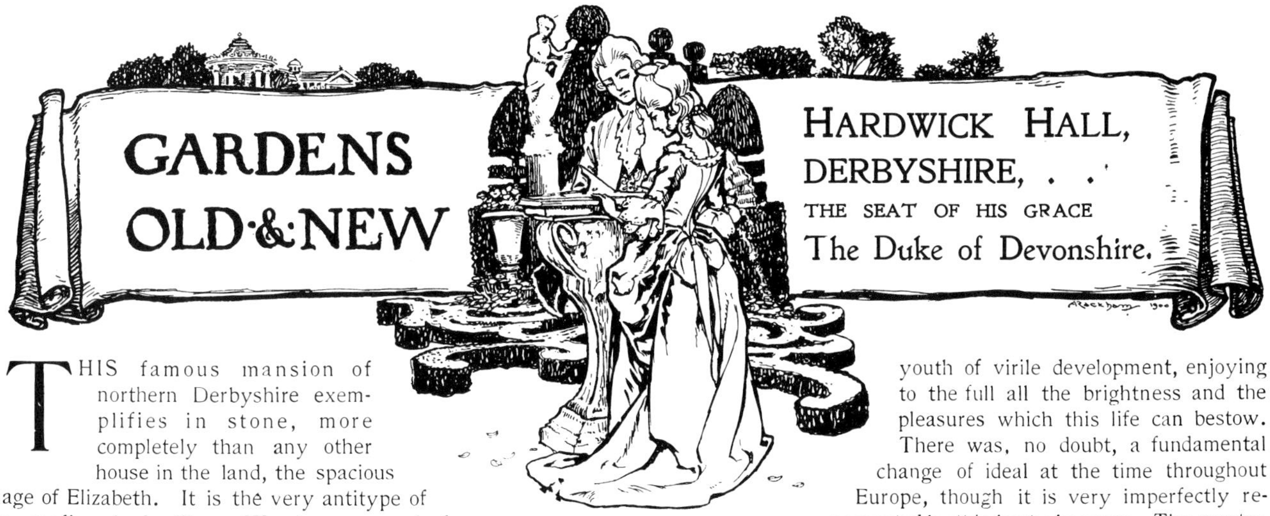

GARDENS OLD·&·NEW

HARDWICK HALL, DERBYSHIRE, . .

THE SEAT OF HIS GRACE

The Duke of Devonshire.

THIS famous mansion of northern Derbyshire exemplifies in stone, more completely than any other house in the land, the spacious age of Elizabeth. It is the very antitype of a mediæval dwelling. We have remarked before in this series of articles that the wide development of the national outlook in that century was accompanied by a rapid change in domestic architecture. In earlier times the strong tower, with its narrow loopholes, cut off from the surrounding land by a moat and a drawbridge, marked the dwelling of those who wished to be secure. There has been a tendency to depict the spirit of mediævaldom in the guise of some gloomy ascetic, hastening tombward with his head beneath a cowl, and looking even upon God's sunlight as unholy, while, on the other hand, we have had presented to us the new spirit, finally exemplified in the Renaissance, as a youth of virile development, enjoying to the full all the brightness and the pleasures which this life can bestow. There was, no doubt, a fundamental change of ideal at the time throughout Europe, though it is very imperfectly represented by this hasty imagery. The greater truth—and this is the matter with which we are especially concerned—is that the change in the houses of Englishmen arose from the more peaceful conditions of the times. The moat was no longer called for as a barrier, the strong tower had lost its office, and it was possible for the country gentleman, instead of looking in upon his courtyard as his ancestors had done, to survey the world around, and in particular to look out upon the gardens with which he beautified his home and to rejoice in the pleasant prospect of his delectable surroundings. It was not a new love, but a new opportunity.

THE OLD SOUTH WALL.

THE HORNBEAM WALK.

Now Hardwick Hall was manifestly inhabited by those who loved the luxury of light and were not afraid to admit it.

> " Hardwick Hall
> More glass than wall."

So runs the rhyming couplet of the Derbyshire people, who perhaps shared the dislike of earlier Bacon to houses "so full of glass that one cannot tell where to come to be out of the sun." But, in addition to the wealth of glass, we are impressed with another peculiarity of Hardwick. The place is very distinctly aggressive. There, lifted aloft upon every tower, are the initials "E. S.," to challenge all comers and to remind them of that very masterful woman, "Bess of Hardwick," the famous Countess of Shrewsbury, who built, not this house alone, but old Chatsworth as well, if the inscription on her

monument in All Hallows, Derby, may be believed, and also Bolsover Castle and the manor house of Oldcotes. It is not to be gainsaid that there is something of dreary vastness about the great chambers of Hardwick. From the huge windows you survey the forecourt, where planted large in the grass in glowing carpet beds are the inevitable initials, and, beyond them, the gatehouse, and the wall with its pinnacles, and outside again the old hall of Hardwick mouldering to picturesque decay, for it was not good enough for Elizabeth Countess of Shrewsbury to dwell in. We have so often in these pages enforced the necessity of carrying the spirit of the house into its garden, that it would ill beseem us to question the good taste of those who cultivate these gigantic initials, since they appear so prominently in the structure itself. On the contrary, we shall maintain that they have their right place in the garden of a house

THE GREEN WALK FROM THE SOUTH.

THE SOUTH WALK.

THE GATEHOUSE AND THE OLD HALL.

which seems in a manner consecrated to the glorification of "Bess of Hardwick." Walpole was displeased with the house, and found the chambers uncomfortably grand. "Pictures, had they had good ones, would be lost in chambers of such houses. Tapestry, their chief movable, was not commonly perfect enough to be real magnificence. Fretted ceilings, graceful mouldings, and painted glass, the ornaments of the preceding age, were fallen into disuse. Immense lights, composed of bad glass, in diamond panes, cast an air of poverty on their costly apartments."

But we are anticipating. *Place aux dames!* There is more to say about the builder of Hardwick. The story runs that her restless activity grew out of the belief that when her masons laid down the chisel and the hammer Time would exact his due. Certain it is that she went on building up to the end of her life, in 1607, and it is believed that she died when frost stayed the work of the mason's hand. When quite a girl, Elizabeth Hardwick had married a Derbyshire squire—Robert Barlow of Barlow. To him succeeded Sir William Cavendish, who, through her persuasion, if not through her actual initiative, began the building of old Chatsworth. Presently. Sir William died, and his widow married Sir William St. Lo, Captain of Elizabeth's Guard ; but the good captain, in his turn, departed, and then the wit and beauty of Elizabeth sufficed to captivate the fancy of that great nobleman, George, Earl of Shrewsbury. It is a matter of history that Mary, Queen of Scots was for some seventeen years in his charge, being mostly detained at Sheffield Castle and at Chatsworth, which the Earl occupied in right of his wife, but there can be little doubt that she also visited Hardwick, where her room is still shown, looking over the woods and garden at the rear of the house. The Countess was continually bickering with her last husband, and it is said that jealousy of the fair captive was at the root of the quarrel.

THE ENTRANCE LOGGIA.

At length Queen Elizabeth interposed in the cause of peace. "Her Majestie," wrote Roger Manners, to his brother John Manners at Haddon, "hath bin sondry tymes in hand with him for his wiffe, but he will nowais agree to accept her"; and again, "Your great Erle is very well, sayfe that he is more stoute agenst his lady than ever he was."

There is no certainty as to the hand that designed Hardwick, but it has been suggested that the house was the work possibly of Gerard Christmas, or Thorp, or one of the Smithsons, though no doubt the character of the place was dictated by "Bess of Hardwick." What manner of gardens surrounded the mansion in her time we can only surmise. There were doubtless the yew alleys and other features of the period;

THE FIR-TREE WALK.

and the great forecourt, with the characteristic gatehouse and the pinnacled wall, still remains to give distinction of character. But we shall probably be right if we surmise that the lady who so completely rejected much that was characteristic in the domestic buildings of her ancestors did not greatly cherish that spirit of enclosure which often ruled in the gardens of the period. Her vast windows, giving a superb view over the country, seem to

suggest that there would be something new also in the character of the surroundings.

The gardens have undergone many changes, but they still retain a good deal of quaintess and individuality, and the stone walls with their ornamental cresting bring the spirit of the mansion into them. The fine leaden figures which fall admirably into the picture are of a later date, and not even at Melbourne in the same county does finer garden leadwork

THE FORECOURT.

exist. The long green walks enframed with tall and dense hedges are a very distinctive feature of the place. The same may be said of the manner in which the fore-court is laid out, though that is comparatively modern. The approach is particularly fine. The visitor leaves the older hall, and entering through the striking Eliza-bethan gatehouse, finds before him a broad flagged pathway, leading up to the noble loggia or entrance corridor before the house, which was a feature characteristic of the time found at Hatfield and other great mansions. The flagged approach is margined by turf, in which are set the decorative ribbon beds. The fine trees are very noticeable, and the woodland surroundings are superb. What may be par-ticularly remarked of the

THE GREEN WALK OF YEWS.

garden front is that it pleases, as the visitor looks round him, by its delightful contrasts of architecture, garden, and land-scape, the cool grey stone of the Hall enhancing the effect of its green and floral surroundings, and these again adding much to its stately and dignified aspect. Then, again, the noble flower border along the old south wall and similar borders in other parts of the gardens are extremely beautiful, and they also add richness and colour to the green lawns and the grey stonework.

For the rest, little description is needed. The Duke of Devonshire maintains the gardens in truly beautiful order, and the park and surroundings are very attractive. Wood and pasture form that foil and contrast to the house and

its pleasaunce, which are so marked a note in the character of Hardwick and its surroundings, and, as at Chatsworth, all is freely thrown open for the public to visit and enjoy. They have the opportunity of understanding a mansion which speaks loudly of a changing time in our history, and that is still the exemplar and representative, in its masterful and distinctive form, of the ideas which inspired our ancestors more than 300 years ago.

The pictures of Hardwick which accompany this article illustrate better than words can tell what are the features of the place, and it will be seen that they are rich, attractive, and very varied. Derbyshire possesses many great mansions, but scarcely any so famous as this.

THE MOUNTING-BLOCK AND GATEHOUSE.

GARDENS OLD·&·NEW

HESLINGTON HALL, YORK, ...
THE SEAT OF . . .
LORD DERAMORE.

THOSE who have examined the long series of pictures of our most famous country homes which these pages contain, will find no difficulty in assigning the Yorkshire house of Heslington to the age to which it belongs. They will know that it could have been built in no other period than the spacious time of Elizabeth and James. The lofty frontage and glorious windows, the plan upon which the house is built, and the gardens that neighbour it, all bespeak the century which saw a change so vast wrought in the structure of our domestic life. The increase of wealth, of refinement, and of leisure, which marked the advance of the time, brought with it a striking transformation, proclaimed in the extinction of the feudal character of the nobles. The buttressed walls and frowning battlements disappeared, and were replaced by the pomp and lighter grace of such places as Knole and Longleat, Burleigh and Hatfield, Charlecote and Audley End. As Green says, we still gaze with pleasure on their picturesque gables, their fretted fronts, their turrets and fanciful vanes, their castellated gateways, the jutting oriels from which the great noble looked on the new Italian garden, on its stately terraces and broad flights of steps, its vases and fountains, its quaint mazes, its formal walks, its lines of yews cut into grotesque shapes in rivalry of the cypress avenues of the South.

In the bold and characteristic front of Heslington Hall we discern the features that mark the change. The many windows suggest that prodigal enjoyment of light and sunshine which was a mark of the temper of the age, but the lofty oriel window throws a flood of light into a great hall—legitimate descendant of those huge structures in which the earlier nobles had kept house with their dependents. The Elizabethan gentleman and his family had retired to their withdrawing-room, but the hall still remained, as Lord Bacon said, "so full of glass that we cannot tell where to come to be out of the sun or the cold." Such halls as this exist at Hampton Court and Haddon, and in many another house of the time. The plan of Heslington is that of the letter E, rightly or wrongly ascribed to adulation of Queen Elizabeth, although its porch has not the bold projection which is found in most of the great dwellings of the time. The proud distinction of country gentlemen was to receive Her Majesty in their houses when she made her many progresses through the kingdom, and almost beyond number are the mansions in which she sojourned. Heslington is associated with her in a singular and unfamiliar way, a way so unusual, indeed, that we know not what measure of credence to give to the assertions of the chronicler. The story runs that it was intended in some manner as a thank-offering of accommodation for her glory, and that its suites of rooms were specially designed for her reception. However this may have been, we may certainly aver that

THE YEWS FROM GARDEN-HOUSE.

THE GARDEN SEAT ON THE BOWLING GREEN.

the great hall, the long gallery, and the other chambers of Heslington were well fitted to receive a royal guest.

We have anticipated a little the history of the house. Lying within a couple of miles of the famous city of York, Heslington was necessarily a place of some importance. Those who have gone far back into its history bring it into relation with the operations of the Angles against Imperial Rome. They say that it was " the residence of the folk at the water hall," since in its name the root words of Old English are found—ea, water ; sœl, a hall or guard-house of justice ; ing, a tribal indication ; and ton, an enclosed residence. Such is

the ingenious and fanciful verbal patchwork out of which they would have us believe Heslington sprang. We are on much surer ground when we reach one Thomas Eymes, a member of the famous Council of the North, who was the builder, and evidently the owner of Heslington Hall in Elizabeth's days. He was succeeded in possession by the Heskeths, belonging to a great Lancashire family, and they by the Yarburghs.

Sir Thomas Yarburgh, the father of the first possessor of that name, had married one Mary Blague, a lady of the Court of Charles II. The fair dame, according to Grammont, had fallen in love with a French gallant of the Court, but, as she had not inspired the like passion in him, she married Sir Thomas Yarburgh instead. Grammont, who does not give a very attractive picture of the lady, describes her as the wife of " a great country bumpkin," who, the very week after their marriage, had bidden her take farewell of the town for ever, in consequence of the five or six thousand a year which he wished to enjoy in the country. " Alas ! poor Miss Blague. I saw her go away about this time twelve months in a coach with four such lean horses that I cannot believe she is yet halfway to her miserable little castle." The castle in question was Snaith Hall, in the East Riding of Yorkshire, and the lady's son, James Yarburgh—a godson of James II., a page of honour, and an officer of the Foot Guards—married the daughter

THE SUNDIAL.

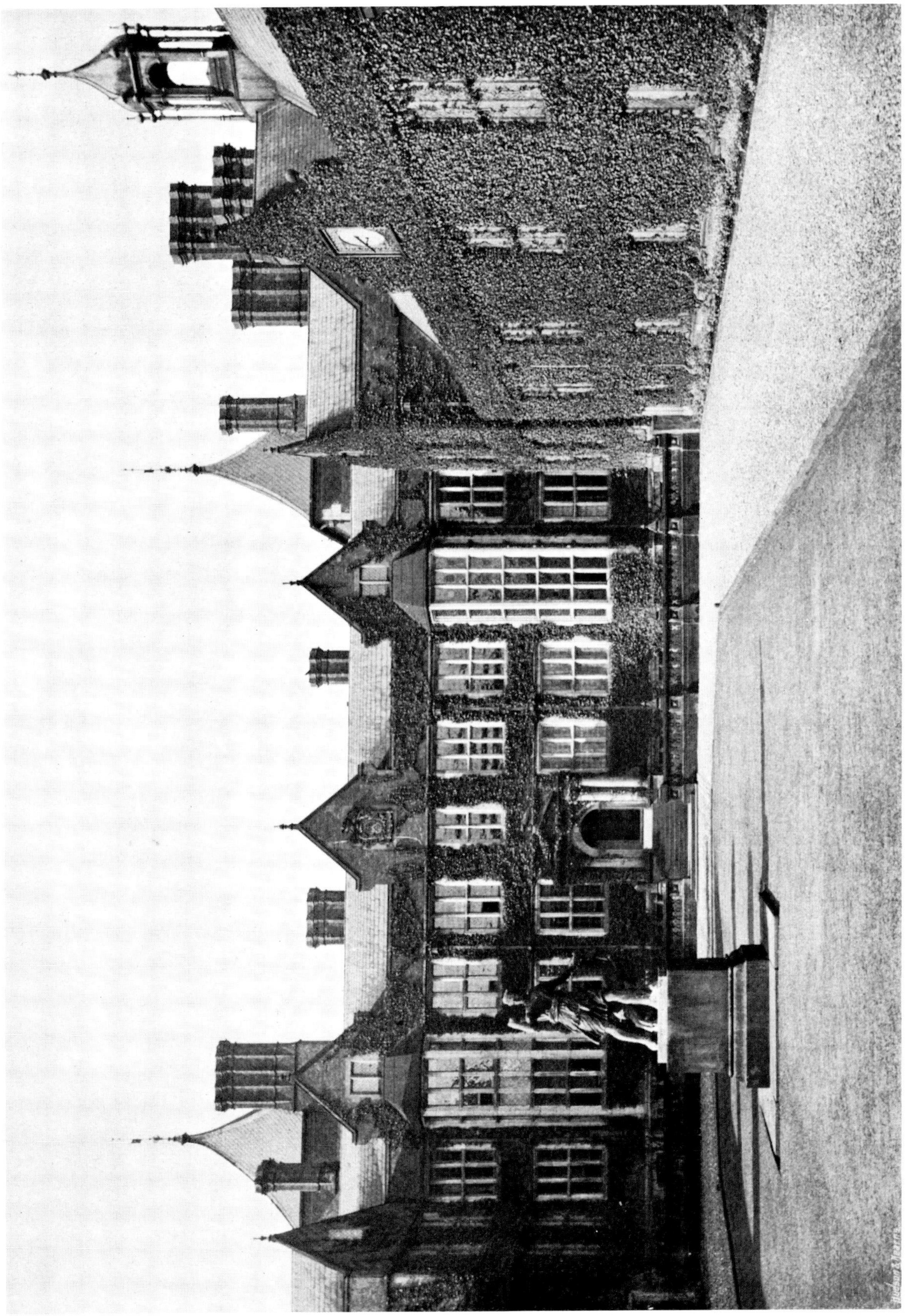

Copyright. *"Country Life."*

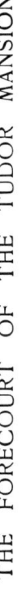

THE FORECOURT OF THE TUDOR MANSION.

and heiress of Thomas Hesketh of Heslington, and thus brought the Hall into the hands of a family with whose representatives it has ever since remained. One of Yarburgh's daughters married the famous Sir John Vanbrugh, soldier, architect, dramatist, and many other things besides.

But Heslington was to pass through heiresses to other families which assumed the name of Yarburgh. Mr. John Graeme married one of the Yarburgh heiresses, and his son, Mr. Yarburgh Graeme, adopted the new surname, but he died, leaving no son, and the estate passed to Mr. George John Lloyd, afterwards Yarburgh, who died in 1875.

THE HOUSE FROM THE LAKE.

The principal front remains scarcely altered since the time in which it was built, though an unfamiliar Diana now hunts in the forecourt. In other parts, however, alterations have been made, for the house was restored and enlarged in 1854. Yet its distinction is that it retains the features of the time in which it was raised. The gardens occupy a notable place in the history of English gardening. Their strange, quaint, and fantastic yews, unlike anything else ever seen on sea or land, are own brothers to the better-known curious creations of Levens. There are no judges' wigs nor royal courtiers shaped out of the ductile yew at Heslington, but only cylinders, globes, and adaptations of beehive forms, with some other odd imaginings carefully kept with the picturesque aspect of the eld. It is a garden world of strange character, such as we like to linger in, but with marked features of a kind that would

not bear too frequent repetition. The old skill of the pleacher and the topiary gardener gave great distinction to the gardens of Elizabeth's reign, and it is something to be thankful for that still at Levens and Heslington garden features exist which belong to a not much later date. The yew hedges are also remarkable, and afford curious vistas through which fine architecture and an old sundial or other such features may be viewed. You may look between these hedges, too, to the more natural charms that lie beyond, to radiant masses of flowers, and to a green park in which are many groups of splendid trees. The old bowling green is still used, and it neighbours a silvery lake, which is an attractive feature in these grounds.

The gardens are not given up to their sombre and curious yews. Embodying much of the rich floral charm which

THE QUAINT PLEASAUNCE WITH ITS WORLD OF YEWS.

THE SOUTH AND GARDEN FRONT.

has been the gift of modern times, brightness is mingled with their quaint old garden imagery. Then, away from the house itself we enter the landscape world, of which there have been many glimpses from the more formal pleasaunce. Here the foliage is fine and the character attractive, wood and water uniting in the effect. And from sundry points of view the Hall, with its many pinnacles,

A VISTA THROUGH THE YEWS.

Appleton when Thomas, the first Lord Fairfax, kept "noble hospitality" there, says that the gardens were laid out in the figure of a fort, doubtless being well terraced for the outlook.

"The sight does from their bastions ply
The invisible artillery;
And at proud Cawood Castle seems
To point the battery of its beams,
As if it quarrelled in the seat
The ambition of its prelate great."

gables and chimneys, is the gem of the garden picture—a simple, beautiful, and delightful composition.

For the rest, there is not much to say. A quaint old garden, with the added charms which belong to modern times, a placid lake, and a splendid park, must needs be famous even among the great domains and fair gardens in which Yorkshire is so rich.

There have been, and there still are, many fine gardens in the level country that surrounds the city of York. Thus at Bishopthorpe, where has been the palace of the Archbishops ever since the time of Walter de Gray (1216-1255), the gardens are large and fine, and the same is the case at Escrick Park, and at many more great places—the "ancient homes of lord and lady"—in the vicinity of York. Andrew Marvell, the poet, who was resident as a tutor at Nun

The gardens at Heslington Hall belong, perhaps, to the same period, though evidently they have undergone changes, and now are very interesting to the garden historian. Such a house could scarcely be without those features which are a distinction of English country houses. The hall is lined with armorial adornments, and there are portraits of Elizabeth, the four Stuart kings, Prince Charles Edward, the Duchess of Orleans, the Duchess of Grafton, and other famous nobles and fair ladies from the hand of Kneller, Lely, and other well-known artists.

The collection includes a considerable series of family portraits also, and Lord Deramore may well be proud of the noble mansion which has descended to his hand, and which is preserved with stately, quaint, and original charm.

THE BOWLING GREEN AND LAKE.

GARDENS OLD & NEW

WOLLATON HALL, NOTTINGHAMSHIRE,
THE SEAT OF . . .
LORD MIDDLETON.

SEE this house of Francis Willoughby, built with rare art, and left for the Willoughbys. Begun in 1580. Completed in 1588." Such is the dedication, in Latin, here done into English, of what a local historian of the day justly called " a wonderful house to be built by a commoner." It stands two miles west of Nottingham, on a gentle rise, among fine trees which do not shut it in. It is even now one of the most marked features in the landscape round the "fair city" of Sherwood Forest and the Trent. The builder was Sir Francis Willoughby, Knight. Even in those days fine houses could not be built without heavy expenditure, and the sources of his wealth at that early period were uncommon. Highly descended though he was, he appears to have been one of the earliest coal kings. "Wollaton," says Camden, "is rich in seams of coal, where Sir Francis Willoughby, Knight, nobly descended from the Greys, Marquises of Dorset, in our days built out of the ground with great charges (yet for the most part levied out of the coal-pits) a stately house with artificial workmanship, standing bleakly, but offering a good prospect to be beholden far and wide." Another account says : "The stone came from Ancaster in exchange for pit coal." The dedication of the place to future Willoughbys was based on a just belief in the merits and high character of that great and good family, of which the present Lord Middleton, owner of Wollaton, is the head. Sir Francis left only a daughter, Bridget, who married Sir Percival Willoughby, who lived at Wollaton and had five sons. One, Sir Francis, was father of the Francis Willoughby who wrote the first good and reliable history of birds, which is still quoted, and from which many of the Latin names for scientific purposes were long used to denote particular species. He wrote this splendid work in Latin, but it was not published until after his death in 1676. He also wrote a "History of Fishes," in four volumes, and thus has a double claim to the regard of lovers of country life. Another, perhaps the best known of the race, was Sir Hugh Willoughby, who perished in the search for a North-West Passage above America to India and Cathay. There is a fine portrait of the lost captain at Wollaton, whose death and that of his crew was due to want of provisions for lasting out the Arctic winter. It is strange that the adventurers, who had the experience of the Iceland cod fishers for at least a hundred years to draw upon, had not realised the chances of having to winter in the region of ice. The first of the family to be ennobled was Sir Thomas Willoughby, who was created Baron Middleton of Middleton in Warwickshire, and whose descendant, the ninth Baron, now holds it. The appearance of the house has been criticised,

A STAIRWAY TO THE LAWNS.

"Country Life."

THE   ROSERY.

as being too much of a stringing together of ornament, without solidity of design. Our readers will form their own conclusions from the appearance of the front presented in these pages, but it is certain that there is no over-elaborate ornament. The pilasters are severe and good, the windows in just proportion to the wall spacing, and the wings so lofty that the florid decoration of the gables is not overdone. The finest feature of the house is the great hall; it is this which occupies the greater part of the square turreted mass in the centre, which dominates the whole. The view of the interior here given shows what was the idea of the builder, and how it fits into the uses of modern occupation. The beauty of the carving on the gallery of stone and the lighting from the windows above,

whose lofty bases are 35ft. from the ground, are also seen. The terrace on which the house stands is reached from the gardens by flights of stairs rounded at the base, and thence mounting straight to the terrace above. The view across the flower garden shows better than words could describe what is that "good prospect to be beholden far and wide" which Camden noted. It is characteristic of the richness of the land round "fair Nottingham," the queen of the Midlands and of Midland shires. The lake and the long avenue make two points of beauty to which the eye is led. If what was anciently called "grace of congruity" can be obtained by art in making landscape on a large scale, this lake is worth remembrance. It forms a curve away from the house at such a distance that it makes a centre of light far beyond the foreground, but instead of stretching out as far as possible parallel with the house front, it curves until it runs directly from it, giving a vista like the bend of a river.

From the evidence of the gardens themselves, and the records of books and pictures, there is reason to believe that they were formerly even more extensive than at present. Before they were laid out in their present form they were designed to satisfy an exacting taste for regularity and geometrical proportion. The date was very early, for the design and plan are shown in a picture in the hall dated 1695. This picture, painted by Liebrichts, is exceedingly interesting and valuable for purposes of comparison, and enables us to see

THE   CONSERVATORY   GARDEN.

THE OLD GARDEN STAIRWAY.

how the formal character of the old garden at Wollaton has given place to the open features of the present landscape surroundings. The taste for the enclosure of gardens was still partly manifest. In this early design the upper terraces were cut up into squares of turf. In the centre of each square stood a statue, and at the corners oranges in tubs. At the east was that indispensable adjunct of the good garden of the Elizabethan time, a bowling green, connected with the park by a succession of terraces. A contemplative game like bowls was probably more enjoyable played on a green commanding a fine view over the country than if pursued in a space enclosed by the high hedges which were generally planted round the greens, perhaps to screen the players from the wind. In this the layer-out of the old gardens showed originality. There is every reason to believe that in other matters of garden design or architecture Wollaton Hall gave a lead to current ideas. South of the bowling

THE GARDEN AT WOLLATON IN 1695.

green stood a building with a glazed roof, in which the oranges were evidently wintered, the tubs being moved there in the autumn. In "Beeton's Garden Management" it is said that Wollaton was the first place in which a glass structure was used for the protection of plants. The date mentioned is 1695, the same as that of the picture, which may have been painted to show the completion of these new and successful efforts at gardening on the princely scale. Next to Chatsworth it is said to have been the finest garden in the country, though who were the designers then, and whether Kent or Brown or any of the famous garden designers lent their aid later, does not appear. The lower terrace was at first devoted to growing fruit, herbs, and vegetables, but after the present kitchen garden was built this terrace was converted into a wilderness garden, and planted with shrubs and rare trees. The cedars, the copper beeches, and the ilexes are among the splendours of Wollaton; the ilex standing at the west end of the upper terrace is said to

THE FLOWER GARDEN.

"Country Life."

WOLLATON HALL FROM THE EAST.

have been planted at the time the hall was built. This would give it an age of about 320 years. The ilex is a native of Italy, and if the hall was built by an architect trained in Italy and Italian workmen—John of Padua is credited with its design—it is more than probable that this is the oldest ilex tree in Britain. The date at which this species of tree was introduced was 1588, which coincides with the completion of Wollaton Hall. Another venerable relic of the ancient, ornamental timber of Wollaton is the trunk of a Pinus maritima, once considered to be among the largest, if not the largest, in England. It died some years ago, and the head was taken off, as it endangered a summer-house near. A boundary oak on the edge of the parish, which coincides with the sunk fence, is 20ft. in girth, but is now failing. Adjoining the terrace is the camellia house, which is one of the most wonderful out-of-date relics of the first efforts at making a winter garden. With the heating apparatus, which also supplied the house with hot water, it is said to have cost £10,000 ; of this, £1,400 was given for the camellias, then most costly exotics. It was in 1823 that this

broken with the pretty art that hides art. To every other pole is wedded not a rose, but a climbing bine of hop, so that the leaves of the hops and their grape-like green flowers may contrast in colour with the masses of Crimson Rambler. It is a beautiful and artistic effect of studied colour and form. Certain beds are also devoted to the old-fashioned cabbage rose, damask and moss roses, the whole being sheltered from cutting winds by clumps of choice rhododendrons.

The flower garden has a glorious southern aspect, with a fine prospect over the park, the lake being in the middle distance, and a background of hills and timber extending far out into the surrounding country. It is laid out with fanciful beds and planted in the freehand style of bedding. Summer annuals and herbaceous plants find a place there as well as the more formal bedding plants. Roses and carnations are always very much in evidence, as these, with sweet peas and lilies, are Lady Middleton's favourite flowers.

Among the notable trees surviving is one we have not so far mentioned, viz., the Lencombe oak, a very fine specimen

THE   FIR-TREE   WALK.

house was raised. It is built mainly of copper, brass, and glass, with iron pillars ; the glass was embedded in copper sash-bars, and the dome and gratings were of brass. The price of thick glass and of copper at that date will account for the prodigious cost of the building. The camellias, some of which are seventy years old, are still planted as they originally stood, in four open beds. One plant has a girth of 24in. They naturally show signs of age. At the south-east end of the camellia house is the rosery, the entrance to which is through a rustic arch of peeled oak, completely covered with climbing roses. The design of this exquisite rosery will be gathered from the picture here shown. The roses are planted in curved beds, circling round an ornamental iron standard covered with a White Rambler, whilst the outer circle of beds holds chiefly tea roses, with white Madonna lilies planted between them Round the outer edges of the beds stand poles of larch, from each of which, looping top to top together, runs a thick rope drooping in curves, and along this simple and rustic tracery the roses run joyfully, showering blossoms over all ; but the effect is

of which is to be seen on the lower terrace. It is a hybrid oak raised from a cross between an evergreen and a deciduous variety. The first tree of its kind was planted in the nursery of its propagator, where it grew to be a fine tree, but from some cause died, was cut down, the timber saved, and when dry made into boards. At the death of its planter the boards were employed to make his coffin, but the tree left survivors to bear his name. Of the kitchen garden, suffice it to say that it contains everything necessary for a house like Wollaton Hall. Some very fine ornamental iron gates mark what was the entrance to the herbaceous garden and American shrubberies. For this kind of work Nottingham has always borne the palm. It was there that the magnificent gates of Hampton Court were made, which were taken to South Kensington Museum, but may now be restored to their proper place at the ancient palace by the Thames. Our readers will gather that Wollaton is among the very first places of interest in central England, that favoured area in which are concentrated the majority of the greatest and finest examples of the great country homes and gardens of this country.

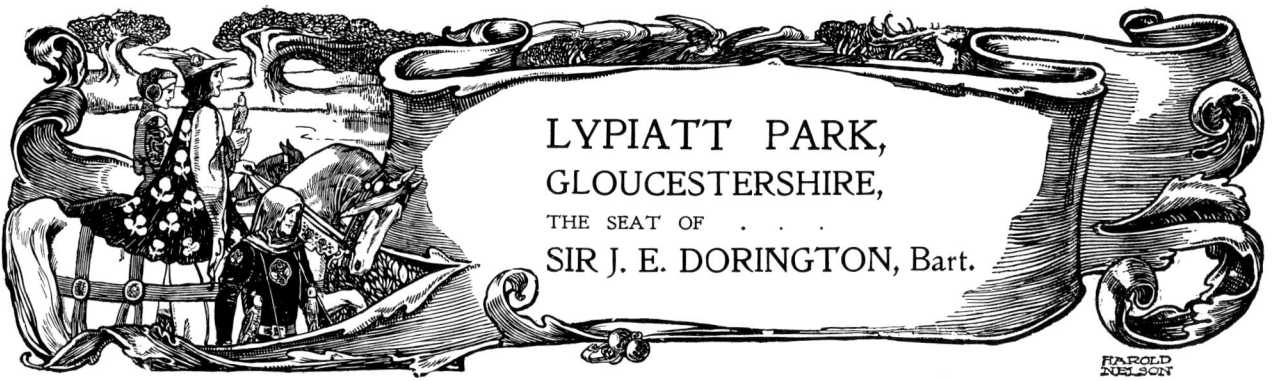

LYPIATT PARK,
GLOUCESTERSHIRE,
THE SEAT OF . . .
SIR J. E. DORINGTON, Bart.

HAROLD NELSON

SIR J. E. DORINGTON'S house in the Cotswolds is one of the finest purely mediæval houses in Gloucestershire. It is not a feudal castle, like Berkeley Castle, or reconstructed on Tudor-Italian lines like Stanway, but a monastic house of the sixteenth century in perfect preservation. The embattled porch and other features have been added later, together with certain other extensions in the original style. But except the curious towers and tourelles in the garden, due to a taste for adding fortifications to the old religious buildings, a taste which the lay owners of Beaulieu Abbey also indulged early in the last century, there is very little at Lypiatt which might not have formed part and parcel of the original. Though built on a smaller scale and at an earlier date, there are many points of resemblance between Lypiatt and Ford Abbey in Dorsetshire. There is the same unity of design, the same half-collegiate look, the same retention of the dwelling-rooms and apartments for their original purpose. The great hall is a feature in both. But at Lypiatt it is in the centre of the building, and is lighted by a graceful and well-proportioned bay window, forming a shallow recess from the ground up to the spring of the roof beam. The chapel is connected with the tower by a short but rich cloister cf the same Perpendicular architecture as the rest of the building. Each wing has its square tower, but the West Tower is of simpler design than that on the east.

The site of Lypiatt is one seldom chosen by the religious when building their houses. In nearly every case they chose a valley for the monastery or abbey, with a river close by to supply fish and fill fish-ponds, and flat meadows to graze their cattle upon. Waverley, Tintern, Ford Abbey, Bolton Abbey, Rievaulx, Jervaulx, and a hundred others occur at once. At Lypiatt the situation of the house is quite modern in feature, on the edge of a lofty hill, instead of at the bottom. The Cotswolds here make a high continuous ridge, with precipitous valleys cutting it obliquely. One of the highest and steepest of these bastions forms the park, studded with fine elms and other timber, full of sweet hill pasture, and little bays and curves in the embosoming hill. On the summit, 800ft. above the sea, and almost at the highest point in Gloucestershire, stands the house. In front runs the great terrace, like a fortification

"Country Life."

THE DOVECOTE AND LAIRD'S BARN.

BASE OF THE GREAT TERRACE.

crossing the summit and commanding the valleys which wind down to Stroud and the Severn, which lies to the right front. To the left are other valleys, in the nearest of which—Bisley— is one of the sources of the Thames. The "Seven Springs" gush out of the rock, now vaulted over and furnished with stone spouts. These springs go down to make the Churn Brook, which flows from the other headwaters of the Thames coming down from the hills behind Gloucester.

The park and woods are full of great forest trees—the beech especially grows to an unusual size. From Bisley a beech avenue nearly a mile long runs to the house. Modern ideas of tree planting are carried out in a large pinetum, in which not only conifers, but all new and rare trees introduced into this country, are planted from year to year. Pines and cypresses shelter the lawns, and three ancient fish-ponds, covered with ornamental water-fowl, are not the least

A SUNNY COURT.

Copyright.

Robert Weana

TOWERS AND TOURELLES.—A GARDEN COURT.

THE GREAT TERRACE.

ornamental features of the high plateau on the hills. Tradition says that the plans which ended in the Gunpowder Treason were discussed in the library of Lypiatt, a story perhaps due to the connection of its former owners, the Throgmortons, with the plotters.

In the Civil Wars, Lypiatt was held for a time by the Parliament. The post was important from a strategic point of view. It commanded the road from Stroud in the valley of the Severn to Cirencester in the valley of the Thames. From Cirencester to Oxford was a short journey and an easy road. The desire to gain the same advantage urged the Cavaliers to make great efforts to take the Gloucestershire garrisons, and chief among them the town of Gloucester itself, which was bitterly hostile and Roundhead, as was the

greater part of the county, the Yeomanry being "most forward and seditious, and, being wealthy, able to redeem their delinquency at a high price." Gloucester was the "only strong garrison the rebels held between Bristol and Lancashire in the north part of England, and if it could be recovered His Majesty would have the men of Severn entirely within his command, whereby his garrisons of Worcestershire, Shrewsbury, and all in those parts might be supplied from Bristol." Lypiatt was attacked in force, and the Roundhead garrison driven out with the loss of fifty men. But the main business of gaining command of the Severn did not prosper. The men of Gloucester sent back, in answer to the King's summons, "two citizens from the town with lean, pale, sharp, and bald visages; indeed, faces so strange and unusual, and in such a gait and posture, that at once made the most severe countenances (among the King's troops) merry, and the most cheerful hearts sad; for it was impossible such ambassadors could bring anything less than a defiance. The men," continues the indignant Clarendon, "without any circumstances of duty, or good manners, in a pert, shrill, undismayed accent, said 'they had brought an answer from the godly city of Gloucester to the King.'" The answer was in keeping with the appearance of the messengers, and Gloucester was held for Parliament till Essex raised the siege, when they had only one barrel of powder left.

The peculiarity of the gardens at Lypiatt is their adaptation to the flat plateau on the hill crest. The ancient façade of the house and the

THE ROSERY.

THE OLD GUEST-HOUSE.

late additions approach so near to the edges of the hill that there was almost no room to develop any garden at all in front of the mansion, unless at great expense, which might not have achieved any better result than the present arrangement of garden and park. At Powerscourt, Lord Powerscourt's fine house in the Wicklow Mountains, which occupies a similar position, the entire front of the steep hill has been cut into a semi-circle of graded terraces, ending in a small circular lake, which the lowest steps of the garden half embrace. At Lypiatt the steep part was left native and wild, so that from the front terrace you may look down into the tree tops and into the blossoms of the hawthorn bushes below. But lateral extension was possible without removing thousands of tons of earth. Consequently, at either end of the house are terraces and gardens, quaint enough, and very characteristic. At one side are the garden court, towers, and tourelles here shown, an effective mixture of house and garden architecture. The small tourelle of one story at the angle of the garden is an example of a favourite device in Tudor gardens. They were set at the angles of garden walls. Some were circular, of which examples may be seen from the South-Western Railway at Old Basing. They are, indeed, the only remnants left of the gardens of Old Basing House. Others were octagonal, though both brick and stone were used in constructing

THE DAIRY.

them; the roofs were nearly always of Durham slate or Gloucester stone flakes. But at Lypiatt the walls of yew hedge and laurel take the place of walls of brick or stone. The yew hedge connecting the tourelle and the turrets has a better effect than any line of masonry could give. On the opposite wing the line of gardens is prolonged parallel with the crest of the hill by the great terrace. Above it the land runs back on a *terre-plein* level with the top, and is planted with ancient cedars, oaks, and beeches. The design is really more of an escarp than a terrace. The idea of fortification given by the tourelles in the garden court is carried out here also. The base of the terrace is marked by a scarp wall and tourelles flanking the line of the lower path. On the west side of the house is a flower garden sheltered by a yew hedge 10ft. high, a necessary and perfect protection from rough winds on this high summit of the Cotswolds. The same yew hedge shelters a pretty lawn, set with raised flower-beds, on the south side. The Monk's Walk, overhung with evergreen oak, is one of the sights of Lypiatt, and is always, though probably incorrectly, associated with its ecclesiastical owners. Modern gardening, with its uninterrupted sequence of colour, is particularly well suited to the precincts of Lypiatt, where the formal garden finds no natural starting point, save in the command given for the terracing.

THE ROSE GARDEN.

THE OLD GARDEN, ETWALL HALL, DERBYSHIRE.

INDEX.